A unique insight into the cause and cure of high
anxiety, phobias, OCD, depression and more...

...

Evolving

Self Confidence

*How to Become Free from Anxiety
Disorders and Depression*

TERRY DIXON

Help-For

Published by Help-For
PO Box 106
Newton Aycliffe
Co. Durham
DL5 4FB
www.help-for.com

A catalogue record for this book is available at the British Library
ISBN 978 0 9558136 0 3

Printed and bound in the US and UK
by arrangement with Help-For

Important: The information in this book is not intended to be used for self-diagnosis nor taken as a substitute for good individual personal professional medical attention. The only intent of the author is to offer information to help you in your quest for well-being and no responsibility can be taken by the author for the way the information is used.

It is strongly recommended that anyone who is thinking, feeling or behaving in a way that they don't understand, any way that is debilitating or is causing pain and unhappiness should consult a medical professional and that a medical doctor should always be consulted for any persistent physical or bodily function problem, in the first instance, to rule out possible physical causes before psychological reasons are explored.

And that, under no circumstances, should anybody stop taking prescribed medication without fully qualified medical supervision.

Dedicated to Dennis, Patricia, Carol and the memory of Linda who made it possible.
And to James and Matthew who make it worthwhile.

...

CONTENTS

...

INTRODUCTION

THIS BOOK IS FOR all those of us who suffer the anguish and despair of loneliness rather than face the perceived rejection that social failure may bring ... it is for those who experience as much fear and panic, in phobia, going into a shop or stepping outdoors as if they were going to face a firing squad ... and for those who are so convinced that they are physically or mentally ill that no medical tests can convince them otherwise. It is for those who scrub themselves hundreds of times a day or repeat phrases and rituals to allay the anxiety and prevent some perceived catastrophe or retribution from 'higher forces' ... and it's for those of us who look back on a life with regret, in depression, longing for the person they feel they could have been or should have been.

This book is for all of us whose own thoughts, feelings and behaviours drive a life of anxiety and fear instead of the adventure and excitement it can be ... it is for all of us because we are all doing the same thing.

With anxiety-related problems (including depression as such a problem), we watch ourselves in everything we do and it's not difficult to appreciate how this self-absorption can lead us to believe that we are the only one with such a problem. This, in itself, strengthens the 'what's wrong with me' beliefs, yet nothing could be further from the truth.

Millions of people worldwide experience these problems; it is estimated that in America alone over thirty million people suffer from some form of anxiety disorder. The most common one is Social Anxiety Disorder (or Social Phobia), closely followed by Post Traumatic Stress Disorder (PTSD) and Generalized Anxiety Disorder. Around one in thirty to fifty people suffer from Obsessive Compulsive Disorder (OCD) and one in ten are reported to have a specific phobia. This doesn't include vast numbers of people who have depression or those living anxious lives ruled by shyness or stress.

Many people feel they are working below their potential and are frustrated, more people are unhealthy and overweight than ever before, greater numbers of teenagers are depressed and problems involving anxiety and stress account for the majority of visits to doctor's surgeries. In a world of better education, food, hygiene and healthcare, emotionally, society is crumbling.

The unique pressures in modern society no doubt play a part in the tension and stress found in these problems, but anxiety problems are nothing new; they are part of the human condition and the following quotation, from over three hundred years ago, sums them up aptly:

'The mind is it's own place, and in itself can make a heaven of hell, a hell of heaven' – John Milton (1608–1674)

For centuries, writers, poets and artists have tried to convey the inner turmoil and conflict that is often associated with existence.

The world we live in personally is dictated by what goes on in our mind, irrespective of what external reality seems to be. Nowhere can this be seen more profoundly than in the case of Anorexia Nervosa. How can a painfully thin girl look in the mirror and see herself as fat? Even to the extent of pointing out which areas of her body are too fat? Anxiety problems are reality to us and later we shall discover just how and why this happens; how we start living a life ruled by anxiety and how, even though we had little power over the creation of the situation, we can change things. Others don't see us as we see ourselves and once we understand this and why we think the way we do, we can start to accept things and change, move forward and evolve beyond the problem to true self-confidence.

Vast resources, in the form of research, therapy and medication, have been used in an attempt to resolve these problems, with, on the whole, a spectacular lack of success. Problems are defined, named, classified, listed, ordered, placed in categories, placed in sub-categories in an attempt to understand and control them – strangely enough, exactly the same attempts to gain control are found in most forms of OCD. And while some argue that benefits of this system include a more accurate diagnosis and subsequent better treatment (which is debatable given such a lack of success) others argue that it is inaccurate, misleading and overlooks the bigger picture. That is what this book is about – the bigger picture.

But for slightly different circumstances, my social anxiety disorder could have been your OCD or your generalized anxiety disorder could have been your neighbour's Bulimia. At their heart, all these problems are the same; they start for the same reason, grow in the same way and are cured by the same methods. Indeed, many people who seek treatment for anxiety-related problems present with a number of symptoms across the whole range of anxiety disorders and the final 'disorder' diagnosed is the one relating to the most frequent or strongest set of symptoms shown. Many people are actually diagnosed as having a number of anxiety disorders!

When we look at the backgrounds of large numbers of people with anxiety and depression problems, they are often strikingly similar in various ways. Negative life experiences and subsequent feelings involving self worth and insecurity occur across the board with such regularity and are so similar that its hard to see how they cannot possibly play a major role in these problems.

Ranging from acute shyness and stress to anxiety disorders and depression, each problem is unique to the individual. Expressions of social phobia vary from person to person just as those of agoraphobia vary from panic disorder and GAD varies from OCD. However, as unique to the individual these problems are and as different to each other they are, these problems develop for similar reasons and strengthen in a similar way. They do so in a manner that reflects the way our mind and body works.

Every human being on the planet (indeed, every animal) is built in such a way as to develop an anxiety disorder given the right (or wrong) set of negative life experiences.

We shall learn how at the heart of these problems can lie neither illness nor disease and not even disorder for these problems aren't irrational, they develop for a good reason – for our survival. As such, anxiety disorders (including depression) will be referred to as 'anxiety-related problems' throughout much of this book.

These problems are, in fact, highly adaptive, given our life experiences and genetic history, but they are not appropriate. In essence, most problems involving anxiety are learned behaviours involving deep-seated survival mechanisms that develop from the ways we learned to cope with negative life experiences. The vast majority of people with these problems are extremely intelligent, more so than the average population, and are aware of the inappropriate thoughts, feelings and behaviours, yet feel powerless to stop them. It's the fact that we are dealing with deep-seated, instinctual behaviours and self-beliefs that make them seem so hard to control.

Long-term anxiety and panic, phobias, OCD and depression can leave us feeling helpless and that there is nothing that can be done or nothing we can do to be free of them. Years of searching, reading books and websites, finding what seem to be answers, trying ways to think, trying ways to behave, 'get-well quick' ideas, therapy, medication etc. can leave us exhausted, without hope and even more anxious about our problem.

And yet, many people do successfully overcome these problems, usually after years and years of experience, research and experimenting with their problem. They find the answer. They don't suddenly wake up one day and their problem has gone; they grow, move forward and change. Their problem weakens and fades as they come to understand it, accept it and develop a new attitude towards it. They start to think and behave differently.

The key to overcoming most anxiety and depression related problems involves understanding how they work. Like everything in life, when we know how and why something works we know how to stop it. To try and overcome these problems without this understanding is exceptionally difficult for whatever we may try, as soon as any symptoms occur, we think that it's not working, that it isn't the answer and we continue with our never-ending search for the 'real answer'. Feelings of no control play a huge part in the development and growth of these problems and without a deep understanding of what's going on, the unknown will always overpower us.

To start to deal with these problems takes courage, for fear and self-doubt play a major part in them. And yet, if you have admitted to yourself that you have a problem, you have already taken one of the most courageous steps.

Although you may not appreciate it at the moment, you do have special qualities that many people don't have, including some that could have only developed out of the struggle with feelings of self-doubt and anxiety symptoms. You have the potential to become a much stronger, wiser person than one who hasn't experienced these problems.

We all learn and grow through our experiences. In anxiety disorders and depression we learn and grow in a negative way. But this can be turned around whenever we choose and we can become stronger, wiser, better for the experience. Armed with the right knowledge it is possible to become free.

The aim of this book is to provide such an insight into these problems that we can stand back and say "that's it, that's what happened to me", and with this knowledge we can stop searching for that elusive ultimate reason (which, as we shall learn later, doesn't actually exist) and start to live.

Research shows that the right kind of self-help can be beneficial with anxiety and depression problems, however, our individuality and uniqueness means that with self-help, 'one size doesn't fit all'. Basic truths apply to all of us, but take the advice given and tweak it, mould and shape it to suit yourself. Use the 'my notes' section at the back for your notes, for anything that strikes a chord with you. Even if you feel that you have (or have been diagnosed with) a particular 'disorder', read about all the disorders in 'The Problem' part of this book – you may learn something beneficial.

When it comes to the mind and anxiety problems, generally speaking, anything that we feel uncomfortabe with and have to force will not work since this merely enhances the 'feeling bad' part of us. Conversely, things that are comfortable to us can work.

Freedom from these problems involves insight, understanding, acceptance, practise and perseverance. With these, we can go from feeling bad about ourselves to feeling great about ourselves and once we feel great about ourselves everything else follows. The foundation for this change is insight, the greater the insight, the greater is the potential for change. So let's look at the ultimate question - just what are these problems and how do they start?

...

PART I

THE CAUSE

"Do not give in too much to feelings. A overly sensitive heart is an unhappy possession on this shaky earth."

JOHANN WOLFGANG VON GOETHE (1749–1832)

The Bear and the Flagpole

... You're running down the road, you are frightened, something is behind you. You can feel its presence *bearing* down on you. It's chasing you, it's *overbearing* and you know that if it catches you it will destroy you. Wherever you run it follows, down every street, down every alley, it's still there right behind you. You run into a house and hide ... still it comes. Managing to glance back you see it, it is in fact a ... *giant grisly bear* ... snarling ferociously and wanting to destroy you. Now tiredness is setting in, you've been running for so long and still the bear is right behind you.

What can you do? How can you escape? You turn a corner and you see it, there in the distance ... your salvation.

Twenty yards in front of you ... *a flagpole* ... you'll be safe up there, the bear won't be able to get you. You make it and climb to the top just as the bear reaches the bottom of the pole. Seeing the bear down there, you breathe a sigh of relief ... you are safe.

Suddenly you feel scared, you realise that you are thirty feet in the air, any wrong movement and you could fall, you must stay alert at all times to prevent this. So there you are ... at the top of the flagpole, unable to go down towards the bear, constantly alert lest you fall ....

The above describes a dream, a dream that symbolises the cause of anxiety-related problems and how we can live our lives ... constantly alert, watching ourselves so that we don't fall (fail), trying to protect ourselves from a greater fear, always anxious to some degree.

But how do we get to this position?

We need to start at the beginning – our lives begin to take shape in infancy and childhood ... and so do these problems.

1

As a Child...

OUR PARENTS ARE GOD to us. We worship the ground they walk on; they gave us life and keep us alive. A father shows his son, what it is to be a man, a mother, to her daughter, a woman, and yet this same parent, the one we worship, can come to make us feel as though we are inadequate, stupid, weak and worthless. Significant others can do the same to some extent – but our parents are different; their genes are a part of us, their behaviour toward us strikes at our very existence, our inner-self, our being and we cannot feel any way toward them without feeling the same about part of our self.

Throughout recent history, there have been changes in thinking about the influence of parents on their children. Parents have gone from being fully responsible or having no responsibility at all to a middle ground, where other things, such as peers, school, society, and media play a major part. And they do, but nothing influences us like our parents; their genes are our genes and from the day we are born we are shaped by their beliefs, attitudes and behaviours, we are moulded by their hopes and fears and many people, well into their middle age, are still trying to please their parents and gain their love.

In her self-help book about depression, Alexandra Massey estimates that around 80% of people that she has spoken to about depression are entangled with their parents and stuck.[1]
And research has shown an improvement in the phobic behaviour of adolescents when relationships with their parents improved.[2]

However, the purpose of this section is not to blame, judge or denigrate our parents. Not to justify anger, resentment or hate, for in doing this – something that plays a large part in most people's problems – we only hurt and damage ourselves. The purpose of this section is to understand what happens and why.

A Parent's Power

Human infants are the most helpless of all the mammals when newborn; immediately after being born we cry in order to be comforted and we come equipped with a number of instinctual behaviours to form strong attachments to those who can protect and nurture us. As we grow, this attachment grows, to ensure our safety.

The power of our parents is unquestionable. They are big and strong, we are small and weak. They can do things we can't: drive a car, mow the lawn, drink beer and change a light bulb – and they teach us how to do things; things that empower us, like how to ride a bicycle and how to swim and the meaning of things. Their knowledge and power shapes our sense of competence, what we can and cannot do, and our confidence. They feed, clothe us and keep us warm. They can do things we can't and know things that we don't; they must be right and we must be wrong.

They make us feel good and make us feel bad; almost all of the rewards and punishments that a child receives are mediated by the parents. They hurt us and they help us get better. To top it off, we cannot avoid them. Even as a small child, certainly as a teenager, if someone was nasty to us or treated us badly, we would soon learn to avoid them – but we can't do this with parents.

Every child faces this situation, totally dependent on their parents who are so powerful and sometimes so rewarding, trying to deal with mixed up feelings about their parents and themselves.

What we do next is something that strengthens the parent-child bond (for good or bad) – we start to identify with our parents.

Identification

The dog, a family pet. Its owner will look after the animal, feed it and take care of its needs. He may become strongly attached to it, but it is unlikely that he will identify with it. However, if the dog is a show dog, a thoroughbred, winner of the best of breed in many dog shows, the owner may identify with the dog in order to gain status that he, himself, lacks. The public accolade that comes with being a winner, through the qualities of the dog, provides a feeling of self-enhancement for the owner.

The child believes that if he or she were more like the parent and shared some of the parent's qualities then they would feel more competent and powerful, feel stronger. At some stage in their lives virtually every son wants to be like his father and every daughter like their mother. As a young child, we can feel immense pride when people comment on how much we look like our father or mother and when identification with the same sex parent is particularly strong, we may even want to look like them; many children actually go through stages of looking remarkably like their parents. (Perhaps, as in the pet example above, there is some truth in the saying that 'the owner looks like their dog').

Identification involves the desire to possess the characteristics of the model. Characteristics such as attitudes, values and qualities not actual behaviours, which involve imitation. Because it relates to such things as values and qualities, identification is associated with our self-concept, and it is seen throughout life. New recruits to the armed forces (or social groups, companies, political parties) will adopt a great many attitudes held by the group because his/her self-image is so dependent upon their relation to the group. We take the values of the model into our own understanding of our self and the world. In essence, we want to be like something we value so that we can become strong like them and liked by them and thus liked by people in general – our self-image becomes linked to our parents.

Identification serves an evolutionary purpose. Through it, the child learns to depend on himself. Our parents, the ones who we see living successfully in the world, no longer have to be by our side. We internalise their successful coping and can start to act as our own caretaker. We develop the ability to control ourselves and we learn to do this, initially, through self-talk.

Self-Talk

Self-talk, the scourge of virtually all anxiety and depression related problems – but only because it is negative, in both content and tone. It's a fairly safe bet that if we use 'you' in our self-talk that it's our parents talking.

When we learn to talk, we learn to self-talk, to direct ourselves. It follows the same development path as learning to read, first we do it out loud and then we internalise it, taking it into our heads. The first stages can be seen in children who will often talk out loud whilst performing tasks. It has a survival value: we only need hear our parent shout, "don't touch that fire" once, with fear and alarm in their voice, in order to direct ourselves not to do it in the same manner in the future.

Through talking to our self, we come to no longer need our parent in such a way, for they are in our head. By using the words our parent uses, in the way that they use them, we can warn ourselves of danger and about the consequences of our acts. We can also punish ourselves by reproving our own behaviour.

We learn and obey roles and behaviour patterns appropriate to our sex and to the standards of our family and society.

I remember well, during a university psychology lecture, a story related by the Emeritus Professor of Psychology at the time about a woman who got off the bus at the wrong stop. When asked by a friend "why?", she replied, "because my mother told me to". Her mother had been dead many years.[3]

As adults, we talk to ourselves silently in our heads all the time, usually in a way that reflects the beliefs, attitudes and qualities of our parents. Unfortunately, for many, and entirely due to what they have experienced, self-talk becomes focused on self-criticism and self-punishment.

But it doesn't have to stay that way; when we understand how and why we identify with our parents and how self-talk facilitates this and when we realise that our parents weren't really that successful, they didn't know everything and most of the time what they said wasn't actually the truth, we can legitimately change the way we talk to our selves. Our self-talk can become encouraging and supportive, a friend rather than an enemy.

* * *

Born out of the instinctual behaviour to form a strong bond with someone who can protect us, for the most part, identification isn't some 'thing' that we consciously decide to do. It's a natural progression that follows from seeing what success means and wanting to be like that, wanting to have it. It is a part of growing and developing and it's a double-edged sword.

The right amount, with a good role model can lead to a well-rounded individual. Someone who is independent and confident, intelligent and well disciplined, respectful of the standards of others, the family and society. Well equipped to move through life successfully; an example of evolution and learning in harmony.

Over strong identification with a good role model may also be beneficial and can lead to great achievement. An article in the Sunday Times in 1997 regarding some of the influences on great explorers described Robert Swan as driven by a father who was extremely strict with high expectations and Ranulph Fiennes as spending his life trying to live up to a father he never even knew.[4] Importantly, we can also identify with strong images and ideals of parents that we don't even know.

However, strong identification with a weak role model can be devastating. Excessive identification can lead to that entanglement with our parents and being stuck, that continues throughout our lives. In childhood, it can lead to over dependency and attachment, desperate for their love and as an adult we can spend a lifetime of perpetual achievement, in order to please our parents.

Excessive identification results from feelings of insecurity about our relationship with our parent. The more a parent makes us feel unloved (in whatever way), the more we need to be like that parent, not only to feel more competent and successful, taking away the insecurity but because we think it will make them love us.

Children will forgive their parents anything to receive their love. It has been shown that children who have suffered incredible neglect and abuse from their parents still want to be with them.[5]

It follows, that since we want to be like our parent, that identification between father and son and mother and daughter will be more intense and have a greater effect than identification between opposite sex parent and child. A son very rarely wants to grow up to be like his mother, she cannot teach him what it is like to be a man. And this is generally the case – father-son and mother-daughter conflicts continuing well up to middle age and sometimes beyond.

It may well be the case that same sex child-parent identification forms the base for many a neurosis, where we take it out more on ourselves, because the connection is so strong. Whereas, opposite sex child-parent identification, due to its corresponding weaker connection, leads to taking it out on others.

Identification, in itself, is not the problem for it is a natural part of development. It is when it becomes excessive, for the wrong reasons that things can start to go wrong. This usually happens due to the way the parent – the one we look up to, the one that we want to be like and to love us – treats us.

How Parents Affect Us

We can see that, from around three years old to the pre-teenage years, part of our self-concept starts to take shape through identification, mainly with our parents and usually one parent more than the other. We look at their qualities and achievements through filtered eyes and we want to be like that.

As all this is happening, we are interacting with our parents, dealing with them daily. And it's this interaction, the way they treat us that also helps to shape what we think about ourselves.

We have seen how identification with a good role model is ideal and how, in certain cases, strong identification with a parent who isn't even present can lead to great achievement. But this book isn't about those things, it's about the other side of the coin; the development and resolution of problems, problems that relate to the way we feel about our self.

When parents treat their children badly, whether directly or indirectly, excessively or mildly, it affects the way the child feels. Being treated badly leads only to one thing – feeling bad.

Without doubt, one of the worst things to make a child feel bad is conflict between the parents.

Parental Conflict

'The most important thing a father can do for his children is to love their mother' – Henry Ward Beecher (1813–1837)

Perhaps a truer word has never been spoken. When our parents argue, we feel bad, simple as that. How many children have sat upstairs in distress, listening to their parents screaming at each other below? And how many adults with anxiety-related problems can recall just a scene from their childhood?

Fighting parents are a threat to the child's security. Their fighting instils feelings of insecurity, worry and self-doubt. Things that feel bad, and – as we will learn later – one of the key elements in developing anxiety and depression related problems – when we feel bad, there must be a reason for it; if there isn't, we will find one.

Our parents are right, they know more than us; if something is going wrong between them or between them and us, it must be something to do with us, it must be our fault.

It doesn't take a great leap in imagination or faith to see how regular and extreme arguing between parents can leave a child in an almost constant state of distress. Indeed, arguing parents may affect a child before it is born. If soothing sounds are beneficial to the developing child in the womb, then raised voices and the mother's stressed body may have a negative impact that sensitises the child to such experiences later in life. Perhaps this plays a part in the different temperaments that can be seen in newborns.

Parental conflict affects us deeply but there is something that has an even greater effect on us: Parent-child conflict.

Arguments between a child and his or her parent not only create stress and anxiety in the child (and probably also in the parent) but also influence how a child begins to think about themselves. As a young child, we don't have the acquired brain development, experience and knowledge to work things out for ourselves so we build our self-estimate solely on the appraisal of others and how they react to us; when these appraisals come from our parents, we don't doubt them.

The most powerful negative influence on a child's self-concept comes from criticism.

Parental Criticism

Constructive criticism, given and received correctly, can be extremely beneficial. But there are no benefits from destructive criticism. It destroys children; it can destroy anyone.

Children have an innate need for protection, support, emotional security and love. Anyone who has children has seen siblings competing for the attention and praise of their parents. To a child, being criticised by a parent is seen a withdrawal of love, which leaves them feeling unprotected and afraid. And we cannot feel this way, for feeling fearful means our survival is under threat and we have to do something about it.

And children will do something about it. We see them doing things to try and please their parent, constantly asking if they are doing things well enough, if they are good enough.

With constant criticism, be it direct or implied, we can never do well enough and eventually we come to think that it's actually us, our self, our very being that is not good enough.

Destructive personal criticism is an attack and it's not just the words used. Being told that we are *'stupid'* or *'useless'*, that *'we can't do anything right'*, that *'we always fail'* and *'will never* amount to anything' or that we are 'pathetic', 'fat', 'lazy" or 'ignorant' is bad enough but it doesn't end there. It is the manner in which such things are said to us that damages the most.

To be called 'stupid' by someone jokingly with a smile is not the same as being called 'stupid' by someone who is angry and exuding hatred and disgust.

Young children, without an understanding of language, have a greater awareness of things that accompany it such as tone of voice and body language. Studies have shown that perception of emotion in the face and voice begins during the first year of life.[6] Necessarily, when vocabulary is limited, a greater emphasis is placed on the way something is said rather than what is said. Children *feel* how their parents are interacting with them. As adults we may still possess these skills, although blunted with time, and use them to judge the real truth behind what someone is saying.

Things said with an aggressive posture in a harsh and accusing tone of voice are attacks which make a child feel physically bad: tense, distressed and anxious. Unfortunately, many parents may criticise their children in just such a way. Harsh words said in a harsh manner.

If only we had known at the time, that the anger and distaste displayed by our parents as they criticised us was what they actually felt about themselves and not us.

* * * * *

The effects of Identification, family conflict and parental criticism are all related to our perceptions of losing the protection and love of our parents. To exist in an environment of conflict and criticism makes us feel insecure and feel as if we are being rejected by our own parents. This perceived loss of love may also occur when parents are absent from the child's life, through, for example: parental separation, being reared mainly by nannies or sent away to boarding school. Indeed, the latter, sending a young child away from their parent's protection to an often hostile environment can have a profound effect on many children.

It is important to realise that it is what the child feels that counts. Feeling bad due to our parent's actions cause us to question what our parents think of us and also what is wrong with us for them to behave like that toward us. Surely, there can be no greater negative life experiences for a child than those that lead to constant feelings of insecurity and anxiety.

Studies on healthy families, in communities where external stress is minimal, over a number of years have found that when a family has problems it sends stress hormones coursing through a child's system.[7]

In extreme cases, those that constitute abuse of the child, we can see how the child's self-identity can be severely damaged. The child's survival is directly threatened and negative feelings regarding safety and self-worth often lead to the child blaming themselves even more, for the behaviour of the parent.

Thankfully, only a tiny fraction of parents really don't love their children and many of these are often severely mentally ill. The majority of parents do love their children but, for a variety of reasons, are unable to show it. Many have their own problems expressing feelings, don't have the time or emotional energy or do mean to love their children but never get around to it. Love is also a verb not just a noun.

Identification involves love; we identify with something to enhance how we feel about our self and we love something that makes us feel good about ourselves.

We wouldn't identify with a parent who never loved us; we would not look up to them nor want any of their qualities. We wouldn't want to be like them and would probably become indifferent to them. It may be that such a situation underpins many psychoses, in which compassion toward others and self-control is rarely shown.

Interestingly, if a lack of love plays a part in psychoses, then receiving love may help these problems, and one study, the Soteria Project, appears to show that it does.[8] Here, acutely distressed psychotic patients were treated with maximum kindness and minimum medication and many of them fared as well as patients treated in conventional psychiatric ways. Perhaps love is all we need?

Strong identification with a parent that we look up to, one that we want to be like, who then starts to treat us in a way that makes us feel insecure and unloved is a situation which can underpin all anxiety-related problems. Same sex parent-child conflicts may have a more profound effect: just how many mother-daughter conflicts are played out on the battleground of Anorexia Nervosa.

Variations in same/opposite sex and present/non-present parent identification and conflict probably shape the problems that develop. Of course, strong love from one parent may make up for a deficit of love from the other.

Over time we are conditioned to feel physically bad and bad about ourselves. A situation that involves alternating periods of being treated well and being treated badly produces the greatest conditioning of all. If we are treated well all of the time we behave accordingly; if we are treated badly all of the time we also learn how to behave accordingly; but if we are treated well and treated badly at random – we just don't know how to behave. Even if we are treated well on successive occasions, we never know whether the next time will be good or bad. Hence we can end up constantly anxious.

Over time, with strong identification and corresponding feelings of withdrawal of love, we can become conditioned into a state that lies at the heart of all anxiety-related problems: *part of our self feels bad about our self.*

The above can explain the core 'feeling bad' found at the heart of many anxiety and depression problems. But this is just the start.

This may be how many people exist, driven by an inner insecurity that promotes a life ruled by shyness or stress. Too anxious to try in case we are rejected or constantly looking for love and acceptance through achievement. Others may go on to develop 'disorders' involving anxiety and depression. But there are other influences and things that have to happen for these problems, these 'disorders', to develop and grow – things we shall come to soon.

It may seem that anxiety and depression problems are therefore ingrained in us and that we cannot do anything about them, but that isn't the case. The past is the past, it has happened and can't be changed; it is what we think about the past and what we do to ourselves in the present because of it, that affects us now – and this can be changed. We need to accept the past and not deny it, to understand it and change our beliefs and attitude toward it so that we can move forward. We need to understand our experiences, the people involved and more importantly, the conclusions we drew about our role in them, for it's not the experiences themselves that do the lasting damage, it's what we make of them. We have to understand how we learnt to think and behave because of our experiences.

Love or the perceived lack of love and the way in which it can relate to our self-concept isn't the only way that we are shaped by our parents. We are also moulded by the things they teach us, either directly or indirectly. From social anxiety disorder through to eating disorders and depression, the type of anxiety-related problem that we develop may, in part, come from what we learn from our parents.

Learning From Our Parents

Our parents teach us things directly, through what they tell us, things we should know and things we should do. Knowing that knives are sharp, fires are dangerous and to be careful when crossing the road, ensure our safety. They necessarily instil apprehension and fear over something that could harm us. Many fears can be taught directly and are beneficial but if we are constantly prevented from taking risks we never learn that we can overcome challenges successfully.

Humans are obedient to authority, the child is taught to be obedient while taught to be good. Fear of authority is a powerful incentive for behaviour change and as children we are often told how to behave correctly (in our parent's eyes). It's not difficult to see how constantly being told to "look your best" and "do your best" or that "nice girls are clean, not dirty" can set the scene for social anxiety or obsessive and compulsive behaviour, later in life. Our parent's attitude and expression can often convey their disappointment in our behaviour.

We are also directly influenced by the way we are rewarded or punished for certain behaviour. Children with parents who may not be warm and loving but reward them for excellence may become over-achievers, afraid of disappointing their parents and teachers initially and later of disappointing their friends, employer and spouse. Academic achievement and self-esteem are linked,[9] and achieving becomes a way to be recognised and validated.

Achievement and wanting to achieve is normal; it drives us to perform well, the best that we can. But when this achievement becomes a desperate need, compensation for lack of love, it can be debilitating. With the need for achievement comes expectation, direct or implied, and this can put anyone under tremendous pressure. A child placed under extreme pressure to perform during his or her education can become an adult who feels bad no matter how much they achieve.

Being punished aggressively can lead us to believe that this is the correct way to act. Witness the little girl smacking and scolding her doll; in the same way her mother did to her.

Within the family, the expression of beliefs may also shape us. Telling us things like "this family are all well-built" or "this family will always have to work hard" can be setting the foundations for our self-image. Stereotypical roles may also be played out. Comments about children who are: "the clever one", "the gifted one" or "the pretty one" can leave other children feeling that they are never good enough. Resentment between siblings, fostered by their differential treatment by parents, can last a lifetime. Parents may also provide conflicting information; preaching one thing yet doing another.

We also learn from our parents by watching them. In children's play we can often see the entire parental role reproduced, including the appropriate mannerisms, tone of voice and attitude.

Children see and copy their parent's behaviour since they feel that it is the correct way to behave.

We may copy our parent's depression in times of sadness, their anxiety or anger when stressed or their concern with things being seen to be right in public. A mother who feels herself to be 'weak' and 'hopeless' may well generate those same feelings in us.

Our parents therefore shape us enormously, through how we come to feel about ourselves and how we learn to behave. As we grow, other influences, from outside the family come into play: school, peers, teachers, society and the media, all play a part, and we'll look at these later.

But it's our parents that touch our inner-self and their influence can last many years. Women marry men who have the qualities of their father and men marry women with their mother's qualities. How many people spend a lifetime following a profession that their father wanted?

Healthy identification with a good role model is ideal whereas excessive identification with a weak role model can be disastrous.

Save those parents with severe mental illness, many of our parents treat us in a way that makes us feel rejected and unloved – but why?

Why They Do It

Some parents can't help themselves. Just as we cannot stop scrubbing our hands clean in the compulsions of OCD, although we know it's wrong, they cannot stop themselves being angry and critical of a child whose imperfections, they believe, reflect on themselves. They are driven by their own feelings of weakness and self-doubt.

Are such parents really weak? Are they not strong and it's us that are weak? Well, consider this ...

Without exception, those who criticise others can rarely take criticism themselves and they never fail to tell us just how good they are as they berate us. Most of them would never (dare) say to another adult, the things they say to us and are often kinder to strangers than they are to their own family.

If we were actually behaving badly or wrongly, a strong parent would explain why it was wrong, they would show us the correct behaviour; they would guide and support us in order to help us improve. They certainly would not make us feel humiliated and ashamed. Many of our parents have greater problems than we realise. They are angry and frustrated at their own lives and they hate it, they don't hate us – it just feels as though they do.

It is not possible for some parents to show love, they were never shown any, so how can they? Some may compensate for this by providing a good home for their children but unfortunately, for our inner-self, material possessions are irrelevant. We may have a nice house, nice car, everything that money can buy, but if there is no love in the house we are the poorest of all.

The hopes and fears of our parents can drive much of their behaviour toward us. Their failures drive us to succeed. A father who is a perfectionist in order to cope may strongly believe that his son needs to do things to perfection in order to succeed. A parent who feels hindered in life by lack of education or one who is successful because of it will do all they can to ensure that their children are well educated.

On the other hand, many a parent may try to obtain success through their children, push them excessively and get angry with them when they fail. Just watch most of the fathers at their child's football game.

At the end of the day, when we look back on our childhood and its connection to anxiety and depression problems, and to a parent that made us feel bad, it may be prudent to think that he or she has probably suffered as bad a problem as we have. And that many are doing the best they can given their problems, trying to give their offspring the advantages they never had.

* * * * *

However, some people think that our parents barely influence us, that these people who create us, control us, help us survive, provide food, warmth and shelter, teach us what is right and what is wrong, reward and punish us, make us feel good and make us feel bad, those who provide daily examples of behaviour, don't really affect us.

They point to studies carried out on adults who weren't reared by their parents and to those on genetically similar twins reared in different families. Evidence of an anxiety disorder in such studies is seen as evidence that the parent's role is limited,[10] and that the problem is due to other influences or perhaps genetics.

But these studies miss a vital point, possibly an inherent flaw with such studies: children who aren't reared by their parents are separated from their parents – the parents are absent, a situation which, in itself, may be experienced as a withdrawal of parental love, a precursor to self-doubt and anxiety problems. Also, many adopted or foster children feel the need to find their biological parents when they are old enough. They need to find the parent to discover where they themselves came from, hence who they themselves are.

Our parents are in our genes; nothing will ever influence what we feel about our self like they do – and while we're talking about genes, let's take a look at something many people feel plays an important role – genetics.

The Role of Genetics

Many anxiety 'disorders' and depression can be seen to run in families, but it's too easy to see this as proof of genetics being the cause of these problems. A depressed or anxiety-riddled parent may treat their child in such a way, and provide such a role model, that the child could develop emotional problems entirely through learning and conditioning.

Human beings are complex. If all the DNA (deoxyribonucleic acid) in your body were laid end to end, it would reach to the sun and back over 600 times.[11] Over 99% of our DNA sequence is the same as other humans.

Genes are made of DNA; our entire DNA sequence is known as a *genome*, which comprises an estimated 20000-25000 genes. They are pieces of DNA passed from parent to offspring that contain hereditary information. A parent and child share 50% of their genes as do siblings. Identical twins share 100% of their genes.

Once the human genome was mapped (the entire DNA sequence that makes up humans) it was hoped to be able to identify and cure the genetic cause of almost everything. But that didn't happen. Whilst ground has been made identifying DNA mutations or variations that may be associated with a higher risk for certain diseases, the actual situation is a great deal more complex. The position of the genes in relation to others and interactions between them may exert as great an influence as the genes themselves. It's the structure as a whole, the system, not just its constituent parts that is important. Anxiety and depression problems are the same, it's the whole system that counts – our mind and body and the environment they are in.

For all we know, such a process may also apply to the hereditary information that passes between parent and child. Not just physical attributes and behaviour traits but emotional elements, such things as hopes, fears and frustrations, things that have played a large part in the whole system of our parent's existence, could, in theory, be passed on too.

If a person has survived in life (and very importantly, survived at the level of his inner-self) despite an existence racked by worry, compulsions or depression, it's not unreasonable to assume that these survival 'tactics' will be passed to his offspring in order to increase their chances of survival. A lifelong depressive, no doubt, passes genetic information appropriate to having depression to his offspring.

However, DNA is our past not our future. Information that is passed between a parent and child does not result in actual behaviours, but predispositions. Not fixed behaviours but ways of behaving we are susceptible to develop given the right stimulation. A parent cannot pass on fixed behaviours, for the environment the child is born into is unknown; the knowledge we inherit has to flexible to enable us to adapt and survive – reacting with extreme anxiety to unconditional love would not be adaptive.

We all come predisposed to learn language, but the main language we eventually learn to speak depends on where in the world we are born. Racehorses are bred to be good runners but they still have to be groomed and trained. Any genetic information that we receive from our parents can only be put into practice if the appropriate environment exists. Inter-family conflict and destructive criticism are two environments appropriate to the development of many anxiety problems.

Complex interactions between predisposition and environment probably influence the development of anxiety-related problems and the strength of the problem. But it's the environment (our experiences) that holds the upper hand. The genetic influence sits quietly in the background, waiting to develop and flourish in the right circumstances or wither and die if not called upon. A severely 'anxiety-disordered' person can, by treating them in the right way, raise a totally emotionally healthy child ... many do.

There is also evidence to suggest that genes can be altered through learning.

The popular belief among scientists has been that, although the environment influenced natural selection, mutation was random. That is, for example, environmental changes may favour certain characteristics of a species such that only those members that possess such characteristics survive to pass on their genes, but genetic changes were purely random, it happened by chance and may or may not confer benefits for survival.

However, experiments by Barbara McClintock in the 1950's showed vast changes in the DNA of plants occurring when they were stressed.[12] A stressful environment actually resulted in whole sequences of DNA moving from one place to another, even inserting themselves into active genes. Not random behaviour, there was a method to their shifting and it was triggered by outside influences such as changes in the environment: extreme heat or drought that threatened the survival of the plant. Initially ignored by her peers, McClintock received a Nobel Prize for her work, some thirty years later.

Genes were changing due to experience in plants – imagine what may be happening within the complexity of humans.

Intuitively, we would expect this to be the case; life is about growing, learning, evolving; genes shape our reaction to our experiences and our reaction to experiences and learning must shape our genes. We need not be slaves to our genes.

* * * * *

In summary:

The helpless infant; we instinctively form attachments to our parents in order to be protected and nurtured, to survive. This is seen in all animals where the infant is born reliant on the parent and also in some adult animals. Wild dogs on the edge of settlements become friendlier in order to be given scraps of food and many family pets have now become so cute and cuddly that some people treat them as babies and children.

The bond between the helpless infant (promoted by sounds, smells and appearance) and the powerful parent (receptive to such things) ensures the survival of the infant and ultimately the survival of the parent's genes.

For the first two or three years or so, the vast majority of parents dote on their children, who feel secure and loved – witness the confidence of most small children. And as the child grows they want to be like their powerful, successful parent – generally, like the same sex parent. The more powerful and successful the child views the parent (or even an image of the parent) the greater their desires to be like the parent. This, in itself, can be a healthy and positive situation, however, as the child grows they become more aware.

We start to notice the arguments between our parents, which affect us deeply, we may even have genetic predispositions how to react to stress or have been sensitised to it in the womb. Constant arguing leads to us feeling unsure about our safety, insecure and afraid. An absent parent can make us feel the same to some extent.

As we grow, the parent who we look up to may then start to criticise us in a harsh way, destructive criticism that hurts.

The word critic comes via the Latin *criticus* meaning 'a judge'. And that's how we feel, judged by our powerful parent and left wanting, feeling that we are never good enough. Be under no illusion, destructive criticism is a destroyer, it has the greatest influence of all. It leaves us feeling not only physically bad: tense, confused, and anxious but also feeling bad about our very self. Actual physical or sexual child abuse can take this to the extreme.

Being made to feel this way by a parent we look up to can lead to an almost obsessive identification with them; wanting to be like them more and more to help us stop feeling insecure and to be loved. Such an entanglement with our parent can last many years.

Unsure about the effect of destructive criticism?

Well, consider this ... If we take two small children; one we criticise constantly, put down, humiliate, exaggerate and ridicule their failures, and mock their attempts; the other, we praise often, support, help, guide and demonstrate behaviour constructively – which will grow up afraid to do anything, totally lacking in self-confidence? And which will have total self-confidence? In fact, we could do the same to two dogs, or any other animal that is smaller than us.

Many parents do a fantastic job in raising their children, but when the main environment of a child comprises, combinations of and variations in, family conflict, destructive criticism, genetic predisposition, and parental absence, the foundation can be laid for anxiety-related problems to develop. This environment can last until we leave home.

Constant pressure and distress, in a child without the maturity and experience to cope, leads to one thing – *feeling bad,* and it's a special kind of feeling bad (as we will learn later), that lies at the heart of a myriad of anxiety and depression problems.

* * *

As we move toward our teenage years into a bigger, bolder, more competitive world, this 'feeling bad' can shape our lives. Some may stay at this stage, to various degrees, and lead lives ruled by shyness and self-doubt or spend lives behaving in self-defeating ways in times of stress, becoming 'stressed out' by their own insecurities in such times. Others may find self-comfort in food with all of its associated problems, but for many, life's progression, coupled with certain circumstances, can make the development of an anxiety disorder almost inevitable.

But before we come to what happens next in the development of anxiety and depression problems, we need to know a bit more about something that's responsible for them all ... *feelings.*

...

2

...Feelings

THEY ARE NOTHING more than feelings, but they rule our lives. What drives someone to scrub the skin from his or her hands or avoid doing things in front of others? Drives other people to starve themselves or harm themselves? Causes many to perform endless rituals and others to believe they are dying or that they are worthless?

Feelings are everything to us; they reflect our inner-self's understanding of what is happening to us in the world and what to do about it. An inner guidance system that tells us how our experiences are affecting us - they are related to survival and being in control. Feeling bad means that we are under threat, either directly or because we have no control. We all want to stay longer and enjoy any situation that makes us feel good and we'll actively seek out such situations, but when something feels bad we are driven to stop it, get away from it as soon as we can or to avoid it altogether.

It is often pointed out that many people actively seek out feeling bad, particularly being scared, through such things as scary movies or theme park rides. But this is different; in these situations we are scared whilst actually being safe, we are scared with control. Millions may pay to watch the antics of a knife-wielding maniac on screen, but nobody would want to be in the real situation. To feel bad with no control is to be really scared.

And we don't need direct experience to feel in certain ways. Our brains are programmed to empathise with others,[1] and how they feel. Feelings are shown by the expression on our faces; to know what another person is feeling can be advantageous, examples include: knowing whether someone is pleased to see us or not, and to sense what others are going through without having to go through it ourselves. In mimicking the feelings of others we feel the same way as they do to some extent. Watching a depressed relative may truly make us feel depressed.

With feelings, we feel something happening to our body; our heartbeat may speed up, our senses may sharpen or blur and we may get 'butterflies' in our tummy. But feelings are not just about physiology, they involve thoughts, experience, memories and associations. The meaning we give to our bodily sensations, a meaning that stems from past experiences associated with those sensations, colours what we feel. A faster heartbeat on a theme park ride may feel scary and exciting, but a faster heartbeat when we are harshly criticised means a threat and may come to be associated with fear more readily than excitement for many. The faster heartbeat of many people with anxiety-related problems, as it increases with anxiety or panic can be an instant reminder of insecurity and fear.

* * * * *

Most people who seek therapy do so for problems with feelings and emotions. Even when our main problem is one of incessant negative thinking, it's what we feel about this and our inability to control it that is actually the problem. How we feel about having anxiety disorders and depression or even illness, for that matter, can make things worse; feelings and emotions are paramount.

Emotions

Dictionaries define emotions as strong feelings but they are more than this, they are a combination of feelings, thoughts and behaviours. Anger may involve feelings of tension in our chest, rapid heartbeat and increased blood pressure. We may think we want to kill someone and waive our arms around or stomp our feet. Conversely, in joy, we may feel warm inside, think how much we love someone and smile or laugh.

Emotions may consist of other emotions: passion may involve enthusiasm, optimism and hopefulness; jealousy may comprise hatred, anger and revenge. We all experience a great range and mixture of feelings and emotions all the time, however, there are some feelings and emotions that seem particularly relevant to anxiety disorders and depression, namely: anger, guilt and shame.

Anger

We need anger to survive. It is the precursor to aggression; all of us may have to fight to protect our loved ones or ourselves at some stage in our lives. Like anxiety, it is an energizer, readying us for action.

Anger can mask anxiety, for example, the first reaction of a mother that has lost a child, on finding the child, is often to scold him or her, getting angry with them masks the fear of what might have happened. Similarly anxiety can mask anger.

It is natural to get angry in conflict, to want to take some action and do something about it. We often see our parents getting angry in dealing with various situations and when they act angrily toward us we want to complain, get angry back and end the conflict. But this isn't possible; we cannot fight a more powerful adult and anger toward a loved one is not acceptable because we love them and need them, so we suppress our anger. The 'angry' situation is also making us scared; anger is associated with being afraid so we suppress it further. From small children to teenagers, severe parent-child conflict often ends in tears (for the child) as the suppressed anger comes out in the form of crying.

In households of family conflict or over-strictness, some parents are angry virtually all the time. How many people with anxiety-related problems have had a childhood dominated by the angry man or woman?

Angry people get angry all the time. They know how to be angry so very well given the right situation (and isn't it strange just how often the right situation occurs for them?). Their voice, stance and what they say, demonstrate their anger impeccably.

Angry people usually want to tell others what to do and then criticise them for their shortcomings; their lack of inner peace is obvious: anger shows on their faces and in their whole demeanour, family and friends tread carefully as not to upset them.

Regarding our parent's anger, we need to realise that although it may often be directed at us, they are really angry with themselves and their lives. Regarding our own, suppressed anger, it shows in various things, such as: temper tantrums, petulance, sulking, boredom and verbal abuse as children; sarcasm, gossip, violent behaviour and illness as adults.

Suppressed anger runs throughout many, if not all, anxiety and depression-related problems. People with OCD often express high levels of aggression toward family or significant others, the release of bottled up emotions in PTSD frequently results in anger and in depression we feel that even getting angry is hopeless. Indeed, getting angry is a good defence against depression; angry people don't get depressed for they are always taking action to some degree.

It is not anger, per se, that's the problem; it's when it is not expressed or resolved that is. In (family) conflicts where the anger is not expressed or not resolved though conciliation, no making up with apologies, hugs, acceptance and compromise – anger festers inside us.

Guilt

Guilt is fear, about punishment and rejection. It involves feeling responsible for our actions and that our actions have broken the rules, rules generally laid down by our parents, grandparents, teachers, society, religion and so on. It is the regulator of the family and of society; without it, rules wouldn't be obeyed and society would break down.

Guilt involves anxiety, apprehension about being found out and punished, and anxiety promotes guilt – *"why am I anxious, what have I done"*. Conflict in families often leads to children feeling that they are to blame and that if they were better in some way, perhaps the conflict would stop. Here, guilt seems to be a by-product of the situation, although it can still affect us throughout our lives, making us feel guilty for almost everything.

Some guilt, however, is thrust directly upon us. Parents often make their children feel guilty as a means of control. Phrases such as: *"after all the sacrifices I've made for you"* and *"you have it so easy compared to my childhood"* are frequently employed and make children feel guilty for just existing.

At the extreme, in families where conflict goes hand in hand with high religious beliefs, it's not uncommon for children to be threatened with the wrath of God. Imagine being constantly under the threat of punishment from God! No wonder many children reared in such environments, feeling bad and fearing punishment from above, go on to develop compulsive rituals as the only means of allaying their anxiety.

It is relatively easy to assuage guilt; we can admit our wrong-doing, ask forgiveness and make amends. The problem is, many of us carry guilt around without actually doing anything wrong – it was just the way we were made to feel. Whereas anger can stay inside us because we are afraid to express it, guilt stays with us because there is nothing to make amends for.

The effects of guilt can mirror those of anger; unresolved guilt cuts a stream through many anxiety disorders: the obsessive-compulsive feels guilty about often-normal thoughts, the bulimic feels guilty about food and guilt, like anger, can be a defence against depression. In depression we feel helpless but at least with guilt we feel we have done something that has had some effect.

Shame

Whereas guilt is concerned with doing something wrong, shame is about feeling wrong as a person. With shame we feel bad about something about ourselves, it strikes at our very core. And it can be nothing to do with our true qualities, for example, the child from a poor background who dresses poorly is often ashamed of it, the overweight child is frequently ashamed of it, no matter how good a person they may actually be.

Shame is so powerful it can transcend death. In the fourth century B.C. in Greece and centuries later in Marseilles, suicide rates were so high that, in an effort to reduce the numbers, laws were passed decreeing that anyone who committed suicide would be dragged through the streets naked. Suicides rates dropped dramatically.[2] It seems that people could not face the public humiliation and shame (even though they wouldn't be around to experience it).

Destructive criticism creates shame, as does being severely chastised and humiliated in public.

Shame is related to a perceived 'self-weakness' and if it is felt often enough and long enough it can set the foundation for the self-hatred and self-loathing that underpins many anxiety and depression problems. These problems, in themselves, are often seen as a personal weakness and we are ashamed of having them.

Shame goes hand-in-hand with humiliation, two things that destroy people ... humiliation and shame can be the greatest form of pain. Unlike guilt, where we can atone for our deeds, shame is not so easily healed. It cannot be expressed as such, only understood and changed. Changing shame lies at the heart of healing anxiety and depression problems.

*   *   *   *   *

We have feelings for a reason, even bad ones. When a person is nice to us we feel good, when someone is nasty to us we feel bad.

Feeling bad tells us that we are in a state of distress and we need to do something about it. And often we can; we may express anger appropriately or even fight if we have to and we can atone for guilty deeds. Problems arise when bad feelings are not resolved and we still have them inside.

It's as though feelings are a form of energy that need to be released and if not released they create a tension, a pressure inside us until they are resolved. We see time and time again, people reliving bad situations, those involving: family confrontations, abusive partners and sexual abuse are common. We are driven to relive painful situations until we gain control and remove any potential threat.

It's as if our inner-self is telling us, "That painful situation wasn't resolved, you are still distressed, not in control, under threat. Go back and relive it again and this time take control, resolve it and everything will be alright, the threat will have gone".

Feelings also shape our memories. With anxiety and depression problems we seem to remember the bad things more than the good. The greater the feelings and emotions involved in an event, the stronger the memories that are formed.[3]And this makes sense; emotional events don't only provide greater chunks of information with which to form long-lasting memories, they affect us in various ways and we need to remember them for the next time. When something makes us feel bad, strong memories of it and the events surrounding it are formed, memories which, when recalled, bring back the associated emotions.

Of course, feelings aren't just about feeling bad. Feeling good reflects the joy of being alive, it relates to feelings of ease and contentment, being happy and safe, free from stress. And we *can* take control of our feelings; we can make ourselves feel good. Experiments have shown that just reading different statements associated to emotions can affect our feelings.[4]

However, this has to be done in the correct way; we cannot suddenly go from feeling terrible most of the time to feeling great, just as we cannot go from being totally unfit to supreme fitness in one leap. For now, it is enough to realise that feelings can be resolved and changed – think about something you have seen in real life, or on television, or have read that was really really funny. Imagine it as strongly as you can – how do you feel?

Feelings are vitally important to our survival; they reflect our inner-self's assessment of what is happening to us or what may happen to us, irrespective of the actual, in-the-moment physical reality.

They are the reason why a painfully thin anorexic girl can look in the mirror and see herself as fat; they are the reason the obsessive-compulsive person can lock a door, turn away from it and have to turn back and check it is locked, turn away from it again and have to turn back and check it again, turn away and back again. In both these cases, based on our previous life experiences, our inner-self is trying to protect us. But just what is this inner-self?

Our Inner-Self

Today, when we talk about being aware, we are generally talking about three levels: conscious, relating to being fully aware of our surroundings and what is happening to us; unconscious, where we aren't aware of these things and subconscious, presumably somewhere in between. The term 'inner-self', is used throughout this book to refer to some part of us, deep within ourselves, that uses all our past experiences and knowledge of the world to protect us.

Comprising all our levels of consciousness and more, perhaps even down to the level of interactions involving DNA and genes, our inner-self aims for our ultimate survival, the survival of our genes.

We are all kept alive by some part of us about which we are essentially unaware; our unconscious regulates the majority of the activities necessary for living. It transforms food and oxygen into tissues and energy, regulates body temperature, heartbeat and breathing, coordinates all the activities of the heart, lungs, liver, kidneys and stomach and oversees all necessary repairs: broken bones knit together and torn flesh heals. Deeper areas of our brain warn us about threats, through the fight-or-flight response, often before we are conscious of them. Nature does not trust man to consciously control his day–to-day survival; would she trust him to control the progression of his genes?

Until recently, the mind and body were treated as separate entities; we are now moving toward an understanding that they are intimately linked. Perhaps in the future we shall come to realise that our genes, mind and body are all intimately linked, for the main part, not fixed, but flowing and adapting – interacting with the environment and nature enabling us to learn, grow and evolve.

How ever we see this inner-self, it is a part of us deep inside, relating to our very being, that effectively assesses what is happening to us, what it means, how it relates to our existence and what we have to do about it. Our inner-self cannot see, hear, touch, smell or feel but it interprets all the information coming from our senses in line with all its stored knowledge (that derived from instincts, genetic information and experiences), and guides us appropriately. We see ourselves through our inner-self, yet our inner-self cannot see.

And the inner-self has the final say, no question about it – vast numbers of thin people look in the mirror and see themselves as fat, many good-looking people look in the mirror and see themselves as ugly. We see ourselves how we feel and when our life experiences make us feel bad continuously, there is only one conclusion that can be drawn – *we are bad*, or more accurately perhaps, we are in some way '*not good enough*' and this is where anxiety and depression problems start.

As mentioned earlier, this is a 'special' type of feeling bad and it is this that causes the problem.

Feeling Bad

Everyone is made to feel bad at times. But when it becomes a constant theme running through the background of our childhood years, it goes deeper. Prolonged family conflict and perceived lack of parental love lead to feelings of badness deep within us – our very being feels in some way not good enough.

It becomes a constant pressure, an overwhelming mixture of tangled emotions and feelings relating to: feeling scared, angry, weak, dirty, sad, bad, unloved, ashamed, guilty, not good enough and helpless, coupled with actual 'bad' physical sensations involving tension, anxiety and stress. It can be relentless and overbearing and its effects probably depend on the intensity and timescale of such pressures and the age, maturity and intellect of the child.

This inner self-doubt, this feeling bad at our core can often be seen directly in many cases of self-harm, where feelings of self-hatred and self-loathing mixed with an interminable inner stress can only find release through blood-letting. Many people with anxiety disorders and depression often look back over their childhood and see periods of being afraid of almost everything. Most, if not all, of these problems are preceded by a period in our lives of extreme nervousness.[5]

There is something 'special' (in a negative way) about this feeling bad, something that sets the scene for the development of anxiety and depression problems. *It is intangible.*

We never were bad, save normal childhood antics; we never did really bad things, yet we were constantly made to feel intensely bad. If horrible situations make us feel bad, then in times when we feel bad it must indicate to us something bad about the situation. But if there is nothing about the situation that is bad, then it must be down to us, it must be something about us that is bad.

Picture it; there was never really anything to attach all this feeling bad to, no bad deeds to explain it and no real reason for it. Faced with all this, there is only one conclusion our inner-self can make – *there must be something bad about us.*

And we never had the power to say to our parents, "you are making me feel terrible, stop it", like our anger and guilt we kept it inside us, we never ever faced the real cause of our feeling bad – this is why entanglement with our parents can last a lifetime.

In one experiment, participants who performed a test were randomly given results showing that they performed either well or badly. Those who had been given a bad result (irrespective of how they had actually done on the test) felt bad for weeks after, even though they were informed that their results were actually made up. The situation was only helped when it was explained to them how the finding out of their results would make them feel.[6] We need a reason why we feel bad; without one, we blame ourselves and the feelings grow. We feel it is due to some 'weakness' in us.

At this stage, it is important to realise that we never were bad – it was just how we were made to feel, over and over again without good reason.

It is also not necessary to reflect and analyse too much on how and why we felt bad: how much anger, guilt or shame, how often we were criticised and attacked or felt unloved or expectations of us were too high. None of this needs to be mulled over and over again once it is understood.

To change, to turn anxiety and depression problems around, all we need to realise for now is that we were, in some way, made to feel bad about our self. An intangible 'badness' or 'inadequacy', a 'not good enough' feeling at the level of our inner-self.

* * * * *

As humans, we cannot exist in a state of uncertainty; things need to have a reason and an answer, to be finalised, to be 'done and dusted' so that we can move on. If they aren't and they remain unresolved, anything could happen, we are not in control and this can lead to constant apprehension. This could be the reason why the 'intangible badness' often results in a prolonged nervousness that precedes most anxiety and depression problems.

We have to find a reason for the feelings of badness, urgently, to alleviate our anxiety; if we don't it just builds up and up.

For some, possibly with a less intense 'feeling bad', they come to believe that they are naturally shy people, a valid explanation for their feelings of insecurity and self-doubt, and they live their lives accordingly. Others may try and compensate for these feelings through eating or amassing wealth and power or they may develop a need for relentless achievement with all the stress that entails.

For many, however, as we progress through life, our experiences seem to offer reasons for our 'badness'. They falsely appear to make the intangible tangible, and mistakenly show us why or how we are bad and what we can do about it.

...

3

As We Grow...

OUR WORLD EXPANDS beyond the family. We meet many new people, develop relationships outside of home, experience more things and are open to various influences.

Initially, school and new friends dominate our learning; we meet others who are similar to us but have different qualities; social awareness and inter-personal skills begin to take shape. Groups are formed and we start to notice the importance of personal qualities. Some qualities are good and likeable and a person with such qualities is liked and accepted by the others. Other qualities are not so well accepted.

For most, early school days pass quietly; we are still relatively small, teachers are friendlier toward us, academic expectation is relatively low and we fall in and out of friendships easily.

However, as we approach the latter years of junior school (probably around eight to eleven years of age) things change. We are maturing and becoming more socially aware, our intelligence and powers of reasoning grow, things become more competitive as we prepare for a new school, academic achievement, new friends and social acceptance. This situation peaks during the first years in the new school (secondary school), and the need for social acceptance and how to achieve it becomes more important - it is probably no coincidence that this corresponds to the onset of puberty. One of the greatest influences on this social awareness is those around us of similar age and position, the people we probably spend as much time with as we do with our parents: our peer group.

Peers

There is no doubt; we can see with our own eyes, that a child's groups of friends hold a strong influence over them. Children talk like their peers (often inventing new words), dress like their peers and act like them. Smoking, drinking and even breaking the law are often regulated by the peer group.[1]

We look to our peers for guidance on how to function in society and they help shape our identity. We begin to associate personal qualities with acceptance and rejection, such qualities as: strength, good looks and fitness for boys, being slim and pretty for girls. Social acceptance is a must; even at this age, competition for survival in the world and sexual attraction is developing; young girls get 'bitchy' toward each other and young boys are competing for leadership. Being accepted by the group feels good, being rejected feels bad. We start to realise how we should be to be liked and accepted.

Our peers do hold great power over us; being shunned by them can only add to inner feelings of badness, but the power we give them relates to how we feel about our self.

The group we belong to often reflects our self-image. If we bring along deep insecurities and feeling bad we may well end up in 'lower' groups, all the while longing to be in the top group in the social rankings: those with the strong boys and the pretty girls. A family background that promotes achievement may well lead to membership of the 'brainy' group, a background of neglect or conflict, the 'rebels'. We all need to be in a group; in the past our ancestors' survival depended on it.

Groups

To not belong is to be alone and to have to defend ourselves. Animals form groups to survive; a lone wildebeest is easy prey, a group of one hundred wildebeest dramatically increases the odds of individual survival. We'll do almost anything to prevent being cast out from the group and many 'follow like sheep' rather than go against the majority and be seen to be different. Numerous studies have shown that a person will give a knowingly wrong answer in agreement with other wrong answers rather than stand out from the crowd by giving the correct answer.[2]

Groups can promote a sense of belonging and identity; there are often codes of dress that distinguishes the group, and they can increase our self-esteem and our sense of being needed. Group membership may go some way in tempering the bad feelings derived from our family. They also provide a collective knowledge, a consensus; if nine people in a group of ten believe something, they must be right (even if they are wrong) because so many people believe it.

Dynamics within groups reflect those between groups; again we see the importance of personal qualities in relation to being accepted or rejected.

Everyone has a role, each bringing their own strengths to the group; to remain in the group we need to provide a benefit to it and be seen to be strong in the group's eyes. We need to conform to the rules of the group to be accepted. The undercurrent of 'how to be' to be accepted, even within our own group is beginning to grow.

Without these specific functions and roles, the group would not survive – there can only be one leader. A soviet army experiment with the elimination of rank was quickly abandoned under combat, as it proved unworkable.[3]

To belong is an essential requirement for successful survival, when we don't belong our troubles are magnified. One of the most insidious things that can happen to us to make us feel that we don't belong is to be bullied.

Bullying

Of course, not everyone is bullied. Nor is it a prerequisite for anxiety disorders and depression, but it is a powerful influence in the lives of many.[4]

When bullied, we are victimised, under attack incessantly and helpless. There is very often little we can do to protect ourselves or prevent attack from people, or groups of people that are more powerful than us. It is helplessness similar to that felt in the conflict with our parents, helplessness similar to those feelings in depression – nothing we do has any effect and we cannot stop it. We have no power to change the situation, we can only suffer it.

It's not just the small and weak that are bullied; many children with desirable qualities are bullied through jealousy. The bully gathers a group to attack the person they are jealous of, often turning the child's own friends against them. Being made to feel bad by a group of people at school can only reinforce any bad feelings at home.

Being bullied is a terrible experience even if we have supportive, loving parents back home, so it's not difficult to see that for a child who is bullied at school then goes home to conflict and criticism, life can seem unbearable.

Schadenfreude – a German word that has no direct English equivalent, broadly means - to enjoy watching someone else suffer. Many bullies do. Others in the group may not and secretly feel sorry the victim, yet conform to the standards of the group, changing their attitude and actions to fit in, more out of survival instinct than true intent, relieved that it is not them that is being attacked.

It may not seem like it as they overwhelm us and cause us pain, but it is perfectly true – bullies are weak and inadequate. Very few bullies work alone, most bully people with the support of others. The support of 'the pack' is often the only acceptance that these sick individuals can get. It shows not strength but weakness, to attack somebody who cannot fight back. Bullies are indeed weak and inadequate where it counts most – in person and in spirit; they are chewed up inside with their own inner conflict and the only way that they can get relief is to make someone else feel worse than them and take pleasure in it.

* * * * *

Outside the home, interactions with our peers shape and mould our development. And our new experiences generally bring with them new authority figures, new role models and new rules.

Significant Others

Significant others are people who have some importance in our lives, some form of power over us. Their power may be related to coercion (force) or knowledge or in their provision of rewards. It may be legitimate due to their position, for example: policeman, doctor, teacher and boss or it may be referent whereby we attach importance to them and their values because we like or admire them. The more significant they are to us the more importance we attach to their opinions, attitudes and beliefs. The more qualities we admire in them the more they can affect us. To be criticised by a teacher we admire affects us more than criticism from one we don't like. Being put down feels different if it comes from someone we respect or from someone we think is a fool. Of course, constant criticism from anyone who has power over us, whether we like them or not, can affect us.

We can also look to other people outside the home as role models. We may admire the qualities of a favourite teacher or youth club leader and want to emulate them and even identify with them to some extent. Famous people: stars of movies, television and music often appear to show us what qualities are necessary for great success in life and many people look up to them and want to be like them.

As mentioned earlier, a favourite aunt who lives with depression or compulsive behaviour could influence how we ourselves learn to behave, particularly in times of stress, as may a grandfather who is always angry. Like our parents, anyone of significance can teach us fears directly.

Without doubt, significant others can affect us and hurt us and we may even identify with certain ones to some extent. They may help weaken or strengthen bad feelings we already have but it is unlikely that they can, in themselves, affect us as deeply as our parents can. They are not in our genes and not part of us.

This may even apply in cases where children are not brought up by their parents. Yes they may affect us, (perhaps even more so if they are a relative and there is some genetic connection) but not as deeply as our parents.

Most of our important interactions with peers and significant others take place in school, an environment that guides much of a child's personal and social development. For some of us, our schooldays 'are the best days of our lives', for others they aren't.

School

For many, going to school is like facing a phobia every day. We head to school knowing that we are going to be bullied again, knowing that we cannot do anything about it. We go to school knowing that we will be expected to perform and not only do we have to perform, but the result of our performance will be seen by all. Every test is an opportunity to show that we are not good enough, another opportunity to let our parents and our teachers down ... to let ourselves down.

Is it any wonder that some children, feeling bad and insecure inside, develop phobias of going to school where they have to face their fears constantly?

School is all about performance, and so is Social Anxiety Disorder. How many have sat in class waiting their turn to speak, to give an answer or recite something, and felt the anxiety and fear build up? Yes, such a situation can be nerve-wracking for anyone but when we bring to it deep feelings of insecurity, weakness and fear of rejection it is much more. It is no longer just mild anxiety but the beginnings of panic.

Of course, school can be great. We can gain new knowledge and understanding about many things. We learn discipline and new skills, cultivate a work ethic and develop a sense of pride and achievement. We progress socially and often make many new friends, some that can last a lifetime.

But there is one more thing about school, more precisely the education system, to consider. School channels our thinking in well defined directions; it is not the best thinkers that are rewarded, but those that think in the right way about the right things that achieve good examination results. Perhaps this is why many of the highest achievers in life fared badly at school.

This conditioning, about what is right and true, continues throughout life, whereby we tend to believe that anything any authority says is correct. Such a situation may hold the fabric of society together, but it has implications for those with anxiety 'disorders'. It influences what we believe about these problems and the hold they have over us. Much of the strength of anxiety-related problems comes from what we believe them to be. When we know what they truly are, much of their power vanishes.

Outside school, other environments impact our development. A child's intelligence and that of their parents, the affluence of the family and the neighbourhood, and the availability of contact with extended family members can all influence the route that inner feelings of 'badness' can take. We may react to it by trying to figure it out (thinking too much – never a good idea) or by fighting in the street.

Society, religion and the media all have a part to play in shaping and moulding us. In a sense, these operate in the background; they are not our main concern at this stage, which generally involves social relationships. They affect us as we grow and continue their effect throughout our adult lives, providing all-encompassing environments that are often supportive of, and even promote anxiety-related problems. As such, we'll take a closer look at them later.

* * * * *

As we grow it's not just our experiences and learning that change. Our body is now changing too, physically, preparing us for adulthood.

Adolescence

Defined by physical changes, awkwardness, idealism, self-consciousness, rebelliousness and mood swings, adolescence, in itself, can involve a roller coaster ride of mixed emotions and feelings. Self-awareness increases and magnifies any self-image problems.

Adolescence marks the transition toward independence, to make our own way in the world. We are moving from being a dependent child to an independent adult. Even in low-conflict families, arguments between adolescent sons and daughters and their parents erupt as parental ideals are challenged in the first step toward asserting independence.

To start to make our own way in the world and rely on our own strengths and abilities can be an enormous pressure, especially if we feel we don't have any. It can be scary to grow up.

It has often been commented how conflict in our childhood may lead to 'being stuck' at some level as a child in relation to some unresolved conflict. But there may be a greater influence on child-like behaviour in adulthood. In parent-child conflict, the child is often scared of the adult. And yet, we have to grow up to be like someone who scares us. How can we grow into something we are scared of? We can't, so part of us is scared to grow up.

Adolescents may cope in various ways. Some research draws distinctions between three types of coping: active coping, internal coping and withdrawal.[5] Essentially; doing something about it, planning to do something about it or avoiding it. Coping styles that reflect our self-confidence: if we feel powerful, we'll do something about the situation; if we don't feel powerful, but not powerless, we'll plan to do something about it and if we feel powerless, we'll avoid the situation. The latter, planning and avoidance reflect elements of many anxiety and depression problems.

The change in our bodies can have a drastic effect and is often the basis for worries and feelings of inadequacy as we compare ourselves with our peers and come up short. Sexual development is a prime concern for both sexes. The size and shape of the genitals for boys and the breasts for girls often create concern for everyone. However, when we tie such worries in with pre-existing self-doubts and feeling bad, they can become obsessive.

And it's not just the sexual areas of our bodies. Any part will do. If we feel intangibly bad about ourselves and some part of our body makes us feel bad, the two can become inextricably linked. Our bad feelings now have a reason: we are bad because some part of our body is 'wrong'.

This can lead to an obsession with the offending body part and fruitless attempts to rectify it, an all-consuming problem in itself. A reaction to life's experiences that has been deemed a 'disorder' and given a name – Body Dysmorphic Disorder (BDD).

Dislike or hatred of, disgust with, or feelings of inadequacy over some part of our body can be one of the early symptoms in the development of anxiety-related problems. It shows that we have an intangible badness and (at the level of the inner-self) we are making associations with personal and physical qualities and what is happening in our life in an attempt to explain and justify it.

Throughout the changes taking place in adolescence, family relationships also change. Existing parental conflict may increase as our youth and striving for independence annoy our parents even more, and conflict with our siblings, probably always present to some degree, may increase. Research has shown that problems such as anxiety were more common in early adolescence in children whose siblings had been more hostile toward them when they were younger.[6] As we grow, relationships with our siblings may become more competitive and potentially more hostile, adding to the environment of conflict.

* * * * *

In summary:

As we move outside the family, we bring how we feel about our self to new experiences and relationships. Significant others, peers and our group of friends can weaken or confirm our feelings of 'inner-badness'. Throughout all this, family conflict may continue or increase.

Society imposes rules to control our behaviour; religion may instil fears over natural behaviours, such as sex, and the media shows how personal qualities and possessions equate to success in life. We are developing socially and begin to realise how our personal qualities and our behaviour determines our popularity and acceptance in society.

Our Family life shapes how we feel about our self, our social life shows us where we stand in the world. From feelings of inner badness and life's teachings of what is good and successful, the formation of 'how to be' takes place. We may feel bad, but we can see what it takes to feel good – what qualities offer acceptance and success. We may feel bad, but we can see 'how to be' to be good.

This 'how to be' often shapes the anxiety disorder, but even at this stage, the development of anxiety-related problems are not a certainty.

The development of anxiety disorders and depression usually requires one more thing, something that 'kick-starts' these problems. Something that connects the insecurity we feel deep inside to seemingly real physical evidence that we are under threat ... the panic attack!

...

4

...Panic Attack

THE DAY OUR experiences result in extreme anxiety or a panic attack about which we become acutely aware, from that day on our lives have changed. From that day on, our inner-self takes over in a way that we previously didn't need it. We now become driven to find reasons and answers, driven to constantly watch ourselves and to look out for failure and negative outcomes, to concentrate on that one bad quality or weakness among the many good and strong ones. We are driven to behave in ways that make us angry or scared, despairing and frustrated, ways that make us more anxious, ways we believe help to protect us.

A panic attack (and to some extent, continuous high anxiety) changes things dramatically. We become extremely self-conscious, more aware of how we feel, our actions, our surroundings and other people. To our inner-self, the physiological symptoms of the panic attack show that we are under immediate threat – but we aren't. Again, like the intangible 'badness', we experience intense, unpleasant feelings without an apparent direct cause. Not surprisingly, for many people, it can seem like these panic attacks come 'out of the blue' – in reality they don't.

To that part of us deep inside, the part that operates with feelings – we are 'bad' and we are in danger; we are, as confirmed by our feelings, inadequate, weak and vulnerable and we need to be alert at all times, prepared for any threat. It is no exaggeration to say that, for many of us, the day we have a panic attack our lives are changed. Our main focus now becomes our self and what could happen to us.

Much research shows that panic attacks are implicated in the development of many anxiety disorders[1] (not just panic disorder), but before we look at why they happen and what they lead to, we need to understand more about the underlying factors, namely: panic, anxiety and fear.

Fear

Fear drives all anxiety; it is an emotional reaction to the threat of being hurt. Dangerous situations (or the thought of them) cause reactions in our body and it's these body reactions as much as the threat itself that guides our behaviour. We don't have to stand up close to a lion and see its teeth and claws to be afraid. One far off in the distance can cause enough anxiousness in our bodies to keep us well away from it.

Some fears are programmed into us for survival. It probably didn't take too many attacks by wild animals on our distant ancestors for them to realise the danger and learn to avoid such animals or be prepared when facing them. An inner 'preparedness' for such dangers increases the chances of survival for the species. Fears programmed for survival include the following categories: -

- Potentially dangerous animals, insects and people
- Naturally dangerous environments (eg. heights, darkness)
- Dangerous situations (eg. trapped in confined spaces)
- Infection and disease / blood and injury

Like much of our genetic information, even survival-promoting fears are mediated by learning. Indeed, most of our fears come to us not through direct experience but by learning. Almost everyone fears snakes, yet few people have actually seen a real snake or been threatened by one. Our fear of snakes comes from what we have learned about them, usually from others, via such things as books and television, or at school.

In one experiment demonstrating this, young rhesus monkeys were introduced to a large, harmless snake. The snake moved freely around the monkeys and they showed no fear. The monkeys were then shown other monkeys reacting in terror to a large snake. Once they had witnessed this, no snake could again be introduced to the young monkeys without them being terrified, even a toy snake.[2] To learn from a parent, anxious or depressed in times of stress, potentially has a survival value to us.

Another way we learn fear is by conditioning; here, we become conditioned to fear certain things.

Conditioning

Through conditioning, repeated exposure to situations, and, importantly, things associated with them, can elicit responses in our body that become 'ingrained' in us; we become 'programmed' to react in certain ways to certain things.

In a classic experiment in the early 1900's, the forerunner of virtually every experiment on conditioning, Ivan Pavlov, a Russian physiologist, demonstrated how this works. Hungry dogs were presented with food and they would salivate, a natural response elicited by the smell of the food. Then a light would be turned on just before the food was presented; this was repeated a number of times; eventually the light would be turned on without any food being presented to the dogs; they would salivate at the light alone.[3]

Light does not induce salivation in dogs, food does. The light had become associated with the food and in itself could produce the body response of salivation. Here we see a classic example of body responses based on associations, and in humans, fear by association forms the basis of most, if not all, anxiety-related problems.

Of course, the properties of the light itself did not cause the salivation; it was the connection to what was coming next (the food). Perceptions of what is going to happen next, and 'what could happen', underlie all fears. With the lion above, we don't have to go any closer to it for we know what could happen.

Nowhere is the fear of 'what could happen' seen more explicitly than in Generalized Anxiety Disorder. Excessive worrying over what could happen defines this 'disorder'. Obsessive-Compulsive Disorder too, shows us the same. Rituals are a last resort; attempts to take some form of control over powerful forces we feel may harm us, to feel in some way in charge of what may happen.

'Fear can, though it is not God, create something from nothing'
- Caspar De Aguilar

In the Pavlov experiment above, the situation could be reversed, the responses extinguished. If the dogs were repeatedly shown a light but no food was presented, salivation would stop. In effect the dogs had been re-conditioned back to normal. Known as extinction, variations in this approach are used in many therapies, whereby exposure to fear-evoking situations whilst remaining relaxed, re-conditions us to be less fearful.

Some types of response are easy to extinguish, but others, those relating to self-preservation are more difficult. Because they are related to survival they form strong connections in our brain, we don't have to learn fear about something that could kill us, twice.

Anxiety-related problems are all about such fears, for example:

- Generalized Anxiety Disorder – fear of bad things happening
- Obsessive Compulsive Disorder – fear of harm (or harming) by unseen forces (eg. contamination)
- Social anxiety Disorder – fear of attack by others
- Panic Disorder – fear that something bad is happening to our body

And so on. Every anxiety-related problem has fear of survival, a fear of existing, at its heart. And these fears are not irrational; they developed for a reason – our experiences, and they exist for a reason – our survival.

Some say that modern living has allayed many of our natural fears, those relating to wild animals and insects, for example. And that these natural fears have become displaced to more various things, resulting in a myriad of weird and wonderful fears and phobias. One website lists over 500 phobias in alphabetical order.[4]

But these fears haven't gone; two hundred years of modern living doesn't wipe out millions of years of evolution. Every single phobia reflects a fear for our survival. We may have good reason to fear clowns (the phobia: Coulrophobia), for we cannot tell in their face, their true intent toward us. That painted on smile could mask mal-intent. And the phobia of peanut butter sticking to the roof of the mouth (Arachibutyrophobia) must be associated to choking.

In a similar argument, if all our fears are survival-related, then why aren't we afraid of such things as electrical sockets, guns and cars? The answer is simple; these things in themselves are inanimate, they cannot approach us and harm us. Everyone would be petrified of touching a live electrical wire, facing somebody shooting bullets with a gun, or standing in front of a speeding car.

The fears involved in many anxiety and depression problems are related to inner survival fears but they are not the actual fears. As such, they are not as strong and, although difficult, they can be changed.

Consider this: Would you face your fears for a day for £10000? Don't scrub your hands or perform rituals; stop worrying; go for a walk outside or shopping to the local mall, for £10000.

Would you? If not, how about £100000?

One thing is for sure. None of us would spend a day standing next to a wild lion for any amount of money – for it would mean certain death. This is a true survival fear.

Once we understand what we truly fear and the reality of why and how it is affecting us, we can change things.

From fear comes: helplessness, hopelessness, guilt, frustration and anger. But fear itself does not mobilise us into action. It shares a behavioural passivity with depression; in fact, fear immobilizes us. For action we need an energizer and that energizer is anxiety.

Anxiety

Imagine you're lying on a beach. It's a beautiful day, the sun is shining and there is a gentle breeze wafting over your body. Sounds of nature fill the air as you chat and laugh with family and friends. You are surrounded by people you love and respect and who love and respect you. You feel warm, contented and happy, totally relaxed, anxiety-free.

Now imagine a very different scene. It's the dead of night; you are alone walking down a dimly lit alley. There are doorways on either side – who knows what's hiding in them, waiting to pounce? You are scared, your senses are heightened – your sight and hearing have become more sensitive, able to pinpoint the slightest movement or sound. Your breathing and heartbeat have become more rapid, you feel light-headed and dizzy, want to go to the toilet or throw up, your limbs feel shaky and your whole body is now charged with energy, full of anxiety, ready to fight or flee, possibly for your life.

These two scenes represent either end of the anxiety scale. In the first we feel warm, secure and safe, we are fully relaxed. In the second we are fully tense, in a state of preparedness, highly alert and scared. Anxiety involves a series of mind and body reactions that have evolved over millions of years and are essential to the survival of all living things.

We need to realise this – anxiety is not wrong, it is an essential part of the human condition. It prepares us and energizes us into action and it is brought to life by fear. It is a part of being alive, and although we may not realise it, anxiety is with us all at varying strengths throughout our lives:

- Without anxiety (fear of being knocked down and killed) we wouldn't be careful when we crossed the road.
- Without anxiety (fear of not having food and shelter, or recognition, status, achievement) we wouldn't go to work each day.
- Without anxiety (fear of failure) the performances of athletes, entertainers, executives, students etc. would suffer.

Everyone has anxiety, even confident people. The problem is not anxiety, but why we have it, why it comes to us so readily and why it is so strong and so persistent. Without insight, this problem seems insurmountable but with what we now know, the answer is clear. Inner feelings of being in some way 'bad' or 'not good enough' combined with evidence of being in danger (from panic or prolonged periods of intense anxiety) leaves us in a constant state of preparedness – acutely sensitive to our surroundings, what could happen and how we are feeling. We are in a higher state of arousal than others, acutely more sensitive and aware. Measures of physiological arousal states constantly show an increased resting heartbeat rate in those with anxiety-related problems.[5]

This constant state of apprehension is the reason we get more anxious than normal in mild-anxiety provoking situations and why we panic in greater anxiety-provoking situations; many of us live our lives with an undercurrent of anxiety.

A timid little mouse, always anxious and vigilant, and with good reason. He is so small, weak and vulnerable that everything is a potential threat to him; every situation offers the opportunity to be attacked. Many children from backgrounds of constant conflict do, indeed, grow up to be 'as timid as a mouse'.

Not due to illness or disorder, the increased anxiousness of many people is purely due to life experiences and learning. Many anxieties and fears are 'given' to us socially; examples include those relating to shame and guilt for behaving badly and the fear of punishment. So many things can seem to be an integral part of us, a part of our nature, when in reality they were actually learned.

Anxiety is a 'protector' and a 'preparer'; the level of anxiety we have, shows us just how much our inner-self feels we need to be protected and prepared. It is related to coping, how we feel we can cope with the situation. The more we feel that we cannot cope, the more anxiety we experience, and when we feel 'not good enough' and 'that everything we do is wrong' we don't feel that we can cope with much.

Anxiety disorders may or may not involve depression, but all depression involves anxiety, usually extreme anxiety and for good reason – when depressed, we feel helpless and that everything we do is hopeless, we feel unable to cope with everything.

Anxiety prepares and protects us in two main ways.

It helps prepare our body for action, makes us more alert, ready to fight or flee from any imminent threat to our survival, just like when we see a wild lion in the distance. This is related to the direct anxiety symptoms such as fast heartbeat, fast breathing, being jittery and on edge, trembling etc. We can go from being totally relaxed to totally tense and prepared in an instant, which is panic. The fight-or-flight response relates to both anxiety and panic and we'll learn more about this shortly.

Anxiety also causes us to plan ahead for any potential dangers and how we may deal with them – an excellent survival strategy (it's better to deal with a danger or avoid it before we get in the situation) but an unfortunate effect of this is that we can get anxious/nervous just thinking about situations; a main ingredient of many anxiety disorders, it is related to symptoms such as persistent negative thoughts and excessive worrying.

Some typical symptoms of anxiety are seen below. These are associated with our body preparing for action; our mind trying to figure out what is happening, what could happen and why, and the resulting behaviours in order to protect ourselves:

Our body:

- Breathing becomes more rapid
- Heart beat speeds up
- We feel dizzy and light-headed
- We get 'butterflies' in our stomach
- We feel sick and/or need the toilet
- Our mouth becomes dry and it feels difficult to swallow
- We sweat more
- We feel 'jittery'/'jumpy'/'on-edge'

Our thoughts:

- We feel frightened
- We think people are looking at us
- We worry that we may lose control or make a fool of ourselves in front of others
- We feel that we must escape and get to a safe place

Our behaviour:

- We hurry out of places or situations where we feel anxious
- We walk to avoid taking the bus
- We cross the street to avoid people
- We make excuses to avoid going places or doing things
- We may have a drink or take a tablet before doing something we find stressful

The above symptoms aptly demonstrate the significance of fearing that we cannot cope and the physiological sensations in our body merely confirm our fears. Our mind, body and behaviour all working together.

Most of our anxiety takes shape in our minds, thinking about events or situations that we have to face in the future and preparing accordingly, it doesn't require the real thing. We can build it up and up through a vicious cycle of thoughts and feelings that confirm and enhance each other, so that it grows and grows until it comes to resemble something that does occur in real-life situations. A response to immediate threats that can occur in an instant ... panic.

Panic

The word panic comes from the Greek *panikos*, which is derived from the name Pan, the Greek God of flocks and herds. Pan, responsible for strange and frightening woodland noises, would jump out at unsuspecting travellers striking terror in them.

Physical symptoms include increased heartbeat and breathing rates. Like anxiety, panic involves edginess and trembling that we feel as our body is energized for action.

This 'jumpiness' is not something we plan to do, but innate bodily reactions based on survival instincts. We don't have to think about jumping out of the way of a charging wild animal or a speeding car; we can go from standing calm to action in an instant. The foundations of the panic reaction are with us from an early age; observe the small child 'jumping' when startled at being caught out in some secretive act.

And this instant energizer is not always helpful and not always the appropriate response to help us survive. A drowning man, panic-stricken, charged by energy to survive, thrashes around in the water when he should really be keeping still and trying to float. Panic, whether helpful or not, can happen automatically when we are in danger – it's our inner-self's way to make us avoid harm. And it's not just about actual immediate physical danger.

In panic our heartbeat can speed up to over three times it's normal level, but panic symptoms are not just physical. We often experience a sense of dread and a fear of losing control; like anxiety, panic too is mediated by our thoughts.

It is a two-way street; panic induces thoughts of dread and fear of losing control; thoughts of dread and fear of losing control induce panic. This can be seen in the potentially confusing situation whereby panic can occur just before falling asleep or as we attempt relaxation. Why on earth should we panic in such situations, where there is no danger?

Well, as we fall asleep or start to relax, we are giving up control; we are letting our guard down, releasing all of our vigilance and preparedness. We could be attacked whilst our guard is down – here the danger is a perceived possibility (again based on our inner feelings), but a potentially very dangerous one.

For some, attacks of panic become the focus of their problem.

Panic Attacks

Our heart beats so fast that our chest shudders. We can hear it, we can feel it; we are breathing rapidly, our shoulders are raised and tense. Our legs feel like jelly and our arms and hands tremble, we can't keep them still. What's wrong with us, why is this happening? We feel sick and want to go to the toilet, our mouth is dry, it's hard to swallow and we are sweating. A dark fog of dread grips our mind.

The more we think about it the worse it gets ... and the thoughts ... we can't stop them ... what if something happens? What if I can't cope? ... what if I fail? Something might happen ... what will I do? Part of us knows we are blowing things out of all proportion, but ... what if?

Once this happens, no subsequent panic attack is really 'out of the blue' – it affects us so powerfully that we will always have an apprehension about it happening again.

And what of our first panic attack? Does this really come from nowhere?

There is little difference between extreme anxiety and panic. Anxiety that builds up and up turns into panic; the physiological changes in our body (which we shall come to soon, as we look at the fight-or-flight response) are the same – one can start slowly and intensify to a high level (anxiety), the other (panic) hits the higher levels almost immediately.

As we have seen, most people who suffer from anxiety and depression problems come to them with a background level of anxiety, usually stemming from conflict. A person who is anxious and alert is already some way toward panic. We are, in a sense, 'primed to panic' and any stressful incident can set it off. Many of these incidents are the normal stresses found in life, as with the previous example of waiting in class to speak at our turn. It causes mild anxiety in many people, but if we already have underlying anxiety, the combined stresses can quickly lead to panic.

Research has shown that negative life experiences precede many panic attacks.[6] This could not be more surely demonstrated than it is with the development of many examples of panic disorder. Here, the first panic attack that leads to this 'disorder' is often preceded by the death of someone close.

* * * * *

Fear, anxiety and panic are all about one thing: survival. It is the main drive of every living thing – to survive and reproduce (so that our genes survive). It drives everything we do – every waking second and every sleeping second, every conscious minute and every unconscious minute. Anxiety-related problems are all formed around this drive.

Survival

Carl Rogers, perhaps one of the most influential psychologists in American history, founder of the humanistic psychology movement, based his client-centered therapy approach on the concept that everything in life strives to 'be', to exist as best they can, given the circumstances. In his book, 'A Way of Being', he describes one of his boyhood memories, that, to him, clearly demonstrates this 'drive to exist' in all things. The family used to store their winter's supply of potatoes in the basement, in a bin that was several feet below a small window. The conditions were unfavourable, but the potatoes would begin to sprout – pale white sprouts, so unlike the healthy green shoots that they sent up when they were planted in the soil in spring. These sad, spindly sprouts would grow two or three feet in length as they reached toward the distant light of the window. To Rogers, these sprouts, that would never mature, never become plants, in their futile, bizarre growth, were striving to become, to live and flourish, even under the most adverse circumstances.[7]

And it's the same for every living thing on the planet; driven from somewhere deep inside; to be, to exist and grow, to survive.

We are all the product of millions of years of evolution, designed to survive at all costs. The child in the womb competes with her mother's body for resources, newborn pups in a litter fight to get to the mother first; from our first conception, we fight to survive.

Basic survival needs include: the need to eat, to eliminate waste and to have shelter. However, what interests us is the need for self-protection. An ability to deal with actual or potential situations that are dangerous and may harm us, it is this ability that is associated with anxiety-related problems.

Nature will not trust us with the survival of our genes (her genes actually), so we are programmed to behave in ways that will help us to protect them in certain situations. Newborns will duck at looming objects;[8] we don't have to learn how to jump out of the way of a speeding car.

As we have seen earlier, we have an internal system that energizes us to take action, either slowly if the threat is in the future or in an instant if the threat is imminent. This energy helps us to deal with the situation or to avoid it – to stand and fight or to run from it.

Fight or Flight

This response, this energizing of our body is responsible for all the anxiety and panic symptoms that we experience. Some of the symptoms may be enhanced by our thoughts, for example, a dry throat with subsequent perceived difficulty swallowing, may be built up into feeling we are choking, but in essence everything that is happening to our body is a result of it being prepared for action.

Physical anxiety and panic symptoms result from the body re-directing resources to the major muscle groups (legs/arms/chest) to provide them with an energy boost to prepare us for action (ultimately to fight or flee):

- Our *breathing becomes more rapid* to get more oxygen for these muscles into the blood.
- Our *heartbeat speeds up* to get the blood to the muscles quicker.
- Blood is diverted from the brain (making us *light-headed* and *dizzy* and from the stomach (causing '*butterflies*').
- Energy cannot be wasted processing any half-digested food in our system so we need to get rid of it quickly — either through the mouth (*feelings of nausea*) or the other end (*wanting to go to the toilet*).
- Other 'energy-wasting' systems (unnecessary in time of danger) are shut down eg. saliva production, giving us a *dry mouth* and *difficulty swallowing*.
- We *sweat more* to cool down all this energy production.
- The energy boost to the muscles makes them '*jumpy*' / '*jittery*' / '*jelly-like*'/ *on edge* ready for action.

Much the same can happen with anger, for in anger we are also preparing for action.

After we have been angry, anxious or panic-stricken this charge of energy needs to be released and it is done so by such things as crying and shaking – often seen after anger and panic.

We need to realise that all the above symptoms are normal and natural. Indeed, when we experience these symptoms, there is nothing wrong with us; our body is, in fact, working perfectly. What is wrong, the core of anxiety disorders and depression, is the reason why we experience these symptoms. What in life are we associating with danger and why? And the answer to this comes from our experiences; our body responses may be programmed and automatic, but the situations that we come to associate with them are learned.

* * *

This 'energization' of our body can be instantaneous. Indeed it can actually start to happen before we are consciously aware of any danger. We don't have to think about jumping out of the way of a looming object, if we stopped and thought about it, it would probably be too late. Information representing a dangerous situation goes directly to the more primitive, deeper areas of our brain, bypassing the parts of the brain involved with higher thinking and rationalisation. This has to be the case; we have to be able to respond immediately.

Not only do we have to be able to react quickly once there is danger, we also need to predict possibly dangerous situations, to give us an even greater advantage. And this is what we do; we use an array of senses and signals to predict what may happen, and our reaction to it can be instantaneous. A positive analogy to this situation can be seen in sports such as tennis and cricket, where the sports stars react much quicker than the untrained in hitting balls that are coming toward them at over 100mph. No one could react in time if they waited until the moment the ball left their opponent's racquet or hand, it is travelling too fast. The batsman in cricket and the receiver in tennis are already moving to hit the ball before it has left the other person. They are picking up subtle information such as body language, stance and gaze and using their years of experience in the sport to 'read' the serve or bowling action and react more quickly.

If we exist in an environment of what seems to be constant danger, we become always on the 'lookout', prepared to respond quickly, ever vigilant for threats. It is seen throughout the animal kingdom – animals at the lower end of the food chain, hyper-vigilant, on guard against attack; as timid as a mouse – they have to be for their lives depend on it.

In anxiety disorders and depression, the fight-or-flight response often comes on more easily and with greater intensity as more and more situations and environments become associated with potential threat.

Like everything that keeps us alive, we are not consciously aware of much of this 'preparedness'. It appears to involve something deeper within us. Evidence relating to survival behaviours and the employment of higher senses range from everyday things such as reading another person's body language and turning around when somebody is staring at us to evolution-driven behaviours that can shape our lives. Women can be unknowingly attracted to certain men by picking up pheromones from the man that indicate he has a different immune system to themselves; no benefit to the woman, but a great survival boost to any offspring that will have a more diverse immune system. Similarly, when a group of women spend a lot of time together, in offices at work, for example, their menstrual cycles often fall in line with each other. Perhaps once again through pheromone recognition, none of them will be allowed the evolutionary survival advantage of reaching the ability to conceive before the others.

These examples, and others such as: not being aware of the background noise at a party but suddenly hearing our name with full clarity if it is used or awaking from deep sleep at a noise in the middle of the night, appear to show that there are forces within us, apparently beyond our knowing, that work to ensure the survival of us and our genes.

But survival is not just about speed of reaction or the processing of information coming from our senses. It involves experience and learning. Fears grow because we learn; dangerous situations multiply because we learn; fears weaken because we learn.

If we face a potentially dangerous situation and we deal with it, we become confident in such situations. However, if we face a fearful situation and don't deal with it (or avoid it), similarly we learn. We learn that we cannot cope with it and as such, all these situations are dangerous to us. But not just that; because we could not deal with it, situations that are similar to it also become a threat, for they too are potentially dangerous – we may not be able to cope with them also. It's a process known in psychology as generalisation. Fears grow and grow, becoming attached to situations with similar characteristics. And it is seen in every single anxiety disorder: the social phobic goes from fearing eating in front of people to fearing talking to people; the obsessive-compulsive rituals become more and more intricate (as does the allowable food criteria for anorexics and the ways and patterns of cutting in self-harm); hoarders feel the need to collect even more stuff as many new things acquire an importance to them; obsessive and worrying thoughts, like rituals, become more intricate and involved and panic attacks can develop into Agoraphobia and beyond, to a situation where only certain parts within the home are considered safe. A fear of spiders can come to elicit fear at photographs of spiders. How can a photograph harm us? – it cannot, but that is not the way our inner-self sees it.

In an ethically questionable experiment in the 1920's an infant, 'little Albert' initially unafraid of a rat, was made to fear the rat through classical conditioning (by making a loud noise whenever the rat was introduced). A fear of the rat developed and the fear extended to furry toys. The child was afraid of the rat and anything that was like the rat.[9] Although critics have questioned the results of the experiment, we know that it is possible, for adults can be scared of photographs.

For now, we need to realise one more thing: our problems are not getting worse because they are such great problems that there is no answer to them – they are getting worse for one reason ... the generalisation of our fears.

* * *

The limbic system of the brain, which comprises in part, the pituitary gland, thalamus and hypothalamus, hippocampus and the amygdala does more than just interpret information coming from our senses and release hormones, such as Noradrenalin, to jolt us into action. It is also involved in the processing of emotions and the storing of memories. Feelings and emotions associated with dangerous situations are retained for future use, information we may need to protect us at a later date, and any situation that causes those feelings and emotions can become associated with danger and survival.

Our inner-self uses everything it has to protect us: direct information from our senses, experience, memories, feelings, programmed responses and genetic information. These resources are used appropriately for situations that our inner-self interprets as a threat to survival, not for what is happening in reality.

In blood phobia we see a survival reaction totally against the fight-or-flight response. Here the person often experiences a rapid drop in blood pressure and faints. The reason?

We have seen blood, someone is injured and losing blood – a low blood pressure reduces any blood flowing from our body if we too are injured, increasing our chances of survival. Unfortunately (for us, in reality) fainting, itself, can result in injury. Our inner-self, in protecting us in its own way could actually cause us harm.

And this is what it does in every anxiety disorder and depression. These problems are so terrible, that there must be some gain in having them, to our inner-self there is: -

- OCD is about surviving, not living
- GAD is about surviving, not living
- Social phobia is about surviving, not living
- Panic disorder is about surviving, not living
- PTSD is about surviving, not living
- Depression is about surviving, not living

Based on all of our experiences and knowledge, our inner-self is trying to ensure its survival, the survival of our genes. Unfortunately, this is often at conflict with daily living. Again, we see this phenomenon throughout the animal kingdom with examples like the huge and elaborate tail of the peacock and the massive antlers of the male caribou. Designed to attract a mate and ensure the progression of the genes, they hardly promote ease of daily living.

Of course, the inner-self is not just working to ensure the survival of those with anxiety-related problems; it is there for everyone, but when intangible 'badness' and feelings of panic interplay, survival becomes paramount.

Thankfully, as pointed out earlier, anxiety and depression problems are only associated with true survival fears; they are not the actual fears. They are learned and they can be unlearned.

'Fears are educated into us and can, if we wish, be educated out' – Karl A. Menninger (1893–1990)

Imagine you're lying in bed, about to fall asleep. Suddenly you hear a loud crashing sound ...

Do you – sit bolt upright, feel your speeding heartbeat, feel scared, wonder what it could be, worry what it could be? You hear it again – fear and panic are rising, what if it's a burglar, what if he's got a knife or a gun ... you become panic-stricken.

Or do you – sit bolt upright, feel your speeding heartbeat, feel scared, then stop and think about it? You listen; there are no other noises, you aren't sure that you checked all doors and windows. You hear it again – it sounds familiar, like a window banging. Still feeling apprehensive, you go and check with caution.

In such a situation we cannot flee anyway. The first reaction involves letting the fight-or-flight response snowball into panic, which leaves us helpless; the second reaction tempers the fight-or-flight response with knowledge and reasoning which gives us an element of control.

It is the same with anxiety-related problems.

Take social anxiety disorder, for example, and a situation that we cannot or don't want to avoid – going to a party. If, when we opened the door, there was a real survival danger, perhaps people in the room had clubs and knives and were going to hurt us, we would run like mad, a totally appropriate fight-or-flight response.

But there isn't a real danger; it's based on our feelings about our self and our experiences. The fight-or-flight response is totally inappropriate – do we let it snowball into panic or temper it with knowledge and reason?

Our life experiences have conditioned us into reacting purely with survival-promoting responses to an ever-increasing number of related situations, based on our feelings. But we can change all this through knowledge and reasoning.

Now imagine that you experienced a childhood of conflict; you felt bad, inadequate and always under attack. You became tense, anxious and prepared and one day, due to all the inner anxiety, and perhaps a real-life stressful situation, the anxiety overflowed into a panic attack. It felt bad, really bad, out of control and made you apprehensive about it happening again. And it did happen again and again. On the next panic attack ...

Do you – feel your speeding heartbeat, feel scared, wonder what it could be, worry what it could be? It confirms weakness and inadequacy; it's hard to control.

Or do you – feel your speeding heartbeat, feel scared, then stop and think about it? You realize why it is there, exactly what is happening and why. How the fears and anxiety build up and what the feelings mean. It does not confirm weakness at all, it is totally based on experiences and how humans work. In fact it signifies that, in a sense, the body and mind are working perfectly.

* * *

Many argue that life is not totally about survival and point to behaviours that seem to go against surviving such as bungee jumping and contraception, or to behaviours that simply give pleasure such as acquiring knowledge or watching theatre.

Survival underlies them all: bungee jumping involves pushing life to its limits, but with control, experiencing a threat to death, with all the heightened senses that entails, and surviving (nobody would do it without the rope – that *would* give evidence of anti-survival behaviours); contraception allows the focus of attention on fewer offspring, better a few surviving well rather than many surviving poorly; knowledge equals control and being in control means surviving well and anything that gives us pleasure indicates contentment, a lack of struggle, no survival threat.

Be in no doubt, survival lies at the heart of everything we do, and whether life is a struggle or one of contentment depends on one thing.

Control

It lies deep within human nature ... the need to be in control of our environment; it must – our very survival depends on it.

We have an innate drive to understand things that influence our lives so that we can have some control over them, some control over our own survival and existence. Any situation that we cannot understand or control remains, in a sense, unresolved, anything might happen; the situation has the potential to cause us harm and as such remains frightening.

This drive has led humans to conquer the oceans, the highest mountains and outer space and we'll search a lifetime to achieve insight into something we feel has power over us. When we have a sense of control over something we feel safe for we know we can handle whatever happens. However, knowing that we cannot control something causes constant anxiety.

Anxiety and panic, phobias, OCD and depression seem so strong because they involve feelings of not being in control; we don't understand them and feel that they control us.

A sense of being in control is reflected in love, joy, knowledge and freedom; lack of control involves fear and despair. Even resistance to and recovery from illness can depend on how much control we think we have. This is why doctors now give us as much information as possible about what is happening to us and why.

77

I remember a couple of years ago, one time that I suddenly developed a bad stomachache. The pain continued for one day then another day. On the third day of pain I was now beginning to worry about it, perhaps it was a sign of some serious illness. The more I worried about it, the greater the situation affected me. By chance, on the third evening, I happened to bump into a friend who asked me if I had been well, since he had suffered terrible stomach pain since we had eaten at a restaurant a few days ago. Suddenly everything changed; the fear, the worry and much of the actual pain just disappeared. I now knew what was happening and why, I was now in control. A similar situation to the experience described above (though greatly exaggerated) fuels much of panic disorder.

When we feel weak and inadequate, with little power or significance we can never feel in control. Studies with groups of baboons have shown that those lower down in the social hierarchy, with little power or influence are in a state of constant stress.[10]

Feeling that we have no control is damaging to us in numerous ways. So much so, that we spend our lives trying to be in control; every one of us, not just those with anxiety-related problems. Everything is ordered and categorised to help us know what we are dealing with. People are labelled: married or single, rich or poor, employed or unemployed; superstition and lucky charms are used to ward off bad luck and gamblers devise systems in attempts to control random outcomes. Lack of control can be so anxiety arousing that we don't want to be in that position. Our inner-self won't let us.

The basis for many optical illusions and magic tricks, our mind will 'fill in' any information that is missing in a situation, rather than leave it incomplete.

A certain amount of control is not only natural and normal, but also necessary. We control what we eat and how we exercise to keep our body fit and healthy and we keep clean to avoid infection and disease. However, an excessive need for control indicates a problem. It's a bit like 'identification' that we learned about earlier; the correct amount in the right way is beneficial but too much, based on insecurity and desperate need, is harmful.

Anxiety and depression problems reflect this desperate need. Without exception, they comprise rigid, set behaviours – we need to be in control, nothing can be left to chance; we cannot stand chaos and inflexibility. Without exception, they involve 'thinking too much' – a constant search for reasons and answers; we have to understand them, we must know what is going on; again, to be in control.

It means nothing to the person with a phobia of flying, that air travel is statistically far safer than travelling by car. What counts is the feelings of no control: being thousands of feet in the air with someone else in charge and no means of escape, where anything going wrong means virtually certain death. In a car, we can stop and get out whenever we want.

Nowhere is the effect of feeling that we have no control seen more greatly than in depression. Nothing we do is any use, we cannot change anything, the world is against us and everything we try fails – what is the point of even trying.

Jewish prisoners in concentration camps, with no control over any aspect of their lives, came to have no reason to pay attention to anything, even life itself. In an experiment in the 1970's, dogs were given electric shocks with or without a control lever being available for them to press and stop the shocks. Dogs that had the control lever quickly learnt to stop the shocks and also learnt new ways (presented to them later) to stop more electric shocks. The dogs that had never had control of the shocks wouldn't learn new ways to stop the shocks when given the opportunity later. They had already learned that they had no control over the situation and simply gave up and accepted all future shocks helplessly – it was a learned helplessness.[11]

Well-meaning friends may bid us "just stop thinking like that" or "just pull yourself together" – of course, if we could, we would. Depression shows us the true extent that a lack of control plays in all anxiety-related problems. It is not only the problem itself that causes us misery but also the fact that we cannot do anything about it – *'oh woe is my woe, it won't let me go'*.

* * *

With control, life is different, and it doesn't even have to be actual control, just a sense of having control will do. As long as we know that there is something we can do, or think we can do, we are less anxious. We don't even have to press a lever to stop electric shocks; just the fact that there is a lever there makes a difference.

If we believe that we can cope with a situation we approach it more assuredly and make better use of our abilities. If we believe that we can manage potential threats we have little reason to fear them.

The key to control is knowledge; once the mystery is removed from a situation it becomes less frightening; the power of the unknown is diminished. A speeding heartbeat is less frightening when we know that it is happening in order to pump the blood to our leg muscles and help us run away. Quite different to not knowing what is happening and thinking that we may be having a heart attack?

Hand in hand with knowledge goes discipline, the right sort of discipline – doing the right things for the right reason in the right way, for example: exercise, diet and sleep. Paradoxically, we can only have true freedom when we are disciplined; otherwise we are controlled by our moods, appetites and passions.

In reality, none of us have much control over our lives at all. Society, government, church, and employers dictate many of our actions. Personal survival and feelings of control are played out within a broader social context. We depend on others.

Social Animals

Human beings are social animals from the moment they are born and throughout their lives. An infant does have not to learn how to cry; it is a programmed survival behaviour to attract others who can provide security and care.

Born into relationships with others, initially with our mother and the rest of our family, successful interactions with other people are essential to our survival. Without a partner, there would be no reproduction and no species!

No individual human can grow and survive without the active help of other humans. The modern family has evolved from the tribes of our ancestors, with extended families reflecting attempts to keep as many members of the unit as safe as possible. We live as we have always lived, in groups, and we depend on our ability to cooperate with others for survival. Finding food, building shelter, warding off predators, bringing up children – pooling of resources means enhanced mutual survival. This is why we need to belong and we need to be accepted. To be rejected and abandoned means to be alone, to have to fend for ourselves, with all the danger and fear it entails.

Hence deprivation of human contact strikes at our very core. The worst punishment of all, saved for the very worst offenders, is solitary confinement. To be alone is to be vulnerable and scared, to fear abandonment and rejection is to be human.

Rejection is painful. Brain-imaging work has shown that the brain's response to pain and rejection is quite similar.[12] The pain of social rejection causes us to fear it, and as we know, from fear comes anxiety and panic.

The need to belong resides deep within us all. We see it displayed daily in the devotion to such things as: religion, countries, companies and football teams. We all want acceptance and soon learn what it takes to be accepted, we are constantly engaged in presenting ourselves to others. Being accepted becomes associated with society's standards.

However, alongside this need for personal protection and survival through cooperation with and acceptance by others, flows another need, one that connects with our inner-self, the need to progress our genes.

Within our group we need to establish some recognition, some success and status to help us develop relationships and gain a 'successful' mate in order to produce 'successful' offspring. (Those enormous antlers of caribou are there to fight each other over females, not to fight off predators – genetic survival dominating individual concerns). The more recognition and status we achieve, the more success we have in the group and it effectively enhances the survival chances of our offspring (to our inner-self).

Competition drives all species, it promotes the production of 'better' offspring, and so we are designed to compete – winning feels good. In fact it feels very good, so much so that some will do almost anything to win, to achieve success, to survive better. The nature of things is such that competition between males usually involves strength and power while competition between females usually involves beauty and attraction.

In order to drive this competition, just as winning feels good, losing and failure feel bad, very bad. So bad that we don't want to feel this way. Cortisol (an hormone released in times of stress) courses through our blood stream; feel-good chemicals ebb away, leaving us extremely tired and we feel sick to the stomach. This serves as a powerful reminder not to make the same mistake again. A similar reaction occurs to 'losing face' – we don't want to fail and be seen to fail, and lose position in the group.

Just like the social norms for acceptance, our knowledge of what constitutes success comes from social learning. This learning, coupled with innate drives and needs, determines most of our behaviour. Nobody has an innate drive for money, but most of us know what having money and the lack of it can mean. Money (something that didn't even exist for our early ancestors) can make us feel a success or a failure.

Feeling 'bad' and feeling a failure can become associated with all the threats to survival seen above. But there is hope – we don't have to be the best (the strongest or most beautiful) to feel like winners. We can achieve this by supporting winners; supporting and therefore, in a sense, helping them to be winners actually makes us feel good. Their success rubs off on us. A classic example of this phenomenon is played out every week throughout the world by millions of people: football supporters and their teams.

* * *

We have seen that survival within the social context involves being accepted into the group for protection and competing for a chance to reproduce with 'better' mates. But there is one more thing to consider regarding our survival and other humans and that is being attacked by them.

Strangers are a potential threat to us. To our distant ancestors, anyone from outside the group posed a danger, either as a direct drain on available natural resources, such as food, or by stealing resources. Hence they needed to be prepared when encountering strangers and that preparation involved exactly what it involves today: fear, anxiety and panic and the fight-or-flight response. They developed an array of abilities and senses to help pre-guess the potential danger that any stranger may represent. Again, those we use today, involving such things as reading body language, tone of voice and facial expressions. Seen across all cultures, certain expressions are indicators of intent. Staring shows aggression – we are advised not to stare into the eyes of potentially dangerous dogs, to these animals too, it displays a potential fight. Grinning and smiling show the opposite – that we are friendly. As we shall see, acknowledging smiles and smiling our self can be beneficial in many ways.

This same fear of attack by strangers is reflected in social anxiety disorder today. Actually, it lies at the heart of all anxiety disorders. Survival within the social context shows us why social anxiety disorder is so painful. We have a desperate need to belong, yet fear other people. We feel inadequate and weak, yet are driven to compete for recognition and status. Until we understand what is happening, the fear nearly always wins and we end up avoiding people rather than being with them. We see them as enemies rather than friends and the end result for many with social phobia is usually loneliness. But we can change this.

* * * * *

Anxiety and panic are normal. It is possible to experience anxiety without it leading to panic, obsessions, compulsions or despair – to experience it and yet still be calm. In fact many people do experience anxiety like this frequently, examples include: going for job interviews, going on dates and in social or sports situations that require performance. They feel shaky on the inside but relatively calm on the outside, this is normal, this is part of anxiety, this is how it feels:

> On a popular TV quiz show, where the contestants answer questions and can double their winnings up to a million, the quizmaster has said to many contestants, words to the effect, "You look remarkably calm". In nearly every instance, the reply has been the same – "On the outside yes, but inside I'm shaking like a leaf ".[13]

Panic attacks, too are normal. Studies have shown that over 30% of 'normal' people sampled have had a panic attack.[14] But like anxiety, in the example above, to many people they are no big deal. Not everyone feels the same about their anxiety and panic.

These 'energizers' are natural reactions to stressful situations, developed over millions of years to help us survive. And most people think of them in such a way – they realise that any anxiety and panic they are experiencing is likely due to external situations, to circumstances in their lives and events that are happening to them. When panic comes, they feel it and let it pass; they don't worry about it and build it up.

However, when we exist in a state of 'preparedness' with an almost continuous background stream of anxiety we come to panic much more easily, so much so that the anxiety and panic seem to 'come out of the blue', we are anxious and panic-stricken for no apparent reason. Actually, stressful situations in real-life cause our anxiety and tension to overflow into panic and after the first attack we become apprehensive about it happening again.

The panic attack feels really bad and we cannot control it – something bad is happening to us over which we have no control.

As we have seen, control relates to survival and a lack of control, in itself, causes anxiety. No wonder panic attacks are so intense for many people. Indeed, for some, this situation may define much of their problem, the whole focus becomes one of waiting and preparing for 'out of the blue' panic attacks, a problem classified as Panic Disorder.

When a background of conflict leads to deep-rooted feelings of being in some way 'bad' or 'not good enough' and all the stress and tension inside us breaks out into panic, there is only one explanation that we can come to, or more precisely, that our inner-self can come to. It's an explanation based on all our feelings and what is happening to us: we are in danger because we are 'bad' or 'not good enough'.

With deep-seated feelings of 'badness' and insecurity, panic attacks mean so much more. The physiological symptoms of anxiety and panic become associated with our inner weakness. And now it's a very public weakness; the blushing, sweating, and trembling all confirm our inadequacy to ourselves and show it to other people.

We relate the threat that anxiety and panic attacks represent, to our very being. They signify to us, and others, that we are weak and inadequate; they confirm our negative feelings and self-doubt and put our acceptance by the group at risk.

Other people don't think like this, they don't have the intense inner feelings of inadequacy and insecurity with which to associate the anxiety and panic. To them, anxiety and panic are due to the external situation; to those of us who develop anxiety-related problems, anxiety and panic are due to something being wrong with us.

The panic attack signifies that we are in danger in some way; our very self is not good enough and we are vulnerable because of it. The situation is untenable, one of constant potential threat, and we cannot go on like this. Now we have to be different, we have to be 'better' in order to feel accepted and not threatened; we can no longer just be ourselves – that is not good enough. We have no confidence in our very being; we are scared to be our self.

This leads to the final stage in the development of anxiety disorders and depression, a situation that can determine the form and type of many of these problems ... 'how to be'.

...

5

...How to Be

WE ARE ALL involved in presenting ourselves to other people continuously. We change our appearance and demeanor to fit the situation and are different in the presence of our mother, boss or lover. Aspects of behaviour and personality are altered to suit all the time; keeping up appearances is a daily task.

It is also natural to admire good qualities in others, qualities that we see lead to successful living, and want to be like them, want to possess those qualities and be successful. And the qualities that are admired the most are the ones we have mentioned, the ones pertaining to survival and reproduction; good-looks, power and strength for men and beauty and attraction for women. It is the basis for every successful story: the handsome hero defeats all the bad guys and gets his girl; the woman gets her man. Millions of people look up to the screen and wish that they were just like the leading man or leading lady, wishing that they looked like them and behaved like them.

But it isn't real life. They are fantasies of the perfect existence, of doing everything right and being admired and respected by all.

Virtually everyone has fantasies of such a perfect existence, it fuels the dreams and desires of many – that's why television shows and films, for example, are so popular and why the stars receive so much adulation, when in real life they are just people acting.

Dissatisfaction with our lives can lead to fantasies about 'ideal' living for many, but for others it becomes so much more than this, it becomes about survival.

When those inner feelings of badness and insecurity become associated with the feelings of danger and threat signified by excessive anxiety and panic, something more happens. We look to all of our experience and knowledge, to other feelings and reasoning to find an answer. We look for what to do and 'how to be' to alleviate the situation, to take away the insecurity, anxiety and threat. 'How to be' becomes much more than a desire, it's a must. The fantasies are stronger, they develop into an aim for something that we must achieve – once we can *be* like that, everything will be alright. With anxiety and depression problems, living is on hold; we live for the future, waiting until we are 'right' … one day.

> … Deformity is daring.
> It is its essence to o'ertake mankind
> By heart and soul, and make itself the equal –
> Aye, the superior of the rest[1]
>
> (From The Deformed Transformed)
> LORD BYRON (1788–1824)

Slim people are not attacked; good-looking people are not attacked; clever people aren't attacked; good sons, daughters, pupils, mothers and worshippers aren't attacked; people who do things right aren't attacked. When we feel inadequate or bad, and threatened because of it, we have to become better – there is no choice in the matter, our inner-self drives us to take control of the situation and survive. Again, it is all based on feelings.

'How to be' is driven by our inner-self's attempt to overcome intangible feelings of badness and threat. But where does it come from? How do we decide just how to be?

This isn't something that just suddenly appears; although, essentially brought about in its extreme and overriding forms by panic attacks, it is something that has been developing as we grow.

Feelings, experience and learning are showing us what qualities are deemed acceptable and successful. If, at the time of our first panic attack, we could have gone to our parents (or someone) and explained how we felt, how scared we were, and received reassurance and support (and love) – many anxiety disorders would have been 'nipped in the bud'. But we could not do this; there was already a part of ourselves that viewed the panic as a weakness and we had to be strong, so we kept it to ourselves. This keeping it in, worrying what was wrong and searching for what was wrong fuelled the initial stages of the disorders and it's a situation that is mirrored throughout life, seen today in the actions of many people, of all ages, that suffer these problems.

Unfortunately, too, for many, we could not approach our parents or others in such a way; to do so could invite ridicule and criticism rather than support and reassurance. To do so would to appear weak in front of someone who is strong; we cannot be weak, we have to be strong just like we perceive them to be – much of 'how to be' comes from our parents (or guardians).

Parents and 'How to Be'

As seen earlier regarding identification, to be big and strong and knowledgeable equates to living successfully, like our parents.

If we can be like this, we will feel better.

Also, being good and helpful may bring us the love we crave from our parents and many people go through life trying to be good and helpful to everyone in order to be loved, liked or accepted.

Not just about perceived parental qualities or how we can behave, direct learning can also shape 'how to be'. Families that stress education or cleanliness or 'doing things right' shape their children's ideas of what it takes to be right. Parents who demand perfection in themselves (because of their own problem) often put pressure, directly or indirectly, on their children to be perfect.

And it doesn't take too many times for a parent to call their child fat, or imply through expression or gestures that being overweight is not acceptable to create problems relating to food.

We can begin to feel that there is a certain way that our parents expect us to be and we will try to be like this if we feel unloved by them. Because we fear losing our parents (or their love) we seem to make a promise to ourselves to be 'good' in the way we believe that they expect us to be. In a similar way that the use of 'you' in our self-talk invariably reflects our parents, 'how to be' invariably reflects the ideals of the person or people we want acceptance from, those whose opinions matter to us, whose adoration and admiration we crave.

Of course, our parents are by no means the only influences on the way we feel we should be.

Other Influences

Many other things supplement the learning from our parents. These may strengthen or weaken what we have already learned or they may suggest new ways to be accepted.

Nature

Concerned with survival and mating as we have already seen, being bigger, stronger and more attractive promotes success throughout the animal kingdom. And concerns over the lack of certain physical qualities can have a profound effect on many people who have a background plagued by insecure feelings.

Feeling that we are: not being big enough, strong enough, tough enough or attractive enough in some way, can dominate many of our anxiety-related problems.

Society

In today's society, looks, power and success are rewarded. Wealth and material possessions reflect these rewards and because they do, their attainment has become associated with success. No matter how we achieve it, to be wealthy or own bigger and better possessions show that we are successful. (Of course they don't really – some of the wealthiest people around are also the most miserable). And so life becomes dictated by 'how to be', what to do to achieve these measures of success.

Many people are working harder than they need, in jobs that they hate to earn enough money, not just to survive comfortably (their earning surpassed that long ago) but also to acquire material possessions and show that they are successful. However, no amount of wealth will change inner feelings of inadequacy; we are trying to overcome the feelings in the wrong way and the result is further anxiety and stress. Although there are other factors to consider relating to job dissatisfaction and work-related stress, studies show that stress-related illness costs employers billions of pound per year[2] and millions of people are dissatisfied with their jobs.[3]

Society, in general, imposes rigid rules in order to fit in, restrictions on our actions in order to be 'right'. And many of these rules are enhanced and adulterated by the media.

Media

We are bombarded by images of 'successful' people and what is required for success. If we don't have these qualities or act in these ways, we are deemed a failure. One thing, in all our lives, can fuel this fear of failure – advertising.

Totally false, advertising shows perfect people with perfect lives; beautiful people with fantastic bodies – if only we buy the product, we too can be like this. If we were perfect like these people, we wouldn't have any problems. Advertising saturates us daily with images of 'how to be'.

We'll take another look at society and the media later, but for now there are two more things that can shape how we feel we must be:

Religion

In all religions, we have to be in some way good. We have to behave in strictly defined ways (different ways for different religions) in order to please the Lord so that we can go to Heaven rather than Hell. And we do, we behave in ways we are told to rather than ways that are true to ourselves.

Religions involve conformity based on the fear of retribution, and what retribution! – punishment by God. But God has never told me how to behave; save those who have spoken to him directly, he has never told anyone how to behave, it's another human being that has done that. Religion helps to keep society together (and is also responsible for the death of untold numbers through war), but it is a sad fact: man-appointed church leaders dictate the behaviour of millions.

Good Feelings

'How to be' is only slightly influenced by information. Like everything we have talked about so far, what truly guides us and determines what we do, is our feelings. Society, media and religion seem to offer us not only an explanation for our 'bad' feelings but also a way out of them. For example, if I feel inherently weak, 'bad' and vulnerable and the church offers me salvation – I can feel good, if I am good and please the Lord ... the scene is set, I will act in any way prescribed in order to take away my bad feelings.

Times that we do feel good greatly influence 'How to be'. Loose-fitting clothes *feel* better than tight ones; making a group of people laugh makes us *feel* accepted, much better than being bullied, and doing things right earns us praise that *feels* good. And we will do virtually anything to feel good and anything to avoid feeling bad.

'How to be', this way to stop feeling inadequate and vulnerable, takes two forms – one relating to our physical presence, seen in the direct aims of Anorexia Nervosa (to be thin) and Social Anxiety Disorder (eg. to be big and strong, for men), and one relating to how we should behave, seen, for example, in the need to be good (in various ways for various reasons) that is found in many obsessive-compulsive and generalized anxiety disorders.

* * * * *

'How to be' develops from the need to take control. We cannot exist in a state of anxiety and vulnerability; we have to do something about it. Even the fantasies serve this purpose – *'one day, I will be ...'* gives an element of control. And it can extend to beyond ourselves; with eating problems, what we feel about our self can be determined by readings on a scale – if we lose a pound in weight, we are good; if we gain a pound we are bad. We must have some control at all costs.

And it can be a heavy cost; trying to get control may cost us our lives; the ultimate paradox: in trying to survive we can kill ourselves. No matter how thin we become it will never be enough; no matter how perfect, or strong, or powerful, or wealthy we are or how hard we work, how often we scrub our hands or how good we are it will never be enough. It will never be enough because we are never in real control – it is just an illusion of control.

It is a 'secondary' control that develops because the feelings of inadequacy and vulnerability are intangible. They don't exist for valid reasons, they are merely an accumulation of feelings and we are associating seemingly valid reasons and answers to them in our attempts 'how to be'.

We attempt to take away these feelings by being in some way 'better', but this attempt is never truly related to any original 'badness', because the badness did not exist. The control that we try and get by being 'right' is not actually related to the intangible jumble of feelings inside us.

With Anorexia Nervosa, being thin will not change the 'inner intangible badness', no matter how thin we become. It is simply that, in this 'disorder', due to our experiences and learning, we find an answer to the badness – it is because we are fat. And all we have to do to take away all our bad feelings is become thin. Any badness we feel is now associated purely to how successfully or not we control our weight.

For many of us, our experiences don't offer a rigidly defined reason and answer (being thin, for example). Here, the 'how to be' becomes associated with ways to behave – to be good in some way or simply 'not to be bad/wrong'. The reasons and answers are more diffuse and we cannot focus our energy on one tangible thing (eg. thinness) to be 'right'. This means that the potential threats if we are unsuccessful are much more varied and free-floating. In essence, we just need to be good in some way or 'not wrong' and if we cannot be this, then threats are everywhere. Generalized Anxiety Disorder and Obsessive-Compulsive Disorder typify this situation.

Take OCD: the rituals of ancient tribes to such things as the sun and moon are attempts to allay anxiety over the power of these phenomena. It bears no relation to actually controlling them, but it does allay anxiety because it provides a sense of control. The compulsive behaviours in OCD offer relief from anxieties relating to a diffuse 'how to be', but similarly they bear no relation to the real anxiety due to inner *intangible* feelings of 'badness'. We can turn and check that the door is truly locked a million times, it won't make any difference, we will still feel insecure. The insecurity is not due to the door being potentially unlocked – it is already there inside us. In this case, intangible insecurities have become associated with a potential threat (being burgled if the door is not locked). Checking the door affords some relief of an associated anxiety, but not the real one. The real one doesn't actually exist, it is intangible – so we had to associate something to the feelings in order to get some control.

* * *

Anxiety, tension and vulnerability lead us into the situation of 'how to be' as a reason and answer. However, this in itself serves to increase our anxiety and tension. We are forcing ourselves to be and behave in rigid ways and we constantly watch ourselves to check that we are being 'right'. It is a performance; a performance where we have to be perfect and this becomes highly stressful (and anxiety-provoking) in it's own right.

Public speaking is the one situation that many people fear the most; surveys constantly indicate this to be the number one fear for the majority of the population. One study reported that over one third of those questioned had experienced severe anxiety when speaking in public.[4] And with good reason; to stand up in front of a number of people who are scrutinising and judging every word and action, where there is no acceptable means of escape, can be a truly frightening experience. As such, we worry about it, prepare for it and approach it with trepidation. Imagine if we attached the same importance to virtually everything we did in public, that everything we did instilled in us the same trepidation and fear – this is what is can be like with Social anxiety Disorder.

As we have seen, everyone has degrees of how to be and behave in varying situations and circumstances. It isn't a problem. Nor is it a problem to try and do things the best we can, to achieve the best and be the best in any endeavour – it is natural and healthy to do such things out of the competition of life and the joy of being good and doing well.

However, it does become a problem, a serious problem (in the same way that identification does) when it is based on fear. When it becomes a 'must' rather than a choice, when it becomes associated with deep feelings of insecurity and vulnerability ... for now it becomes related to our very survival.

'How to be' shapes and drives almost all anxiety and depression 'disorders'. The physiological symptoms of the fight-or-flight response in anxiety and panic are the same for everyone. Yet we all choose particular symptoms to focus on. Some choose the heartbeat, some the blushing or sweating and some the trembling. The ones that we focus on are the ones that represent our weakness and reflect failing at how we should be.

We all have to be in some way strong, not weak – only 1 in 5 young people aged 16 to 24, depressed enough to have suicidal thoughts, would seek help from a GP.[5]

Unfortunately, 'how to be', seemingly providing a reason for our bad feelings and presenting us with the way out of them, actually makes the whole situation a lot worse. It creates a way of living and being that actually fuels the inner feelings of insecurity and badness. When we are at this stage we now have a self-perpetuating problem, a vicious cycle of feelings, thoughts and behaviours that feed themselves ... the anxiety disorder (including depression).

Before we take a closer look at individual anxiety disorders and depression there's just one more thing that we need to understand. That is why these problems feel so powerful and why they become so entwined with our existence – how they are part of us.

...

6

...A Part of Us

ANXIETY-RELATED PROBLEMS can be with us in such a way and for such a long time that we come to feel they are a part of us, part of our personality, that they are us. And in a way they are, but only because of the way we feel, how we think and the things that we do.

Part of our parents are a part of us, whether we like it or not. Biochemist George Wald's reply, when solicited for a semen sample by William Shockley's sperm bank for Nobel Prize-winning scientists, " if you want sperm that produces Nobel Prize winners, you should be contacting people like my father, a poor immigrant tailor. What have my sperm given to the world? Two guitarists!"[1] sums things up aptly. We are a product of our parent's experiences and learning, hopes, fears and perhaps most important, drives and struggles. Their genes are our genes; without doubt, their lives shape ours. However, genes are our history not our future and when we understand what is happening, we can change things.

Save genetics, these problems feel so powerful and become so entwined with our existence for two main reasons: how we work as humans and the environment that we find ourselves in.

The Brain

Everyone's brain looks the same, feels the same, weighs approximately the same and works in basically the same way. Yet we all have different views and attitudes, likes and dislikes, pleasures and pains, hopes, fears and dreams.

Our brains comprise billions of cells; around 90% of them make up the supporting structure, known as the *glia,* the 'glue' that holds everything together, the other 10% are *neurons*, the cells that do the work of thinking; there are roughly 100 billion of them. Neurons have a long extension, called an *axon*, which is used for sending messages and a number of branching extensions called *dendrites*, which act like antennae for receiving messages. Each neuron has around 10,000 connections (*synapses*) with other neurons; it has been estimated that the number of possible interactions between neurons exceed the number of atoms in the universe! Such is the complexity of our brains and our thinking – a trembling web[2] of activity; connections and interactions between neurons that define each and every one of us.

Not necessarily specific connections between neurons, more so patterns of connections between neurons reflect our experiences and learning. Experience changes our brains; patterns of neurons interacting with each other represent all the information we are absorbing from our experiences. And the more we experience the same, the more that same pattern of neurons work together and the stronger the links between those connections become. For example, brain scans of violinists show the area of the brain devoted to his or her left fingers (the right primary motor cortex) to be 2 or 3 times larger than that of non-violinists; constant use of these fingers in playing the violin have formed and embedded the associated pattern of connections in his or her brain.

The connections in our brain are also influenced by thought:

Whatever we dwell on strengthens and grows (a pain in the tummy gets worse if we dwell on it); we hold on to anxiety and depression problems, strengthening them, as we attempt to find answers and reasons; PET (Positron Emission Tomography) brain scans of people with OCD show increased energy use in the orbital cortex of the brain, compared to those who don't have OCD.[3]

As we have seen earlier, the lower primitive parts of our brain can make us react with fear, anxiety and panic before we even realise the danger, making anxiety-related problems seem a great (and uncontrollable) part of us. Most animals only have relatively primitive brains and so live their lives ruled by such behaviours: survival instincts and behaviours, fear and aggression, but we are different, through logic and reasoning, using the higher levels of our brain, we can temper these behaviours.

Our brains are incredibly complex and man's understanding of the actual physical entity is still in its infancy. The brain itself and the way it works can lead us to believe that our behaviours are an inherent part of us rather than something we have learned which can be changed. But there is more to the brain than just its structure and constituent parts, something that involves thinking and thought processes, something that creates our reality ...

The Mind

'To be human is to go beyond physics.' – Diderot (1713–1784)

There is much more to learning than mere vibrations, we do not hear music as vibrations any more than we see faces as mere lines of contrast. Sensory information interplays with the information stored in our brain and involves past experience, contexts in which it occurs, feelings and emotions, to influence what we perceive.

Take reading and writing, for example. Words are no more than organised squiggles on a page, yet a good novel can transport us into a different world.

Our memories, more stored patterns of neural connections, determine our view of the world, irrespective of reality and the memories most easily recalled are the ones with the greatest number of connections, those formed by our most influential experiences. Filled with experiences of conflict and criticism, that is what we see. We can only approach new situations based on knowledge gained through past experience so we approach life accordingly: people are seen as a threat and critical, rather than accepting; our mind shapes the perception of the present situation to confirm our experiences and feelings – something true for almost everyone with anxiety-related problems: we can accept criticism without question, compliments we just cannot accept ... they don't fit in with our experience.

This utilisation of stored memories to shape our perceptions happens all the time. It is the basis of many optical illusions. For example, the fake room with sloped floors illusion: our mind won't let us see the mis-shaped room in front of our very eyes; because we are used to seeing nice regular square rooms, that is what we see. Similarly, our mind won't let there be any 'incompleteness' to what we perceive since this equates to lack of control – if there is any information lacking in what we see (or hear, feel, smell or touch), the mind 'fills in' based on our stored knowledge.

Memories are the result of active, creative processes and are not fixed but changeable. As we live our lives with anxiety disorders, our memories adapt accordingly to fit: good ones are forgotten or minimised and bad ones are enhanced, all to fit in with how we see our self and what is happening to us.

And our thoughts work in the same way since they, too, are based on patterns of neural connections. Influenced by such things as: emotions, feelings, values, principles, experiences, learning, morals, ethics – the list goes on, they reflect what is happening to us and how we feel. When we feel of little value and afraid, all our thoughts revolve around this: we look for reasons and answers in the past; we worry about how we feel at present and we fear the future. We fear the future because all we have to guide us is our past experience – how many times has the thought of some feared forthcoming event caused us to argue in our head with our parent?

With our thoughts, feelings, memories and perceptions working in such a way, is it any wonder that living with feeling bad and insecurity represents a very large part of us?

But remember, all the above is not just some way our mind is working because we have anxiety-related problems – it is the way everyone's mind works, how the human mind works. It is just that (for the main part) our experiences have caused our brain and mind to revolve around feelings of inadequacy and anxiety.

When we have feelings of high self-worth and confidence the mind uses stored memories (and 'fills in') to support those beliefs. And uncontrollable thoughts aren't always negative: when we 'have a crush' on someone or are in love, we often cannot think about anything else!

Of course, even with anxiety–related problems we still have times of happiness and joy and positive feelings, it's just that they can be overshadowed by all those connections in our brain relating to feelings of low self-worth and insecurity.

Thoughts, memories, and sensory information all interplay with our feelings and when we talk about feelings we usually relate them to another part of us ... our body.

The Body

The racing heartbeat, quickened breathing, disruption to our digestive processes and tension in our muscles as they are made ready for action, signify the fight-or-flight response. Essential for immediate survival, these processes can take their toll on our body if we don't allow it to recover through sufficient rest. When we are constantly anxious, constantly prepared, the body never gets a chance to recuperate and it will often warn us to slow down. Constant stress and tension can lead to headaches, and general aches and pains. Being in a constant state of tension (readied for action) uses up all our energy and leaves us tired for most of the time. And tiredness and 'having no energy' feed on themselves; if we don't need energy our body won't give us any, the less we do, the less we feel we have the time to do or feel able to do. The opposite also applies, the more energy we use, the more our body gives us – something often seen after exercise; yes the exercise tires us, but we also end up with much more energy.

Regular aches, pains and tiredness become part of the way we are.

And the physiological symptoms, themselves, come to shape our thoughts and behaviours. As soon as the heartbeat quickens or we feel shaky, we associate it to the problem, strengthening our beliefs, – even if it has nothing to do with anxiety. Shivering in cold weather is often seen as being anxious as the increased muscle activity due to shivering (which burns the sugar stored in the muscles and creates heat) is associated to the 'energizing' of the muscles in the fight-or-flight response; similarly, tingling and numbness of the fingers, whether due to the cold or anxiety, can become linked (in both cases the body draws blood away from the extremities to protect the major body organs), and the speeding heartbeat in excitement is often perceived as fear (something that underlies many non-physical sexual problems).

Indeed, heartbeat rate may be one of the main indicators of anxiousness. In the results of one experiment: what distinguished those bomb disposal volunteers (all heroes) that had been decorated for gallantry from those that had not was their heartbeat rate. The ones decorated maintained a lower cardiac rate when making stressful decisions.[4]

Long-term, the regular anxiety responses experienced in anxiety disorders could play a part in many illnesses. Relationships may exist between: IBS and regularly needing the toilet due to anxiety; Diabetes and the constant release of sugar into the blood for energy through anxiety; auto immune problems due to 'over-use' of the immune system through constant 'on-off' preparation to deal with any attack (particularly relevant to stress), and high blood pressure related to tension in the small muscles in arteries.

Of course, many factors contribute to illness, such as diet and lifestyle and perhaps other physical causes but the natural state of our bodies is one of wellness; generally something has to make it go wrong, it doesn't just go wrong itself.

With anxiety-related problems, illness may result (usually after a long time) due to the stresses and strains on the body but it can also happen another way; very often we may develop illnesses psychologically. The illnesses are real, but we make them.

Something often seen in children, physical symptoms are used to express psychological distress. Being ill can give us a tangible reason for our inner bad feelings and may promote sympathy and care in others but, most importantly, it tempers the fear of failure associated with 'how to be'. Being ill serves as a reason for not being 'how to be', a legitimate reason that is nothing to do with us.

Indeed, it can also eliminate the need 'how to be' to some extent with feelings of weakness and inadequacy being attributed to the illness rather than some inherent flaw that needs correcting.

Some people come to focus solely on related illnesses. We have an illness, that's how we are – unfortunately this does nothing for the real underlying problem ... the inner feelings of 'badness'.

Psychologically–based illnesses developing with anxiety-related problems show us something vitally important – we cannot treat the mind and body separately, they are intimately linked.

Mind and Body

We talk of our feelings being hurt in the same way we do about our body. Mental anguish is painful and if it cannot be released it is often expressed through physical pain. Virtually all the pain that we feel has an emotional element to it. One recent study that compared brain areas involved in processing osteoarthritis pain and experimental pain indicated that emotions play a strong role in how patients feel arthritis pain.[5]

And it's not only the body that causes the lack of energy we talked about earlier; the mind, too, plays a part. Twenty percent of the all the 'fuel' (food) that we put into our body goes to supply the brain. No wonder the constant thinking, ruminating, comparing and despairing seen in depression, coupled with a lack of activity from feelings of helplessness, can result in having no energy at all.

The link between mind and body is often reflected in the skin. Seen in blushing, the skin responds to emotions and many people can suffer skin problems for years due to underlying emotional issues. It is well known that stress often plays a large part in such problems as: acne, eczema, rosacea and psoriasis.

What we think about ourselves and how we feel and, of great importance, our sense of control has a profound effect on every illness we suffer. Feeling that illness controls us and that there is nothing we can do gives the illness power over us, which only makes things worse. Many people may also feel that they deserve to be ill, as inner feelings of low self-worth become linked to the bad feelings of illness. We can become ill in many different ways for many years because of how we feel about ourselves. The good news is: when we feel good about ourselves, illness is a rarity.

Feelings of having no control over the way we think and the things we do lead us to believe that 'that is just how we are' – but only when we don't know what is happening.

Everyone's mind and body protect them in ways that they aren't fully aware of: the fight-or-flight response 'kicks in' before we even realise the danger and the mind shapes perception and behaviour to preserve our self-concept.

It is seen in defensive ploys used by everybody. We all: project flaws onto others, rationalise and intellectualise behaviour, distract ourselves with activities and deny or repress unpleasant facts. Every single one of us does such things; self-protective behaviours orchestrated by lower levels of awareness.

However, once we experience panic, the self-protection drives go much deeper, they come from a deeper level and are extremely powerful. Uncontrollable thoughts and behaviours such as: worry, 'how to be', perfectionism, fears and compulsions, driven from deep inside, come to feel like problems that are a natural part of us – but they aren't, they developed through learning.

When we feel 'down' it is reflected in our posture and the way we dress. But it is not only reflected in our own behaviour, it is also reflected in the behaviour of others toward us – our own attitude shapes the attitude of others. And so we can come to exist in an environment that reflects how we feel about our self, which brings us to that second main area of influence relating to living with anxiety-related problems.

* * *

Our world can often support, enhance and strengthen those inner feelings of low self-worth that develop as we grow.

Society

Society represents a struggle against true nature for almost everyone. The rules, regulations and laws temper evolutionary survival instincts (most of us will renounce murder, rape and genocide, despite them being potentially beneficial for the progression of our genes) and instil a conformity that holds populations together. Conflict between instincts and the rules of society exists in all of us.

Fear is an undercurrent running through all our lives; most of the rules and regulations are based on fear, fear of being punished or cast out from the main group (imprisoned) and real fears over being attacked personally or about society being attacked are often overplayed by leaders to impose control. Indeed, we have very little real control at all: government, the church, employers and educational systems direct much of our lives.

In earlier times we strove to survive through finding shelter and enough to eat and defending our family. Today, survival has become one of achieving and possessing and winning.

During the 2006 World Cup, the topical joke about seeing more dives than at an Olympic diving competition, illustrates the point: society has become one of winning at all cost – if we don't win, we are a loser, so much so that many people will do anything to win.

The Media

The media not only reflects society but also drives it. Hand-in-hand with success and failure comes criticism. Today's society is also one of criticism. We love to criticise; to build people up then knock them down. Perhaps the negative feelings we all feel when criticised as children find expression later in life by such means.

The media is extremely powerful; TV sits there in the corner of the room, day in and day out, bombarding us with messages, many of which are negative. (An interesting aside: many psychotic problems involve 'hearing strange voices' – well we all hear strange voices everyday, they travel through the air as radio waves and come out of small electronic boxes in our homes).

Bad role models abound, ratings of the more base TV shows soar and sex and violence rules – perhaps reflecting our true instincts rebelling against society's constraints?

Culturally defined ideals of body image are often manipulated by the media and one of the most insidious, negative influences in our lives comes from advertising. Here, we are deliberately made to feel inadequate; that nothing we have is quite good enough. But we can feel better, indeed we can be perfect and have perfect lives, just like those attractive people we see in the adverts – if only we buy the product! Society is now obsessed with body image.

Most adverts play on our deep instincts relating to attraction and procreation. We all have instinctual concepts of beauty (even infants) for it is seen as an indicator of health and good genes and advertisers use this for profit. Combining winning and losing and possessing with attractiveness and beauty, the media and society forge a strong bond between body image and success in our minds. One study in 1999 reported a five-fold increase in the symptoms associated with eating disorders among Fijian girls (normally robust and happy about it) since the arrival of TV to Fiji in 1995.[6]

If we don't conform to these society-and-media-imposed standards of attractiveness, age and weight we feel different and are treated differently and may feel 'not good enough' even more – our inner feelings enhanced by manufactured images and ideals.

* * *

Today, more and more people are angry; incidents of road rage and attacks on people increase; stressed and bewildered youths, lacking in discipline and support, mimic the extreme violence of video games; 80% of women are unhappy with their bodies and girls of nine and ten are on diets; bullying flourishes; teenage depression increases; lives ruled by anxiety-related problems or stress describe virtually everyone – perhaps we are all so sick because society is sick?

Religion

Like society, religion pervades our very existence, dictating standards and ideals of beliefs and behaviour in order to promote conformity. If we don't conform, threats of punishment by God induce anxiety and fear in many.

* * * * *

We are products of our environment and learning; what we learn shapes our brain and our world – patterns of neural activity.

Virtually all of our learning takes place within a social context and initially strong connections form in response to interactions with our parents; childhood experiences that guide us later in life. Our self-talk mimics those interactions and comes to us when we feel the same way we did as a child. In times of stress we may argue with our parent (or significant others) in our head or scold and criticize ourselves – the harshest criticism there is.

Memories shape our world, all we can bring to a new experience is what we have learned; automatic body responses and self-protective behaviours become a regular part of our existence and interplay with how we feel about ourselves; feelings of inadequacy and insecurity lead to 'how to be' that fuels incessant comparing and self-watching in order to judge our progress.

We have been conditioned to think, feel and behave in the way we do. And conditioning is extremely powerful: In India, when they train elephants, they take a baby elephant and tie it with an iron chain to a huge tree. Then they start reducing the size of the chain and the tree. Eventually a huge elephant can be tied with a flimsy rope to a green plant, but it is unable to escape – it has been conditioned, and the belief forged between mind and body that it is imprisoned.[7]

Behaviours that we do over and over again become automatic, a part of us, so we can attend to other things. Repeated behaviours strengthen patterns of neural connections and when they become strong, once the sequence of 'firing' neurons is started it continues automatically. After hours and hours of practise, violinists don't have to think about every note they are playing in a song – it comes automatically. Many of the things we do are like this.

Take tying a tie, for example; we learn how to do it then it becomes automatic; once we start the sequence of steps we just do it. If, for some reason, we stop half way through we usually cannot remember the next step and have to start again at the beginning. It was a long time ago that we actually learnt what to do and we have just been performing it automatically; so we have to start at the beginning in order to initiate the automatic sequence again.

This forms the basis of habits; behaviours that we do so often that they become automatic. Initially done for good reason, they continue now out of habit. Often this initial reason is no longer appropriate but once started, habit behaviour is hard to stop – just like tying a tie, once the sequence is initiated it continues automatically. This can play a part in anxiety-related problems where the first sign of any symptoms associated with anxiety can often escalate into panic automatically.

Those thoughts, feelings and behaviours often reflected in, and supported by, our world lead to what we believe about ourselves.

A man found an eagle's egg and put it in a nest of a barnyard hen. The eaglet hatched with the brood of chicks and grew up with them.

All his life the eagle did what the barnyard chicks did, thinking he was a barnyard chicken. He scratched the earth for worms and insects. He clucked and cackled and would thrash his wings and fly a few feet into the air. Years passed and the eagle grew very old.

One day he saw a magnificent bird above him in the cloudless sky. It glided in graceful majesty among the powerful wind currents, with scarcely a beat of its strong golden wings. The eagle looked up in awe. "Who's that?" he asked.

"That's the eagle, the king of the birds," said his neighbour. "He belongs to the sky. We belong to the earth - we're chickens." So the eagle lived and died a chicken, for that's what he thought he was.[8]

AWARENESS ... Anthony de Mello

We come to truly believe that we are weak and inadequate and can often produce a long list of what is wrong with us but not one thing that we truly believe is good. Beliefs shape our moods and attitudes; they become our living reality and we will only do and accept things consistent with them. They dictate our future: we shy away from challenges, won't approach members of the opposite sex, don't try for jobs we would like ... because of what we believe.

But beliefs are not reality, they are just the mental acceptance of an idea, they are just one view of reality and can be changed. Much of what we believe about others having things better than us just isn't true: some of the most beautiful people are the shyest; many with fantastic physical abilities never come close to fully utilizing them and geniuses end up in menial jobs – the opposite of what most people believe.

Imagine the world of difference it can make changing the belief of 'I am a bad person' to 'I am really a good person that has been made to feel bad' (actually the truth!). Just accepting this truth can start to change our lives.

PART II

THE PROBLEM

"I had gone through life thinking that I was better than everyone else and at the same time, being afraid of everyone. I was afraid to be me."

DENNIS WHOLEY

The Bear and the Flagpole

... The bear represents that churned up mixture of intensely powerful negative feelings and emotions we feel inside. It is an overwhelming collection of fears, pressures, worries and doubts that cause us to be afraid and reflects the tremendous stress that we feel. It is overpowering and overbearing and it's unshakeable, everywhere we go it stays with us; we just can't seem to get rid of it. Arising out of conflict and the resulting insecurity, the anxiety and panic we feel is played out in the dream through the bear chasing us and wanting to destroy us. Many people who experience regular anxiety-provoking situations often dream about running from (though never being able to shake off) large frightening animals.

The flagpole represents 'HOW TO BE'. If we are at the top, the best, the biggest, the strongest, the most beautiful, the thinnest, the most intelligent, etc ... if we are perfect, we will be safe. But if we aren't these things then we are doomed, our very survival is threatened for we will fall and the bear will consume us.

To be at top of the flagpole is itself scary; we have to be constantly alert, checking that we are safe – making sure that we don't fall – the constant watching and comparing to monitor our standards.

When life means that we have to be at the top of this flagpole, constantly alert, afraid of falling and being destroyed by the bear down below, we have an 'anxiety disorder'.

This dream also gives us insight into the workings of our inner-self, our feelings, our existence and dreams in general. There are no words to explain the level of our inner-self and the way it operates – we can only get glimpses into it through the symbols in our dreams.

7

The Problem

WORRYING, BINGEING, STARVING, constant anxiety, panic and phobias, obsessions and compulsions are *symptoms* of an underlying problem. Anxiety disorders (including depression) are not disease processes; they follow a normal and predictable psychological evolution relating to the experiences in our lives.

Genetics have a part to play in these problems but it is limited;[1] by far the greatest influence comes from our life experiences and how we learn and grow in response to them.

A childhood lived within a background of conflict, pressure and stress, one in which the child feels unloved by his or her parents, sets the scene for the development of emotional problems later in life. Much of the perceived lack of love comes from actual conflict, either between parents or between the parent and child but many situations can lead to children feeling unloved and unprotected by their parents. The absence of a parent being one such situation: parental separation and divorce has been linked to various forms of psychopathology later in life.[2]

The stress remains constant and it is a stress that we are too young to face. We don't have the maturity of mind or body or the experience to understand what is truly happening. It just feels bad, we feel bad for much of the time and these feelings are confirmed and enhanced every time we experience more stress. Psychological problems are rarely linked with one incident in a person's life; what defines them are continual, interlinked negative experiences and feelings. Our childhood can make us feel bad for much of the time.

At the core of anxiety disorders and depression is our feelings of 'badness'; but there is something strange about these feelings – they don't actually exist for a valid, real-life reason and that's the problem, they are intangible. They are not an illusion, they are real feelings and emotions, but they are not really related to us being bad, for we never were bad, we were just made to feel that way, usually by someone of great significance to us. They are a tangle of emotions, feelings and associations that our inner-self relates to our very being. And because of this inner badness, so bad that even our parent doesn't love us, we cannot love our self. Anxiety and depression problems often reflect an inner 'self-dislike', 'self-hatred' and in extreme cases 'self-loathing'. Virtually all of us with these feelings find it hard to look in the mirror.

The elusiveness of these feelings can be reflected in the way we strive to 'be', gain, and achieve – often for what, we know not; some elusive quality that others seem to possess and we don't. Feeling 'bad' and 'not good enough' leads to us questioning our worth and the constant comparing of ourselves to others that follows. Watching, measuring and judging ourselves against our peers and, since we feel inexplicably bad, we always come up short. When we feel bad we look for supporting evidence; indeed, we usually only take note of anything that confirms (or may confirm) the way that we feel. Factors involved in our conditioning influence our selections for comparison.

Not only do we feel bad and find supporting evidence that confirms our worth (or lack of it) but we keep it all to ourselves. This *what is wrong with me* and *why* becomes a solitary struggle, an inner burden. Partly due to what we are already learning about 'how to be', we cannot be weak - weakness means possible rejection and further hurt.

Unsurprisingly, all this conflict, inner feelings, comparing and questioning take their toll, we now become tense and nervous, for much of the time. This period of anxiety and nervousness often precedes many anxiety-related problems.

Some people may live their lives in much this way, ruled by shyness or stress; others may take this anxiety and nervousness and try to reduce it through anger and resentment – that angry man or woman, mentioned earlier, that eclipse many of our lives – or build it up and up until it overflows into panic. Often influenced by stressful life events, this marks a turning point, from this moment on, everything changes.

* * *

Panic feels horrible, it's meant to – we need to get out of the situation quickly and once we have, the horrible feelings dissipate. The physiological sensations become salient, we begin to notice our heartbeat, breathing and trembling as they energize us into taking action. Experiments have shown that making physiological sensations conspicuous can cause individuals to reflect about themselves, their qualities and standards of their behaviour more intensely.[3] When we bring feelings of inner badness to this situation it isn't surprising that we come to associate the panic with our own feelings of inadequacy. This is why the panic means so much more to us than it does to many people.

One survey suggested that approximately 14% of the population has experiences uncued, unexpected, 'spontaneous panic.[4] A build up of tension and resulting panic can be a normal part of modern stressful living, but when we associate it to our own self-worth it takes on a new importance.

Panic now confirms that we are weak and vulnerable and in danger because of this weakness. To add to this, we also have no control over it. The fear builds up and up and there is no means to escape, not without looking as weak as we feel. Yet once the heartbeat quickens, the hands tremble and the legs shake – that's it, we have to escape at all costs. Even safer – don't get into this position in the first place, avoid the situation and all those like it, where we might panic and lose control.

Fear, anxiety and panic are nothing more than forms of energy; it is what we think of them that makes it wrong.

If we are walking down the street and see a large dog in the distance growling and baring it's teeth – fear, anxiety and panic are totally appropriate to the experience. We will avoid the dog quickly and it could save our life. But if we are sitting at home and we feel afraid, for no apparent reason, it feels wrong; it shouldn't be like this, there must be something wrong with us. Yet it is all happening for good reason; we have been made to feel scared and weak in ourselves, open to attack and anything could have set it off – something we thought, or read, or saw on television; perhaps a minor stressful event in the present or imagined in the future. The feelings are right – the meaning we give to them is wrong. We are scared and vulnerable, not because we are bad or wrong ... but because we have been continually made to feel that way.

To our inner-self the feelings of badness and weakness, coupled with the experience of panic, indicate a threat to our survival. We are weak and open to potential attack. Just as our lives revolve around social affairs, so do many of the fears – the core of virtually all anxiety-related problems – they often relate to abandonment, rejection and attack by other people. When we feel intrinsically bad, we can never be at ease with other people lest they discover how bad we really are.

Throughout all of this the original conflict usually continues. The comparing and questioning increase and we become more apprehensive, on the look out for potential threats and danger. Our lives are governed by the future, not what is happening here-and-now but by what might happen.

There is no way that we can live like this, in this state of uncertainty, for it means almost continual anxiety. We need to find a reason and an answer. Why we feel like this and what we can do about it. The answer and our salvation comes from 'how to be' – or so we think.

* * *

As we grow, various sources show us those qualities and behaviours that are successful in this life. Our own experiences with others, our feelings, society, religion and the media all play a part in guiding us how to be in order to be liked and accepted.

Generally a part of everyone's life and development, in the context of anxiety disorders, it becomes a 'must', not a choice – it becomes 'how we should be' and can feel as though we are expected to be like this. It becomes connected to our very survival, to be more precise; to the survival of our genes ... this drive is so strong that it overrules normal daily living. In a sense the 'how to be' is the anxiety disorder.

Living like this is a constant pressure, a constant fight, a struggle to prove our worthiness – imagine approaching some important forthcoming event (a wedding, for example) and being nervous, preparing for everything to be right, full of trepidation and anxiety. This is what it is like living our lives as 'how to be'. Everything is a performance, watched and judged by the harshest critic of all – us. And the end result of such a situation, a performance carried out under pressure, with a desperate need for success, is seen all the time. How many sports stars and indeed whole teams end up performing poorly, often worse than they usually do, under such conditions?

Those feelings of 'not being good enough' and 'not doing anything right' may originally come from our parents but when we have to do everything to perfection, we soon prove to ourselves that we are not good enough and cannot do it.

But this isn't the only pressure; there is a greater one (which also applies to the example above) – that is the fear of failure.

The consequences of failure are so great that we must not fail; to do so means returning to that vulnerability and weakness which we cannot bear – so we will not fail, at any cost. A devastating result of this, the inner drive to promote and progress our genes, based on the feelings generated by our experiences, over and above daily living (and real survival) can be seen in some cases of Anorexia Nervosa, where a person will starve themselves to death.

Thankfully, such extreme cases are rare, but every single anxiety disorder and depression reflects this inner survival drive trying to protect us at the level of the inner-self, yet actually causing us great suffering and harm. This desperate need 'how to be' and the consequences of not achieving it is seen in all these problems. Examples being: the person with social anxiety disorder can never be tough enough; the anorexic can never be thin enough; the obsessive-compulsive can never be clean enough and the person with generalized anxiety disorder can never plan enough.

* * *

With 'how to be', we are trying to take control, to find an explanation for the bad feelings and vulnerability and stop them.

Unfortunately, the sense of control is an illusion. We never felt bad because we weren't thin enough, or tough enough, or clean enough etc. – these are just things that we associated to our problem because they seemed to provide a possible explanation and a possible solution. The control we feel in 'how to be' only allays an associated anxiety, not the real one. It actually makes the real one worse.

When we fail in our attempts 'how to be', and fail we must because perfection is unattainable, it actually increases the inner feelings of 'badness' and 'uselessness' at our core – we found a way out, yet we cannot do it. We are trying to be 'right' yet still feel bad; we are trying to do 'right' yet still feel bad. The feelings of badness increase, as does the anxiety and the panic and the 'how to be'. It becomes a vicious circle of bad feelings → anxiety/panic → how to be → bad feelings → etc. (see fig.1, P.127).

This shows us why these problems become so strong and how they become more and more intricate and involved through the generalisation of our fears.

We feel bad... discover a reason why and how to stop it ... we do it ... but it doesn't stop it, it makes it worse ... the underlying fears and anxieties are strengthened so we need to do it more and better. This is what is happens with all anxiety disorders and depression – the fears and anxieties grow and diversify (whilst still related to the original) and the attempts to control it ('how to be') become more and more intricate.

We can see from this that there are really two parts to anxiety-related problems. Inner feelings of badness and trying to stop them but not being able to. It's the second part that defines the problems that we know as those 'disorders' classified today. Accordingly, there are two main fears – the underlying one (existing at our very core) involves feeling bad and survival and the second one (arising from our attempts to control things) relates to performance and failure. Both fears support and strengthen each other. How many times have we not even seemed nervous or scared yet had to avoid something just in case it came on?

Trying to make something intangible tangible lies at the heart of all anxiety disorders and it is based on how we all are as human beings – the human mind and body (inner-self) has to have a cause for things. To have something happening without a cause is unbearable since it relates to unpredictability, loss of control, potential threat and insecurity.

Looking for that ultimate cause, that ultimate reason is what we all do with anxiety and depression-related problems and we'll search a lifetime for the answer ... but there isn't one, it's intangible. The only answer is that the badness is not the truth; we were never that bad, we were just made to feel that way.

* * * * *

Figure 1 gives a basic idea of how anxiety-related problems can develop, strengthen and grow due to negative life experiences.

THE VICIOUS CIRCLE

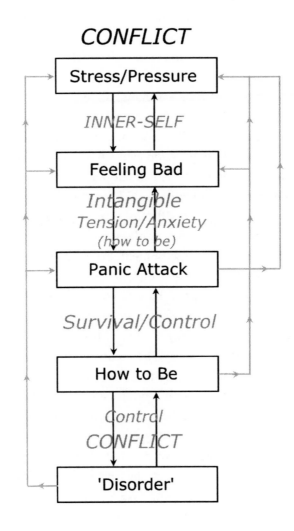

Figure 1: How anxiety-related problems can develop.

Although we can see distinct phases that influence the progression towards and development of anxiety disorders and depression, we need to realise that they all interplay with each other and that they develop in parallel. For instance, the panic attack: where we experience it and in relation to what, is already forming along with ideas of 'how to be' as the inner feelings of badness increase. If we are feeling bad and we look to our parent as being big and strong, showing us already that we cannot be weak (the reason we don't make our panic attack known) then any life experience that requires an element of strength (for example – that reading out loud in class, mentioned earlier) can initiate the first panic attack and it's from this first attack that the context of 'how to be' and consequently the type of 'disorder' takes shape. Everything is related and interplays – a whole system developing and growing based on environment, experience and learning. This shows us why these problems are so powerful (and why previous attempts to deal with them have faltered) – they are a part of us, the way we learned, developed and grew from our experiences. They are a part of the way we think, feel and act and can be no more removed than can, say: the ability to drive a car, or to bake a cake, for they are a learned part of who we are.

Our life experiences have conditioned us into these problems ... but knowing exactly what is happening and why, we can condition ourselves differently. Indeed, we can become stronger for them; we already have more strength, knowledge and wisdom about existence than those without our experiences. How can we be weak? How many other people have endured as much physical and mental pain? How many could endure it? Be in no doubt, you are not weak but strong.

These problems develop from conflict and are maintained by conflict. Anxiety disorders and depression are based on the ultimate fear of being attacked and ceasing to exist because of our badness. And the ultimate conflict: we are bad, and to stop being bad we have to be in some way good, but how can we possibly be good when we are so bad. This conflict drives all of our inner turmoil. It is the basis for problems ranging from shyness and stress to obsessive-compulsive disorder and severe depression and there is only one answer to it – stop feeling bad about ourselves. Of course easier said than done, but we will learn how and why we can do it later ... and we can do it, we have every right to do it, it is our birthright and underpins all of our existence ... we have to learn to love ourselves, so that we can be ourselves.

...

8

Symptoms

BEFORE WE TAKE a look at many of the symptoms that run through the whole range of anxiety-related problems and then at the individual 'disorders' themselves, let's pause for a brief moment and consider how what we have learnt so far relates to some of the most influential ideas and theories of the past about personality and it's problems.

The psychoanalytic theory of personality, by Sigmund Freud (1856–1939), remains one of the most comprehensive, far-reaching and influential theories of personality ever created.[1] The first to give primary importance in everyday functioning to the unconscious – a storehouse of impulses, passions, inaccessible memories and drives that affect our thoughts and behaviour – Freud postulated three main systems involved in personality. The *Id*: consisting of basic drives and impulses; the *Ego*: a part of us that tempers our basic instincts in line with demands of reality and the *Superego*: the internalised representation of the values and morals of others. These three elements are often in conflict.

In line with what we have learnt so far, we can see how, in those with anxiety-related problems, a deep level of the self (inner-self) struggles with the overbearing demands of an inflated superego (parent-driven for the most).

Like Freud, Carl Roger's (1902–1987) developed his theory from his work with emotionally troubled people.[2] As mentioned earlier, Rogers believed that the driving force behind every living thing was one of 'actualization' – to 'be', to flourish, using all available resources.

Central to Roger's theory of personality is the *self*, consisting of all the ideas, perceptions and values that characterise '*I*' or '*me*' and includes an awareness of '*what I am*' and '*what I can do*'.

To Rogers, emotional problems developed when a person's actual beliefs about himself or herself differed from real-life experience and also from some idealised self – the greater the differences, the greater the problem.

With what we now know about feeling 'not good enough' (to deal with real life) and a survival/control-driven 'how to be', we can see how conflicts relating to the self versus some ideal self originate.

Abraham Maslow (1908–1970), in a similar manner to Carl Rogers, promoted actualization as the primary aim of man. Self-actualization represented living at the peak of existence and to achieve this level, a hierarchy of needs had to be met. Seven needs ascending from physiological ones (hunger, thirst etc.), through safety needs (security, out of danger), belongingness and love, esteem and achievement, the need to know, and a need for beauty to the peak: self-fulfilment.[3]

In our story, a one of conflict and subsequent negative development, we can see that even our most basic needs, those at the second level, safety, are not met, and so none of those following, needs relating to the meaning and purpose of life, can ever be fully satisfied.

Of course, this hierarchy of needs is not a fact; it is Maslow's theory. Neither are Freud's three systems or Roger's actualising tendency, though they all do reflect elements of the human condition that we can relate to from experience.

However, they all emphasise the same: conflict and perceived weakness at a deep level within the self.

Other theories do the same, examples include: introverted versus extroverted personalities (Hans Eysenk –expanding on the personality traits work of Gordon Allport and Raymond Cattell) and the 'inferiority complex' -based work of Alfred Adler.

What seems fairly certain, a common stream running through the theories and ideas of those working with the emotionally troubled, is the importance of survival and perceived weakness, a 'not good enough' experienced at a deep level within the self – a feeling bad.

* * * * *

This perceived inner weakness or inadequacy, this 'feeling bad' lays the foundation for all the symptoms found in anxiety-related problems.

The Symptoms of Anxiety-Related Problems

The following list is an example of some of those symptoms associated with anxiety and panic, phobias, OCD and depression. They can be numerous, encompassing our thoughts, feelings and actions, and may be related directly to anxiety and panic at a given moment and long-term (physical symptoms) or generally to the way we feel about ourselves and our attempts to deal with it (psychological symptoms). Many of these symptoms can be present whichever 'disorder' exists.

Physical Symptoms

We have already discussed the physical symptoms associated with these problems, what they mean and how they develop. Ranging from those immediate bodily sensations involved in the fight-or-flight response of anxiety and panic energizing us into action through to ailments and illnesses caused by the long-term stresses on the body of continuous anxiety-related problems, they include: -

- Breathing becomes more rapid
- Heart beat speeds up
- We feel dizzy and light-headed
- We get 'butterflies' in our stomach
- We feel sick and/or need the toilet
- Our mouth becomes dry and it feels difficult to swallow
- We sweat more
- We feel 'jittery'/'jumpy'/'on-edge'
- Numbness and tingling
- Feelings of unreality and depersonalisation
- Raised resting heartbeat
- Raised blood pressure
- Tiredness and lethargy
- Aches and pains
- Digestive problems
- Bowel problems
- Skin problems

In addition to the immediate 'energizing' sensations; stresses and strains of long-term anxiety-related problems can cause many physical problems. However, there are a number of medical conditions that can produce similar symptoms, examples include:-

- Cushing's Syndrome – palpitations, chest pain
- Hyperthyroidism – anxiousness, sweating, tremor
- Hypoglycaemia – dizziness, weakness
- Mitral valve prolapse – palpitations, chest pain

There are more. It is therefore extremely important that a medical doctor be consulted in the first instance, for any persistent physical or bodily function problem, to rule out any possible physical cause of such problems.

Psychological Symptoms

The whole process that we have talked about regarding the development of anxiety 'disorders' and depression can be seen in the following symptoms. Feeling bad, not good enough, vulnerable to attack, and having to be good is reflected in them all.

Avoidance

The safest option of all to prevent danger and harm is to avoid being where it is. Based on one of the self-protecting roles of anxiety, we think about any forthcoming situation that may pose a threat to us and start to get anxious about it. Without fail, this ensures that we either prepare for the situation (for many with anxiety-related problems this means to take a tablet or a drink) or we avoid it. Avoidance promotes our safety. Unfortunately, it makes things a lot worse; the situation (and any similar ones) will always hold fear for us and we will (have to) avoid more and more things. The common notion 'to get straight back on a horse after falling off ' is good advice for this very reason. If we don't get back on the horse straight away, before the fear of the potential hurt and pain builds up, we never will.

"Cowards die many times before their death; the valiant never taste of death but once." - Shakespeare in " The Tragedy of Julius Caesar".

Avoidance affords a moment's relief, yet causes a lifetime's suffering. But don't worry about avoidance, or any of the other symptoms that follow, soon we won't need them anymore.

* * *

Avoidance, like all the psychological symptoms that we are about to consider, actually makes things worse. It increases the underlying feelings of inadequacy – 'we cannot do something, yet we should be able to; we need something but we cannot get it; we should be good but we cannot be ... so it confirms our inner weakness. All these symptoms illustrate this inner conflict.

* * *

Child-like

When faced with tasks that are too hard, or situations that are unfamiliar or may involve competition, the insecure child often becomes panicky, gives up easily or runs away.

We may feel like a child in an adult's body, having never achieved independence from our parents, being 'stuck' at some unresolved conflict in childhood or simply, perhaps the most significant of all, being too afraid to grow into our parent.

Other child-like behaviour includes that desperate need for the love and approval of our parents and others, a situation that can last most of our lives, – to make up for the lack of love that we felt.

Comparing

Spending a lifetime comparing ourselves with others and always coming up short. We compare ourselves to others to find an explanation for how we feel; how we stand in relation to others and in society. Unfortunately, when we feel bad about ourselves, all our comparisons become about justifying these feelings. We find what we look for. A man who feels small and weak compares himself unfavourably against those who are bigger and stronger – he never considers those who are smaller and weaker; they cannot justify his feelings of weakness and inadequacy. The more we feel bad, the more we compare ourselves unfavourably against those people we believe have the qualities and attributes that we think we should have and the more we feel bad – again, a vicious circle, misguided reasoning and explanations hurting us.

And our comparisons are never based on full knowledge – the majority of people in this world are not naturally successful, they have to work extremely hard to achieve it and the flawless skin, beautiful hair and sparkling white teeth of the models whose pictures we see are usually the result of pictures being 'touched up'. Nothing is what it seems!

Whether we are happy or dissatisfied in life usually depends on what we compare our life to. Believe me; if you have regular food and a shelter, enough money to buy this book and the ability to read it ... you are better off than 90% of the people on this planet.

Denial

It's not nice having anxiety-related problems, not nice thinking bad thoughts and feeling bad. Denial and intellectualisation both reduce stress somewhat. Likewise; studying, researching, writing a book or website, planning, working long hours, making money instead of making friends all give us valid reasons not to face our problems. All the above help us to avoid facing the problem whilst giving the appearance (and feeling) of actually doing something about it. I don't know how many times when I was sitting examinations that I would spend hours making revision timetables rather than actually doing the hard work of revising.

Fantasising

Discussed earlier. Of one day being rich/famous/great, loved by all. Fantasies provide hope and an element of control over the outcome of our situation. A normal way of easing everyday stresses for many people, in anxiety and depression problems they become much more important and associated with 'how to be'.

Hypochondria

Constantly visiting the doctor, every ache and pain becomes a worry about having a serious illness. Now called health anxiety or Hypochondriasis, millions of people suffer from this.[4]

The troublesome aches, pains, minor illnesses etc. that everyone experiences become associated to inner feelings of badness and doubt. We feel bad; illness feels bad. It comes to explain our feelings. If we haven't yet developed a strong sense of 'how to be' to associate with feeling bad, then illness provides a reason. We feel (very) bad because we have a serious illness; it stands to reason; it doesn't matter what medical tests and examinations fail to find, there must be something seriously wrong with us to feel this bad.

Hypochondria is reflected in Panic Disorder, where the symptoms of panic become associated with something really bad happening (or going to happen) to our body.

Illness

We have seen that, in the context of anxiety-related problems, illness may arise as a consequence of actual physical damage or through psychological processes. One thing is for sure; every illness is made worse by stress. Take IBS (Irritable Bowel Syndrome), for example, no one is quite sure whether its cause is physical or psychological, it's probably a combination of the two, but there is no doubt that stress can both initiate it and make it worse. Anxiety-related problems may not only cause illness but also make any illness worse. Many people (myself included) believe that virtually every illness (except those with a direct cause eg. infections, viruses, poisoning) is psychologically based.

Ordering

Ordering reflects the way all our minds work. We order and categorize all incoming information in order to store it and use it. Witness young children organising their toys and the collector organising their display.

It represents a form of control – everything is in order, we can understand it, get to it easily and use it, nothing is left to chance. Reflections of this need for order, excessive tidiness and symmetry (what is done by [happens to] one side of the body must be done by [happen to] the other side) can be seen throughout all anxiety-related problems to some degree, not just OCD. They are attempts to bring form and order to our world, to gain a sense of being in control.

Paranoia

Mild paranoia over 'being picked on' or 'others are treated better' can be experienced by anyone who is feeling insecure.

Again, it offers an explanation for feeling bad. Indeed, all anxiety disorders and depression are based on a greater paranoia, one that has been shaped by our life experiences; the belief that we are going to be attacked and destroyed ... it is the basis of all our fear.

Paranoia isn't just thinking in a strange way, we cannot tell the psychotic person to just stop believing it. Paranoia is a reality, based on experience and feelings, it is what we *feel* is really happening to us. What is going on in our heads is reality, not what is happening in the outside world. In the same way, Hypochondria is reality to us too – it doesn't matter what medical examinations reveal ... we know the truth because of our feelings.

Perfectionism

Perfectionism, in itself, need not be a problem, and the right measure may actually be beneficial. It has been found to be related to better learning strategies, self-esteem and a sense of personal control.[5]

Like almost every symptom we have covered (and will cover), this behaviour is a normal part of being. Perfectionism is about control and safety, to do things right, beyond reproach or criticism – in the correct amount, perfectionism helps us to feel safe.

It is when it becomes a 'must' that it is a problem, we must be perfect to prevent attack. Needing to be the strongest, the most beautiful, the cleverest, the most handsome, have the best body, to do the best, to be the best et cetera.

* * *

This 'needy' perfectionism is driven by self-protection, to be safe and although related, and seen in many with anxiety-related problems to some degree, it is not the same as being an out-and-out perfectionist. The perfectionist uses this as a guise to hide their perceived weakness. Based on a pretence of intellectual and moral supremacy, such people externalise their failures, constantly finding others stupid and generally at fault. Having such high standards can give them a sense of mastery, but because they can tolerate no imperfection, being forced to admit their own errors commonly results in self-hate. It is often the perfectionist that leads us to a life of perfectionism.

* * *

The need to be perfect can actually stop us from even trying – what's the point if we cannot do it right or are going to fail? Children frequently think that they can master a new skill straight away, but often, when they don't get it right first time, they feel totally discouraged and never try again.

Waiting for the perfect time to start ensures that it will never happen – there is never a perfect time for anything.

Perfectionism drives procrastination.

Procrastination

Everyone puts off difficult tasks – just like preparing exam revision timetables, rather than actually revising. However, when we expect everything we do to be completely right, everything is a difficult task. Hence we end up putting off virtually everything.

Self-consciousness

Just as with procrastination, the roots of self-consciousness lay in perfectionism and the need to be 'right' and thus safe. Here, we constantly watch ourselves. Monitoring all of our actions to ensure that we don't slip up. "Am I doing it right?" "Am I doing well enough?" "What are the others thinking about me?" The self-consciousness in shyness mirrors the perfectionism in 'how to be'.

They both subject us to the pressures of performance and failure and increase our anxiousness. Nobody could do anything if they were subjected to the same pressure that we put ourselves under!

Self-worth

Worth equates to value. When we have been made to feel bad, feel as though nothing we do is right and that we can never be good enough, we feel of little value. Self-worth, self-confidence, self-esteem all relate to the same ... our perception of our value.

Feelings of low self-worth underpin all anxiety-related problems and remember, that every time 'anxiety-related problems' is mentioned in this book, it also includes depression. In one of the only studies to control for baseline depression, it was shown that, during a one-year follow-up period, women with negative self-esteem were twice as likely to become depressed after a stressful life event.[6]

Low self-worth and low self-esteem show in all that we are and everything we do. They are reflected in: -

Posture

Standing shoulders down, feet inwards with our arms in front of our body, trying to be small, almost apologetic for being there.

Dress

The way we dress makes a statement to the world of who we are. Groups wear similar dress to show belonging. How we dress and how we behave are closely related, dressing down usually shows a lack of confidence, not wanting to stand out or be noticed. We are what we wear. Almost!

Dressing up may hide a lack of confidence or it may give us a sense of control. If we feel conspicuous and that people are watching us, it can be scary. But if we dress outrageously we can attribute their attention to our dress. Attributing their perceived attention to our dress and not just 'something about us', eases our anxiety.

Social Interactions

Many of the ways we interact with other people reflect our feelings of low self-worth and uneasiness in the presence of others. They are all based on the underlying fear that we are going to be rejected or attacked: -

- **Eye contact**
  As covered earlier, the gaze is of innate importance throughout the animal kingdom. Staring signifies threat and conflict and submissive animals look away from more dominant ones to prevent attack. Feeling of little self-worth, maintaining eye contact is usually difficult.

- **Anger and aggression**
  Many people attempt to overcome their insecurity by turning it into action – 'to attack first rather than be attacked'. Dissatisfaction with ourselves may be turned inward or out toward others. This can also be observed in the way that we communicate with others.

- **Communicating styles**
  Sarcasm; putting our self down before others do (submission); belittling; putting them down before they put us down (attacking first); being argumentative (always needing to be right); gullibility (easily influenced) and lack of assertiveness (too scared to stand up for ourselves) all show our true feelings. Interestingly, so can conversation where we end sentences with questions; here we shift attention from us to the other person, thus taking the pressure off ourselves.

- **A problem with authority**

The perceived greater significance and influence of people in authority can cause apprehension in most people, even more so when we feel insecure. We cannot be guided and shaped; this represents being controlled and causes conflict since we need to be free to act in the way that we deem is right to be accepted and safe. Here lies one problem with authority: authority figures have the publicly sanctioned power to tell us what to do ... and we cannot take it.

- **Loneliness**

The fear of rejection and attack (and subsequent destruction) lies at the heart of all anxiety-related problems, as we know them. The ultimate threat is from other people and the end result of many of these problems is loneliness. How many people with feelings of low self-worth are working at jobs well beneath their ability because of this very fear? Avoiding people, and avoiding interacting with people because of fear, ultimately results in loneliness. It is better to be alone than to be attacked. It's an awful situation, very stressful in itself, because it involves an inner personal conflict almost as powerful as the ultimate conflict. We are social animals; we need others to survive, yet we are scared of them.

- **Psychological sexual problems**

Like it or not, sex with a new partner involves issues relating to performance and judgement. It is no surprise that sexual problems are often related to social anxiety disorder.[7] Just like that sportsman performing under the pressure of expectation and judgement and the fear of failure, the situation can provoke extreme anxiety (and ultimate lack of performance). As with everything in life, we generally perform according to the pressure we put ourselves under and with inner feelings of low self-worth and inadequacy, that pressure is usually extremely high – for we have to be perfect, we cannot fail.

Sex also involves a lack of control (losing ourselves in our emotions) and as we are now well aware, a lack of control relates to safety and insecurity. Having to perform perfectly and keep control is not conducive to good sex!

- **Timekeeping**

Rushing around and being late all the time can be explained by much of what we have learned above. Partly in fear of the forthcoming event or meeting, we would really rather avoid it. Also, partly due to our need to perform well and if we cannot, to not perform at all (related to procrastination), again, we would rather avoid the situation.

Rushing around makes us anxious. If we are already feeling anxious about some forthcoming event, then the physiological sensations elicited by rushing around can be used to explain our anxiety. One of the reasons to 'slow down' when facing anxiety-provoking situations because rushing around, in itself, causes feelings similar to anxiety.

* * *

Sleep Problems

Although the role of sleep is not fully understood, there is little doubt that one of its functions is to give us a rest, a break from activity to replenish both body and mind. The body is no longer subjected to the stress and strains of living and can restore itself and the brain is no longer subjected to streams of incoming information that it has to decipher, store and use. During sleep, our mind processes, organises and stores information, newly acquired during the day, in relation to existing knowledge and experiences. An extremely active time for the brain, shown by the increased electrical activity of the rapid eye movement (REM) stage of sleep and often reflected in our dreams. Indeed, even neurons normally involved in walking and seeing are activated, even though the body itself is doing neither.[8]

Sleep problems involving the inability to get enough sleep (not being able to fall asleep and/or waking up early) plague many people, not least those with anxiety-related problems. A day spent obsessing, despairing, fearing, questioning, researching and reflecting produces a multitude of information for our brains to make sense of at night. Yet part of us does not want to go to sleep, it represents that relinquishing of control that we have seen in the examples of panic that can arise from falling asleep or trying to relax. This association between sleep and giving up control can be observed when we do wake up. For a few moments it is peaceful ... but suddenly, with a jump, we realise that we are not in control ... we become instantly alert and steel ourselves for the day ahead.

Perhaps, since a part of us does not want to go to sleep and give up control (something seen in babies, by the way, who often fight going to sleep) our mind attempts to process all the daily information without us being asleep? This may explain the deluge of encircling thoughts that, in themselves, prevent us from getting to sleep?

Sleep is very important to us, we spend a third of our lives doing it and so we'll look at it again later.

Thinking too much

Ruminating is associated with persistent 'unstoppable' thoughts similar to those seen in worrying and insomnia. Constantly going back over things are attempts to find out why we feel as we do, why we behave as we do and why these things happened to us. They are also attempts to find out how we can behave, how we need to 'be' and what we can do to resolve the situation. They are, in all their forms, essentially attempts to understand and master the problem.

* * *

Other symptoms experienced to some degree throughout the whole range of anxiety-related problems include: body-image fears, depression, obsessions and compulsions, over-eating, shyness, stress and worry. However, these will be discussed in the next section as they relate to the main focus of many of the problems we know as anxiety disorders.

* * * * *

Hopefully, it is becoming clear that whatever the so called 'disorder', anxiety and/or depression related problems all involve the same set of symptoms for the same reason. One person can show many of these symptoms; indeed, every person in the world shows many of them to some degree, it is not indicative of having many disorders.

Which anxiety disorder symptoms exist, the number of symptoms, the extent to which they occur, the situations in which they appear and the way they interact with each other are as complex as the individual and the events experienced. They can support and confirm each other and strengthen until they become part of the make up of an individual. It is not surprising that we tend to use such phrases as '*It's just the way I am*' and '*It's just part of me*'.

However, such behaviours do make up JUST PART of a person. Someone who is sad – is also at times happy, weak – is at times strong, scared – is at times brave and unconfident – is at times confident! What we need to do is reduce the bad feelings and increase the good ones. No matter how small they exist at the moment – THEY DO EXIST.

"Inside of me there are two dogs. One of the dogs is mean and evil. The other dog is good. The mean dog fights the good dog, all of the time." When asked which dog wins, he reflected for a moment and replied "The one I feed the most."

The above is often attributed to an unnamed Native American elder. We can replace 'evil and good' with 'weak and strong', 'sad and happy', 'insecure and confident' or any two opposing qualities we prefer ... the one that wins, the way we are, is the one we feed the most.

* * *

Since one main cause underlies all the symptoms that we have discussed (feeling bad and insecure deep within ourselves and consequently vulnerable to attack), is it not the same for the disorders themselves? Aren't they all actually the same problem at their heart?

Before we look at the individual disorders themselves, let's consider just how similar anxiety disorders are.

The Similarity between Anxiety-Related Problems

Similar ways of thinking, feeling and behaving are seen across the anxiety disorders. They all involve a state of higher than average physiological arousal, a nervousness – greater alertness, shown by heightened senses and a higher than normal resting heartbeat rate.

GAD and OCD both involve self-perpetuating thoughts relating to insecurity and attempts to gain control. Phobias and OCD entail panic when confronted by the feared object or thought.

Feelings of inability to cope with negative events occur with anxiety and depression, but those with depression feel responsible and helpless about the events while those with anxiety generally do not.

Panic Disorder, Phobias and PTSD all involve some form of avoidance. Ranging from that due to the overwhelming urge to escape in phobias (physical avoidance) to the cognitive avoidance strategies used in panic disorders (mental avoidance) and the emotional numbing seen in PTSD to avoid painful feelings (emotional avoidance). In both social phobia and agoraphobia the fear is increased in places where we feel trapped. For example – waiting in queues (eg. at the checkout) and in the hairdressers or dentists chair. All disorders involve feelings of not being in control, particularly panic disorder and agoraphobia where exaggerated fears of losing control are prominent.

Almost all anxiety disorders are preceded by negative life experiences. From the short duration, high-intensity traumatic events associated with some forms of PTSD (eg. violence-related) to the more prolonged long-term stressors involved in many disorders. The most common symptom at the start of many disorders is usually a period of 'nervousness'.

* * *

Read any Internet website or book relating personal accounts of living with these problems and one thing stands out – just how bad the author feels within himself or herself.

Anxiety-related problems are truly fascinating. The same basic fear can cause us to binge or to starve, be spotlessly clean or be filthy, rise to the top of the tree or descend to the bottom of the pile ... it's to the individual 'disorders' that we now turn.

...

9

Anxiety-Related Problems

WE WILL SEE over the next few pages how those problems classified as anxiety disorders and many others relating to anxiety and stress can develop by the process seen in Figure 1. (Page 127).

An undercurrent of feeling intangibly bad, fear over our survival being threatened and 'how to be' to get out of the situation can be seen in all the anxiety-related problems that follow (which are arranged in alphabetical order).

At their heart, these problems are the same – only the outward expression of our attempts to deal with the inner problem differs. It is these outward expressions, the main areas where we focus our attention that defines the 'disorder'.

Bearing this in mind, we can see that – but for slightly different circumstances, my OCD could have been your social phobia or your generalized anxiety disorder could have been your neighbour's BDD ...

Body Dysmorphic Disorder (BDD)

Most of us are not happy about some feature of our body or face and have fantasised about having a better nose or better eyes, for example. A survey of college students found that 70% of them indicated some dissatisfaction with their appearance.[1]

But with BDD it is much more than this. We are repulsed by some feature of our appearance, it is wrong and we hate it. Like everything we have seen so far, a desirable situation becomes a 'must' based on fear. The intangible inner badness becomes linked to the offending feature – *if only my nose was better, I would be right and acceptable*'; 'how to be' is linked to having better eyes, or ears, or breasts, or hips, or ...

We *feel* that the offending part is wrong. Feelings based on experience, examples may include: continual taunting, observing others with better features or simply through anything that made an impression on us about part of ourselves being wrong.

Body dysmorphic disorder involves a total preoccupation with the offending part of our appearance or body. Others probably don't even notice anything wrong, but it is all we can think about.

Attempts are made to hide, disguise and draw attention away from the unacceptable feature. As with social anxiety disorder, we may avoid social situations where we can be seen and rejected. Just like in OCD and GAD, the obsessive thoughts themselves perturb us.

An appreciation of beauty and attractiveness is innate, we all want to be attractive (just like those peacocks with their tails) to attract 'better' mates and produce 'better' offspring. Society and the media play on this innate need for their own ends. We are bombarded by messages that promote attractiveness and beauty as a way to happiness. Women undergo plastic surgery, for the most part, on their lips and breasts, two of the main areas associated with sexual attraction. One of the best predictors of how we feel about ourselves is how we rate our attractiveness.

But attractiveness is subjective; some of the most attractive people have many less than perfect features. When we look at others we see them as a whole – their attractiveness projected through their expressions and demeanour. Attractiveness (and beauty) comes from within.

For us it is different; we cannot see ourselves as a whole. The feelings of 'badness' ensure that we check for anything that could be causing it, everything is scrutinised to the utmost detail. A nose that is too long or too short, too pointed or too flat, or perhaps slightly off-centre can confirm the feelings of low self-worth for many people.

Futile attempts are made to 'correct' the problem part. A person may undergo so much plastic surgery to 'correct' a nose that the real nose collapses, a situation analogous to the ever more extreme dieting observed as Anorexia Nervosa progresses.

Analogous too, to that persistent turning back to check that the door is locked in OCD. No amount of checking will change how we feel, as will no amount of plastic surgery. We are only alleviating an associated anxiety, not the real one. We are not dealing with the main problem ... the intangible feelings of badness inside.

Trichotillomania (Hair Pulling)

Like BDD, deep insecurities that become attached to our appearance and attractiveness lie at the heart of this problem.

The hair holds a special place relating to innate attractiveness. Comparable to plumage, manes etc. in other animals it reflects health and vibrancy. Most men don't want to be bald and will do anything to delay/disguise it. Women 'fiddle' with their hair when flirting and constantly adjust it when they feel insecure about their appearance. Both sexes spend a considerable amount of effort to get their hair 'just right'.

Pulling at hair is similar to the 'picking at our self' seen in milder forms as nail biting and stronger forms as biting the skin of the fingers – it reflects our feelings of 'something wrong with me', 'something not quite right'. Adjusting our hair in order to be 'right' and picking at it 'for not being right' become related.

Linked to innate personal need for attraction and society's endless pursuit of it, hair coming out and going bald becomes associated with our self-value. The more we feel bad the more we pull our hair and the more that comes out, the more we feel bad. It becomes obsessive – adjusting, picking, and pulling, rather than alleviating our insecurity, just makes it worse. So the obsession increases; pulling hair transforms into ever more intricate rituals: pulling out single hairs, sucking or eating them, eating the root – more and more intricate procedures, providing some element of comfort but ultimately linked to chasing the control that we cannot find, the control we desperately need to take away our feelings of insecurity.

Depression

In the 2004 health report for the United States, The Centers for Disease Control and Prevention (CDC) found that 10% of women and 4% of men, over the age of 18 were taking antidepressants.[2]

That's almost 1 in 7 of the adult population of the United States considered depressed enough to warrant medication. Add to this the widespread usage of alcohol and barbiturates to alleviate frustration and disappointment plus the ever-increasing numbers of teenagers depressed and the overall picture emerges of a deep dissatisfaction with life for many people.

Society, as we know it today, promotes and fosters the problem. Perhaps much depression is, as James Hillman observed, 'a special problem in a society hell-bent on happiness'.[3]

Life throws many things at us that give us good right to be depressed. Grief, loss, frustration and disappointment reflect our helplessness regarding many life experiences, such things as: death of a loved one, illness or incapacity, relationship and work problems demonstrate our lack of control. Indeed, some feel that the beliefs of mildly depressed people actually reflect reality – the struggle, loss, pain and effort of life.

Perhaps they do, but there is a situation where depression goes much deeper. It becomes associated with those inner feelings of badness that we have discussed; something more than just the bad life events that are uncontrollable and happen to everyone ... yes the same bad things happen, but they become related to our very self, our 'badness/weakness' and the belief that there is nothing we can do about it. If we believe that bad things happen to us because we are in some way 'not good enough' and that there is nothing we can do about it, how can we not become seriously depressed?

Nothing sounds good, nothing feels good; thinking processes are slowed down and replaced by a lack of concentration, indecisiveness, and rumination. 'Dullness' descends; even colours can appear faded. This can be exacerbated during the winter months when it is darker and duller. Higher depression rates have been observed in some areas of Finland, where there are only 6 hours of daylight during winter months.

Depression results from a 'pushing down' of emotions and feelings, particularly anger. Our mind and body symbolise this dullness and 'pushing down', and makes it real to us through physical sensations such as 'a weight on our shoulders' or 'a fog surrounding us'. It may involve tiredness and body aches, lethargy and procrastination; our depressed immune system can also result in constant colds, flu's and viruses. The only real things we do feel include anxiety and fear, worthlessness, hopelessness and guilt.

Although they involve excessive anxiety, depression-related problems take a different route to anxiety disorders. Comprising the same inner doubts and fears, they show inactivity, unlike the taking action that defines such things as phobias and compulsions.

More than just sadness and anxiety, depression embraces hopelessness and fear, immobilizing fear. Perhaps resulting from the inability to express any anger at all during childhood conflict; direct learning (being told that we couldn't do anything and/or observing the 'depressed' coping styles of significant others); experiencing bad significant life events or a combination of all these things, we have been conditioned to *feel* that nothing we can do is of any use, so we give up. And as we know, when we don't need energy, our body doesn't give us any. Lack of 'doing' and lack of energy typify depression, that is why getting angry and exercise – both examples of 'doing something' – can help to alleviate the problem to some extent.

The combination of feeling bad and feeling that there is nothing that we can do is potent enough in itself; being afraid all the time and not being able to do anything about it is a helpless situation.

However, 'how to be' still plays a part. Not a direct 'how to be' but a more diffuse, vague ideal. A sense of worthlessness and failure are only meaningful when compared to some measure of 'how to be' and success. Depression, perhaps more than any other anxiety-related problem involves constant comparing against some ideal. Perhaps much of this ideal stems from society's desperation for happiness?

Depression and its associated behaviours may have some evolutionary advantage. A slowing down of systems (both mind and body) in times of over-excitability (anxiety and stress) may give us a chance to recuperate. The fact that some minor forms of depression fade over time without treatment may support this.

But deeper depression goes beyond this, life's knocks are associated to our badness – there is nothing we can do about it; we are bad and we deserve it. Not only strengthening in winter months, depression can also become worse in springtime, where the vibrancy, growing and flourishing of new life contrasts profoundly to our despair.

Most anxiety disorders come to include depression over time as we begin to realise our inability to do anything about the problem. And just as these problems get worse and worse (through generalisation) so does depression. As we feel less and less able to influence situations (and more worthless because of it), more and more situations come to have power over us until it gets to the stage where we feel that there is little point in doing anything.

That intangible badness and feelings relating to the inability to have any significant effect on anything we do because of it, lie at the heart of many depression problems. But we can change it.

Eating Disorders

Food is one of the main sources of fuel that keeps us alive, without it, none of us would live very long. It is essential for our survival and because of this, nature (as is her way) does not leave the finding and consuming of food to conscious control.

To ensure that we eat it, tasting and eating are pleasurable, it feels good and being hungry feels bad. To ensure we find it, we crave food and actively seek it out; the greatest cravings are for fat and sugar.

High calorific foods such as fats (found in meat) and sugars (found in fruit) provide the quickest, greatest and longer-lasting energy and offer the greatest survival value. They were hard to come by for our ancestors and craving provided the drive to find them. Unfortunately, today they are exceptionally easy to come by in the fast and convenient foods that overrun the modern food supply. For millions of years our ancestors struggled to find such foods; only in the last hundred years or so have they become so readily available – obesity was never a problem for our ancestors!

Once our cravings are satiated we feel good. This not only keeps the craving-satiation (drive-satisfaction) going but also makes us happy and content. Many parents use food (quite innocently) to calm their children, to make them feel better and, perhaps not so innocently, to reward them for 'good' behaviour. From our early days many of us are conditioned to associate the consumption of food with the alleviation of many problems, not just hunger. In her book about the problem, emotional eating, Geneen Roth describes an interesting phenomenon. On returning to the parent's home as adults, the first thing that she and her brother would do was walk straight to the refrigerator, the freezer and pantry and stand there gazing before doing anything else, making some connection between food and security.[4] I do the same, how many other people do?

With food's connection to survival and being, the abstinence of food and eating has long been linked with perceptions of control and goodness. Throughout many religions, fasting is demanded as a show of faith, control over pleasure or repentance and hunger strikers, with no other means of control, make their point through starving themselves, occasionally to death.

The importance of food and its consumption lies deep within the human psyche, so it's not really surprising that when we have deep feelings regarding our self-worth, many attempts to self-comfort and take control involve food.

Anorexia Nervosa

There are many things in life that we cannot control but we can control our body size. Taking control underpins much of Anorexia Nervosa and so does entanglement with our parents. We may wish to punish our parents for what they have done to us but underneath lays the desire to please them and be loved and we may at times relinquish the control we have and eat something if they plead enough. A fear of growing into an adult may also be at play.

All of it based on insecurity, and very often due to conflict and pressure related to having to maintain a 'quiet', 'good', 'obedient' child image, Anorexia Nervosa gives us one of the most clear examples of the role of a direct 'how to be'.

To be thin means to be good, all the badness and insecurity gone if only we are thin. Thin people are liked and accepted, fat people are made fun of – the direct association between 'goodness' and thinness is made. This association comes from many sources, not least from society and the media's relentless pursuit of thinness as the ideal. The achievement of totally ridiculous body sizes (size '0' and even '00') is promoted as successful living.

But Anorexia is not just about wanting to be thin like the 'models', it's much more – again, it is about a 'must' and a need: thinness has been inextricably linked to being liked and accepted; being thin will take away all the insecurity and fear. The association is so strong that our mind shapes our experiences to fit in with it. This is why the skeletal girl can look in the mirror and see herself as fat.

Emotional Eating

Just as we can never be thin enough, we can never eat enough to erase the inner badness. But we may try. Inside we feel weak, scared and insecure, void of love, empty. Eating makes us feel full and eases the emptiness; it comforts us, offering a sense of control over our bad feelings. We can do something to feel good instead of bad; it's addictive. But like all addictions, it fails to address the real problem ... those inner feelings. This illusory control, as we now know, only makes the real problem worse.

Constant Dieting

In the long run, diets don't work! Ask anyone who has spent a lifetime trying them. When we starve ourselves (diet) our mind and body believes that we really are starving and so fat burning slows down. Once we start eating again, our body stores fat quicker and more easily in order to ensure a readily available supply of energy, in preparation for the next time of starvation (diet). We can spend years and years on the merry-go-round of losing and gaining weight and eventually end up weighing more than ever.

A lifestyle that includes sensible eating and exercise is the real answer, but there is also something equally as important.

When we feel good about ourselves we naturally look after our body, we eat the right things and exercise out of self-respect and self-love. Not just eating for comfort, being overweight can make us feel unattractive and unlovable, offering a tangible reason for the intangible badness. It is hard to imagine just how many people believe that they don't like themselves because they are fat, when in reality they are fat because they don't like themselves.

Bulimia

Bulimia appears to combine elements seen in both emotional eating and Anorexia. Attempting to take away the bad feelings through bingeing, which is then controlled by expulsion of the offending food.

* * * * *

Eating disorders involve many elements of gaining control using the body. Being big can make us feel secure or unattractive, being small may punish others or make us feel acceptable. Whatever the form and reason, they are all related to feelings of inadequacy and self-protection. They are 'must do' actions to eliminate our bad feelings and in themselves promote further guilt and shame.

Unfortunately, all of these problems only make the underlying feelings worse, for the control they offer is an illusion. Just like an obsessive-compulsive disorder; the bingeing, starving, weighing, exercising, food preparing etc. become obsessive and turn into ever more intricate rituals as the inner feelings, fears and true lack of control increase.

No amount of bingeing or starving will change what we really feel about ourselves.

Generalized Anxiety Disorder (GAD)

Our thoughts are racing; they're unstoppable – what could happen? What might happen? What would I do? What could I do? … what can I do? … *what if ?*

Generalized anxiety disorder does not mean worrying about all things. Everything we worry about has a common theme – some potential threat to our safety or that of our loved ones.

We all worry about bad things that could happen, to some extent, things that we cannot control, such as: falling ill; accidents happening; losing our job, which could mean losing everything; financial troubles, we cannot just get money when we need it, and being attacked. To make things worse, we are bombarded daily by reports of real-life negative events in the news programmes and newspapers. Indeed, events are only newsworthy if they are bad. Being alive means being available for bad (and good) things to happen to us regularly.

GAD involves all the symptoms of anxiety that we have discussed and also many of the physical symptoms (such as tiredness, aches and pains) associated with being constantly tense and anxious. How long can you hold your arm stretched out in front of you with your fist clenched as tight as you can, before it begins to ache? GAD shows the mind and body working in unison – an anxious, jittery mind and an anxious, jittery body. It can also involve panic, but unlike panic disorder, the panic is not the main focus of concern. The main focus is on the worrisome thoughts.

Worry

Worry stems from that role of anxiety involved in planning and preparing for forthcoming events. An appropriate amount of planning is adaptive and conducive to survival, worry is not.

Planning reflects attempts to be in control. Armies plan and plan for possible future events to have some idea of what to do if they arise. Planning does indeed instil a sense of knowledge and competence in the face of unforeseen events. Planning turns to worry for one reason – the attempts at control aren't working.

* * *

The uncontrollable, racing thoughts in GAD are just like those seen with insomnia; they reflect what we did and should have done in the past and what we should do in the future. A major part of the problem stems from not being able to control or 'switch off' the intrusive thoughts.

In an experiment in 1970, a group of insomniacs were given a placebo (a harmless pill with no effect); some were told that the pill would help them to relax, others were told that the pill would make them more alert. Surprisingly, the ones who were told that the pill would make them more alert went to sleep faster.[5]

It isn't really surprising, given what we now know. The group who thought that the pill made them more alert, had a reason for their insomnia – it was the pill's fault so they went to sleep. All their feelings and racing thoughts were perceived due to the pill and not to themselves. It was no longer their fault; it was no longer something about them that was causing the problem. A similar situation is reflected in generalized anxiety disorder.

The intangible feelings of insecurity and badness become associated with perceived potential threats to the safety of us or others. Something might happen because of us or that we could have prevented. A part of us knows that this is not sensible and we cannot control the future but the two sets of bad feelings have been linked. Something might happen to us (or our loved ones) because of us, so we must do something about it – it isn't sensible, but ... what if?

We cannot control the future so we plan, but the planning is not real control, it doesn't help the future and it doesn't make us feel better or safer. It isn't real control, it's that illusion, that secondary control and it isn't working. So we plan more, feel worse and plan more. It is now no longer planning, it offers no control, it is worry. And we cannot stop it (just like we cannot stop needing to be thin) because we *feel* it is the answer, the way to get control, the way to stop potential bad things happening and to ease our bad feelings.

GAD reflects our insecurity; we cannot stop worrying - just in case (it's the same in OCD rituals), a prime example of 'what if?' The fact that we cannot control our thoughts makes us feel as bad, if not worse, than the thoughts themselves. And it can often creep toward obsessive-compulsive disorder as we start to develop mental rituals to ward off bad things happening, as the worrying fails. It also involves an element of inactivity, like depression, thinking about rather than doing. Affecting more women, they are less likely or less able than men to take physical action against threats and, in one sense, have no option but to attempt to take control through planning rather than action.

Again, a more diffuse 'how to be', it seems to relate to a vague 'not good enough' and should be 'better in some way'. Often (but not always) developing later than other anxiety disorders, perhaps the focus is less on the identity of the self (seen in the direct need for better personal qualities and traits associated with BDD, Anorexia Nervosa and Social Phobia which develop as our identity develops in the teenage years) and more on roles, for example: we are not a good enough Mother or son or parent. We cannot be these things perfectly no matter how hard we try and so the fears associated with failure are everywhere, all around us, more diffuse, even in the future in the form of bad things that could happen.

Manic-Depressive Illness

Many people that suffer from manic-depressive illness attach great importance to the role of genetics in this problem. However, we will look at it within the context of everything we have learned so far.

Symptoms can range from the extreme highs of mania to the terrible depths of severe depression. The highs can encompass: elevated mood, boundless energy with little need for sleep, rapid thinking and speech, inflated self-confidence and grandiose thinking. Lows generally display the opposite: apathy, lethargy, hopelessness, slowed movement and thinking, and self-hatred.

However, it's not usually as clear cut as this, symptoms often overlap, undulating and flowing, reflective, perhaps, of some inner turmoil. Even the highs generally have an irritable underpinning.

Like all anxiety-related problems, it generalises more and more as the lack of real control becomes evident. Manic-depressive cycles increase in frequency and intensity, the amount of 'normal' time becomes less and less and the periods of depression grow longer as hopelessness takes hold.

The highs often produce periods of intense production and creativity and manic-depressive illness has often been linked to this creativity – the madness of genius? Is creativity the cause or the result? Or both? Some of the greatest artists: poets, writers, painters and musicians have been thought to suffer from it with many of their works reflecting inner turmoil, making associations with anxiety and panic to fears over madness and death.

The creative genius, riddled with insecurity and self-doubt; recent examples include Spike Milligan and Tony Hancock. Just like many of the most famous artists throughout history: brilliant, but consumed with self-hatred.

Substance abuse (alcohol and drugs) is also implicated in manic-depressive illness. In various ways: as self-medication, creating and strengthening mood symptoms or as an indicator of susceptibility[6] – not just by the sufferers themselves, but in many instances by their parents also. The highs and lows of the illness mimic the highs and lows of substance abuse and a family run by an alcoholic parent generally produces extreme conflict.

Extreme self-hatred results in an extreme 'how to be' and many desperately crave not just love and acceptance, but public adulation. Only this can make up for such self-hatred. But fame comes at a high price; fans love the image, not the real person. It can result in a terrible conflict, something that, in itself, can lead to substance abuse, as seen in many disturbed 'stars'.

Not just the need for love but adulation, extreme 'how to be' also shows through a need for not just achievement, but ultimate achievement. Only the best will do, but it is not achievable and even if it was, it is not an answer to our inner self-hatred, it's just that illusion. Many of those who suffer from this problem look back on a life and, no matter how successful or brilliant, see only failure.

And when life revolves around such a creative mind, the fears of failure know no bounds. Extending beyond the normal survival-based fears that lie at the heart of most anxiety disorders and depression, they are as limitless as our imagination; our creativity contributes to our punishment. Figurative or poetic forms of speech become literal; feelings of conflict, anxiety and panic become demons (the intangible mixture of pressures a bear that pursues us!) and remember, what is in our mind is reality. The paranoia and hallucinations are real to us. We have to be the ultimate best and adored by all – if we cannot the devil, demons and untold horrors await.

Obsessive-Compulsive Disorder (OCD)

If God is going to punish us, what on earth can we do about it? Nothing – it is an unbearable situation of apprehension and no control.

Ancient tribes, with no understanding of the natural forces that dictated their lives (eg. the sun providing light and heat and life itself), often performed rituals to these forces in order to allay the anxiety of having no control whatsoever over the awesome power that controlled their existence. The sun, moon and the elements were often seen as Gods in many civilisations and today, all religions perform rituals to God in order to feel a sense of control and gain favour with the ultimate power that can determine our future for eternity. Rituals are basically attempts to control the uncontrollable, to gain a say in the unpredictable.

Religion, itself, can play a large part in the obsessive thoughts and compulsive rituals for many people – a preoccupation with sin and religion. The only thing that we can do to allay anxiety over fear of punishment by God is to feel some sense of control through the order and structuring seen in rituals. But how do we come by such a fear of God? From God himself? ... No, it is always from another human being. How dare any human speak for God and tell us what God is going to do?

We all have an innate connection to something more, some greater power we feel may be good to us or do us harm; nobody wants to tempt fate. Rituals are a part of everyday life, seen in such things as: saying 'touch wood' to not tempt fate; throwing salt over the shoulder; saying 'bless you' after sneezing (to protect from attack by the devil in a vulnerable moment) and all those pre-performance 'ceremonies' of sports stars and entertainers to enlist the help of some higher force and be successful. There are worship rituals, greeting rituals, bedroom rituals and eating rituals – all performed so that things 'go right'. Just like food and eating, an appreciation of higher powers and rituals resides deep within the human psyche and so does something else ... cleanliness.

Cleanliness

'Cleanliness is next to Godliness', many religious ceremonies involve 'holy' water and washing away the sin; being clean is good and being dirty is bad our parents tell us and generations ago character was assessed by cleanliness. One of the basic human emotions, disgust, reflects a fear of something dirty, something rotten and bad, that may contaminate us and cause illness and disease. We 'wash our hands of' blame, responsibility and the past.

Not only is this cleansing related to the physical but also to what we say. How many mothers in the past have threatened to wash their children's mouths out with soap and water for saying bad things? Words for cleanliness and dirt, such as 'pure' and 'tainted' are also used for virtue and sin and modern society, flooded in antiseptics and disinfectants, is obsessed with germs.

* * *

In the early 16th century, obsession referred to a 'siege' or 'laying siege to' and that's just what our intrusive thoughts do to us. They besiege us.

Constantly intruding into our mind against our will, we cannot prevent them, change them or make them go away. It can be extremely distressing. Common obsessions include: blasphemous thoughts; harming a loved child; obscene thoughts and fears over contamination and dirt, aggression and violence, religion and sex.

Yet, like everything else we have discussed (and will discuss) in relation to anxiety-related problems, the behaviour only reflects an extreme form of normal behaviour. Bad thoughts, in themselves, are normal; we all have bad, horrible, disgusting thoughts to some degree at some time in our lives. No sane parent would hurt their child but all of us, at sometime, suppress rage when driven to extremes of frustration and anger by our children. Virtually everyone has occasional intense thoughts relating to aggression or sex, for these drives underpin our existence. In one study, fully 80% of the 'normal' people (without OCD) questioned, reported having obsessive thoughts.[7] The difference is, not everyone relates these thoughts to an inner badness.

Bad thoughts give us a reason for our badness and their content confirms how we feel about ourselves. For some the badness equates to being dirty and contaminating other people; for others it equates to being punished by God; possibly due to the continuous religious ranting of someone telling us what God will do to us or from perceived blasphemous thoughts. It's not difficult to see how an innocent comment of 'religion is stupid' from a child in defiance of a strict religious parent can turn into worries about being blasphemous, once inner self-doubt comes into play. Normal (but infrequent) thoughts about sex or violence can intensify in a similar way, once they become linked with our inner badness.

Also, potential real-life threats become linked to our insecurity – something may happen to us because we are bad. Possible threats that exist for everyone are exaggerated as the bad feelings become linked: a switch left on may cause a fire, as could an iron or oven, a door left open may result in burglary, unseen germs may give us a disease or illness.

In OCD, 'badness' is related to thoughts, not tangible things that we can focus on to put things right, such as our nose (BDD) or our weight (Anorexia), but thoughts – a higher force, uncontrollable, the only thing that will help us to feel in control is a ritual.

Not only that, but unlike GAD where the potential threats we focus on are in the future (so that all we can do is plan for them), these threats are here, now, there is something we can do about them, we can take action and the actions that we take constitute compulsions.

We all go through a stage with a compulsive element in our development. Children like repetitive games, watch the same things over and over and have 'magic' rituals that make them feel safe. Ordering is part of our nature.

I remember my eldest son, when he was around four years old, lining his toy cars up in perfect order on the windowsill. If anyone moved one car out of place he would scream until it was put back, perfectly aligned. Today, his younger brother and their cousin spend hours lining up toy cars and toy soldiers, deriving great satisfaction just from the ordering and arranging involved.

When fears involve intangible thoughts and higher powers, the only thing we can do to allay anxiety involves ordering and rituals. If we associate them to unseen threats, then taking action against the threat eases our anxiety to some extent. Contamination fears (of ourselves or others) leads to cleaning and washing; cleanliness does prevent infection and disease. Vague fears lead to associating possible reasons for them and related actions, examples include: checking doors, checking switches, and checking appliances.

But yet again, any control is merely secondary; washing and scrubbing doesn't ease the fears over inner badness, just the associated fear of contamination. When deep insecurity and fear is associated to the potential threat of a door being unlocked or a switch being left on, the checking does not affect the deep inner insecurity – we check and still feel insecure, so we check again, but we still feel afraid and insecure, so we turn and check again ... and so on. As the rituals and checking fail, the inner fears increase and so the actions to allay the anxiety increase. Rituals become more intricate; washing turns into rituals (eg. number of times, order of fingers etc.), the actions become compulsive in frantic attempts to get control but they don't give us control. It is not just the thoughts that distress us in OCD, but the fact that we cannot do anything about them. And as the compulsive behaviour fails to ease our 'badness' and the associated thoughts, the thoughts themselves, reflecting the badness, begin to strengthen in content, frequency and intensity – the vicious circle tightens its grip.

Like generalized anxiety disorder, OCD can occur later in life. The 'how to be' can again be more vague and, in some cases, not related to self-identity and some direct personal quality that needs to be 'put right', but a general 'badness' a 'not good enough in some way' that fuels the problem'. We know our compulsive behaviour is wrong, but we have to do it just in case ... what if?

Of course, we are not 'bad in some way', we never were and once we know, accept and believe this, all associated fears fade away.

* * *

Compulsive and Addictive Behaviour

Including: food, alcohol, drugs, shopping, work, sex, gambling, virtually anything that we derive pleasure from can become compulsive and addictive. They represent immediate gratification; taking away the bad feelings and replacing them with good ones. But they don't take away deep inner bad feelings; although they give us some pleasure, we still feel really bad. The fleeting pleasure can never erase the inner badness, but it does allay some anxiety and give us some control so we try more and more. Eventually the attempts to ease the pain and get control become habit, indeed, they often no longer give us pleasure (after a while, the binge eater doesn't even taste the food) and only serve to enforce our inner feelings of badness, insecurity and lack of control.

Hoarding

Here, our inner insecurity has become linked to possessions. Perhaps not surprising in this materialist world, 'owning' and 'having' imply security. The more deeply insecure we feel, the more we collect or hold onto. Items that just might be useful to us, which we may need in the future. We are what we own; hoarding can fill the emptiness and loneliness felt inside. However, as the collecting and holding onto things fail to offer real control and security, it becomes more and more detailed – until we have to keep or collect virtually everything.

Tourette Syndrome

Obsessive-compulsive behaviours such as checking, counting and tapping can often be seen with this problem. Grunting, coughing, tics and sniffing may seem more physical than psychological yet even these can become linked to rituals. Attempts to gain control can take the shape of such things as: doing the best cough or a perfect sniff – there is often a 'need' or compulsion to perform the tic or cough.

Outbursts of foul language and shouting, whilst possibly helping to break free from restrictions and constraints, are also linked to a need for attention. Usually occurring by the late teens, this problem has associations with self-identity, with the severity of the symptoms depending on the presence of other people, the importance of the other people and how stressful the environment.

Trichotillomania

As we learned earlier, this also involves obsessive thoughts (relating to hair and appearance) and associated compulsive behaviours.

Panic Disorder

"My nerves have more phases than the moon – *varium et mutibile semper femina:* I seem to be moon struck, and infected with her changeful disposition – but her changes are all lovely, mine all distressful."[8] – SARA COLERIDGE (1802-1852)

The works of many great writers and poets reflect the eternal struggle with anxiety and panic that affects us all. For some it is a part of life, for others it becomes a part of their very being.

Those people with inner self-confidence accept that their panic stems from external events and are relatively unaffected by it; for others, riddled with self-doubt, it becomes associated with inner weakness and survival and leads to that preoccupation with the various reasons and answers, for those inner feelings, that define many 'anxiety disorders'.

However, for some people, filled with self-doubt and insecurity, the panic itself, the physiological sensations in the body and fears over what they may mean, becomes the main focus ... something bad happening to our body becomes associated with our inner feelings of intangible badness.

The pounding heart, rapid breathing and trembling associated with the fight-or-flight response become much more as the doubts and worries about what is happening and why, take shape. Fears over choking, having a heart attack or stroke or going mad, build up. The panic grips us, and there is no reason for it; no wild animal chasing us, no speeding car or knife-wielding maniac – the only reason we can find for it is our self. The fear that something terrible is going to happen to us (we are going to die, or going mad) and that there is nothing we can do about it is one of the greatest fears of all. It's no wonder that many people visit hospital emergency rooms at such times and refuse to believe that there is nothing wrong; just like, to a lesser degree, the Hypochondria that

173

plays a part in many of those anxiety disorders, where panic ceases to be the main focus of concern.

We may feel that the first panic attack comes 'out of the blue', but it never does. It results from pre-existing anxiety and tension coupled with stressful events. Many people panic 'out of the blue' when giving a speech (one of the most feared situations for virtually everyone) or after a bereavement (a highly stressful and emotional time). It is no coincidence that fears over our own body going wrong and that we are going to die can come to those of us with deep inner insecurities just after the death of someone close, where actual death and loss have come to the fore.

And it doesn't have to be highly stressful events or situations, anything stressful will do. Once we have such a panic attack, more are inevitable; we become anxious and scared of it happening again, an apprehension which, in itself, increases our stress and tension, two precursors of panic. Essentially we develop a fear of the panic, indeed, a phobia of panicking.

Physiology, important in all 'disorders', reigns supreme in panic disorder as we become exquisitely sensitive to the sensations in our body; the first sign of increasing heartbeat rate or breathing, or shakiness can set the ball rolling toward panic. We look out for signs of it starting and avoid places where it may happen. The panic starts to happen more easily and more frequently and in many more situations as our fears and feelings of having no control increase. Situations from which there is no (dignified) escape are avoided at all costs, much like social anxiety disorder.

In panic disorder, 'how to be' can appear minimal. Associations with explanations for the feelings remain solely with the workings of our body. Yet there is an element of 'how to be' in that we have to be strong, we cannot be weak. We don't tell of that first terrible experience but take it inside and keep it to ourselves. And those situations that we must avoid through fear of no escape, they are not just about the panic, a large part of the fear includes making a public spectacle of ourselves ... of being humiliated and ashamed.

Panic disorder is not just about the physiological symptoms. It is what we associate them with. When we attach them to some inner weakness, an inner badness, it becomes something about us that is to blame. In experiments where panic disorder patients were made hypoglycemic (causing panic-like physiology), they reported 'nervousness' along with somatic symptoms of panic, but no panic.[9] As we have seen before, when something tangible can explain our 'weakness' we no longer have the weakness.

A similar explanation can be given for the apparent 'strange' phenomena of a decrease in panic attacks, in those with panic disorder, during pregnancy. Despite all those 'nasty' bodily sensations experienced during pregnancy, panic attacks decrease, not increase – pregnancy offering a valid (non self-related) reason.

The more and more we suffer panic attacks for no apparent external reason (but not out of the blue) and the more and more we cannot control them, the fears build up and up and generalise to an ever-increasing number of situations. Eventually there are very few situations that we dare face. We become too scared to go anywhere and need to stay somewhere safe; for some of us, we become too scared to leave the safety of our home.

Agoraphobia

Anxiety and panic, through the fight-or-flight response drives us desperately to either fight or escape.

Yet there is nothing to fight nor anything to flee from, only the situation or place. If we flee (or avoid) a particular place, we will soon have to avoid anything similar.

Agoraphobia reflects only having the confidence to deal with a restricted number of situations, those where we feel safe. This can limit us to our homes or, in extreme cases, even to certain parts of the home. We just cannot bear to go anywhere that a panic attack may occur.

Feelings of low self-worth and insecurity lie at the heart of all panic-related disorders. With it being more socially, and innately, acceptable for females than males to avoid situations, Agoraphobia is seen predominantly in women; many men tending to self-medicate with alcohol or drugs and face the situation rather than avoid it.

The lack of control over our own body and the perceived implications of what is happening and why, only serve to fuel the underlying insecurities, ensuring more and more panic.

Once we know what is happening and why, we can start to retake control of our body, to control it instead of it controlling us. In whatever we face in life, self-confidence grows as feelings of control grow.

Phobias

Spiders, snakes, heights, the dark; all of us have specific fears of a variety of objects and situations and according to some surveys, for between 5% and 10% of the population these fears are severe enough to be classed as phobias.[10]

We fear anything that may cause us pain and learn to avoid these things and so avoid pain. Based on innate apprehensions, fears where an object has to do something to us have to be learned (as we saw with the monkeys and the snake); fears to prevent us getting ourselves into harm are already encoded in us, for example: heights – even babies are scared of heights.

We can learn fears from others (children can learn them directly from their parents) or through direct experience. Being attacked by a dog can lead to a fear and avoidance of dogs which can, quite understandably, generalise to all similar four-legged animals with sharp teeth, in order to protect us.

And it's not just the object itself; the surrounding environment can play a part, anything about it that may mean possible danger can also become fear provoking. If the dog attacked us in an alley, alleyways could invoke fear, if it were in a field, open spaces will have a similar effect. We will notice, remember and use any information necessary to protect ourselves.

Fear becomes a phobia when it balloons out of all proportion to the actual danger. Although still related to potential threats to our safety, such fears have an added ingredient ... our thoughts.

Akin to generalised anxiety disorder and the fears over what could happen in the future and those unseen potential threats obsessed about in OCD, we scare ourselves through associations and feelings rather than the physical reality of what is happening, and usually end up getting more distressed over being scared and panicking than over the feared object. This can happen at any age.

In themselves, when not too extreme, simple (or specific) phobias need not be much of a problem for us. We are usually only anxious in the presence of the object or situation and can generally avoid such things without too much disruption to our life. And they can easily be resolved; with a few hours of graduated exposure (done correctly) we can usually learn to overcome them.

However, some phobias are more complex. They are related to feelings about our self and insecurity rather than the actual object. The object is (like all we have seen before) merely an associated reason, something that could explain the feelings.

In such a way, we can see how a typical phobia can develop: A child, full of self-doubt and insecurity through family conflict, sees his Mother run from a harmless house spider. Inner feelings, innate genetic apprehensions over real poisonous spiders, and the experience of a reaction to a harmless spider become associated. The small spider offers an explanation for the feelings of being afraid and when running from the spider doesn't alleviate the true inner insecurities (being only illusory control) the fears generalise, often in many cases, even to pictures of spiders.

When fears are not directly learned or they are totally inappropriate to the actual danger, perhaps it is the degree of our inner self-doubt and insecurity that, coupled with experience, influences the type and severity of the phobia we develop.

Without doubt, any phobia can develop in such a way, for all the phobias that exist are based on innately-real potential danger and when this becomes linked to inner self-doubt, these phobias are no longer specific or simple. They are complex and varied; overcoming one usually means developing another, for the real fear lies within us and when the secondary control (avoidance) fails, the fear generalises to more and more things.

Post Traumatic Stress Disorder (PTSD)

Not everyone who witnesses or experiences traumatic events develops PTSD; there must be something else at play other than just the trauma. Like everything we have looked at so far, it is not just the experience but what it means to us that counts.

Fear, anxiety and feelings of insecurity are normal reactions to traumatic events, not just in war (although potentially much greater in this case) but also in everyday life with situations such as: rape, assault, accidents, injury, the sudden death of someone close and natural disasters – anywhere the fragility of life becomes evident to us through real experience.

Symptoms include all those related to anxiety and panic; the usual alertness and apprehension. More than this, there can be a pervading sense of doubt regarding our safety and security that becomes almost pathological. In one sense, of course, this is totally justified, we have been brought close to death and it could happen again. Similar situations induce fear and we avoid them. The more we avoid, the more we have to avoid. As with all fears and phobias, the lack of control over our feelings results in a generalisation of the fears.

Inner fears over survival, being harmed in some way or attacked lie at the heart of all anxiety-related problems, but when they are evidenced through actual experience, the anxiety and insecurity can come to mean much more. One comprehensive study in the 1980's found that over 15% of the 3 million men who served in Vietnam still had PTSD over ten years later.[11]

Coming face to face with our own mortality, depersonalization (the mind and body's removal of our self from the situation, away from the horror of reality) serves to protect us, to minimise the pain. As does suppressing the extreme emotions involved and the emotional numbness that results. The suppression of emotions flows throughout all anxiety disorders. Our fear of attack or displaying weakness for expressing how we feel helps to form that intangible mixture of feelings and fears inside us. In PTSD, with actual experience relating to harm or death, the emotions can be stronger and the subsequent suppression stronger, however these suppressed emotions usually find a way out in dreams – the plague of many people with this problem.

Not just dreams, but flashbacks and re-living the event, perhaps there is also another reason for them. We have had real-life experience of injury or death with all the resulting feelings and emotions that entails. But the event has passed, the cause has gone but the feelings and emotions remain. To explain how we feel, a reason for it, the mind, once again, 'fills in'. A reason for the way we feel comes to us through the flashbacks and nightmares ... re-living the cause.

Our response to traumatic events and whether we develop post traumatic stress disorder or not, probably depends on where we start emotionally. If we bring inner doubt, feelings of low self-worth and insecurity, a history of 'being attacked through conflict', suppressed emotions and a need to be strong to the situation, the die is cast. Real-life experience relating to the fragility of life and mortality become linked to our perceived inner weakness.

Self-Harm

Biting nails and fingers or pulling our hair are all examples of self-harm; behaviours driven by insecurity and offering a sense of relief from, and a reason for our feelings. However, when the intangible mixture of feelings and fears becomes more extreme, greater measures are needed for relief. If life doesn't provide us with a plausible reason or answer for our bad feelings, (no experiences showing us 'how to be'), with no means to alleviate or control them, they build up and up inside. These feelings of self-doubt and worthlessness, fear and having no control can easily turn into self-hatred.

Self-harm in the form of cutting often develops as a way to release the intolerable pressure of the feelings inside. Bloodletting, (also a legitimate though misguided medical practice in earlier times used as a 'cure' for many illnesses ranging from fevers to hysteria), 'lets it out'. It is also seen throughout the animal kingdom: under conditions of extreme stress, such as isolation, overcrowding and confinement, many animals will inflict great damage upon themselves; they may bite themselves, gnaw through limbs or tails or relentlessly bang their heads against a wall, something often seen in zoo animals.

Not only a relief, the physical pain inflicted gives a reason for the emotional pain. Intangible pain made tangible. In the United Kingdom alone, over 170,000 people visit the emergency wards of hospitals each year as a result of self-harming.[12]

Paradoxically, (though not surprising, given what we now know) hurting ourselves does offer relief and a sense of control; we feel that we can take charge of the emotional pain. But it soon becomes addictive, for it isn't real control; the relief we feel through bloodletting does not change those inner feelings, it only makes them worse. Guilt and shame over doing this to ourselves only add to the inner badness.

We don't actually have real control and the true lack of control ensures that we have to do it more and more – cuts become deeper, more numerous and more intricate in pattern; a futile obsession and compulsion associating secondary relief and control to the inner problem.

Intangible feelings of badness are clearly reflected in those of us who can find no other answer than to harm ourselves.

Social Anxiety Disorder (Social Phobia)

Just the mention of a forthcoming event can evoke anxiety. That vital role of anxiety, the one that protects by making sure that we avoid potentially dangerous situations, kicks in and the more we think about the future event, the more anxious we get; we even imagine ourselves 'failing' in the situation.

Of course this happens to almost everyone to some degree at various times in his or her life. Ask most people to give a public speech and they will go through the same. However, with social anxiety disorder, doing almost anything in public can come to instil such fear in us.

Public speaking involves putting our self up for judgement and possible rejection by others, with nowhere to go if we are not up to standard – no wonder it is the number one fear for many people.

Fears over rejection, abandonment and attack form the basis for all anxiety-related problems: we believe this will happen to us if we are not 'how to be'. With social phobia, these fears come to the fore. In one study, over 60% of males with social anxiety disorder reported that the situation they feared most was being introduced to other people.[13] Here, again, some form of judgement, and possible rejection, is implicit in the situation.

Paradoxically, the fear of being rejected, cast out and alone, usually ends up in loneliness as we avoid people rather than face the pain of rejection. Self-protection ensures that we withdraw from people and maintain only those relationships where we feel in control. Unfortunately, the walls we build to protect ourselves also keep us in; loneliness and avoiding people only serves to strengthen the inner bad feelings. But to our inner–self, the unbearable pain of loneliness is nothing compared to the potential threat to our survival that interacting with others may mean.

It is not hard to understand how a child that suffers constant destructive criticism can become conditioned to expect rejection and attack when dealing with others. And with social phobia, that is what we do; we approach others and situations expecting to be judged and criticised, our past experience dictates it. Everything has to be just right; perfect, to ward off negative assessment and criticism. Perfectionism staves off attack; the word meticulous originates from the Latin word *metus* meaning fear.

And we do fear attack. Eating in public or even signing our name in public – two common social phobias – represent letting our guard down, we are being watched whilst we concentrate on something else and are thus vulnerable. It's comparable to the anxiousness of many animals seen at watering holes – as they concentrate on drinking they are often attacked.

Destructive criticism often goes hand-in-hand with over-concern regarding social evaluation; this, too, can be instilled in us and it often feels as though we are expected to be perfect. A perfectionism that is reflected in a direct 'how to be'.

To be the best, the biggest, the strongest, the cleverest, the most beautiful ... Often related to innate needs: strength for males, beauty for females, social anxiety disorder begins in adolescence and affects men and women equally. It sits at the very heart of our self-identity; we must be these things, anything less is a failure and will meet with rejection, humiliation, shame and pain.

So everything becomes a performance under scrutiny, with the utmost pressure which, in itself, makes us anxious and tense. And every symptom indicates a sign of our weakness and failure; whether it be shaking or sweating or blushing or stuttering, the one we focus on is the one that, we believe, most represents our publicly visible display of weakness.

Just the fact that we get anxious and scared in the first place confirms our weakness and inadequacy to us. The increasing heartbeat and breathing, the trembling and the feeling on-edge confirms that we are indeed 'weak' and 'not good enough'. This only increases our inner feelings of inadequacy, which strengthens the need to be better ('how to be') which in turn increases the performance pressure and the anxiety and tension symptoms it produces – the vicious circle is set.

With social anxiety disorder we don't really have to do much for it to strengthen and strengthen. A desperate need to be 'right' produces performance anxiety and tension that confirms the weakness and thus the desperate need – it is self-fulfilling.

We can never get control, we can never be better enough in the way we feel we have to be (just as the anorexic can never be thin enough) and so the fearful situations increase in number and intricacy.

Just like panic disorder, the most feared situations are the ones in which we feel trapped. But actually, in both cases, it is psychological entrapment. We can actually walk away at any time, but dare not, for to do so would only display our weakness to everyone – something that to us is unbearable.

Of course, those intangible inner feelings of badness rule the show. The feelings of weakness and badness come from within, and feelings of not being strong or beautiful enough are only associated reasons and answers.

We know that, generally, people are not going to attack and reject us. In many cases we are probably bigger and stronger than them and they couldn't hurt us even if they wanted to. It is the associated fears in our mind, our reality and the links we have made through our experiences that are our downfall. The basis of social phobia – that we are not good enough and so we are going to be attacked and rejected, is based on what we feel, not reality.

Perhaps social anxiety disorder (and life) can be reflected in the performance anxiety of the musician ... if we try to achieve perfection, we will fear every note and be consumed by anxiety. However, if we just play for the joy of playing ... the performance may be brilliant.

Shyness

People with social phobia may hold down jobs well beneath their capabilities, possibly due to fears over interviews or dealing with the public. They can be considered quiet, introverted, or obtuse. The same can apply to those who are shy.

As we are grow, we are bombarded by a phenomenal amount of 'don'ts' and 'can'ts', 'mustn't' and 'shouldn't' – perhaps it is no wonder that surveys regularly indicate that a high percentage of the population considers themselves to be shy.

Shyness involves negative feelings relating to our self and our abilities, but it doesn't involve panic. There is no desperate need 'how to be' related to survival. Levels of self-doubt and insecurity appear lower, perhaps due to lower levels of conflict and pressure in childhood or possibly due to any conflict being tempered by love from others, extra support or positive life experiences. However, self-doubt still remains as does fear of attack from other people; shy people find it difficult to maintain eye contact.

Drastic 'how to be' isn't necessary for we have accepted the reason for our nervousness and fears – we are shy, a shy person. This is reason enough to confirm and support our inner feelings.

And so we live our lives accordingly, lacking in confidence and daring, being safe rather than taking chances simply because we are shy. Avoiding 'difficult' situations, though all the time longing not to be shy, wanting to be confident like everyone else.

Social phobia to a lesser degree? Inner self-doubt, insecurity and fear of interacting with other people lie at the heart of shyness.

Stress

In the Western World, a host of illnesses, rarely seen in the past, have now become commonplace and widespread. Heart disease, strokes, cancers and degenerative diseases such as arthritis and the 'myalgias' have become more prominent, in part, due to stress.

Imminent threats (eg. a charging animal) or actual threats (eg. a virus invading our body) result in a mobilization of the body in order to deal with the threat. Hormones such as Adrenalin and Cortisol flow through the body to help us overcome such threats, via the fight-or-flight response and attacking/killing invading viruses etc. The short-term effect of this body mobilization is beneficial, in that we survive the threat, but long-term, frequent and prolonged stress responses weaken our immune system and other important body functions. It can lead to loss of appetites, weight loss, sleep disturbances and memory problems.

Stress involves a threat and whether we feel we can cope or not. If we can cope it is a challenge, if we cannot it is seen as a threat. In today's society, much of our stress comes from threats that are psychologically based. It is not the event, per se, that causes us stress, but what we make of it. Yes, many life situations cause us distress (eg. loss and bereavement) but we have the appropriate responses to cope, such as grieving. It is the way that we ourselves perceive events as a threat to our security (in some way) that produces psychological stress. Our body mobilizes to deal with the threat, but there is no threat, no charging animal or virus.

Not 'real' threats, events like separation and divorce have been shown to be related to a depressed immune system.[14]

Many people feel the need to be 'active' when stressed as a result of this body mobilization – showing us why exercise can be beneficial in helping stress. In exercising we are doing something.

With others controlling a large part of our lives (government, employer, teacher, church), many feel unable to cope to some degree. Add to this the breakdown of communities and family life and we see more and more people having to deal with events alone, lacking support in hard times. Bereavement, divorce and separation, social and financial problems – how much they affect us depends partly on our sense of control and the support available. However, whether we perceive an event as a threat, hence stressful, or simply more stressful than normal depends mainly on how we feel about our self. Our reaction is determined by where we start emotionally (just like with PTSD).

True stress is a normal part of existence and has a role in our survival. Intermittent stress reactions build up our resistance and resilience to many diseases. If we didn't experience stress and overcome it, we wouldn't be able to withstand any stress at all.

However, when we bring a background of anxiety and insecurity to a situation, feelings of not being able to cope already in us, the stress we experience increases greatly. We build up potential threats due to the insecurity inside us. When we link the bad feelings associated with negative life events to our inner bad feelings, any potentially threatening event becomes stressful.

Many of us *feel* that the answer is to do more (that body mobilization need to be active), to get results – doing, achieving and 'completing' are seen as answers to the 'stressful situation' and thus answers to our inner insecurity, but, of course, they aren't.

And everything must be done in a certain time or by a certain time, even our leisure activities – everything we do is governed by deadlines. Society sets them, companies set them and we set them. A 'must do' not too far away from that 'must be' of 'how to be'.

One area of our lives provides a classic (and extreme) example of all the above ... the workplace.

Stress at Work

Here, a potential threat is ever-present; we could lose our jobs, thus our livelihood and possibly, therefore, the life we now know. Our whole life could change and it is scary, so we have to do what we are told, when we are told, how we are told.

In the workplace, many factors add to our feelings of low self-worth and thus the stress we suffer. Things such as: being treated as a number, having no say, and corporate identity overshadowing our own all make us feel worse. And as profit rules, fewer and fewer people are expected to do more and more within tighter deadlines, by many companies. The extreme amount of stress suffered in the workplace today reflects the lack of worth and need to do more, that many of us feel, coupled with ever-increasing demands. Some people won't work like this and get out, other people try to comply and make themselves fairly ill, others feel that they must do everything that's demanded of them, whatever the cost, and make themselves really (life-threateningly) ill.

Deadlines can be beneficial in moderation; many people thrive on such pressure to help produce the work and there is nothing wrong with wanting to achieve and be successful in a company. As always, the problem lies in it becoming a 'must' rather than a desire or choice. Inner self-doubt and experiences can lead us to associate the failure of not getting results with our insecurity. When 'getting results' doesn't relieve our inner feelings we can end up doing more and more, still believing that it will.

Seen in many people (often classed as Type A personalities), we must get results at all costs and can end up trying to do everything. But we can never do enough, achieve enough or make enough money. It isn't the answer and all we end up doing is damaging our health as the constant stress on our body takes its toll.

In stressful times, anxiety disorders get worse and those people without anxiety disorders often show an increase in behaviours associated with them (such as checking). When we view situations as related to a weakness in us, they are a threat and we will become stressed. When we are truly confident, no event is ever associated to inner weakness and we don't have to accept every demand that is made on us.

Our individual personalities probably develop from a mixture of genetic makeup, experiences and learning. As such, how we behave depends on using the knowledge that we have gained from past experience and how and why we apply this to present situations (based on situational clues, knowledge at that time, assumptions and reasoning). Differences in, and complex interactions between, the above factors give rise to our individuality. We are all different, and yet, in one sense we are all the same. We all have similar body structures; we all have similar mind structures; we all have the same five senses and we receive and process information through these senses and structures in a similar manner. Therefore, it is not surprising that we all tend to deal with certain situations in roughly the same way.

Anxiety-related problems vary from person to person, within similar disorders and between different ones, each reflecting the nuances of individuality and experience. However, just below the surface, they are the same.

Developing to varying degrees at different times, probably depending on the amount of conflict/pressure experienced and the ability to deal with it, they all involve inner feelings of intangible badness and efforts to deal with the feelings. Efforts that are based on associated reasons and actually make the inner feelings worse.

Some don't involve great panic and show a lesser need for 'how to be'. These can include: shyness, overeating, hair pulling, self-harm, susceptibility to stress and the need to achieve.

Others involve great panic and 'how to be' is a must.

A direct 'how to be' is seen in BDD, Anorexia Nervosa and Social Anxiety Disorder. Here, it can be a survival 'must' and becomes directly related to self-identity.

In OCD and GAD, for example, the 'how to be' is more diffuse and related to a vague, living up to some ideal, prey to unseen threats if it is not achieved. Depression, too, forms around 'not being good enough'.

Some 'disorders' form early (usually those related to self-identity), others can start later in life. In these cases, perhaps a weak self-identity is brought into play by later-life experiences. A fragile self-image damaged by an over-critical spouse, for example, can often play a part in OCD and GAD. Negative life experiences and work pressures can also interplay with a damaged self-image. Specific (and more generalized) phobias can start early in life or later, depending upon experience.

Some focus mainly on the body and the physical (eg. Panic disorder and social phobia) others, the mind (generalized anxiety disorder and Obsessive-compulsive disorder). In PTSD there can be equal focus on both.

All involve an element of 'deserving it'. Often in OCD, rituals can be stopped when there is a sense of 'having done enough' (to make up for being bad) similarly with Anorexia, many feel that they only deserve to eat once they have exercised enough.

These problems are all based on exaggerated normal behaviours due to deep inner intangible feelings of being in some way 'not good enough' and that we will be attacked (destroyed) because of it. Our inner-self is only protecting us – but before we look at the answer, lets look at some of the things that influence our current attempts to deal with these anxiety-related problems.

...

10

Making Things Worse?

A NEGATIVE THOUGHT is a negative thought. Unstoppable thoughts of the teenage anorexic girl and the panic associated with eating and being fat works just the same as the uncontrollable thoughts of the man or woman with OCD and the panic they feel when they don't perform their rituals. The heightened anxiety associated with constant worrying and planning in generalized anxiety disorder is the same as that which we feel with social anxiety disorder when we think about facing a fearful situation. Excessive shaking in panic is the same whatever gives rise to the panic, as are the depressed feelings of frustration sadness and despair, whatever their cause.

There is no doubt that these problems are very powerful since they relate to inner self-protective drives that shape our thoughts and actions, but we ourselves increase the hold they have over us by the way we think about them.

There's a story on a website relating a medical experience that illustrates this nicely. It shows how beliefs about powerful forces that we don't understand, hence cannot control, can affect our life (and death) ... the awesome power of belief:

'The patient, ill for many weeks, looked wasted and near death. Tuberculosis or cancer was considered the cause. As he approached death, his wife informed the doctor that around four months before hospitalisation, the patient had had an argument with a local voodoo priest. The priest had summoned him to the cemetery and announced that he had 'voodooed' him and that he would die very soon.

Dr. Daugherty pondered long how to save this man. What followed was more like theatre than medical treatment, but it saved the man's life. The next day the doctor gathered 10 or more of the patient's kin at the bedside and announced in his most authoritative voice that he knew what was wrong. He described how he had confronted the voodoo priest and demanded to know what he had done. He announced, to the man and his family, "the priest had made some lizard eggs climb down into your stomach and they hatched some small lizards. All but one of them died, leaving one big one that is eating all your food and the lining of your body". He informed the group that he would remove the lizard.

He then gave the man a powerful emetic to induce vomiting and within a few moments the man started to vomit. After several minutes of continued vomiting, Dr. Daugherty pulled from his black bag, carefully and secretively, a live green lizard. At the height of the next wave of retching, he slid the lizard into the basin and called out in a loud voice, "look what has come out of you, you are now cured, the voodoo curse is lifted"...

The man then fell into a deep sleep and awoke the next morning ravenous for food. Within a week the patient was discharged home.'[1]

The belief systems about voodoo[2] in the man's community had almost killed him. Belief and fear is a potent mixture and can lead to many self-fulfilling prophecies. Something that not only applies to anxiety-related problems but to many illnesses – Cancer isn't regarded by many as 'death by diagnosis' for no reason.

Conditioned in ways to think by the educational system, many of us blindly believe information that comes from experts and authority without question.

The Classification of Anxiety Disorders

Categorization reflects the way the brain and mind works and forms the basis of everything we understand. New information is analysed, compared and stored by reference to what we already know so that we can use it to predict and control our environment. The classification of anxiety disorders is no different; it serves to describe and order various symptoms into well-defined categories to help to manage them. It has promoted much research and expanded our knowledge of these problems. However, most of the research is limited to what can be physically measured and we can truly measure very little indeed in our universe.

The names given: OCD, GAD etc. are only descriptions of ways of thinking, feeling and behaving but naming them gives them a life of their own, a whole new power. Suddenly they are an entity, they exist and what we think of them is influenced by what we are told. Thoughts and behaviours fundamental to human existence and survival, (experienced by all in times of insecurity), that have become exaggerated due to extreme negative experiences are now a 'disorder'. And we believe everything that the experts and authorities tell us about them: they are irrational (not correct), due to genes (partly correct), due to chemical imbalances (probably not correct). Feelings, beliefs and well-meaning mis-information can interplay to make these problems seem insurmountable – a prime example of fear and belief creating self-fulfilling prophesies!

Classification also obscures the bigger picture. When we focus on individual categories, separate reasons and answers are often proffered for different problems yet we have seen how they are all related: feeling bad, uncontrollable negative thoughts and images, physiological symptoms of anxiety, panic and tension lie at the heart of all anxiety and depression problems ... they also lie at the heart of their cure.

Anxiety-related problems are not illnesses, diseases or even disorders. Our mind and body are perfectly ordered, trying to protect us from potential threats inferred from our experiences.

A self-protection extreme and mis-guided, for we were misled: feeling bad not due to our badness but to how we were treated.

The Medical Model and Medication

Most of us trust everything the doctor tells us. If he or she tells us (in good faith) that we have an illness we generally accept it. And it may appear to serve us well to accept it; a name for our problem and, in one sense, a relief – it's nothing to do with us; just a faulty gene or a chemical imbalance, an illness we were just unfortunate to contract, nothing at all to do with us being weak and inadequate. But it's an illusion and it doesn't last for long. Such explanations don't adequately explain or deal with those inner bad feelings – there is no real control and so they get worse.

Synapses, those connections between the neurons in our brain (around 10,000 for each neuron), are tiny spaces that are occupied by chemical messengers called *neurotransmitters* which carry information between neurons. Serotonin and Dopamine are two neurotransmitters regularly mentioned with regard to anxiety and depression problems. And chemical imbalance, usually referring to deficiencies of these neurotransmitters, is often proffered as a reason for anxiety disorders and depression. Well, anxiety and depression deplete our body of many resources, including: energy, vitamins and no doubt neurotransmitters. Surely, any chemical imbalance is the result of these problems not the cause. Balancing chemicals in the brain through the action of drugs may alleviate some symptoms to a degree, but never touches the cause.

And findings from gene research suggest that mental 'illnesses' do not occur because of a single gene.[3]

The medical model, one in which physical abnormalities explain our mental processes, goes hand-in-hand with classification and treatment. A neat set of symptoms, well defined and named with a neat, specially prepared drug to cure them – which rarely works. Often, placebos (pills working on belief alone) are just as good.[4]

It seems as though classification has gone crazy: new disorders springing up all the time, many of which are only slightly different from existing ones or represent mildly exaggerated normal behaviour; people are classed as having many different problems instead of one with various symptoms and the incidence of 'mental problems' in the population has sky-rocketed, with some studies purporting that one in seven of us has a mental problem. Many people believe that 'new' problems are being created in order to increase drug sales. In the United States of America, lawsuits have been filed claiming that the definition of ADHD (Attention-Deficit Hyperactivity Disorder) has been made inappropriately broad to encompass more children and so increase the numbers requiring treatment.

The medical model ignores the incredible power of the mind and in doing so doesn't even come close to providing an answer. One recent experiment involving anorexic teenagers found that nearly all of those tested had reduced blood flow to the part of their brains that controlled vision.[5] Now, we could use this to promote the idea of physical brain problems causing Anorexia Nervosa or we could go beyond this to the core problem: the mind controls the body in order to justify feelings. Similarly, regarding an overactive thyroid gland producing anxiety-like symptoms – perhaps for many, it is the other way around: the mind causing over activity in the gland to justify constant anxiety.

We need to understand the system as a whole - brain, mind, body, spirit and environment all interacting ... our whole being.

In viewing it as merely brain and body and individual parts that have gone wrong and need fixing, we are ignoring the bigger picture. Many refer to the stomach as the body's second brain and there have been reports of heart transplant patients changing personalities[6] (presumably in tune with that of the donor). We are all much more than just that which man can measure!

Currently, one of the main ways we attempt to 'fix the parts that have gone wrong' is through medication.

Medication

Under no circumstances should anyone stop taking prescribed medication without medical supervision.

Medication has its uses. When we are overwhelmed by anxiety and fears and despair, appropriate short-term medication can alleviate the symptoms, giving us the relief we need to begin to deal with the problem correctly.

For some people, those with an unshakeable belief in a physical cause for their problem, a lifetime of medication can offer relief.

Short-term medication can be a lifesaver; long-term usage of medication generally serves to make things worse, for it fuels the very core of the problem – it strengthens our inner feelings of inadequacy and weakness. We have to take a tablet to be ok, therefore we must be weak; having to take medication at all (to be 'normal'), confirms our inner self-doubt.

Medication also represents that illusory control that we have talked about so often; there is a sense of some control, the symptoms may lessen, but it never touches those inner feelings hence we need more and more as we try to get real control. This psychological dependency, coupled with any physical dependency (that many medications induce) can entrap us.

If medication has calmed us, once we stop taking it, any anxiety we experience will feel greater for we are used to being calm. Withdrawal from medication can result in many anxiety–related symptoms feeling worse, again strengthening the underlying problem; yet we have become a medication-dependent society: emotional and life issues have become illness that merit treatment, usually in the form of a pill.

With problems that are defined by anxiety, fear and despair, it would nice if they could be just taken away, removed from us without further struggle – but they cannot. Medication may have some short-term benefits but it is never a cure, nor will it ever be, as millions can testify.

* * *

Alcohol and Drugs

Many people with anxiety-related problems self-medicate using alcohol and/or recreational drugs. These can take away the pain for a while and offer us that sense of control, replacing the bad feelings by good ones. Not real control, so they become addictive – more and more achieving less and less. And physical effects of alcohol/drugs often intensify our feelings and moods.

The use of alcohol and drugs can show us the effects of altering the balance of chemicals in our brain as they produce unpleasant symptoms, both physical and psychological; chemical imbalance in the brain does have an effect on both thought and behaviour. And studies with brain-damaged patients show us, too, that physical changes in the brain produce many 'abnormal' thoughts and actions. Both of these: chemical imbalance and physical problems in the brain can obviously affect the way that we think and behave, but when we bring to our problems a background of conflict, fear and self-doubt – this is where the answer lies.

Therapy

There is a certain knowledge that only comes from experience. Most therapists, whilst highly qualified, professional and caring people probably don't know as much about the problem as we do.

Problems with therapy can come when our experiences and responses are forced to comply with some theory. Most theories are ideas, not fact and in doing this, some therapies have made many people worse. One survey found that 28% of practising psychologists were unaware of negative effects in psychotherapy.[7]

Of course therapy can be extremely beneficial, but as we will note later, it's not so much the therapy as the therapist that counts.

Self-Help

All progress in anxiety-related problems involves self-help. Yes the guidance and support of another can be truly beneficial, but we have to change ourselves, nobody can do it for us. Self-help (the right kind) is the only way to change these problems – but the right knowledge is essential.

Most current self-help focuses on the symptoms not the cause: we can spend a lifetime struggling to fight anxiety and panic symptoms, a struggle often as great as the problem itself, and alleviating symptoms has little effect on the underlying problem. Take perfectionism, for example, how can we practise not being perfect when we have an inner self-protective drive to be perfect. It is the reason why we have to be perfect that we need to change.

When we understand and change the problem at its core, everything else follows. There is no more need for general fear and anxiety or self-protective behaviours – they are no longer relevant.

How to deal with the core of our problem is where we head next.

PART III

THE ANSWER

"This above all; to thine own self be true."

WILLIAM SHAKESPEARE (1564–1616)

The Bear and the Flagpole

... We've spent a long time at the top of the flagpole and have grown weary, but we have discovered the truth ... we don't really need to be here. We now know what to do and start to slide down the pole slowly, feeling anxious as we go but controlling it. We are apprehensive about meeting the bear at the bottom but we have a new strength and a new power, insight into everything that has happened and why.

We reach the bottom and face the bear; it is roaring and snarling ferociously and all our survival instincts tell us to flee ... but we don't, we know the truth and our true worth, we know just how good we really are, so we stand and face it.

Then something amazing happens ... as we look deeply into the bear, standing before us, roaring and growling, we see just how wrong we have been ... it's not a bear at all, and the roar is not a roar ... it is just a group of timid little mice, all clinging together and squeaking in fear. As we approach, they loosen their hold on each other, fall to the ground and scurry away ... we are free.

* * * * *

Anxiety-related problems may be partly influenced by the role of genetics via predispositions and possibly through some learning in the womb, but by far the greatest contribution comes from experiences and learning and how we were made to feel because of them. Life experiences have made us feel afraid, worthless and unable to cope. Not usually single frightening instances (with the exception of some forms of PTSD) they more likely develop from general living situations which involved such things as: constantly being put down or ridiculed, being made to feel ashamed, guilty, or of little value and unloved – we were made to *feel* bad.

But this is all we need to know; we don't need to mull over the *'why's'* and *'where's'* of the anger, shame and guilt or search for reasons any longer – doing so only serves to keep the connections strong. The 'feeling bad' was never connected to us as a person, so we need to stop looking for reasons for our 'badness', we'll never find one, for the badness doesn't really exist – it is intangible.

This feeling bad, anxiety and stress and ultimately panic led to the conclusion that something about our very self was not good enough and that we would be rejected/attacked because of it. So we had to be different, better, much better and this need resulted in a relentless pursuit of 'how to be'. A pursuit that only offered the illusion of control and merely served to fuel our inner feelings of worthlessness since it could never be the real answer. There is only one answer: we don't need to be anything ... just our self.

We cannot change the past for it has happened and is a part of us, but we can change the way we think about it and what it means to us. We now have the insight and understanding to enable us to turn these problems around, evolve and grow through them, beyond them to become the unique, worthy individual that it is our birthright to be.

11

Weakening the Connections

VIRTUALLY EVERYTHING THAT we do in our lives, we have learned. Some reflexes, behaviours, predispositions and aptitudes may result from evolution but even these can be modified and developed by learning. Learning involves change in the nervous system and gradual automation.

Change in the Nervous System

Experiences shape patterns of neural connections within our brain and in doing so change us. When we learn something, new connections form within our brain and nervous system; the more things associated with the learning the greater the number and more varied the patterns of connections that form. Repetition of the learning and regular usage leads to the connections occurring more frequently and becoming stronger.

Similar to the violinists we mentioned earlier, studies on London taxi drivers showed that the longer they did the job, the bigger became the spatial navigation regions of their brain.[1] The stronger the learning, the more it becomes part of our make-up.

Take the following simple example: learning the colours of the rainbow.

If we simply learnt the seven colours: Red, Orange, Yellow, Green, Blue, Indigo and Violet, making no associations, the knowledge would not remain in our memory for very long. (Try it and see – write down seven different colours (not the ones in a rainbow) and, without making any associations to aid memory, learn the list until you can repeat it. Put the list somewhere safe and see if you can remember the list one week later). However, when we associate the colours of the rainbow with the popular acronym – Richard Of York Gave Battle In Vain (introducing elements of wonder: Who was Richard of York? Which battle did he lose? and surprise - the cleverness of the connection) the learning becomes that much stronger. In fact the first thing that comes to mind for most people when asked to name the colours in a rainbow is the association – Richard Of York Gave Battle In Vain.

It is not really surprising then, that anxiety-related problems involving learning associated with: thoughts, feelings, emotions, confirmations, reasoning, comparisons, evidence and expectations do strongly shape our brain and nervous system, do shape our thoughts, feelings and behaviour and do become part of us.

However, this part of us is not an inborn quality (we are not born with low self-confidence and phobias) it develops from learning and the conclusions drawn from our experiences.

Gradual Automation

Behaviours and thought processes that are repeated over and over again gradually become automatic, that is, they can be performed 'without thinking'.

Again, related to survival, this has to be the case. Things that we do regularly (that we have learnt strongly) can be carried out 'automatically' so that our attention is available for anything else that may require it and we are ready to learn new things.

Imagine having to learn from scratch how to drive a car every time you wanted to use it, how to ride a bike, how to swim, how to tie a tie or a shoe lace or having to relearn how to write every time you wanted to write a letter.

For those who can drive, remember the concentration and practise and more practise required when you learnt to coordinate the clutch, gears and accelerator – now you do it without even thinking about it – it's automatic.

This process not only applies to behaviours but also to thoughts and memories. Anyone who has ever revised for examinations will have experienced forgetting that section you learnt until you remember the first few words, then the rest comes flowing back – automatically.

When behaviours or thought processes are repeated over and over again the associated connections in the brain become so strongly linked that once the behaviour is started the rest follows in sequence as these strongly connected areas of the brain work together. Something seen in habit behaviours: when started, the habit is continued even though any initial rewards or good feelings associated with the habit may no longer apply.

We can see this process at work in anxiety-related problems in that, once the initial image of 'failing' in a situation occurs, all the associated feelings, emotions and behaviours come into effect. Often leading to avoidance behaviour, that initial mental image of facing the situation can lead to: memories of past 'failures', expectation of impending 'failure', feelings of anticipated shame and rejection, feelings of being 'not good enough' or 'bad', and all the physiological signs of anxiety (increased heart rate, shaking, dizziness etc.). These thoughts, emotions and behaviours can occur, repeat, interact and strengthen to such a degree that the resultant panic can cause us to avoid the situation in order to obtain relief.

* * *

This understanding of learning shows us how it is possible to change. We need to reduce the strength of previously learned thoughts and behaviours and learn new ones. That is, we must weaken the strength of the connections in the brain and nervous system associated with low self-confidence and anxiety and develop and strengthen new connections associated with more positive (and incidentally closer to the truth) beliefs.

But how can connections in the nervous system be weakened? Consider the following examples: -

Top golfers, snooker and darts players practise their skills relentlessly for many hours every day. This, along with some natural ability, can keep them at the top level, perhaps in the top ten, of their sport. Connections in the brain associated with such things as: hand-eye-muscle coordination, balance and judgment of distance and speed need to become strong and stay strong for them to remain at that level. But what happens if they don't practise?

A top class player that does not practise for a month will probably fall out of the top twenty rankings and one who does not practise for a year will probably not make the top one hundred. The connections associated with the behaviour have diminished through lack of use and so has the behaviour. That part of the person that was a top class sportsman no longer exists.

This weakening also applies to thought processes. The ability to do simple mathematics can be easily lost through lack of use, as anyone who has forgotten how to do multiplication and division since the advent of the personal calculator can testify.

Memories, if not recalled, fade with time. Similarly, limbs can diminish if not used. A broken leg in plaster for six months loses both size and function to some extent and usually requires extensive physiotherapy once the cast is removed.

As the adage goes: *If you don't use it – lose it!*

* * *

Connections in the brain and nervous system can be weakened by... **not using them**.

If we don't think those thoughts and don't do those behaviours they will gradually weaken and fade. Of course this is easier said than done; people with feelings of low self-worth and anxiety problems can be likened to those top class sportsmen, continually strengthening the connections by daily practising – but there is something we can do, something that stops us bringing all the associated connections into play.

ACCEPTANCE

When we *truly* accept the bad thoughts, feelings and drives we can stop strengthening the problem. And we are now in a position to truly accept these things because we know exactly what is happening and why. Acceptance without such insight is doomed to failure for the unknown will always overpower us – but we are accepting the truth as we know, and that truth is: we never were bad; the feelings come from how we were treated in the past; how we interpreted the behaviour of others and how we developed ways to protect ourselves. We feel bad because of the problems of other people and not some inherent badness.

And from this truth we can form an acceptance statement: -

> *"I know that I feel scared and insecure and inadequate because I was made to feel bad; so bad that I feel I will be rejected and attacked. My inner self is only trying to protect me but I now know it was all just how I was made to feel; I am not really bad, I never was, I am good."*

This acceptance statement, this underlying truth forms the foundation for change, you need to adapt it and make it personal to you – something that you firmly believe.

Whenever we are thinking bad or feeling bad we can stop the process through acceptance. Take any of the symptoms listed in the symptoms section and we can start to weaken them in the following way: -

When the symptom is present, we can say to ourselves:

"I realise that I am... (the explanation given in the symptoms section) and that... (the acceptance statement)" – for example, when we find we are thinking too much we would say to ourselves, something like: -

> *"I realise that I am trying to understand what happened to me, trying to get control and that I know that I feel scared and insecure and inadequate because I was made to feel bad; so bad that I will be rejected and attacked. My inner self is only trying to protect me but I now know it was all just how I was made to feel; I am not really bad, I never was, I am good."*

If possible say it out loud (or under your breath), this gives it form and presence. Doing this can also form the basis of a more understanding and positive self-talk, which will come to be internalized giving us an inner reassuring guide rather than a critic.

When you compose your own acceptance statement (or use the one given if you prefer), write it in the 'my notes section'. One written statement that you believe in and use can change your life.

You don't have to use the same words (eg. realise), just state an understanding of what is happening and the inner truth. And the understanding of the symptom shouldn't be long- winded, just the core reason, which usually boils down to trying to get control, associating bad external events to inner feelings and our inner-self trying to protect us.

* * *

Accepting in this way changes the pattern of connections in our brain. Old patterns weaken and fade; new ones take shape – ones that represent a whole new belief and attitude about our problem. The problem as we know it is changing, it no longer means the same to us or has the same hold over us.

We are not simply removing the problem of feeling and thinking bad (something that cannot really be done) but changing it. The thoughts and feelings come to us but we let them fade and weaken through acceptance rather than build them up and strengthen them by fighting.

And this is how we work as humans; confidence and 'holding ones nerve' comes from not dwelling on the negative, not thinking about (hence strengthening) the doubts and fears and feelings. Many confident people when asked about some forthcoming 'big event' (for example, a wedding speech or a work presentation) will reply 'I'm trying not to think about it'.

As a pop star recently replied, when asked about an imminent awards ceremony, "I try not to think about it otherwise I get too nervous".[2]

In the past our problems have revolved around building up and strengthening all those bad thoughts and feelings: ruminating, worrying, comparing, despairing, looking for reasons and answers all served to keep the problem alive. These behaviours can be compared to 'picking at a scab' preventing healing. The natural state of body and mind is one of health if we don't fight and block it; if we don't keep picking away they will heal.

Through acceptance, we allow our mind (and body) to heal; we accept the thoughts and feelings instead of fighting and picking at them. Of course the effects of acceptance take time; but this too has an analogy with how we work as humans: building up acceptance is analogous to building up a muscle, the more we take control of our thoughts and feelings, the stronger the ability becomes until it is a part of our nature and self-belief – a new belief in our strength and ability is taking shape, and belief is everything.

"The thing always happens that you really believe in, and the belief in a thing makes it happen"
– Frank Lloyd Wright (1867–1959)

* * *

Through acceptance, we are taking control of our thoughts and feelings but it doesn't stop there; we can actually use it to weaken the 'disordered' behaviours themselves. The principle is the same – we need to experience the anxiety and panic in order to master them, to learn control and gain confidence. Once we feel the anxiety and panic we need to accept the true situation and stop fighting it and building it up.

But we cannot just face the extreme anxiety and panic related to obsessions and compulsions, worrying, phobias etc. – it is too great and will overwhelm us. What we need to do is face it in stages.

Facing Fearful Situations

To weaken the connections regarding our 'disorder', we can: -

- Grade anxiety and panic arousing situations on a scale from 1 to 10 (more if you need to). Where 10 = mildly frightening and 1 = extremely frightening.
- Start with number 10
- Feel the anxiety, thoughts, feelings etc.
- Truly accept it – through realising that it is actually only our inner-self protecting us because of feelings, and saying the acceptance statement.
- Gradually move up the levels of difficulty. **But** only move to the next level when you have mastered taking control at each level. (Taking control is feeling scared but not letting things progress to panic).

Grading the situations may include such things as: delaying worrying for progressively longer times, or not worrying about milder fears; delaying compulsions in a similar manner or reducing the repetitions in rituals or stages of the ritual; throwing less important stuff away (or not collecting it) in hoarding; facing more and more fearful social situations; doing more and more in depression; going further and further in Agoraphobia etc. You know what you fear doing or not doing and can grade it accordingly.

Success will take time and practise, for remember, our inner-self is protecting our very existence and the progression of our genes. Until new beliefs and attitudes about our true goodness (hence no need for protection) develop and strengthen, it will not give up its job lightly.

With this method we are not doing anything extraordinary, no magic technique; what we are doing mirrors life. Everyone masters difficult situations in stages; it is the only way to do it.

Picture a young child approaching the ocean for the first time. First they let the water cover their feet; then, when they feel more confident they move deeper, up to their knees. As confidence develops they move up to their waist and so on ...

We are doing nothing more.

However, there is something else that we can use to enhance the effect of acceptance in weakening those neural connections forged in our brain through life experiences, something that, once again, reflects how we work as humans.

Distraction

Our brains are incredibly complex, comprising around 100 billion brain cells and 100,000 billion connections. But for all this complexity there is an ability we don't possess. That is the ability to pay real attention to more than one thing at a time.

We can do 'automatic' behaviours and attend to something else, (that is the whole point of behaviour becoming automatic) but we cannot give only part attention to something that is of importance for this represents lack of control.

Try the following simple example.
Can you solve the two equations in your head at the same time?
Not one then the other or part of one then part of the other but both together simultaneously!

$$84 \div 16 =$$
$$24 \times 17 =$$

If we try to work out $84 \div 16$, we cannot think about 24×17. If we then shift our attention to 24×17, we stop thinking about $84 \div 16$, and if we try and do them together, we can't do either. In fact, we cannot do much when we are prevented from attending to something fully.

Some may proffer examples such as: people who read on a plane to try and take their mind off phobias about flying, supporting the notion that we can attend to two things at once – reading but still thinking about the fear. In truth, their mind has never been taken off the fear, it is the main focus of attention and the reading has never been given true attention, shown by what usually happens: they have to read the same sentence or paragraph over and over again because of lack of attention. The fear indicates a threat, reading doesn't and so real attention is given to the fear. Such people are generally attempting to overcome the fear by distraction alone, which will never work, for this is simply fighting it. Truly accepting the fear and the reason for it first, then distracting attention would be a better way.

Distraction should be used to supplement acceptance. Once we have accepted the bad thoughts, feelings or behaviours and stopped them building up and progressing automatically, the distraction can enhance this by moving our thoughts etc. to a different set of neural connections entirely.

Distractions that may be helpful include such things as:
Reading a book or article, doing a crossword or puzzle, doing something creative – draw or sculpt, speak to a friend on the phone, listen to music, take a bath or go for a walk ... anything we can become absorbed in.

* * * * *

Not all 'bad feeling and thinking' comes from our problem; they may stem, in part, from situational or environmental reasons, things such as: being tired after a late night, a hangover, arguing with someone, the onset of flu, cold weather etc. can all have an effect. An effect that we usually amplify by associating them to our inner feelings – again, just realise and accept what is happening.

Our life circumstances too, may not help. Doing a job below our ability or living with an abusive partner cannot be put right overnight. Here, we need to accept why we are in the position (because of our low self-worth), know that we can now change and that soon these circumstances can be changed. Know also, that with abusive partners etc. – the real problem is theirs.

The power of this acceptance comes from knowledge and insight; it grows through understanding. Numerous studies have shown how panic can be tempered through understanding what is happening.[3]

Acceptance, using insight into the truth about what is really happening can help us to change. But don't fight to accept or fight to distract, fighting only strengthens the connections – just move on and try again next time. Only acceptance that is true (not forced or a 'must do') can work.

To take control we have to let go; acceptance helps us to do this and confidence grows as the feelings of control grow. However, there are other things that we can do to reduce the negativity we hold inside, relatively simple steps to take that can have a positive effect deep within us.

12

REDS

OUR MINDS AND BODIES are so interlinked that in some ways it is difficult to distinguish between them; thoughts generate feelings and feelings generate thoughts. Nowhere is this interplay between mind and body demonstrated so convincingly as in the person with low self-confidence and anxiety-related problems. Bodily sensations such as tension, shakiness, aches, pains and dullness (whatever their actual cause) can become associated with the thoughts confirming worthlessness, leading to an increase in those sensations, which further increases the confirming thoughts, which further increases the sensations ... and so on, the circle is set up. It is not surprising that people can spend virtually all day thinking and feeling bad!

If we are good to our mind our body feels good and if we are bad to our mind our body feels bad. Similarly, treating our body badly hurts our mind just as treating it well can promote a sense of well-being. We know that we feel worse when we are tense, unfit, eating poorly and not sleeping well and these factors can all play a part in the physiological symptoms that we experience.

Hence, there are things that we can do which will influence our nervous system in a deep, positive way. These include: Relaxation, Exercise, Diet and Sleep (**REDS**).

Relaxation

Anxiety leads to tension but also tension leads to anxiety. Many people with long-term anxiety and depression problems exist in a higher than average state of tension and a tense body is already making associations with anxiety, 'prepared' to spark off a worrying thought or image and start the ball rolling towards the panic, phobia, OCD, despair.

The upper chest and shoulders are one area where many people with anxiety-related problems maintain tension in their body. They constantly have raised upper chest and shoulders. For two reasons: first, this is a defensive posture (I would raise my shoulders if somebody went to strike me) - second, it stems from conditioning associated with the body's attempt to relieve tension naturally - sighing (letting out a deep breath) is a natural way to relieve tension.
Many people with these problems hold their breath a lot (especially before going to sleep) in order to sigh. This can lead to conditioning the body to have the chest and shoulders raised and also the development of breathing from the chest rather than the diaphragm.
Try this:- throughout the day notice how high your shoulders are and drop them down (as in Yoga - 'roll them over and back').
When your shoulders are lowered - do you feel ever so slightly more relaxed? Do this a number of times throughout the day and when you are in bed before you go to sleep.

Relaxation is the opposite of tension.
A muscle that is relaxed cannot be tense.
We can reduce tension by learning to relax.

This is something that we must do; we have to reduce all the tension inside of us for when we exist in a state of 'background' tension our anxiety-related problem is with us all the time.

We may feel that being unable to relax *is* the problem. But it is not that we cannot relax, it is just that it is very, very difficult given that we have learnt so strongly to be tense.

Learning to relax involves learning how various parts of the body feel when they are tense and relaxing them.

Numerous methods exist, one of the most widely used being the Progressive Muscle Relaxation technique,[1] first described in the 1920's by Edmund Jacobsen. It involves systematically tensing and relaxing groups of muscles.

You need to find a method that you feel comfortable with and then practise, practise and practise some more until relaxing becomes a strongly learned behaviour and being calm and relaxed becomes the natural state rather than tension.

Other good, tried and tested ways to help us relax include: -

Breathing

Oxygen, from the air, is the other main fuel that our body and mind needs to survive. We need clean, oxygen-rich blood to function correctly.

Fear and anxiety can lead to rapid, shallow breathing, which, like tension, can become our state of existence. A state, again like tension, that keeps us 'primed' toward panic (shallow breathing reduces the level of CO_2 in the blood and can lead to further panic inducing symptoms). We can address this through breathing more deeply and slowly.

Diaphragmatic breathing (breathing from the diaphragm [the muscular wall separating the lungs from the stomach] as opposed to breathing from the chest) shows us one way in which it is possible to positively influence the nervous system by physical action. This breathing redresses the oxygen-carbon dioxide balance in the body and promotes a feeling of calmness.

Try this:-
- Take a deep breath in through your nose for a slow count of four (imagine the air filling your stomach, not lungs, and feel it expand)
- Hold for a slow count of four
- Breathe out through your mouth for a slow count of four (imagine you stomach pushing the air out)
- Hold for a slow count of four
- Repeat three or four times [no more]

How do you feel?

With practise, this should make you feel more relaxed. If it doesn't, try again later. Keep practising at various times until it does.

This demonstrates how we can take control of our body and make it relax.

Meditation

Methods such as: breathing awareness, body awareness or even walking awareness can help promote relaxation.

Visualisation

Imagining calm and peaceful settings or previous times when calm and relaxed (or feeling good) can enhance relaxation.

Relaxing the mind relaxes the body. This is shown at times when we are engrossed in some activity such as reading, writing, painting or watching a movie and our mind is taken off the problem. When we are not thinking about the problem we are more relaxed mentally and physically. Conversely, relaxing the body relaxes the mind.

Exercise

Exercise helps us to keep our bodies in good condition. It can, however, place a great deal of stress and strain on the body and in order to counteract this the body produces its own stress-relieving chemicals, including endorphins – Morphine-related painkillers. These chemicals, produced to relieve the stresses and strains of exercise, act on the nervous system in general and help promote feelings of relaxation and well-being.

Like relaxation, exercise is a way that we can physically make our nervous system work positively for us.

Exercise offers many benefits. We have seen how anxiety, anger and stress mobilize us into action, usually when we aren't in a position to act. Exercise can fulfill this inner generated need for action and in doing so can relieve anxiety, anger and stress to some extent. In generalized anxiety disorder, too, it can prove beneficial for the antidote to worry is action.

Experiments have shown that exercise can help to alleviate depression, often more so than antidepressants,[2] and we know why – the activity counteracts the feelings of inability to act with depression and it also gives us back some of the energy that this problems robs us of.

Pushing that bit extra in exercise (taking care to build up fitness levels slowly), and learning to master the fatigue and pain involved (essentially by relaxing through it) flows through into our lives.

It builds mental strength and resilience to the stresses of living and the feelings of achievement it can promote empower us.

Other benefits of regularly exercising include: -

- Increased fitness
- Weight control
- Improves appearance and self-image
- Increased social contact
- Helps to relax us
- Improved posture
- Promotes a positive mental attitude
- Improved function of all vital organs (including the brain)

Exercising regularly really is one of the best things that we can do to improve many areas in our lives, however:
ALWAYS CONSULT A MEDICAL PROFESSIONAL BEFORE STARTING ANY EXERCISE REGIME.

Generally speaking: -

- Do something you enjoy – exercise should be enjoyable (and challenging). Setting goals, short workouts, listening to music, doing it with friends can make it more enjoyable.
- Start slowly, don't overdo it
- Do it regularly – 3 to 4 times a week (10 – 60 mins.)
- Don't focus on the aches and pains during exercise – think how good you will feel when you have finished

And:
ALWAYS SEEK QUALIFIED ADVICE TO ENSURE THAT YOU EXERCISE AT THE APPROPRIATE LEVEL FOR YOUR AGE AND FITNESS (eg. from a gym instructor).

As we get fitter our resting heartbeat rate becomes slower, something that, in itself, makes us calmer.

Even gentle exercise such as walking (briskly and often) can provide many of the same benefits. Or consider Yoga, which combines both relaxation and exercise.

Diet

There's a small grey tree frog that lives in the Baskett Wildlife Area, near Ashland, Missouri. In the late 1990's the population of tree frogs began to die out. Locals blamed a then new pesticide that had started to be used in the area, but the makers of the chemical conducted tests in the laboratory, exposing the frogs to the pesticide, and showed that it didn't affect them. However, later experiments conducted by the University of Pittsburgh showed something extremely interesting: the pesticide did indeed appear harmless to the tree frogs in the tranquil setting of the laboratory, but when the frogs were exposed to the pesticide *and* the stress of daily living in their natural environment, particularly those stresses related to predators, the combination proved lethal.[3] The compound effect of environmental stress and pesticide chemicals proved too much for the frog's immune system.

Such a situation may underpin the drastic increase of once uncommon illnesses that we see in society today.

One thing is for sure: when we are struggling with conflict and stress and the resultant damage they cause, the last thing we need is any additional stress on our system.

In order to minimise the stress we suffer we need to reduce the burden of man-made chemicals (compounds that the human body never had to deal with for millions of years) in our body.

Dietary advice for everyone (not just those with anxiety-related problems) really is clear-cut: reduce or eliminate refined and processed food. The more something is processed, the more we should avoid it.

We have seen how anxiety and depression can deplete our body resources, something that is particularly relevant to vitamins and minerals, and perhaps taking supplements of these (under suitably qualified supervision) may be helpful.

However, there is really only one thing that we need to do: eat fresh, wholesome (organically produced if possible) foods. Eating a good, well-balanced, varied diet that includes the six essential nutrients: water, minerals, vitamins, carbohydrates, proteins and fats can help us tremendously. As with relaxation and exercise, a good diet can promote not only physical but mental health.

Remember:
ALWAYS CONSULT A MEDICAL PROFESSIONAL BEFORE
STARTING ANY NEW DIET REGIME

Sleep

Although the exact function of sleep is still under question, one thing we can be fairly sure of is that it performs a restorative function. People that go for long periods without sufficient sleep can be irritable, on edge, unable to concentrate and feel confused.

Lack of sleep may affect our emotional ability to withstand stress and most people believe that we 'feel better' after a good night's sleep. It appears that most people require 8 or 9 hours of sleep to be free from daytime sleepiness.[4]

When we have difficulty in falling asleep, it may be a good idea to accept what is happening (our mind is trying to sort out all the information (see sleep problem section) and that we are not really 'bad' (acceptance statement). In doing so, we realise what is happening and that it is not due to something wrong with us.

Some helpful tips, regarding getting a good night's sleep, are: -

Don't (just before bedtime): -

- Take alcohol or caffeine – these can disrupt the sleep cycle and cause you to wake early
- Eat heavily – this causes the digestive system to be active during the night
- Perform heavy exercise or brain work or rush around

Do: -

- Slow down around one hour before going to bed
- Try and relax – engage in soothing activities (eg. warm bath, light reading, soft music)
- Establish a regular routine – go to bed around the same time each night and wake up around the same time each morning
- Ensure the bedroom is a comfortable temperature and not too light or dark

There are many other things that you can find to add to both of these lists – do the ones that you find comfortable and helpful.

* * * * *

In learning and maintaining good habits regarding relaxation, exercise, diet and sleep we can take practical steps to positively influence our body, mind and nervous system. You need to explore ways that are comfortable and beneficial to you and do them regularly until they become good, strong, habitual behaviours.

Incidentally, people who feel good about themselves do these things as a matter of course, out of self-respect.

Take care not to treat these things as 'how to be'; we are not doing them to be 'right' in any way. Remember you don't have to do anything to be right for you are right just as you are.

We do these things to reduce and change what has happened to our body and mind over the last few years; simple practical steps that, when coupled with insight and acceptance, can have a long-lasting, profound effect deep within us.

In learning to do these things we are learning to take control and practising a more positive way of living, one that's beneficial to our whole being. It cannot directly help any socioeconomic or relationship problems that may exist but it may lay the foundations for taking control in all areas of life.

Regaining control tackles one of the fundamental causes of anxiety-related problems, but we still have the other one to deal with. Change involves not only weakening existing connections but also developing and strengthening new ones. We've spent a large part of our lives feeling bad ... it's about time this changed.

13

Feeling Good

IF 10,000 PEOPLE say we are good, but we feel bad, we will believe we are bad. Conversely, if 10,000 people say we are bad, but we feel good, we believe we are good ... we are what we feel.

Countless bad experiences caused us to feel bad and believe that we were bad, not good enough in some way; everything else followed. To turn this around, we can do the opposite: feel good as often as we can, in as many varied ways that we can until our world starts to revolve around feeling good instead of feeling bad.

However, our feelings, thoughts and actions (the anxiety-related problem) all support feeling bad, the connections are many and strong. Feeling good doesn't fit (just like not being able to accept a compliment); it goes against everything we are.

Therefore, we need to wait a while, to practise acceptance and distraction and develop good habits regarding relaxation, exercise, diet and sleep until the connections weaken. When they do, we can start to shape new ones, strong connections around good feelings and everything else will follow.

To do this, we need to do countless things that make us feel good naturally (not using artificial stimulants which represent false control) to forge many new and varied connections.

And we don't need to think about anything, we are not trying to be good or having to be good, we just need to experience the feeling – all we have to do is notice and accept the feeling, just *feel the feeling good.*

Here are some ways we can feel good: -

- **Surround ourselves with beautiful things**
Pictures, paintings, photographs, furniture, furnishings – things that make us feel good when we look at/use them.
- **Hobbies and activities**
Finding something that we sincerely, unreservedly and guiltlessly enjoy doing and doing it often.
- **Reading**
Depending on what we read, it can calm, inspire, amaze and empower us.
- **Listening to music**
Studies have shown that listening to music can relieve stress and is good for the heart and mind. It can affect us in many ways similar to reading. Singing and dancing provide even more good feelings.
- **Walking**
Can clear the mind; give us some fresh air and a break from the many chores of life. Try walking barefoot in the grass occasionally and break down society's barriers between ourselves and nature. Feeling the earth beneath the bare soles of our feet can make us feel secure – if we let it.
- **Dress**
When we feel down we may often dress correspondingly. Conversely dressing in fine clothes can make us feel good.

The more and varied the information we can provide, the stronger will be the connections that we form.

So we need to use as many senses as possible in the things we do to feel good. Others ways include: -

- **Touch**

The skin, the largest organ in the body contains around 500,000 receptors for touch and pressure. Touch is directly related to the emotions (think how you feel when you are touched by someone who loves you); babies fail to thrive if they receive little or no affection in their early days and stroking produces friendly, loving animals.

Massage makes us feel good and we can get many of the same benefits through self-massage. Learn how to do it; self-massage of areas such as: the head, tummy, and abdomen can produce pleasant feelings inside. Do it with no preconceptions, associations or expectations – just experience the feelings.

- **Smell**

Like touch, smell has deep connections to our emotions. We are only beginning to discover the power of it; take, for example, the unconscious recognition of immune systems through pheromones mentioned earlier. Researches have found that up to 10,000 proteins are used in our smell receptors and that each has its own genes,[1] an awful lot of genes for one sense. Perhaps whenever we're feeling good, we should pay particular attention to any associated smells?

- **Taste**

Eating nice things is pleasurable, we should enjoy it more.

With the power many of the above hold it's not surprising that they can be used as therapy for emotional problems.

Massage and aromatherapy make us feel good but they could never be the answer in themselves, for the hold our problem had over us was just too great. But with the insight that we now have we can allow ourselves to feel good, and anything that makes us feel good can be beneficial. Similarly, more things (and therapies) that generate good feelings within us include: -

- **Creativity**

Paint, draw, write, sculpt ... produce something. It strikes at our very core to create (life) and progress our genes. Some of the greatest artistic works have been produced by people suffering from immense inner turmoil. Perhaps attempting to get beyond their suffering to the essence of existence.

- **Laughter**

Laughter may be one of the best medicines there is. It is a display of emotion, can be infectious – watching someone else laughing makes us laugh – and represents emotional bonding between people. A group laughing together feels at ease and safe. It has been shown to reduce the amount of the stress hormone Cortisol and increase levels of infection-fighting lymphocytes in the blood stream,[2] giving us a less stressed, stronger immune system. We should really laugh as often as we can.

But we cannot talk about laughter without mentioning the other side – crying. Whenever you feel like crying, cry. That's what it's there for, why we evolved it – to express those feelings.

* * *

All the above can help us tremendously; the more and more we can feel good within ourselves the more we will come to know that we are good, and the more we believe that we are good, the better our world will become. But it doesn't end there, there are some things we can do that are extremely powerful and cannot fail to generate intense feelings of goodness deep inside us – we can remember them by the acronym – **HAPPY.**

HAPPY: -

- **Help**

Whenever we help others we help ourselves.

- **Appreciate**

When we appreciate something or someone, we are feeling the good in them. A goodness in ourselves generated from what we think about others. Next time you see something or someone that is beautiful just appreciate the beauty (don't make any comparisons) – see how you feel.

Hand-in-hand with appreciation goes gratitude – when you feel good and good things happen to you, be thankful.

- **Praise**

If we genuinely give deserved praise, it makes others feel good and when we make others feel good, we cannot help but make ourselves feel good.

- **Present** (to, or give)

Whatever we give with a good heart (examples include: a smile, compliment, letter, phone call, visit, gift, love, kindness) we will get back tenfold.

- **You**

When our personal space is invaded we feel threatened; notice the uncomfortable feelings that people have when strangers get too close, as in lifts or on public transport. Take a few minutes each day just for you, in your own space.

Remember, don't force anything, just be true to yourself. We are not trying to be good; we are not trying 'how to be'. We don't have to be anything for we are good as we are – all we have to do is generate the good feelings and accept them.

* * * * *

Of course, life isn't just about feeling good, there will always be times when we feel stressed, down and inadequate – the mistake is trying to resist, deny or fight the bad times. Negative things will always happen, they are an inevitable part of living, but we now know that they are nothing to do with any deep down badness in us, for there is no such thing, it doesn't exist.

Conflict too, is inevitable; at some time or other our wishes, interests and convictions are bound to clash with those of others around us and we often have to decide between two sets of values, wishes and obligations. We are a complex bundle of feelings and may often hold conflicting emotions, such as: like/dislike, and anger/kindness toward the same person at different times. We need to realise that our feelings are justified and related to the situation at the time; experience the feelings, and express them appropriately, letting them go. Feelings are meant to arise within us (appropriate to the situation), be used (guide us) and go (through expression) – it is because we fight them (worrying about/analyzing/questioning/comparing etc.) that they persist and strengthen. In reality, never again do we need to associate any feelings that we have to our own worth.

Moods reflect this bundle of emotions and feelings and, like anything, if we dwell on them they strengthen. However, these can also be alleviated by acceptance and distraction – good ways to make negative moods fade fairly quickly. The same applies to anger: dwell on it and it builds up, distract from it and it fades. Kicking a football or hitting a ball with a bat or racquet and perhaps hitting a cushion can also be good ways to express anger for they represent action (which anger prepares us for).

Essentially, we are learning to let go and the more we practise it, the stronger our ability becomes. True control comes from letting go and as the old connections in our brains weaken and new ones develop, we begin to let go of the struggle.

It is ok to be 'weak': to ask for help from others, to apologize; we don't have to be strong all of the time.

Indeed, a powerful way to generate inner good feelings can come from asking others for help. It feels good, not just because of the help but because we can let people – and it makes others feel good helping. We can add this to the 'H' in HAPPY – feeling good, not only by helping others but also by asking for and accepting help.

Also, let others 'win' occasionally; as Brian Tracy, in his book 'Maximum Achievement', so correctly points out, "would you rather be right or liked?" [3]

Paradoxically, being 'weak' in such ways doesn't represent weakness at all, but strength. When we have to be strong and right and perfect (how to be), we are riddled with anxiety and weakness and cannot do anything. Conversely, not having to 'be' or 'do' for self-protection represents true strength, true confidence in our self. We don't need to be anything; we are fine just as we are.

* * * * *

As we practise acceptance and distraction, maintain good habits regarding relaxation, exercise, diet and sleep, and generate good feelings about our self our world starts to change.

Relationships with others become more positive as we begin to see ourselves differently and others differently. Our social world takes shape around feelings of acceptance and belonging rather than rejection and fear. The 'buzz' that we get from others becomes a good one.

When we interact with others there are things happening at deeper levels within us than we realise; we get an emotional 'buzz' from other people. Patients with Capgras Syndrome[4] don't get this buzz due to malfunction in certain areas of their brain. Such patients can see someone that they know but because they don't get the emotional 'buzz' associated with that person, the person seems somehow different to them, not real. Because of what is happening in their brains being their reality, those with Capgras Syndrome often truly believe that people they know are imposters or have been taken over by aliens or robots.

When we feel good about ourselves many of the exaggerated social fears regarding rejection and attack fade naturally, however, there are still things that we can do, on a daily basis, to assist the process.

Daily Living

Mixing with people that make us feel good changes our environment and experiences and can support our new positive world. Unfortunately, this means avoiding people that bring us down and fill our world with negativity. Remember that they behave in such a way because of their own problems, really nothing to do with us, but if we cannot help them (which we should try first) then the only thing to do is to let them go.

*

We should always try and treat people as we would like to be treated. When dealing with others, take a few seconds out, think and then practise this. Old sayings survive for such a long time for a reason; the sentiment they express is true. Treating people as we would be treated can turn our lives around.

Essentially, we would like others to treat us kindly and being kind to them can bring this about. Research shows that the act of being kind (and receiving kindness) has a beneficial effect on the immune system and overall health.[5]

Similarly, if we want others to like us, show interest in us, and respect us, the answer is really quite simple: all we have to do is like them, show interest in them and respect them.

*

Taking notice when others are nice toward us also helps. A nice smile or pleasant gesture feeds our feelings of acceptance. Thinking to ourselves, "that was nice smile" or "she/he was pleasant" can lead to associated positive thoughts. Similarly, if someone is unpleasant toward us, thoughts such as, "they must have problems", reflects the true situation.

And speaking of smiling, it's a good idea to smile often (with friends and colleagues and those who smile at us, not strangers). When we feel good we smile and it is a two-way process: smiling can make us feel good. The brain circuits which control particular expressions are closely linked to the brain circuits for the experiencing of the emotions themselves – activation of the facial muscles involved in smiling sends feedback signals to the areas of the brain associated with pleasure.

It can be difficult to be happy or have something to smile about with long-term anxiety-related problems and a sorrowful expression can in itself help strengthen the effects of anxiety and despair.
(We all feel better when we are laughing).
Try this:- Imagine a big grin on your forehead (just imagine it - don't try and make your forehead smile). You should feel the corners of your lips raise ever so slightly
Try it a number of times throughout the day.

As we start to feel good about ourselves, smiling and dealing with others more positively becomes a matter of course. And while we are treating others well, let's not forget about us – let's treat ourselves well, like we would a friend.

* * *

Hopefully the process is becoming clear: through insight and knowing the truth we can turn our world around. We can acknowledge the past, accept it and let it go; we are now much stronger for it. The old bad feelings are fading and new, more positive ones are growing, ones that actually reflect our true worth.

And we don't really need to concern ourselves with ways to think; new thoughts arise from inside us as our world changes. Trying to think ourselves different usually means trying to force things and rarely works for thoughts are connected to feelings and emotions and most of ours were related to feeling bad. Trying to force good ones goes against all of our experience, learning and evidence – it's like trying to run a marathon after 20 years of no exercise and will just harm us. But if we just let thoughts come they will soon begin to reflect our new world.

Take the example above of a good way to think about when someone smiles at us: If we think, for example "she is smiling at me, she must like me", we are trying to force the good thoughts, however, when we think, "that was a nice smile" and nothing more, making no associations or connections, our inner-self does it for us and connects a nice smile to our newly developing feelings of goodness. We generate reasons for receiving a nice smile (because of being in some way good) from within. Our self worth is developing from deep inside; we are evolving in a new direction.

And when new thoughts and beliefs develop from within (hence stronger) as we begin to weaken existing ones and start to regain control, we need to treat them in a similar way to 'bad' thoughts. Accept them (feel good about these ones for the moment) and let them pass. They should not be treated in the manner – "that thought made me feel good, that's what I should be thinking". In doing this, we are going back to 'how to be', in this case trying to restrict our thoughts to thinking the 'right' way to be 'right'.

Remember, you don't have to 'be' or 'do' anything to be right, for you are already right just as you are.

And as we start to feel better, there is one more thing we can do ... act.

As If

Here, we don't have to be good, we are not trying to be good, there are no reasons or justifications for or against it, we are merely acting ... acting as if we are...

Not being the greatest, most successful, most confident etc. for this, like strongly opposing thoughts, will not work.

Just acting as if we are ok, as if some benevolent higher power has taken away all our turmoil. Indeed acting as if... "I am good enough" (no further elaboration needed) and/or as if... "most people really like me" addresses the two main fears and can drastically change our experiences. In both of these, (which probably reflect the truth in reality) our inner-self will start to make it's own connections as to why we are good enough and people really like us.

* * * * *

We have seen that, as the old connections weaken and begin to fade there are many things we can do to form and strengthen new ones. They involve letting go of fighting and blocking and require trust and faith in life and in our goodness. Experiencing, feeling, adapting and growing; this is how life should be: learning and flowing not rigid and stuck in 'how to be'.

And we see evidence of flowing and the results of 'not fighting and blocking' all of the time: whenever we want/need something – it rarely happens, but if we feel ok if it doesn't happen – it usually appears. It is the wanting, the desperate needing that is blocking the flow of life.

Nature and life is one of adapting and flourishing (just like those white potato shoots in the cellar). It is one of positive growth and development, when we allow it. If a caterpillar can trust nature to break down all of it's body cells and form new ones to transform it into a butterfly, can't we trust her to break down our old connections and build new ones?

It really is down to us. Now we know the truth we can create our own positive world; we have everything we need to bring about change.

But before we consider what change is, there is one more thing to consider, something that has helped millions of people ...

Faith

We have spent an awful long time under the shadow of perceived higher forces that are harmful to us, why don't we now consider that there are higher forces that are good and supportive? Many people do. Witness football players that make the sign of the cross on their head and chest as they come out onto the pitch. Such people are never alone and they don't have to do anything by themselves; they firmly believe that all-powerful help is on their side. The same is true for all of us.

14

Change

WE ARE THE sum of our life experiences so far; childhood experiences never leave us, they are our history, a part of us. However, we can look back on these experiences with a new understanding and give it a new meaning.

We are not trying to hide, deny, fight or change the past; this cannot be done, we are making peace with it and letting it go. We cannot move forward clinging to the past, just as we cannot move anywhere when we cling to something.

And we don't have to undo years of hurt, just understand what happened and accept it. Our experiences have given us a unique strength to move forward that many people don't have, a profound insight into life. Bad experiences shape our character and make us stronger (not bad feelings which weaken us) – perpetual sunshine produces only desert.[1]

We had no choice in what happened to us, no say whatsoever; as young children we were not responsible in any way. But we are responsible now; it is up to us: we either continue to use the past to hurt ourselves or use it to move forward stronger, wiser, better for our experiences.

"He has not learned the lesson of life who does not every day surmount a fear" – Gaius Julius Caesar (100–44 B.C.)

Courage is not the absence of fear; it is feeling afraid but keeping those feelings sufficiently under control to be able to act appropriately. Research has shown that: although self-confidence predicted fearless performance in combat (in U.S. World War II veterans), many of them still experienced intense fear reactions to the combat.[2]

Fear and anxiety are normal; it's when they spiral out of control due to inner beliefs about our self and our inability to control them that they become debilitating.

Anxiety is a part of being human, part of being alive; it has evolved over millions of years and is essential to our survival. The goal is not to remove anxiety (which cannot be done) but to understand it and learn how to master it through insight and acceptance. We need to experience the bad feelings and thoughts and anxiety at appropriate levels and *feel* controlling them.

Actually, most things we learn in life are initially frightening, such as: learning to ride a bike, learning to drive a car and take, for example, learning to swim. Most children, and some adults, go from being petrified of venturing into open water, clinging desperately to the side (a perfectly logical reaction since at the beginning they have no control and could drown) to being able to jump/dive in the water, swim under water, tread water and swim wherever they want. Learning to swim involves learning what to do to be in control and confidence grows as the feelings of control grow. It is no different to anything we do in life.

Change involves thinking, feeling and 'doing'. We cannot learn to ride a bike just by thinking about it! It is only in the 'doing' that the knowledge is used and becomes part of us. We can only get the feeling of "yes, I did it", by doing it and it only takes a few "yes, I did it" feelings for confidence to soar.

And we need to start now, life won't wait for us. Don't spend a lifetime waiting to begin, looking to feel better or when things are better before beginning. Things will only get better once we start; the 'doing' is the change and the 'things getting better'.

Regret for things we did can be tempered by time, regret for things we don't do can last a lifetime.

Of course change can be scary; if we stay as we are the dream stays intact: of one day being good, great, loved by all. And that illusion of control does offer us some feelings of control, whilst change is new and frightening – thankfully we now know the truth about the real effect of those dreams and illusions.

Children often have 'comfort toys' that they take everywhere as they undergo the constant changes in their lives: something old and reliable and 'known' to fall back on. In a sense, it is less frightening to be something that we know than something we don't; change equals unknown and is inherently scary.

But another way to look at it is: not as scary but a challenge, and life is all about challenge. Extremely popular computer and video games actually reward success with greater challenges - offering insight into what achieving success in life takes?

Life isn't a bowl of cherries and things don't always go right. Again, it's what we make of what happens to us that determines how it affects us.

Setbacks

Setbacks are inevitable when we try to weaken strongly learned behaviours, just as they are inevitable in all walks of life. We are often quick to attribute setbacks to personal weakness (and success down to luck), which couldn't be further from the truth. We do this because of how we feel about failure.

Failure

The fear of failure is really the fear of punishment. To a 'normal' person failure may mean 'embarrassment', 'feeling a bit silly' and 'giving a poor performance' but to us it can be a crushing blow. It can mean 'public disclosure of weakness' and confirm our inner 'badness' and lack of ability, increasing the bad feelings associated with rejection and punishment.

But there is no such thing as failure; it is only what we make of it. Accept why we feel so bad about it and let it go.

* * *

Setbacks can actually help us to learn! They have to be accepted for what they are – attempts that didn't quite work out. We can learn from them and move on, they don't reflect our quality as a person. Learn to accept them for what they are – changing strongly learned behaviours is difficult (any habit is hard to break), do not associate them with 'inherent weakness'.

At times you may feel more anxious (as you face your fears) or depressed (as you feel that all your efforts are not working, or as you come down from your heightened state of arousal); these feelings are normal, unpleasant but normal. View them positively, they give you the opportunity to practise accepting, distracting and learning just how to take control.

Practise and Perseverance

Successful people are the ones that keep trying in the face of adversity. The key to success is practise and perseverance.

Practise, practise and practise some more, keep practising, keep trying. Whether your attempts succeed or fail, learn from them and keep trying. Nothing in life worth having comes easy.

Acceptance calms the mind, relaxation calms the body; learn to use them together and practise regularly. And as things improve make sure to practise feeling good in various ways, often.

Know that any success is due to your efforts, things did not happen by chance, you made it happen. Eventually the successes will outnumber the failures and when this happens your confidence will increase.

* * * * *

Remember, most things in life are difficult when we first start but they become easier with effort and practise. For example, it may seem impossible to many to jog 5 miles, but if we build up slowly by: walking half a mile regularly, then walk a mile, then jog 200 yards, then jog half a mile, then a mile etc. jogging 5 miles becomes easy – the task has not changed, but we have.

Start easy; behaviours developed over a number of years cannot be changed overnight, but they can eventually be changed through practise and perseverance. Set goals, realistic ones and when you achieve them congratulate yourself; you deserve it.

If some areas of change seem too hard at the moment (eg. acceptance and distraction) focus on the more practical things that you can do such as exercise, eating and sleeping habits. Build up to relaxation and the mental aspects later. Remember, improvement on any level can have an overall benefit; things are easier when our resources are high: when we are well fed, rested, fit and relaxed.

Regarding fearful situations; start at the least frightening, only move to the next level when you feel confident that you were in control – remember the child approaching the ocean for the first time.

It's never too late; age is irrelevant – our brains are continually learning and adapting with experience. The mature mind can think and adapt in ways that a younger brain cannot, thanks to the myriad of experiences within.

And we don't have to do it all alone; help and support can be beneficial from: -

- **Trusted Others** – let them help us to accept the past, the truth and to feel good about ourselves
- **Therapists** – with a good therapist, a significant other that accepts us; someone who understands our problem and us; one with whom we can be 'weak' and yet still feel accepted; one who can guide and support us appropriately – the type of therapy is often irrelevant.
- **Higher Powers** – life is about growing and flourishing with love and confidence ... if we let it.

What we do today influences us tomorrow as new connections form in our brain and strengthen to become part of us.

* * *

There will be no fanfare, no sudden change. Just as these problems develop in stages, they fade in stages. There is no "when I get there I'll be happy", no destination; the journey is the change.

It is gradual; fears and doubts fade and recovery happens in hindsight: we look back and realise that we no longer fear certain things, notice how we have changed and are amazed at what we used to think and how we used to act. The problem stops becoming the focus of our life.

It is not that fear, anxiety and panic are no longer there, they are still with us, but what they mean to us has changed – we never, ever relate them to being bad, for we aren't bad, we are good and we feel it.

Happiness really is an attitude toward life. It is not something that we can actively look to find; it just happens, generally through living positively. As things improve: the need for evaluative comparisons becomes less; social interactions and relationships improve as we begin to tolerate others (and ourselves) more; appreciation grows and we feel a deeper connection to humanity; we become generally more relaxed and enjoy life more.

In changing we move forward, experiencing and enjoying, learning and growing, adapting and flowing.

* * *

With anxiety-related problems there is often a deep inner need to get back to how we used to be; " the person I once was".

It is important to realise that throughout all that we have learned through insight, and all that we practise through such things as: acceptance, REDS and feeling good, we are not changing our core. We are not trying to change into some new, fantastic, super person – that is merely 'how to be'.

What we change is all the conditioning that our life experiences have imposed on us; removing all the fears and anxieties, and all the obstacles and blockages that have prevented us from being ourselves ... we are changing so that we can be ourselves.

...

15

Love Love Love

WHEN WE STAND at the end of the word: e-v-o-l-v-e and look back along it and read the four letters furthest away, in the order that they appear to us, they form the word: l-o-v-e.

Love makes the world go round; its power is unquestionable as millions of songs, stories, poems, films etc. describe. It helps us to develop and grow; being involved in a satisfying relationship is one of the most powerful predictors of health and happiness.[1] Love is as important to us for survival as the food we eat and the air we breathe. It represents the growing and flourishing of life.

Before we can know true love, we have to love ourselves. We have to have the capacity to love our self before we can trust in the love of another. When we feel worthless, we feel not worth loving and our own love is not worthy to give. Our life experiences made us feel this way; they made us, quite literally, scared to be our self.

Scared to be ourselves, we lived in fear of being rejected and attacked; love is the opposite of fear; it represents being wanted and being part of. As we let the old connections fade and new ones grow, and develop good feelings about our self and the strength to let go, our world begins to change. In doing things for others and expecting nothing in return (eg. helping them, letting them win, sharing their pain and joy) we give a part of ourselves. And when we do this, we get much more back – we get a little part of others. Through this we feel a 'belonging' and become more connected to others and the world. The more we feel wanted and belonging, the more we feel a part of things and the more we feel like this, the less we fear rejection and attack. The more we can be ourselves and love ourselves, the less we fear everything.

Self-love and self-confidence go hand-in-hand. It's not about brash, overt confidence, conceit, arrogance or self–grandiosity; these are merely masks that hide the truth. It's about accepting and being confident in who we are and liking (loving) who we are, secure in the knowledge that we are basically good and worthwhile human beings. We don't have to be anything for we now know where all that came from and we don't need it any more.

However, there is one more thing that we need to do: forgive those that have a hold over us, for most of us ... our parents.

Forgiveness

Forgiveness is not denying that someone hurt you or letting them get away with it, it involves acknowledging that you were hurt and your feelings were justified – but then we have to let it go.

It is only natural to want to 'get back' at the people who hurt us, we don't want to feel powerless, and often 'not forgiving' is used to achieve this. But it's only ourselves that we are hurting; the person that we really want to get back is the one at that time (many years ago) not the often, old and weak person that stands in front of us today.

Part of us wants them to suffer and be miserable for what they did to us, but believe me, there is probably little we could do to them that would make them more miserable than they truly are. And there is a deeper part of us, the part that wants them to be happy, joyous in themselves and toward us, probably they way they were when we were very small children.

In not forgiving and blaming, we are only hurting ourselves, not just mentally but also physically; research has shown forgiveness to be associated with fewer negative physical health symptoms.[2] With respect to our parents: however we feel about them, we feel the same way about a part of our self.

It may be wise to realise that those we need to forgive had problems of their own and to consider how they may have lived their lives with a desperate need 'how to be'. Many parents driven by perfection often see 'flaws' in their children as reflecting negatively on themselves, conflicting with their own 'must be'.

At the end of the day, most parents do show some love toward their children in the only way they know how.

With the insight we now have, we can give our children a good start in life and allow them to grow happy and secure rather than miserable and afraid. A loving parent lets the child grow to become independent – the only way we will become independent of the parent inside us is by forgiveness.

And when we can forgive our parent we can forgive ourselves, and we need to forgive ourselves for suppressed anger can play a large part in long-term stress-related illnesses. We are only human and we all make mistakes and hurt people. If we have hurt people we should make amends if possible, if not, then all we can do is apologise to them and wish them well, to ourselves (out loud or under our breath), accept the situation and let it go.

* * *

In this world of profit-driven, success-orientated goals of false materialistic happiness the incidence of feelings of 'not being good enough' and anxiety and depression can only increase; yet in one sense it is the people that have experienced these problems that reflect the truly good human qualities.

Soul-searching and introspection can lead to an understanding of our own behaviour and that of others, acceptance of our own 'faults' and those of others and an appreciation of the effect of our behaviour on other people. Without doubt, if the excessive anxiety, panic and despair could be reduced for sufferers of these problems society would benefit greatly.

Remember, you're not alone. Think of all the other people who are in the same position as you: what they have gone through, what they have learned and how they can change; if you do this you can be sure that someone is thinking of you.

* * *

When we can look back over our lives with insight and understanding and let go of the past through acceptance and forgiveness, and use what we know to practise and develop good strong behaviours regarding relaxation, exercise, diet and sleep, and to generate good feelings deep inside – our world changes.

An old part of us weakens and fades and a new part takes shape, strengthens and grows. All that we do, feel and think begins to revolve around love and acceptance rather than rejection and fear.

When we can learn to be ourselves and love ourselves in spite of all that has happened, there is nothing that we cannot achieve. When we can do this ... we are truly evolving self-confidence.

Unique You

"At bottom every man knows well enough that he is a unique being, only once on this earth; and by no extraordinary chance will such a marvellously picturesque piece of diversity in unity as he is, ever be put together a second time."

Friedrich Nietzsche (1844–1900)

* * *

"You are the amazing product of centuries of evolution and experience; one in six billion that can never be repeated. No other on this planet can experience the things the way you do. You are _____, _____, _____, _____ and _____. You are yourself; that's all there is; that's all there needs to be, just you ...for you are unique.

*

Write out this last statement and fill in the blanks with some of the following qualities. Those that you feel apply or will apply soon or how someone who knows you well would describe you.

Read it often.

intelligent   honest   kind   considerate   friendly   loyal
supportive   strong   wise   sensitive   sincere   good

As things improve: write it out again and add your name in front of the word 'you'.

As things improve even more: write it out again and replace the word 'you' etc. by 'I', 'am', 'myself'.

When you can stand in front of the mirror, look yourself in the eye, read the statement and know in your heart that it is true ... you'll never need to be anyone else.

My Notes:

My Notes:

My Notes:

My Notes:

My Notes:

My Notes:

My Notes:

NOTES AND REFERENCES

CHAPTER 1: As a Child
1. Massey A. *BEAT DEPRESSION AND RECLAIM YOUR LIFE.* (2005) London: Virgin Books. p. 72
2. For example: Prinz, R. J. et al (1979). Multivariate assessment of conflict in distressed and non-distressed mother-adolescent dyads. *Journal of Applied Behavior Analysis, 12,* 691–700
3. Counselling Psychology lecture, University of Sunderland (1994)
4. Driscoll, M. (1997) Against all Odds. An article in *The Sunday Times.*
5. Feral Children from the Channel 4 *Mindshock* series (2006)
6. Lamb, M.E.& Sherrod, L.R.(1981) *Infant Social Cognition: Emperical and Theoretical Considerations.* New Jersey: Lawrence Erlbaum. p. 103
7. 13-year study on the Island of Dominica by Mark Flinn, anthropologist at the University of Missouri, on www.discovermagazine.com (2000)
8. Leon Mosher and the Soteria project, commented on by Richard Bentall in *The Psychologist, 20, 11,* 658
9. Holly, W. (1987) Self Esteem: Does it Contribute to Student's Academic Success? On www.self-esteem-nase.org
10. See for example: Carey, G. (1982) Genetic influences on anxiety neurosis and agoraphobia. In R.J. Matthew (Ed.) *The biology of anxiety.* New York: Brunner/Mazel
11. Dr. Hsien Hsien Lei. 100 Facts about DNA from the website: www.eyeondna.com (2007)
12. See description in: Moalem, S with Prince, P. (2007) *SURVIVAL OF THE SICKEST.* London: HarperCollins. pp. 136–141

CHAPTER 2: Feelings
1. For example: Greene, J. D. et al (2001) An fMRI investigation of emotional engagement in moral judgment. *Science, 293,* 2105-2108
2. Described in: Kay Redfield Jamison *Night Falls Fast* (2000) New York: First Vintage Books Edition. p. 277
3. For an example see: Robertson, I. H. (1999) *MIND SCULPTURE: Your Brain's Untapped Potential.* London: Bantam Press. pp. 191–193

4. In: Robertson, I. H. (1999) *MIND SCULPTURE: Your Brain's Untapped Potential. London: Bantam Press*. p.194
5. Throughout: Barlow, D. H. *Anxiety and its Disorders: The Nature and Treatment of Anxiety and Panic* (1998) New York: The Guilford Press
6. Ross, L. et al (1975) Perseverance in self-perception and social perception: biased attributional processes in the debriefing paradigm. *Journal of Personality and Social Psychology, 32,* 880-892

CHAPTER 3: As We Grow
1. Harris, J. R. *The Nurture Assumption: Why Children Turn Out the Way They Do* (1998) New York: Free Press. Chaps 9–13
2. Asch, S. (1951) Effects of group pressure upon the modification and distortion of judgments. In H. Guetzkow (Ed.) *Groups, Leadership and Men*. Pennsylvania: Carnegie Press. pp. 177–190
3. Seay, B. M. & Gottfried, N. W. (1978) *The Development of Behavior*. New York: Houghton Mifflin. p. 315
4. Around 1 in 3 secondary school children are bullied at some point in their school life, from BBC News 24 on www.news.bbc.co.uk. Nov 2004
5. Seiffge-Krenke, I. (1995) *Stress, Coping and Relationships in Adolescence*. New Jersey: Lawrence Erlbaum
6. Dunn, J. et al (1994) Adjustment in middle childhood and early adolescence: Links with earlier and contemporary sibling relationships. *Journal of Child Psychology and Psychiatry, 35,* 491–504

CHAPTER 4: Panic Attack
1. Barlow, D. H. *Anxiety and its Disorders: The Nature and Treatment of Anxiety and Panic* (1998) New York: The Guilford Press. p. 97
2. Mineka, S. et al (1984) Observational conditioning of snake fear in rhesus monkeys. *Journal of Abnormal Psychology, 93,* 355–375
3. Pavlov, I. P. (1927) *CONDITIONED REFLEXES*. New York: Oxford University Press.
4. www.phobialist.com. Copyright 1995-2007 Fredd Culbertson
5. Holden, A. E. & Barlow, D. H. (1986) Heart rate and heart rate variability recorded in vivo in agoraphobics and non phobics. *Behaviour Therapy, 17,* 26-42
6. Keyl, P.M. & Eaton, W.W. (1990) Risk factors for the onset of Panic Disorder and other panic attacks in a prospective population-based study. *American Journal of Epedemiology, 131, 2,* 302
7. Rogers, C. R. *A Way of Being* (1995 New Ed edition). New York: Houghton Mifflin Books. p. 118
8. Yonas, A. (1981) Infants' Responses to Optical Information for Collision. In *Development of Perception: Psychobiological Perspectives, Vol, 2: The Visual System* (Eds. R. N. Aslin, J. R. Alberts and M. R. Peterson). New York: Academic Press

9. Watson, J. B. & Rayner, R.(1920) Conditioned emotional reactions. *Journal of Experimental Psychology*, *3*, *1*, 1–14

10. Research by R. M. Sapolski, described in: Victoroff, J. (2003) *SAVING YOUR BRAIN*. New York: Bantam Dell. p.79

11. Maier, S. F. & Seligman, M. E. P.(1976)Learned helplessness:Theory and evidence. *Journal of Experimental Psychology: General*, *105*, 3–46

12. Eisenberger et al (2003). Does Rejection Hurt? An fMRI Study of Social Exclusion. *Science*, *302*, 193

13. ITV plc. television show: *Who Wants to be a Millionaire*.

14. Norton, G. R. et al (1985) Characteristics of people with infrequent panic attacks. *Journal of Abnormal Psychology*, *94*, 216–221

CHAPTER 5: How To Be

1. Lord Byron, George Gordon, "The Deformed Transformed" part1, scene1.

2. CBI research 2001 – stress-related illness costs employers between £3.75 billion and £7 billion per year.

3. For example: A Statistics Canada study in 2002 reported that 1.3 million Canadian workers were dissatisfied with their jobs.

4. Stein, M. B. et al (1996) Public speaking fears in a community sample. Prevalence, impact on functioning and diagnostic classification. *Archives of General Psychiatry*, *53*, 169–174

5. Biddle, L. et al (2004) Factors influencing help seeking in mentally distressed young adults: a cross-sectional survey. *British Journal of General Practice*, *54*, 248–253

CHAPTER 6: A Part of Us

1. As described in: Pinker, S. (2002). *THE BLANK SLATE: The Modern Denial of Human Nature*. London: BCA edition. p. 153

2. Fantastic description used throughout: Robertson, I. H. (1999) *MIND SCULPTURE: Your Brain's Untapped Potential*. London: Bantam Press

3. Shown in: Schwartz, M. J. with Beyette, B. (1996) *BRAIN LOCK: Free Yourself from Obsessive-Compulsive Behavior*. New York: Regan Books. intro p. xxxiii

4. Rachman, S. J. (1983) Fear and courage among military bomb disposal operators. *Advances in Behaviour Research and Therapy*, *4*, 99–165

5. Kulkarni, B. et al. (2007) Arthritic pain is processed in brain areas concerned with emotions and fear. *Arthritis and Rheumatism*, *56*, *4*, 1345-1354

6. Fiji study by Anne Becker, Anthropologist at Harvard Medical School in BBC News (May 20 1999) from www.news.bbc.co.uk

7. As described in: Deepak Chopra (2004) *THE BOOK OF SECRETS*. London: Rider edition.

8. As quoted in: Roet, B. *The Confidence to be Yourself.* London. Piatkus. intro p. viii

CHAPTER 7: The Problem

1. James, O. W. (2003) They muck you up. *The Psychologist, 16, 6,* 295
2. Juby, H. & Farrington, D. P. (2001). Disentangling the link between disrupted families and delinquency. *British Journal of Criminology,* 41, 22–40
3. Duval, S. & Wicklund, R. A. (1972) *A theory of objective self-awareness.* New York. Academic Press.
4. Rapee, R. M. et al. (1987) Emotional reactions to physiological sensations: comparison of panic disorder and non-clinical subjects. In Barlow, D.H. *Anxiety and its Disorders.* New York:Guilford Press. p.104

CHAPTER 8: The Symptoms

1. Atkinson, R. L. et al (1990) *Introduction to Psychology, Tenth Ed.* Florida. Harcourt Brace Jovanovich. p. 511
2. *Introduction to Psychology, Tenth Ed.* (as above) p. 523
3. *Introduction to Psychology, Tenth Ed.* (as above) p. 525
4. Salkovskis, P. M. (Ed.) (1996) Frontiers of Cognitive Therapy. New York: Guildford. pp. 48–74
5. Mills, J. S. & Blankstein, K. R. (2000) Perfectionism, intrinsic v's extrinsic motivation, and motivated strategies for learning: A multi-dimensional analysis of university students. *Personality and Individual Differences, 29,* 1191–1204
6. Brown, G.W. et al (1986) Social support, elf-esteem and depression. *Pychological Medicine, 16,* 813–831
7. Barlow, D. H. *Anxiety and its Disorders: The Nature and Treatment of Anxiety and Panic* (1998) New York: The Guilford Press. p. 555
8. Hobson, J. A. (1988) *THE DREAMING BRAIN.* New York. Basic Books.

CHAPTER 9: Anxiety-Related Problems

1. Fitts, S. N. et al. Body dysmorphic disorder. Implications for its validity as a DSM-III-R clinical syndrome. *Psychological Reports, 64,* 655–658
2. Centers for Disease Control and Prevention (CDC): Health, United States, 2004
3. James Hillman, American Psychologist, developed Archetypal Psychology
4. Roth, G. (2003) *Breaking Free from Emotional Eating.* London: Penguin Books. p. 86
5. Storms, M. D. & Nisbett, R. E. (1970) Insomnia and the attribution process. *Journal of Personality and Social Psychology, 16,* 319-328

6. Strakowski, S.M & DelBello, M.P(2000) The co-occurrence of bipolar and substance use disorders. *Clinical Psychology Review, 20,2,* 191–206
7. Rachman, S. J. & de Silva, P. (1978) Abnormal and normal obsessions *Behaviour Research and Therapy, 16,* 233–248
8. From Sara Coleridge letter to H. N. Colridge (1986). Quoted in Jamison, K. R. (1994) *Touched with Fire.* New York: Simon & Schuster.
9. Schweizer, E. E. et al. (1986) Insulin induced hypoglycemia and panic attacks. *American Journal of Psychiatry, 143,* 654–655
10. For example: Myers, J. K. et al. (1984) Six-month prevalence of psychiatric disorders in three communities. *Archives of General Psychiatry, 41,* 959-967
11. National Vietnam Veterans Readjustment study (1984)
12. Statistic revealed by the National Institute for Clinical Excellence (NICE) (2004) in *The Psychologist, 17, 10,* 556
13. Amies, B. L. et al.(1983) Social phobia: A comparative clinical study *British Journal of Psychiatry, 142,* 174–179
14. Kiecolt-Glaser, J. K. et al (1994)Stressful personal relationships: immune and endocrine function. In R. Glaser and J. Kiecolt-Glaser (Eds.) *Handbook of Human Stress and Immunity.* San Francisco. Academic Press. pp. 321–339

CHAPTER 10: Making Things Worse?

1. From the article: Aids and the Voodoo Hex by Matt Irwin MD on the www.virusmyth.com website in Feb 2002
2. "A religious belief system involving witchcraft and communications with ancestral deities" as defined in Collins English Dictionary. (2005) London: BCA edition.
3. Hyman, S. E. (1999) Introduction to the complex genetics of mental disorders. *Biological Psychiatry, 45, 5,* 518–521
4. Piercy, M. A. et al (1996) Placebo response in anxiety disorders. *The Annals of Pharmacotherapy, 30, 9,* 1013–1019
5. Article by Burne, J. in *Brainpower, The Sunday Times, wk4,* 21
6. Transplanting Memories? Channel 4 *Mindshock* series (Jun 2006)
7. Boisvert, C. M. & Faust, D. F. (2007) Practicing psychologists knowledge of general psychotherapy research findings. *Professional Psychology Research and Practice, 37,* 708–716

CHAPTER 11: Weakening the Connections

1. University College London study reported in BBC News (March 14, 2000) from www.news.bbc.co.uk
2. From memory, Spice Girl Mel C's reply when asked about a forthcoming music award ceremony in TV interview.

3. Rapee, R. M. et al (1986). Cognitive mediation in the affective component of spontaneous panic attacks. *Journal of Behavior Therapy and Experimental Psychiatry*, *17*, 245–253

CHAPTER 12: REDS
1. First described in the 1929 book Progressive Relaxation by American physician Edmund Jacobsen.
2. Dimea, F. et al (2001) Benefits from aerobic exercise in patients with major depression: a pilot study. *British Journal of Sports Medicine*, 35, 114-117
3. Relyea, R. A. & Mills, N. (2001) Predator-induced stress makes the pesticide carbaryl more deadly to gray treefrog tadpoles (Hyla versicolor) *Proceedings of the National Academy of Sciences*, *98*, 5, 2491–2496
4. Kripke, D. F. & Gillin, J. C. (1985) Sleep disorders in *PSYCHIATRY (VOL 3)* (Eds. G.L. Klerman, M.M. Weissman, P.S. Applebaum, & L.N. Roth).Philadelphia: Lippincott.

CHAPTER 13: Feeling Good
1. Article by Burne, J. in *Brainpower in The Sunday Times, wk2*, 5
2. Article by Girling, R. in *Brainpower in The Sunday Times, wk6*, 18
3. Tracy, B. (1993) *MAXIMUM ACHIEVEMENT*. New York: Simon & Schuster.
4. Named after its discoverer, French psychiatrist Jean Marie Joseph Capgras, often the main delusion is that a close relative or friend has been replaced by an impostor, an exact double,
5. Luks, A. & Payne, P.(cont.)(2001) *The Healing Power of Doing Good: The Health and Spiritual benefits of Helping Others*. iUniverse.com

CHAPTER 14: Change
1. Quotation attributed to unknown author
2. Rachman, S.J.(1978) *Fear and courage*. San Francisco: W.H. Freeman

CHAPTER 15: Love Love Love
1. Cohen, S., Underwood, L. & Gottlieb, B. (2000) *Social support measurement and interventions*. New York: Oxford University Press.
2. Toussaint, L. L., Williams, D. R., Musick, M. A. & Everson, S. A. (2001). Forgiveness and health: Age differences in a U.S. probability sample. *Journal of Adult Development*, *8*, 249–257

INDEX

265

Index

Personal Note from the Author

I have spent over thirty years researching anxiety-related problems; how and why they develop and how to resolve them. A search that involved qualifications in psychology; courses on different treatment methods and reading hundreds, if not thousands, of books and websites both academic and personal stories. During the search it suddenly struck me: everyone was saying the same thing.

I would like to thank all of those who have ever contributed to the collective wisdom of these problems, through: researching, teaching, writing about, treating and experiencing – without our collective knowledge this book could not have been written.

* * * * *

"If you have no confidence in self, you are twice defeated in the race of life. With confidence, you have won even before you have started."
MARCUS TULLIUS CICERO (106 B.C.– 43 B.C.)

Lightning Source UK Ltd.
Milton Keynes UK
01 February 2010

149384UK00001B/126/P

An adorable preschool-age boy came in the barn.

A bright red snowsuit enveloped his thin frame but instead of a stocking cap, a cowboy hat was perched on his head. A battered black Stetson that looked a lot like the one Lucas used to wear.

He smiled shyly, pressed his cheek against Lucas's leg and pointed to the foal. "Thatsa baby horse."

Erin couldn't help but smile back.

"This is Max," Lucas said.

"Hey, Max. I'm Erin. It's nice to meet you. Do you like horses?"

"I like trucks better," Max declared.

"We'll have to work on that." Erin winked at the boy. "So, who does this little cowboy belong to?" she asked Lucas.

"He belongs to me," Lucas said.

Rocky Mountain Heirs:
When the greatest fortune of all is love.

The Nanny's Homecoming—Linda Goodnight
July 2011

The Sheriff's Runaway Bride—Arlene James
August 2011

The Doctor's Family—Lenora Worth
September 2011

The Cowboy's Lady—Carolyne Aarsen
October 2011

The Loner's Thanksgiving Wish—Roxanne Rustand
November 2011

The Prodigal's Christmas Reunion—Kathryn Springer
December 2011

Books by Kathryn Springer

Love Inspired

Tested by Fire
Her Christmas Wish
By Her Side
For Her Son's Love
A Treasure Worth Keeping
Hidden Treasures
Family Treasures
Jingle Bell Babies
*A Place to Call Home
*Love Finds a Home
*The Prodigal Comes Home
The Prodigal's Christmas Reunion

Steeple Hill

Front Porch Princess
Hearts Evergreen
   "A Match Made for
   Christmas"
Picket Fence Promises
The Prince Charming List

*Mirror Lake

KATHRYN SPRINGER

is a lifelong Wisconsin resident. Growing up in a "newspaper" family, she spent long hours as a child plunking out stories on her mother's typewriter and hasn't stopped writing since! She loves to write inspirational romance because it allows her to combine her faith in God with her love of a happy ending.

The Prodigal's Christmas Reunion
Kathryn Springer

Love Inspired

Special thanks and acknowledgment to Kathryn Springer for her participation in the Rocky Mountain Heirs miniseries.

 ™ LOVE INSPIRED BOOKS

Recycling programs for this product may not exist in your area.

ISBN-13: 978-0-373-87710-2

THE PRODIGAL'S CHRISTMAS REUNION

Copyright © 2011 by Harlequin Books S.A.

www.LoveInspiredBooks.com

Printed in U.S.A.

Lord, you have assigned me my portion and my cup; You have made my lot secure. The boundary lines have fallen for me in pleasant places; surely I have a delightful inheritance.
—*Psalms* 16:5–6

This book is dedicated to Linda, Arlene, Lenora,
Carolyne and Roxanne—
an amazing, gifted group of authors it was
a pleasure to work with. Your encouragement,
prayers and unfailing patience were a blessing!

Chapter One

Lucas Clayton could have driven down the streets of his hometown blindfolded.

The thought was tempting.

Because not even a moonless night and the light snow sifting onto the windshield of his pickup could conceal the silhouettes of the businesses that sagged against each other in a tired line along Railroad Street.

Jones Feed and Supply. The grocery store. The post office.

Each building held more than just sacks of grain or canned goods or stamps. Each one held a memory. Or two.

Or a hundred.

The town of Clayton, Colorado might have been named after one of his dusty ancestors, but Lucas had never taken any pride in that. Growing up, having the last name Clayton had only been one more expectation weighing him down. One more invisible shackle holding him in place.

Lucas had broken free at eighteen and left home with a beat-up canvas duffel bag, a chip on his shoulder as solid as a chunk of rock hewn from the Rockies themselves and a vow never to return.

As he traveled from job to job, eventually landing in Georgia, both the duffel bag *and* the chip on his shoulder had remained constant companions.

But now, after seven years, he'd broken the vow.

Not that he'd had a choice.

His grandfather, George Clayton Sr., had passed away during the summer, leaving behind a will that had caused new splits in an already fractured family. George's brother, Samuel, and his offspring had made life unbearable for years, but they stood to inherit everything—if Lucas and his five cousins didn't satisfy the conditions of the will.

That didn't surprise him. Leave it to good old Grandpa George to attempt to control people's lives from the grave—he'd certainly made a habit of it while he'd been alive. As a lawyer, George Clayton had a reputation for being ruthless, manipulative and self-serving. As a grandfather, he hadn't been a whole lot better.

Lucas still couldn't believe his cousins had agreed to put their lives on hold and return to Clayton for a whole year. But he was the last one to return.

Lucas hadn't exactly had a choice about that, either.

A promise made to a dying friend had taken him to places that no sane person would have chosen to go, but loyalty to his sister had brought him back to Clayton.

Cruising through the lone signal light at the intersection, Lucas saw a soft glow in one of the windows farther down the street.

He didn't even have to read the faded sign above the door to know which one it was.

The Cowboy Café.

Lucas struggled against a memory that fought its way to the surface. And lost.

An image of a girl's face materialized in front of him, clear as a photograph. A heart-shaped face. Hair that glowed like the embers in a campfire, shades of bronze and copper lit with strands of gold. Wide brown eyes that had a disconcerting tendency to see straight into his soul.

Lucas's fingers bit into the steering wheel.

He couldn't think about Erin Fields.

Wouldn't think about her.

She'd made her choice. Before he'd left, Lucas had asked Erin to go with him but she'd refused, choosing loyalty to her family over her love for him.

Maybe she'd been willing to put her dreams and her future on hold, but Lucas knew he wouldn't *have* a future if he stayed in Clayton. The confines of the small town would have served as a mold, shaping him into something—someone— he didn't want to be.

His father.

Vern Clayton, medical missionary and well-respected pillar of the church and the community, had died in a car accident when Lucas was a teenager, but his mother had insisted he follow in his father's footsteps by serving God and becoming a doctor.

Instead, Lucas had turned his back on both.

Disappointing people seemed to be his gift.

As if to underscore the point, an image of Erin's tear-streaked face returned. He could almost feel the touch of her hand on his.

I'll always love you, Lucas. And I'll wait for you.

Lucas pushed the memory aside.

He'd be crazy to think Erin had stayed true to the promise she'd made that night. They'd been kids. That kind of vow didn't stand the test of time.

From his experience, not a whole lot did.

Turning onto a side street, he pulled up to the third house on the left. Completely dark. Lucas hadn't expected a welcoming committee—especially when he hadn't told his mother or Mei the exact date of his arrival.

Lucas's fingers curled around the keys in the ignition,

fighting the temptation to shift the truck into Drive and take off into the night. The way he had seven years ago...

A soft rustle came from the backseat.

Twisting around, Lucas summoned what he hoped was a reassuring smile. "It's okay, Max."

A pair of hazel eyes blinked at him from the shadows. "Daddy?" came the sleepy response.

Lucas's throat tightened, preventing him from responding. Not that he even knew *how* to respond.

For the past few months, he'd provided the little boy with food and shelter. The basic necessities. What he hadn't been able to give Max Cahill was the thing he needed the most. His parents.

What were you thinking, Scott?

His former college roommate hadn't been. That was the problem. Scott's addictions had led him down a path that had ultimately cost him his life—and if Lucas hadn't stepped in, the life of an innocent child.

Max lifted his arms toward Lucas and grinned. "We gettin' out now?"

Lucas shook his head. They'd been on the road for more than forty-eight hours and yet his pint-size passenger, who recently turned four, somehow managed to display a more cheerful disposition than the driver.

"Yup. We're getting out now."

"French fries?" Max stifled a yawn even as his eyes brightened with hope.

"I can't make any promises, buddy." And there we have it, Lucas thought. Another one of his flaws exposed.

A raw December wind stung Lucas's face as he hopped out of the truck cab. The crisp temperatures and falling snow felt almost surreal after traipsing through the Florida Everglades, dodging the men who had killed Scott Cahill. Unbuckling the booster seat, he scooped Max into his arms, blankets and all.

The boy burrowed against him and Lucas felt a familiar burst of panic. The one that gripped him whenever Max turned to him for comfort.

Lucas anchored Max against his chest with one arm while fishing for the spare house key his mom always stashed behind the mailbox. Before he had a chance to slide it into the lock, the porch light came on.

He had only a second to react before the front door swung open and a petite, dark haired whirlwind launched herself at him.

"Lucas! You're home."

"Home," came a muffled chirp from inside the cocoon of blankets.

Mei's astonished gaze dropped to the quilt. Lucas could see the question in his adopted sister's ebony eyes and knew exactly what she was thinking.

He'd given Jack McCord, his sister's new love who'd tracked him down in Florida, permission to offer the family an abbreviated version of what he'd gone through to retrieve Max from the thugs who'd snatched him away from his dying father during a drug deal gone bad. But judging from the expression on Mei's face, they had expected Lucas to return to Clayton alone.

And why wouldn't they? an inner voice mocked him.

He'd been MIA for years, communicating with his family through emails and the occasional phone call. That way, he stayed in control of the relationships.

It was a little unsettling to admit that maybe, just maybe, he and Grandpa George had something in common other than their DNA.

"Hey, Erin, I'm supposed to let you know that we're getting a little low on ground beef…"

Erin Fields jumped at the sound of a voice behind her.

She pasted on a smile to cover the guilty look on her face before turning around to face Kylie Jones. Which was a little ridiculous, given the fact that it wasn't a crime to be caught putting on your coat.

Unless it was the middle of the day.

And your name was Erin Fields.

Kylie zeroed in on the coat clutched in her hands. And then her gaze shifted to the clock on the wall.

"The lunch crowd is thinning out so I thought I'd leave early," Erin explained.

"You're leaving. Early." The waitress repeated, her green eyes widening in disbelief.

Maybe because Erin never left early. As the owner of the café, she was the first one to arrive in the morning and the last one to leave at night.

"Only a few hours." Erin winced at the defensiveness that crept into her tone.

She never got defensive, either.

Kylie tipped her head. The movement sent a tumble of light brown curls over one shoulder. "Is everything all right?" she asked hesitantly. "You've been a little…distracted…lately."

Lately being the past forty-eight hours, Erin thought. And if pressed, she could take it a step further and pinpoint the exact moment it had started. When she'd overheard a customer casually mention that Lucas Clayton was back in town.

As much as Erin had both dreamed of and dreaded the possibility of that happening, nothing had prepared her for the reality.

Lucas. In Clayton. For a year.

Erin knew all about the conditions of George Sr.'s will.

It had been the talk of the town since July. One by one, the Clayton cousins had returned to their roots—all except Lucas.

Every time the bells above the door of the café jingled, Erin's nerves would jingle right along with them. It didn't matter that the logical side of her brain knew he wouldn't seek her out. When it came to Lucas Clayton, the hopeful side had always prevailed.

Which proved she still hadn't learned her lesson.

Which, in turn, made her pathetic.

Harboring feelings for a guy who'd claimed to be in love with her—and then left without a backward glance.

Erin was tempted to confide in Kylie, but even now, after all these years, it felt as if she would be breaking a promise. At Lucas's request they'd kept their high-school romance a secret from friends and family. He'd claimed he didn't want his reputation to cast a shadow on her and Erin had reluctantly agreed, afraid her mother wouldn't approve of her dating that "wild Clayton boy."

Even when the truth about their relationship would have squelched the malicious rumor that Vincent Clayton, Lucas's cousin, had started about him and Susie Tansley, Lucas had held Erin to that promise. That's when she'd started to wonder if there was another reason he had insisted on keeping their relationship a secret. A reason that had more to do with his being ashamed of *her* than some of the things he'd done...

Kylie snapped her fingers two inches from Erin's nose. "See what I mean? *Distracted.*"

"I'm fine. Really." Even as she said the words, Erin wondered who she was trying to convince. Kylie? Or herself? "It's Diamond I'm worried about. She seemed a little agitated this morning before I left for work, and she's due to drop her foal any day now. I'd feel better if I checked on her." It was the truth—and a legitimate reason to escape the memories pressing down on her.

"You're such a softie." Kylie chuckled. "You treat those animals of yours like children."

Erin knew her friend was teasing but the words still stung. She was twenty-five years old. Her friends were either engaged or already married and starting a family, something she'd always dreamed of.

With Lucas.

Stop.

For Kylie's benefit, Erin mustered a smile. "So, I'll leave everything in your capable hands for a few hours."

Kylie reeled her in for a quick hug. "Don't worry about coming back to close up. I'll take care of it."

"We got six hours 'til then." A gravelly voice snarled from the kitchen. "So how about you take care of the orders piling up in here before you talk about shutting the place down for the night?"

"Be right there, Jerome," Kylie sang out. Lowering her voice, she winked at Erin over her shoulder. "From the way that man carries on, you'd think he's the one who signs my paychecks, not you."

The two women exchanged a grin. Everyone in town knew the old cook's bark was worse than his bite.

"I'll see you tomorrow, then." Erin shrugged on her coat and shook her ponytail free from the sheepskin collar. "And Kylie...thanks."

"No problem. Zach is meeting me here after he gets off work. He claims he can't pass up one of Gerald and Jerome's famous barbecue rib dinners, but I have a hunch he wants to keep an eye on me." Kylie's expression clouded. "Now that Lucas is back in town, Zach thinks it's going to rile up Vincent and the rest of his family even more."

Erin kept her expression neutral, although her heart plummeted at the mention of Lucas's name. "Samuel's side of the family has always enjoyed causing trouble," she murmured.

"You're telling me." Kylie couldn't suppress a shudder. "I almost married into it. I thank God every day that He saved me from making a huge mistake—and brought Zach into my life."

So did Erin. Zach Clayton, the second of the cousins to return to Clayton after the reading of the will, treated Kylie the way she deserved to be treated. With love and respect.

Unlike Vincent, who Kylie had caught kissing another woman on the day they were supposed to exchange their vows.

"Vincent can put on quite a show." No matter how many times he'd denied it, Erin had known that Vincent, George Sr.'s nephew, had been behind Susie Tansley's attempt to destroy Lucas's already shaky reputation by claiming he was the father of her unborn baby.

Erin hadn't believed the malicious rumors flying around town about Lucas's relationship with Susie, but Lisette Clayton did. The fact that his own mother hadn't believed the truth had finally pushed Lucas over the edge. By the time the truth came out and Susie's claim had proved to be a lie, the damage had been done.

He'd shown up at Erin's house a little after midnight with a beat-up duffel bag, eyes dark with pain and a reckless offer that had quickly deteriorated into their first—and last— argument.

In the end, Erin had watched Lucas drive away, praying with all her heart that he would change his mind and stay in Clayton. And stand up to the people who'd spread rumors about him.

She'd watched the brake lights on his truck glow red at the stop sign. Left would take him home. Right would take him out of the city limits. He'd turned right.

Toward his dreams. And away from her.

"…Better get back to work before Jerome fires me." Kylie's teasing voice tugged Erin back to the present as she breezed toward the door of the office.

Erin's heart clenched as she followed Kylie into the dining room and her gaze swept from table to table.

Be strong, she silently lectured herself.

Clayton boasted a population of less than a thousand people. Eventually, she and Lucas were going to come face-to-face.

And when they did, Erin knew exactly what she would do.

She would hold her head up high and look him right in the eye. Her polite smile would show Lucas that she was doing all right. She'd moved on, too.

He'd never have to know that he'd taken her heart with him when he left.

Chapter Two

"Easy girl." Erin ran a soothing hand over the flank of the mare stretched out on the floor of the stall. "Hang in there and you'll be a momma in no time."

The horse thrashed weakly in response to the sound of her voice, and Erin felt needle-sharp tears poke at the back of her eyes.

Where was Tweed?

She'd put in an emergency call to the local large animal vet over an hour ago.

Maybe she'd been running away at the time, but Erin was glad she'd left the café early because the moment she'd arrived home from work, she'd known something was wrong. Winston, her corgi, had been standing at the door of the barn instead of ambling down to the mailbox to greet her the way he usually did.

Erin had discovered Diamond lying down in the stall, already in the throes of what looked as if it were going to be a long and difficult labor.

The blue roan was Erin's first rescue. She'd attended an auction one summer afternoon and spotted the horse tied to the back of a rusty trailer, half-starved and abused. One look into those sorrowful, liquid brown eyes and she couldn't walk away. No one had bothered to mention the mare was expecting.

Even with a good diet, a warm place to sleep and daily doses of tender loving care, Diamond had been slow to regain her strength. Erin had been afraid all along that the horse wouldn't be able to handle a difficult birth. She'd shared her concern with Dr. "Tweed" Brighton, who'd promised to help deliver the foal if necessary.

If only she could get in touch with him.

A plaintive whinny split the air and Erin placed a comforting hand on the mare's belly.

"Not much longer now," she whispered, hoping it was the truth.

As the minutes ticked by, helplessness and frustration battled for control of Erin's emotions, swept along on a tide of "what ifs." What if she'd become a veterinarian instead of taking over the café from her mother? What if she hadn't chosen duty to her family over her dreams?

Then she would be able to offer something more than simple comfort or encouraging words as Diamond struggled to bring her foal into the world.

A ribbon of wind unfurled through the barn, carrying the sweet scent of pine and new-fallen snow. Erin's knees went weak with relief when she heard the soft tread of footsteps coming closer.

The stall door slid open behind her.

"Thank goodness you're here, Tweed," Erin said without turning around. "She's in a lot of pain but nothing seems to be happening."

Instead of a response marked by a crisp British accent, something the veterinarian wore as proudly as he did the tweed cap that had earned him his nickname, there was silence.

Erin shifted her weight and glanced over her shoulder. Her gaze locked on a pair of snow-covered hiking boots and traveled up. Over long legs encased in faded jeans. A flannel lined jacket. Broad shoulders. Sun-streaked blond hair. Chiseled features that formed the perfect setting for a pair of denim-blue eyes.

Lucas Clayton's eyes.

Lucas blinked several times, but the young woman kneeling in the straw didn't disappear.

And she looked just as shocked to see him.

The years melted away, burning through the layers of defenses Lucas had built up until all that remained were memories.

Memories of the one person who'd never stopped believing in him at a time in his life when Lucas had stopped believing in everything.

When Tweed had sent him on an emergency call, Lucas had only been given the address—not the name—of the person who needed help with a pregnant mare.

Erin Fields's unexpected presence not only stirred up emotions Lucas had buried long ago, but also created a few new ones.

The image frozen in his mind had been that of an eighteen-year-old girl. This Erin looked the same…but different.

The knee-length corduroy coat didn't quite conceal her willowy frame, but the sprinkle of ginger-colored freckles he'd often teased her about had faded. Windswept tendrils of copper hair framed features that had matured from a wholesome prettiness into a delicate, heart-stopping beauty.

He knew Erin hadn't left Clayton, but she wasn't supposed to be *here.* Inside an old barn adjacent to a dilapidated farmhouse a few miles outside of town. They'd both grown up in Clayton—their houses only a few blocks apart.

The mare tossed her head after sensing an unfamiliar presence, reminding Lucas why he was there.

Focus, buddy. In a town the size of Clayton, you knew you would see Erin sooner or later, he told himself.

Later would have been better.

The expression on Erin's face told him that she felt the same way.

"What are *you* doing here? Where's Tweed?"

"He had another call." Without waiting for an invitation, Lucas stepped into the stall. Kneeling down next to Erin, he caught a whiff of her shampoo, a light floral scent that reminded him of mountain lilies.

A scent that had no business lingering in his memory.

"I don't understand. Why would Tweed send you?" Erin shifted, putting a few more inches of space between them.

"He hired me." Lucas ran a hand over the horse's neck and felt the muscles ripple under the velvety skin.

"Hired…" Her gaze dropped to the medical kit he'd set down in the straw.

Lucas watched the myriad emotions topple like dominoes in a pair of eyes the color of warm gingerbread. Confusion. Disbelief. Denial.

"I'm here to help," Lucas said curtly. Being this close to Erin had opened a floodgate to his past and it was his way of trying to put a cap on the memories flooding in. "But if you'd rather wait for Tweed—"

"*No.* I just wasn't…" Erin averted her gaze. "Go ahead and do whatever you need to do."

Lucas opened the med kit and began to prep for an exam. "She belongs to you?"

Erin nodded. "I didn't realize Diamond was pregnant when I rescued her from the auction."

Diamond. It figured. Only Erin Fields would see potential in an animal as battered and broken as this one. The number of scars crisscrossing the washboard ribs hinted at invisible ones below the surface.

Lucas worked quickly, aware that the woman beside him

was watching every movement. He tried to keep his expression neutral, but she must have seen something there. Erin had always been good at reading him. Sometimes too good.

She leaned forward. "How is she?"

"In distress." Diamond's ears twitched at the sound of his voice, but she didn't even bother to lift her head. Lucas silently weighed his options.

"What can I do?"

"Keep her calm."

Erin had always been good at that, too. How many times had she listened to him as he vented about his mother's unreasonable expectations for his future plans? Taken his hand to absorb his volatile emotions, her lips moving in a silent prayer on his behalf? Been there for him without asking for anything in return?

Don't leave like this...

Lucas ruthlessly shook off the memory of the last night they'd spoken. A hundred miles down the road he'd realized that Erin had done the right thing when she'd refused to run away with him. He hadn't been fit to be a good husband back then.

Any more than he was fit to be a father now.

He turned to reach for a syringe only to find that Erin had anticipated his need. Their fingers brushed together and Lucas couldn't help but notice she wasn't wearing a ring. The realization that Erin wasn't married sent equal measures of relief and terror skittering through him.

"Talk to her." Lucas's voice came out sharper than he'd intended. "She's not going to like this."

Erin scooted closer to the horse and spoke to her in the same gentle, soothing voice she'd once used on him.

Lucas worked in silence for the next few minutes, administering a sedative to relax the horse while he performed a brief but enlightening internal exam.

He stood up after it was over and tried to ignore the pain

that rattled down his spine, a subtle but persistent reminder of a conversation he'd had with a cranky bull the year before.

Erin looked up at him. "The foal is breech, isn't it?"

Lucas didn't miss the catch in her voice and he gave a curt nod, mentally bracing himself for the inevitable—telling her there was a good chance she would lose both the mare *and* the foal.

Lucas took a step toward her, shrinking the space between them. He could see the faint spray of ginger-colored freckles on her nose. The eyelashes spiked with unshed tears.

Something twisted in his gut. His sigh came out in a puff of frost. "Erin—"

"Don't say it," she said fiercely.

"You might have to choose," Lucas pushed.

"All right." Erin's chin lifted, warning him that she was willing to push back. "I choose both."

Lucas stared at her in disbelief. The girl he'd known in high school hadn't been a fighter. It was one of the things Lucas had accused her of the night he'd asked her to run away with him.

"When it comes right down to it, you're a coward, Erin. Your problem is that you have all these plans, all these big dreams, but you aren't willing to fight for them."

"And your problem is that you want to fight everything and everybody," Erin had said, her voice cracking under the weight of his accusation. *"You think if you leave Clayton, you'll leave behind your grief and all the regrets over your relationship with your dad—"*

"Don't bring my dad into this."

"Why not? You do it all the time. Every minute of every day. But if you leave Clayton like this, it's all going to follow you until you give it to God—"

"Leave Him out of it, too."

"Oh, Lucas..."

"Lucas?" Erin stood up. The top of her head was level with

his shoulder but she didn't back down. "I'll help. Just tell me what I need to do."

"Leave." He didn't want her to witness what might happen. Or see him fail.

"Give me something else to do."

Was that a glimmer of humor in her eyes? Lucas couldn't be sure but the warmth of it momentarily chased the chill away, if not the doubts.

"Diamond is strong," Erin whispered. "She's going to get through this."

There was a time when Erin had believed the same thing about him.

Before he'd walked away.

Erin tried to keep her thoughts centered on delivering the foal and her eyes off Lucas.

He worked with a calm efficiency that astonished her. As a teenager, Lucas had reminded Erin of a caged mountain lion. Filled with restless energy. Eyes fixed on some point in the horizon that no one else could see.

She didn't know this man. The one with the patient hands and soothing voice. It had taken Diamond several months to trust Erin enough to accept a treat from her hand, but in the space of five minutes Lucas had gained the mare's trust.

She still couldn't believe that he'd gone to college. Become a veterinarian.

Her dream…

"Erin?" Lucas's voice tugged at her.

She realized he'd caught her staring and blushed. "Sorry. What did you say?"

"The foal turned." In spite of the temperature outside, beads of sweat dotted Lucas's forehead. "I think we can let Mom take it from here."

Five minutes later, Diamond delivered a tiny, jet-black replica of herself.

Erin closed her eyes.

"Thank you, God," she murmured.

When she opened them again, she found Lucas staring at her, a wry expression on his face.

"Are you going to send Him the bill, too?"

Erin couldn't prevent a smile. And to her absolute amazement, Lucas smiled back. A faint quirk of his lips that carved out the dimple in his left cheek, a trait passed on from Clayton to Clayton like a family legacy.

Lucas hated it. Erin, however, had referred to it as the "Clayton brand" and teased him about it.

Pressed her lips against it.

Swallowing hard, she turned her attention to Diamond, severing the fragile connection that had sprung up between them. "There's a bucket of water and a clean towel in the tack room if you want to wash up."

"Thanks." The smile had disappeared.

Two polite strangers. That's what the years of silence had accomplished.

It's what Lucas had wanted, Erin reminded herself.

Diamond's soft whicker was a welcome distraction. The mare was nuzzling her newborn foal, who lifted its head in response to the attention.

Caught up in the wonder of the moment, Erin watched the two interact until Lucas returned and began to collect his medical supplies.

"Everything looks good but I'd keep a close eye on her for the next twenty-four hours." He turned to her, his gaze once again distant. "I'll give you my cell number in case there's a problem."

Erin caught her lower lip between her teeth. She didn't want his phone number. Didn't want to see him again and deal with the stampede of emotions those denim-blue eyes triggered.

"That's not necessary. I'll call Tweed if I have any questions. He's treated Diamond since I brought her home."

"Tweed…" Lucas hesitated. "He's planning to retire around the first of the year. Until then, he wants to stay in the clinic and limit his practice to pets."

Erin sucked in a breath, hoping that didn't mean what she thought it meant.

"I'm taking over the large animal side of his practice."

That's what she'd thought it meant.

"You're staying in Clayton?" Erin tried to keep her voice steady.

"It looks that way. For a year." Lucas didn't sound happy about it, either.

So the rumors she'd heard about George Sr.'s will had been true. Until now, she hadn't quite believed it.

"Yoo-hoo! Is anyone home?" A feminine voice floated through the barn.

"We're in here," Lucas called back.

A few seconds later, Mei Clayton appeared in the doorway, holding the hand of an adorable preschool-age boy. A bright red snowsuit enveloped his thin frame but instead of a stocking cap, a cowboy hat was perched on his head. A battered black Stetson that looked a lot like the one Lucas used to wear.

He smiled shyly, pressed his cheek against Mei's leg and pointed to the foal. "Thatsa baby horse."

Erin couldn't help but smile back. "Babysitting today?"

Lucas and Mei exchanged a look that Erin couldn't decipher.

"This is Max," Mei said.

"Hey, Max." Erin experienced the familiar pang that happened whenever a cute little kid came into the café. *Someday.* "I'm Erin. It's nice to meet you. Do you like horses?"

"I like trucks better," Max declared.

Erin winked at Mei. "We'll have to work on that."

"What's up, sis?" Lucas shrugged his coat on. His sister slanted an apologetic look in his direction.

"I know I promised to watch Max this afternoon, but the high-school secretary called and asked if I would be available to attend an emergency parent-teacher conference after school. You didn't answer your cell so I called Tweed to track you down."

"That's okay." The affectionate smile Lucas gave her told Erin the siblings still shared a close bond. "I'm finished here."

Max broke away from Mei. And to Erin's astonishment, he headed straight for Lucas.

Her gaze bounced from Lucas's sister to the boy, who'd wrapped both arms around Lucas's knees and was clinging to him like a burr on a wool sock.

Lucas looked so uncomfortable with the attention that Erin had to stifle a smile.

"So, who does this little cowboy belong to?" She directed the question at Mei but it was Lucas who answered.

"He belongs to me."

Chapter Three

Lucas saw the flash of hurt in Erin's eyes before she could disguise it.

"I see," she murmured.

Lucas doubted that. How could she? Even he wasn't sure how he'd ended up with custody of someone else's child.

He could almost guess what she was thinking. He was the guy who avoided family obligations like a disease. Sure, he'd been willing to marry Erin, but Lucas had come to realize that the proposal had been offered out of selfishness. He'd claimed he didn't want to lose her, but what he hadn't wanted to lose was the sense of peace she had brought to his life.

Which made him *that* guy.

The guy who had no business taking on the responsibility of a wife. Or a child.

"Oh, before I forget, here's the Realtor's number." Mei fished a business card out of her coat pocket and handed it to him. "I ran into Bev yesterday afternoon and mentioned that you're anxious to find something."

Anxious to move out of his childhood home, Lucas thought. The last few days hadn't been easy. Mei had done her best to ease the tension between him and their mother, but Lisette made no attempt to hide her disappointment in him. Something Lucas should have been used to by now.

Not only did his mother barely interact with Max, she'd refused to care for him when Lucas went out on a call. Mei babysat when she was available, but Lucas knew he couldn't count on her generosity much longer. When his sister wasn't substitute teaching at the high school, she was spending time with Jack McCord, the local search-and-rescue worker who had crossed state lines to bring him and Max to safety.

Lucas still couldn't wrap his mind around that relationship. Mei and Jack, Charley Clayton's stepson, had been at odds in high school but now they claimed to be in love. There seemed to be a lot of that going around, now that he thought about it.

So he wasn't going to think about it.

"Thanks, Mei. I'll try to give her a call after Max goes to bed tonight."

Max frowned. "Don't wanna go to bed."

"You have to learn to spell things," Mei whispered to Lucas.

"Spell things?"

"You know. B-e-d." Mei closed one eye in a saucy wink and blew Max a kiss before breezing out the door. "Bye, partner. Bye, Erin."

"Bye." Erin's smile, when aimed at his sister, was relaxed and genuine.

Lucas couldn't help but feel a little envious.

There'd been a time when they were completely at ease in each other's company. Now, she could barely look at him.

"I'll drop a check off tomorrow." Erin's gaze drifted to Max again.

"No hurry—" Lucas found himself talking to her back. He took Max by the hand and followed Erin out of the barn. "I'll swing by in a few days to check on Diamond. Is there someone around here during the day?"

"I'm usually at the café." Erin veered toward the shoveled pathway leading to the house.

"I know that, but the owners won't mind if I stop by, right?"

She whirled around and sent a spray of snow over the tops of his boots. "What do you mean, the owners?"

Now it was his turn to be confused. "The people who board Diamond for you."

"I don't board her here. I *live* here."

Frowning, Lucas peered at the two-story eyesore with the dingy white clapboard siding, crooked shutters and a wrap-around porch that sagged like an unbuckled belt around its middle. The small outbuildings and barn were in a similar state of disrepair.

"What happened to your house in town?"

Erin looked away. "I sold it after Mom died."

Lucas felt his stomach turn inside out. Erin's mother had battled diabetes for years, but no one had bothered to mention that she'd passed away. When had it happened? And why had Erin stayed in Clayton?

She'd been as anxious as he was to leave their hometown, her goal to become a large animal vet. Lucas's goal had been to break every household rule his parents established.

Did Erin realize she had been instrumental in his choice of a career? Every retired, broken-down ranch horse within a twenty-five mile radius of Clayton had received her loving attention and he'd been right there beside her, currycomb in hand.

His willingness to work with the animals had caught the attention of the local vet on the ranch he'd worked in Georgia.

"You have a way with these critters, Clayton," the doc had said. *"Ever think of making a living at it?"*

Until that moment, Lucas hadn't. But he'd taken the words to heart—and didn't mention that his "way with critters" had been encouraged by a slender girl with big brown eyes and a luminous smile.

He pulled his thoughts back in line. Looking back had the power to make a man stumble.

"I'm sorry." The words sounded inadequate but they were the best Lucas could do.

"So am I," Erin said softly.

"So you bought a…" Lucas searched for the right word. One that wouldn't offend her. "A…house…out here."

A shadow of a smile touched Erin's lips. She'd read his mind. Again. "I'm planning to fix up the place a little at a time and add a few more stalls so I can rescue more horses like Diamond. I think the place has potential."

Lucas didn't have the heart to tell her that she was wrong. The same way she'd been wrong about him.

"I can help. I gottsa hammer," Max announced.

"Really?" Erin reached out and tapped a finger against the tip of his wind-kissed button nose. "You'll have to show it to me sometime."

Max looked troubled and Lucas knew what was coming next.

Sure enough, tears welled up in the hazel eyes. "Hammer's at home."

And home, no matter how rough it had been, was a place that existed only in Max's memory now.

A familiar feeling of helplessness once again threatened to swamp Lucas, reminding him that he was in way over his head. He didn't know what to do about the fresh pain in Max's eyes…or the shadows that still lingered in Erin's from the loss of her mother.

Maybe because he'd never figured out how to deal with his own grief.

Losing his father in the car accident that had also claimed the life of his uncle, George Jr., had changed him. Outwardly, no one could see the damage. On the inside, it was a different story. Like tempered glass, Lucas absorbed the impact of the blow but hadn't been able to stop the tiny cracks from spreading below the surface. Sometimes he felt as if they'd changed the very structure of his soul.

"Wanna go home," Max choked out.

"We're setting up camp together, remember? You'll have your own room and a shelf full of toys."

It was bribery, plain and simple. The parenting books would disapprove, but it was the best Lucas could do.

Glancing at Erin, he braced himself for the reproach he probably deserved.

The compassion in the golden-brown eyes rocked him to the core.

"You're looking for a place of your own?" she ventured.

"Mom isn't used to little kids in the house anymore." Especially a little kid who woke up in the night, caught in the throes of a waking nightmare.

"There's a place just down the road for sale," Erin said, almost reluctantly. "The couple who lives there wants to relocate to Florida to be closer to their daughter."

Lucas didn't bother to tell her that he was interested in a house he could rent, not buy. Buying a house meant putting down roots and he was only in Clayton for a year. He silently corrected himself. *Eleven months and three weeks.*

"I didn't notice a For Sale sign on the way here."

"There isn't one yet." Erin pushed her hands into her coat pockets. "I heard it's going on the market this weekend."

The only place Lucas remembered seeing was a log cabin set back from the road a ways. Small and cozy and surrounded by a yard large enough to appeal to an active boy.

But way too close to Erin.

Seven years ago she'd been both confidante and conscience. His best friend and his first love.

After the way they'd parted, Lucas wasn't sure what they were anymore. But there was one thing he did know.

The thought of staying in Clayton for a year wasn't nearly as terrifying as the thought of being Erin Fields's closest neighbor.

"How long does it take for a guy to get a cup of coffee around this place?"

Erin's back teeth ground together.

Vincent Clayton had sauntered in five minutes before closing time, leaving a trail of mud and slush across her freshly mopped floor before taking a seat at the farthest table from the kitchen.

He loved to do that.

Erin found herself wishing that she hadn't sent Gerald and Jerome Hicks home early. Business had been slow so she'd convinced the two cooks that she could handle any last-minute customers and shooed them out the door.

Help me be patient, Lord. Erin sent up the silent prayer as she made her way to Vincent's table. He smiled at her, his casual pose as deceptive as that of a rattlesnake coiled up in the sun.

She didn't trust him for a second. This particular snake was always ready—and willing—to strike.

Erin suppressed a shudder as she filled his coffee cup. "Sorry for the delay," she said automatically. "I had to put on a fresh pot."

Instead of looking at the menu, Vincent's gaze swept around the empty dining room. "I guess it's just you and me, isn't it, Red?"

"What would you like?"

The sudden glint in the shifty blue eyes made Erin regret the way she'd worded the question. "Now that's an interesting question," he drawled. "Could be that I want the same thing my cousin wants."

"Leave Zach and Kylie alone," Erin warned. "They're happy."

"Who said I was talking about Zach?"

Erin sensed the rage simmering just below the surface of his smile and knew if she followed it to its source, it would lead her to the one family member who had always been Vincent's greatest rival.

Lucas.

It was hard to believe the two men were related. They didn't resemble each other in looks or personality. Whereas Lucas had frequently been blamed for his role in things he'd never even taken part in, his cousin had somehow managed to come out smelling like the proverbial rose.

Even now, Vincent had no qualms about using his father Pauley's title as part-time mayor to throw his weight around.

"It's late. What would you like to order?" Erin somehow managed to keep her voice steady.

"I heard he brought a kid back with him. Wonder how long that'll last?" Vincent leaned back, hooking the heels of his snow-covered boots over the rung of the wooden chair beneath the table.

Erin stiffened. "I imagine it will last awhile. Max *is* his son."

"His son?" Vincent hooted. "That kid ain't got a drop of Clayton blood in his veins. Lucas took him in like a stray pup after the boy's daddy died."

Erin fought to hide her reaction.

When Lucas had said that Max belonged to him, Erin had searched for a resemblance between the two, some trait passed on from father to son, but had come to the conclusion that the boy must favor his mother.

Vincent's claim would explain why Lucas had looked so uncomfortable when Max had clung to him in her barn that day.

Bits and pieces of rumors that Erin had heard over the past few months began to fall into place.

The sudden silences and worried looks she'd seen pass between the Clayton family had led her to believe that Lucas was refusing to come back and fulfill the terms of his grandfather's will.

Now she wondered if the delay hadn't had something to do with Max.

"Lucas says he's going to legally adopt the kid, but that won't happen," Vincent went on. "We both know that Lucas was never what you'd call a 'family man.'"

Erin had had her fill of the man's poison. "He came back, didn't he?"

The triumphant look in Vincent's eyes told her that she'd made a mistake. It didn't matter if he'd been bluffing or if he had somehow known about her and Lucas all along. She'd stuck up for Lucas—the way she always had. If Vincent's plan was to force Erin into admitting that her feelings for Lucas hadn't changed, she'd just delivered the answer. Giftwrapped and ready to use against her.

"But he won't stay long." Vincent shook his head in mock sympathy. "Not for old man Clayton's money or his land. Lucas ain't wired that way and everybody with a lick of sense knows it."

His tone implied that Erin Fields didn't fall into the "people with a lick of sense" category.

"If you don't want anything, I'm going to close up for the night."

Vincent's hand shot out, his fingers curling around her wrist. "I want what's mine and Lucas isn't going to cheat me out of it."

Erin and Vincent might have played in the same sandbox once upon a time, but that didn't prevent her knees from locking up in fear as the pressure tightened.

She sucked in a breath. "Let go."

Vincent released her and sprang to his feet. "Mark my words. A lot can happen in a year." The gleam in his eyes was more intimidating than the grip of his hand had been. "He won't stick it out."

"People change."

"Some do…and some don't." Vincent leaned in close, enveloping her in a cloud of pungent cologne. "If I were you, I wouldn't be getting any ideas about a happily-ever-after with my cousin. You weren't enough to make Lucas stay back then, Erin, and you won't be enough for him now."

He sauntered to the door and the moment it snapped shut behind him, Erin was there, fumbling with the lock. She squeezed her eyes shut and pressed her forehead against the frosted glass.

Her heart had instantly rejected Vincent's claim that Lucas planned to leave Max with someone else. Yes, he'd appeared uncomfortable with the way the preschooler had clung to him, but she hadn't missed Lucas's awkward but tender attempt to comfort him, either.

No matter what Vincent said, Lucas cared about Max.

But unfortunately, Erin knew what Vincent had said about her *was* true.

She was still the same woman she'd been seven years ago. The woman that Lucas had left.

Chapter Four

"We goin' to Erin's house?"

In the rearview mirror, Lucas saw Max point out the window. The wide smile on the boy's face hadn't been there a few seconds ago.

Max must have met half the population of Clayton since their arrival. The fact that he remembered Erin's name proved she'd made an impression.

Maybe it hadn't been such a good idea to bring him along.

An overweight corgi rounded the barn, sounding an alarm as his pickup rolled down the snow-packed driveway.

A moment later, Erin stepped out of the building, her copper hair a bright spot of color against the faded timber siding.

Lucas's heart stumbled at the sight of her.

There had always been *something* about Erin Fields. Some elusive quality that went beyond simple chemistry or the way she looked—although she was more beautiful at twenty-five than she'd been at eighteen.

When Lucas returned to Clayton, he knew it would be awkward to see Erin again. Even though they'd parted in anger the night he left, they had a history. Shared memories.

The trouble was, Lucas hadn't been prepared for the emotions tangled inside of those memories.

Erin was a complication he didn't need. He'd left Clayton once, and after he fulfilled the terms of his grandfather's will he planned to leave it again.

"Wanna get out, Lucas!" Max tugged on the strap of his booster seat.

"Hold on." Lucas hopped out of the truck cab and opened the door.

Giggling, Max made a break for it as soon as Lucas unbuckled him. The kid was smart enough to know where to seek sanctuary, too. He made a beeline for Erin, who swung Max up in her arms as if she'd done it a hundred times before and tucked him against the curve of her hip.

"How are you doing today, cowboy?"

"I wanna see the baby horse." Max pointed to the barn.

"She's with her momma right now," Erin said. "And they're both doing great."

Lucas figured that last bit was meant for him.

"Max and I had a few errands to run this morning so I thought I'd stop by." He hadn't called to let Erin know that he was on his way over. In fact, he'd planned the morning visit because she'd told him the majority of her time was spent at the café. Apparently, however, that didn't mean today.

As he followed her into the barn, Max chattered on about the "black-and-blue" pancakes Lucas had made for breakfast.

"Cowboys like 'em the best," he told her matter-of-factly.

"Really? I didn't know that." Erin glanced at Lucas. "How do you make, ah, black-and-blue pancakes?"

"It's easy," he said ruefully. "The blue comes from the blueberries and the black when you forget to flip them while you're stirring the orange juice."

Erin's laughter swept through the barn…and his defenses. Lucas found it difficult to take his eyes off her.

Not a good sign.

Erin put a finger to her lips before sliding open the stall door. "Shh. Diamond likes it quiet so her baby can sleep."

"I'll be quiet," Max promised, staring up at Erin as if she were a fairy-tale princess come to life. A fairy-tale princess in faded corduroy and denim.

She looked totally at peace in her surroundings, something Lucas had never quite managed to achieve.

Maybe because it didn't seem to matter that he'd juggled classes and work during the day and studied long into the night to earn his degree in veterinary science, graduating a year earlier than his classmates. No matter how much Lucas accomplished, he always heard his father's voice tell him it wasn't enough.

"You have a rebellious nature, Lucas. If you don't listen to me and do what I say, you're never going to amount to anything. You'll disappoint everyone who cares about you and you'll be alone. Sometimes I think that's what you want."

The words had cut deep, embedding themselves in Lucas's heart. He'd discovered that nothing, not a steady paycheck, not pats on the back nor praise from his boss, could erase the words his father had spoken to him on the night he'd died.

They'd taken root and grown. Crowded out his ability to commit until he'd become the man Vern Clayton had predicted he would be.

"God loves you, Lucas, and He won't turn His back on you. You'll never be alone."

Erin's voice sounded sweet and clear, as if she'd just spoken the words out loud instead of years ago.

What would his life be like if he'd believed her, not his father?

Something shifted inside of Lucas and he struggled to regain his balance. "If you have something to do, go ahead," he said curtly. "Max and I won't be here long."

That was one promise Lucas would make sure he kept.

"That's all right." The wary look in Erin's eyes had returned. "I'll introduce Max to Butterscotch and her kittens while you check on Diamond."

Because she didn't want to spend any more time in his company than necessary.

Lucas should have felt the same way. So why did he have the overwhelming urge to follow Erin as she led Max away?

Diamond greeted him with a snort as he stepped into the stall.

"Yeah, I know," Lucas muttered. "The sooner we get this over with, the sooner our lives can get back to normal."

As normal as life in Clayton would ever get, Lucas silently amended. And with Erin Fields less than fifty feet away, she was out of sight but definitely not out of mind.

The music of her laughter echoed through the barn and Lucas paused to listen until Diamond swung her head around and nipped his sleeve.

He was definitely out of his mind.

Ten minutes later Lucas found Erin and Max in a corner of the barn, playing with a litter of half-grown calico kittens with lime-green eyes. Max ambled over and tugged on his arm until Lucas bent down.

"Haveta go, Lucas," he whispered.

"We will, buddy. As soon as I put my things away."

"No." Max shook his head vigorously. "Haveta *go*."

Oh, *that* kind of go.

Lucas silently calculated how long it would take to get the nearest gas station without exceeding the speed limit. "Five minutes, Bud."

"But I haveta go *now*."

Erin sighed. "I do have indoor plumbing, Lucas."

"Are you sure?"

Erin didn't bother to grace that with a response, just closed the barn door and strode toward the house. They followed her inside, where the scent of cinnamon and apples permeated the air.

She pointed to a door at the end of the narrow hall. "Come into the kitchen when you're done. I have to take a loaf of bread out of the oven."

Lucas scooped Max up to hasten the trip but as they passed the living room, the boy let out a squeal that practically drilled a hole in Lucas's left eardrum.

"Look at Erin's tree!"

Lucas blinked. It wasn't just a tree. The entire room resembled a Christmas card come to life.

The roundest balsam fir Lucas had ever seen took up an entire corner of the room, decked out in dozens of shimmering ornaments that caught and reflected the twinkling lights woven between the branches. A pine garland braided with gold ribbons ran the length of the fireplace mantle and a hand-carved nativity set graced the coffee table in front of the green corduroy sofa.

Lucas wanted to smack himself upside the head.

Christmas was only three weeks away and until now it hadn't even appeared on his radar. His mother hadn't decorated for the holiday. Maybe she didn't bother anymore. But after what Max had been through...well, he deserved some of this.

The scents and sounds of the holiday.

A home.

Unfortunately, Lucas didn't feel equipped to give the boy either one of them.

Erin appeared beside him. "I decorate the house the day after Thanksgiving every year. It's a tradition Mom started."

"I remember," Lucas said without thinking.

Erin's lips parted but no words came out. Maybe because there wasn't anything to say that would banish the memories that crowded the air whenever they were together.

Max broke the silence. "What's that?" He pointed at the nativity set, but Lucas shook his head.

"Sorry, buddy. First things first."

Fortunately, Max accepted Lucas's decision without a fuss, but there was no stopping him from taking a detour into the living room on their way back. Erin must have known that because she was waiting for them in the hallway.

"Do you mind?" Lucas needed permission before turning a four-year-old boy loose into her Christmas wonderland.

Erin shook her head. "There isn't anything he can damage."

"I'm not so sure about that," Lucas muttered. As well behaved as Max was, he'd managed to turn Lisette's home upside down in the space of a week. Fingerprints on the walls. A broken dish. Plastic trucks making roads in her potted plants.

Lucas had heard about it all. Which was why they had to find a place of their own. Soon.

His cell phone rang and he glanced at the name on the screen. "It's Tweed," he murmured, keeping a watchful eye on Max. "I should probably take it."

Erin nodded. "Come on, Max. I have a special ornament on the tree. Let's see if you can find it." She took the boy by the hand and led him into the living room.

By the time Lucas returned, he found Max snuggled up on Erin's lap, one of the nativity pieces clutched in his hand.

"Is everything all right?" Erin asked.

"One of Fred McKinney's steers sliced its leg open and he thinks it's going to need stitches."

"What about Max?" Erin frowned. "Is he going with you?"

Lucas didn't get a chance to answer because Max sat up straight and began to shake his head.

"Nope. I'm stayin' with Erin."

"Listen, buddy—"

"Bye, Lucas. See ya later." Max flashed an enchanting smile that Erin matched with one of her own.

"I guess he's staying with me."

Lucas wondered if the preschooler wasn't smarter than he was. Because looking at Erin, at the warm light in her eyes and the arms wrapped protectively around his adopted son, he was suddenly having a hard time remembering why he'd ever left.

Erin ran a damp dishcloth over the refrigerator door and erased another smudge of green frosting.

The table resembled an artist's palette and flour dusted the floor, making it look as if her kitchen had been the target of an early snow. By the time Erin pulled the last batch of cookies out of the oven, Max had been coated in a thin layer of frosting and sprinkles, looking a bit like one of the gingerbread men lining the counter.

She couldn't help but smile at the memory.

Max was one hundred percent boy. Bright. Energetic. Inquisitive. And heartbreakingly sweet.

The trouble was, Erin had already had her heart broken once.

She turned the handle of the faucet with a little more force than was necessary.

Maybe she shouldn't have been so quick to agree to babysit.

But somehow, Max's wide, little boy grin had pushed every one of her doubts about keeping her distance from Lucas aside.

She padded down the hallway to the living room, where she'd left Max playing with the nativity set while she straightened up the kitchen. The wooden figurines had fascinated him. Erin had answered a dozen questions about each piece and tried to explain, in a way that a four year old could understand, why there was a baby sleeping inside the miniature barn.

Max's lack of knowledge about the Christmas story made her heart ache.

As the son of a medical missionary, Lucas knew the Bible inside and out, but he had turned his back on his faith when they were in high school. He'd told Erin that he probably wouldn't be able to live up to God's expectations any more than he could his father's, so why even try?

And even though Lucas had walked away from her, too, Erin had never stopped praying that he would eventually find his way back to God. Over the past few days, she'd felt the burden to pray for him even more.

There's a reason You brought Lucas back to Clayton, Lord. Show him that You love him and help him let go of the past. Max needs Lucas to be a loving father...and Lucas needs You to show him how.

Peeking around the corner, she spotted the boy curled up on the sofa next to Winston, sound asleep, the ragged tail of his blanket clutched in one small hand.

An image of Lucas, holding the rumpled square of bright green fleece, rose up in her mind. He'd retrieved the blanket from the truck and brought it up to the house to give to Max before he'd left. Erin had been touched by the gesture, but the self-conscious look on Lucas's face told her that he wasn't comfortable with his new role.

Erin wasn't completely comfortable with it, either.

He belongs to me.

Lucas. A father.

How many hours had she spent doodling their names in her notebook during study hall? Planning their wedding? Their family?

Their *future*.

Until he'd set out on his own and crushed every one of those girlish fantasies. Erin's faith had been the only thing holding her together during those first few days. And as those days turned into months and the months became years, new dreams eventually began to kindle from the ashes of the ones that had once revolved around Lucas.

If you keep looking back, you might miss something good that's right there in front of you.

One of her mom's many pearls of wisdom. And one that Erin had finally taken to heart. It was the reason she kept a smile on her face and her calendar full. Every morning she asked God to teach her contentment—to show her the good that was right in front of her.

And right now, no matter how conflicted her feelings for Lucas Clayton might be, the "good" in front of her was Max.

As Erin leaned down to tuck a corner of the blanket more snuggly around his thin shoulders, she heard a soft knock on the front door.

By the time she reached the doorframe, Lucas already stood in the front hallway. And once again, her traitorous heart stalled at the sight of him.

Lucas had always been good-looking, but the last seven years had wrought subtle changes. At six foot two, he still towered above her, but he was no longer the lanky teenager that Erin remembered. The sun had permanently stained his skin a golden-bronze, a striking contrast to those incredible blue eyes. *Clayton blue,* Erin had heard someone call them once.

Erin remembered Lucas rolling his eyes when she'd repeated the comment.

"First we get a town named after us and now a color. What's next? A mountain range? A national monument?"

"There's nothing wrong with the name Clayton." Erin had given him a playful swat on the arm.

Lucas had smiled that slow smile that never failed to melt her heart like butter in a hot skillet. *"I'm glad you feel that way."*

Erin had been afraid to read too much into the statement. Until Lucas had leaned forward and kissed her.

Her first kiss…

Don't. Look. Back.

Erin silently repeated the words. Lucas Clayton happened to be part of her past and, thanks to George Sr.'s will, an unexpected part of her present. But he was definitely *not* a part of her future.

That's what she needed to remember.

"Lucas." She flashed a polite smile—the same one that every cowboy who came into the café received with a cup of coffee.

He drove a hand through his hair and snowflakes drifted down like bits of silver confetti. "I'm sorry it's so late. Is Max ready to leave?"

"He's sound asleep."

"Right." Lucas sighed. "He usually takes a nap around this time. I'll carry him out to the truck."

Something in the weary slump of his shoulders tugged at her conscience.

"Would you like to thaw out with a cup of coffee first?" Erin couldn't believe she'd said the words. Out loud.

And Lucas hesitated just long enough to make her wish she could take back the invitation.

Chapter Five

"Sure." The husky rumble of Lucas's voice scraped away another layer from her defenses. "I appreciate it."

No problem.

Erin wanted to say the words but they got stuck in her throat. She was all too aware of Lucas as he followed her into the kitchen.

He let out a low whistle. "Max must have slept a long time."

"What makes you say that?"

One eyebrow lifted. "The ten dozen Christmas cookies on your counter?"

"It's only five dozen." Erin reached for a clean coffee mug in the dish drainer. "And Max wasn't sleeping. He helped me."

"Max *helped* you?" Lucas repeated in disbelief.

"Technically, we divided the work. I baked the cookies and Max decorated them."

Lucas's lips twitched. "I guess the three-eyed snowmen should have given it away."

Erin filled the mug, trying to keep her wits about her. Which wasn't easy with Lucas three feet away. Close enough for her to breathe in the scent of leather, crisp mountain air and the hint of soap that was uniquely his.

You can do this. Just pretend you're at the café and he's a customer, remember? "Do you take cream or sugar?"

"Just black."

So far, so good. "How did it go out at the McKinney place?"

Instead of taking a drink, Lucas folded his hands around the steaming mug, as if trying to absorb its warmth. "Ten stitches."

"Ouch." Erin winced.

"Don't feel too bad for the steer," Lucas said drily. "He only ended up with six of them."

"Then who..." For the first time, Erin noticed the gauze bandage peeking out from the cuff of Lucas's sleeve. "*You* got the other four?"

"That's why I'm late. Arabella called my cell when I was on my way back and I happened to mention the injury. I'll know better next time. Jonathan Turner was waiting in the driveway when I got back to the clinic," Lucas said, his expression rueful. "I heard she was dating a doctor but I didn't think I'd meet the guy while he was stitching up my hand."

"What happened?" Erin was almost afraid to ask.

"Apparently he didn't like my bedside manner—the steer, not Mr. McKinney." Lucas shrugged. "It comes with the job, you know."

"I'll have to take your word for that."

An awkward silence filled the space between them. Was Lucas remembering how she'd once dreamed of being a veterinarian?

Their eyes met across the table and Lucas set the cup down.

"I should go. Thanks again for keeping an eye on Max."

Just like that.

Erin's throat tightened. Apparently Lucas found it no more difficult to walk away from her now than he had all those years ago. Further proof that his feelings hadn't been as deep as hers.

You weren't enough to keep him here...

Vincent's mocking words cycled through her mind and she turned away so Lucas wouldn't see her expression. In her heart of hearts, Erin might wish for Lucas to still feel *something* for her, but she didn't want it to be pity.

Poor Erin Fields. Still hung up on her first crush.

She needed to pray that God would help *her* let go of the past, too.

"I'll pack up some cookies for you to take home." Erin reached for a decorative tin on the second shelf and began to pack it with three-eyed snowmen and pink reindeer, hoping Lucas wouldn't notice that her hands were shaking.

Which wouldn't have been as obvious if he'd remained sitting at the table. But no. He got up, closed the distance between them in two short strides and began to help.

"You've got green and red sprinkles in your hair."

"Christmas decorations," Erin shot back, a little surprised that she could do polite *and* funny. "I get a little carried away."

Lucas, however, didn't appear amused. His eyes narrowed, searching her face as if he were looking for something. Or someone.

What did he see when he looked at her? The girl he'd claimed to have loved? Or one more mistake he'd made?

The air emptied out of Erin's lungs as his fingers brushed against her hair. "Erin—"

Whatever he'd been about to say was lost in the high-pitched scream that pierced the air.

Not again.

Not *now*.

Lucas sprinted down the hall, vaguely aware that Erin was right behind him, already apologizing for something he knew wasn't her fault.

He should have warned her this could happen, but he

hadn't anticipated being gone so long. And the truth was, he never knew when a dark memory would emerge and trigger another one of Max's episodes.

The social worker had encouraged Lucas to give Max time to adjust to all the changes in his life. He'd gone through a lot for someone of his tender age, but he didn't have the ability to process what had happened. Reality and imagination had a way of becoming tangled. The result was a waking nightmare for Max and a sleepless night for Lucas.

He rounded the corner and spotted Max bolt upright on the sofa, his small body rigid with terror, eyes wide and riveted on some unseen threat.

Erin's soft gasp punctuated the air and Lucas remembered how he'd felt the first time he'd seen Max like this. The way he *still* felt when he saw Max like this.

He glanced at Erin to gauge her reaction. To his astonishment, she didn't rush over, pick Max up and rattle off a bunch of questions that he couldn't answer. She stopped in the center of the room, as if she trusted that Lucas knew what to do.

Yeah, right.

When it came to stuff like this, Lucas would have loved to defer to an expert. Unfortunately, there was never one around when you needed one. Max was stuck with a guy who knew more about four-year-old horses than four-year-old boys.

He lowered himself onto the sofa next to Max as casually as if they were going to watch Monday-night football.

"Hey, buddy." Lucas didn't expect a response. He'd learned that words couldn't penetrate the invisible wall that separated them, but talking to Max made *him* feel better.

He slanted a quick look at Erin. She was watching them but her lips moved in a silent plea.

This was the second time he'd caught her praying. Erin's faith had been strong as a teenager and it looked as if she'd held on to it over the years.

That made one of them.

Lucas felt a stab of envy that a close relationship with God had always seemed to come so naturally to her. Over the past few months, when he'd tried to get Max to safety, there'd been times he had wanted to call on God but figured he no longer had the right. He'd made a decision a long time ago to make his own way—it seemed a little hypocritical to ask for help when things got tough. Still, it was comforting to think that God might intervene on Max's behalf because Erin was the one doing the asking.

Ignoring the dull ache from the stitches in his arm, Lucas carefully drew Max against his chest and waited. The only sound in the room came from the crackle and spit of the logs in the fireplace.

As if Max were a frozen statue coming back to life, Lucas gradually felt the thin shoulders relax. The rapid drumbeat of his heart began to even out.

"Lucas?" Max whimpered.

"I'm right here, buddy."

"It's dark."

The fireplace cast plenty of light, but Lucas didn't argue. He wasn't sure if Max had always been afraid of the dark or if it had something to do with the fact that when Lucas found him, he'd been locked in a windowless room not much bigger than a closet.

Erin moved across the room, and Lucas assumed she was going to turn on another light. Instead, she reached down and plugged in the Christmas tree. Hundreds of tiny lights, in a rainbow of colors, began to wink in the branches.

Max hooked two fingers in his cheek and settled against Lucas's shoulder, his gaze focused on the lights rather than the dark memory that had held him captive in its grip.

"Something sure smells good, Erin." Lucas sniffed the air appreciatively. "Like...cookies?"

Erin caught on immediately. "That's right. Gingerbread," she said, her light tone matching his.

Max looked up at him. "Me and Erin maked 'em."

Lucas felt the knot in his chest loosen. "I'll bet they're delicious."

"I ate a tree with sprinkles," Max informed him. "Erin eats the frostin' with a spoon."

"Is that so?" Lucas bit back a smile as color bloomed in Erin's cheeks.

"Someone has to taste test it." The concern in her eyes remained, but she reached out and playfully tweaked Max's toes. "You can take some cookies home for your grandma and Aunt Mei. How about that?"

"An' Jamie an' Julie an' Jessie?" Fear dissipated like a morning mist, unveiling a familiar sparkle in Max's eyes.

"Ahh." Erin looked at him in understanding. "He met Arabella's triplets."

"Yesterday." Lucas winced at the memory.

For an entire week after his arrival, settling Max in and working out the details of his new job had been handy excuses to avoid his extended family.

He'd gotten good at dodging them until Mei cornered him in their mother's kitchen with a message from his cousin, Arabella Michaels. It was time he "make the rounds" and introduce Max to his new family.

Starting with her.

Lucas had braced himself for that first official reunion with a member of his extended family, anticipating anything from awkward silence to outright hostility that he'd returned to Clayton so close to the deadline.

Instead, Lucas had been shocked by the warm welcome he'd received. Something had changed in his family but he wasn't sure what it was. And probably wouldn't be around long enough to find out...

"They're sweet little girls," Erin was saying.

"They're trouble in triplicate," Lucas muttered. "They were playing 'wedding.' If I hadn't stepped in, they would have painted Max's fingernails pink."

Erin's lips curved into a smile. "I'm not surprised, with Jasmine and Cade's wedding coming up in a few weeks."

"Mei mentioned they were getting married on Christmas Eve."

She nodded. "Everyone has been chipping in to help. Kylie Jones has been acting as Jasmine's unofficial wedding planner, and Vivienne is planning the menu for the reception. Arabella is baking the cake and Zach is going to walk her down the aisle."

Lucas was stunned into silence—and not only because Erin knew more about what was going in his cousins' lives than he did.

"You don't approve?"

"I guess I'm surprised *they* do," he admitted. "Nothing against Jasmine or Cade, but they just graduated from high school last spring. They're pretty young to tie themselves down like that. They have their whole future ahead of them."

He saw Erin's expression change and wished he could take back the words.

But it was too late.

Jasmine and Cade weren't much older than they'd been the night Lucas had shown up at her door and proposed. No candlelight or flowers. Not even a ring.

Erin had deserved better than what he'd offered the night he left town.

She still did.

Erin tried not to let Lucas see how his comment had affected her.

If she'd ever wondered if he'd regretted leaving her behind, she didn't have to wonder anymore.

Once he'd crossed the Colorado state line, he'd probably

turned a few cartwheels, relieved that he didn't have anyone "tying him down."

She turned her attention back to Max, who had been listening to their exchange with wide-eyed fascination, and tapped a finger against the tip of his nose. If Lucas could pretend everything was fine, so could she.

"How about I make sure you have enough cookies for the whole family?"

"Okay." Max reached for a wooden camel on the coffee table and held it up in front of Lucas. "This one's Bob."

"Bob, huh? That's a good name." Lucas kept a straight face as he examined the carving.

Erin watched the exchange, still not exactly sure what had happened.

When she'd heard Max scream, she assumed that he had rolled off the sofa in his sleep. But Lucas had brushed aside her apology, as if he'd known something else had happened.

Erin's stomach had dropped to her feet when she'd seen Max sitting on the sofa, the color stripped from his rosy cheeks and his pupils dilated with fear. She'd seen wounded animals in that condition but never a child.

But Lucas didn't appear shocked by the sight. He'd looked…resigned.

Because he'd gone through it before.

The thought struck her with the force of a blow. It was all she could do not to gather them *both* in her arms.

"I'll be right back." Feeling Lucas's eyes on her, she retreated to the kitchen and wilted against the sink, resting her forearms on the old-fashioned porcelain basin for support.

A few minutes later, she sensed Lucas's presence and quickly straightened. "How is Max doing?"

"Fine." Lucas glanced over his shoulder. "Racing the wise men's camels across the rug. When I left, Bob was in the lead."

Erin tried to summon a smile but failed. She waited for Lucas to explain. He waited for her to ask.

Lucas's ragged exhale finally broke the silence that stretched between them.

"I should have…" He paused and tried again. "I'm sorry you had to see that."

"What, exactly," Erin said carefully, "did I see?"

Lucas looked away and for a moment she thought he wasn't going to answer.

"Max went through a recent…trauma." He lowered his voice. "I think some of the things he remembers work their way into his dreams. He wakes up screaming but doesn't seem to be aware of anything around him. It's like he's still stuck in the nightmare."

Erin remembered the terror locked in Max's eyes. "Does it happen a lot?"

"Once or twice a week up until a month ago, but he's been fine since we got to Clayton. I hoped things were getting better. Time heals all wounds, you know." Some dark chord in Lucas's voice told Erin that he didn't believe it. "Max won't talk about the dreams. Or what he…saw."

"What he saw?"

Lucas shook his head. "Trust me, it sounds like the plot of a movie of the week."

Trust *me,* Erin wanted to say. Because whatever had happened to Max had affected Lucas, too. All her good intentions of keeping a polite distance between them crumbled beneath the weight of the pain in his eyes.

She waited, silently praying that he would open up to her the way he had in the past.

"His father, my old college roommate, Scott, was shot during a drug deal," Lucas finally said. "The men responsible were afraid Max would be able to identify them. They took him with them when they left."

Cold horror squeezed the air from Erin's lungs, making it

difficult to breathe. "Are you saying Max was with his father when it happened? That he witnessed the shooting?"

"Scott called me that morning and said he needed help. I got there as fast as I could but…" Lucas's voice trailed off, leaving Erin to fill in the blanks.

She could barely process what he was saying. "You were there, too?"

"Not in time to save Scott's life. If I'd stayed in touch with him after college, maybe I would have known how bad things were. How deep his girlfriend had gotten him into drugs." Guilt banked in Lucas's eyes, casting a shadow that darkened them to cobalt. "Scott hung on long enough to tell me about Max. He made me promise that I would find him."

"What about Max's mother?"

"Died of an overdose last winter." Lucas's lips twisted. "I promised Scott that I would take care of Max, but I had no idea he expected it would be a permanent arrangement until he asked for a piece of paper."

"I'm sorry." Erin couldn't imagine what he'd gone through. Max hadn't been the only one touched by the trauma of Scott's death.

"I'm sorry, too." Lucas's fists clenched at his sides. "I'm not sure what Scott's biggest mistake was. Getting mixed up with a bunch of cocaine dealers or giving me custody of his son."

God, help me find the right words to say.

"He knew you'd take good care of Max."

"Okay, *that* was his mistake," Lucas said bitterly. "You can tell I'm clueless when it comes to kids. I have no idea what to do when Max experiences one of those episodes. He doesn't respond to me when I talk to him. I can't distract him." He sighed. "It's like there's a wall between us. He can't see me. Or hear me. The only thing I can do is set him on my lap and hold him until he comes out of it."

The raw pain in his eyes propelled Erin across the

room. Before she thought it through, she took his hand and squeezed.

"It sounds to me like you know *exactly* what to do."

He glared down at her. "I'm not a real parent—I'm a phony. Max would be better off with someone who knows what they're doing. I'm totally winging it here."

Erin dared to smile. "From what I've heard, winging it is exactly what parents do."

Chapter Six

"I smell french fries."

Lucas glanced down at Max and saw his button nose quiver in delight.

He should have known better than to walk past the Cowboy Café at noon, when the tantalizing aroma of burgers and fries—Max's favorite food—permeated the air.

"Are you hungry? We'll go back to Grandma's house and rustle up some lunch." Lucas wasn't ready to see Erin again so soon. Not when he hadn't totally recovered from the conversation they'd had the night before.

Erin might be under the delusion that he had something to offer Max, but Lucas knew there would come a day when he disappointed the boy, too. The way he'd disappointed his parents. The way he disappointed everyone.

"Yup. French fries." Max repeated the words and flashed a confident smile, certain that Lucas would come through for him.

Trouble was, Lucas kept remembering that Lisette's freezer contained neat little stacks of plastic boxes filled with nutritional things like chicken soup and spinach lasagna.

"How about a grilled cheese—"

"Lucas!" The door of the Cowboy Café swung open and

his cousin Brooke bounded out, a sweet-faced toddler balanced on one hip. "I saw you through the window. Are you and Max coming in for lunch?"

Max's eyes lit up and Lucas figured a grilled cheese sandwich was no longer on the menu.

"We are now."

Brooke's blue eyes sparkled. "Macy Perry is with me and Gabe's son, A.J., but there's plenty of room at our table."

"Great." Just great.

As if Brooke were afraid he would change his mind, she linked an arm through his and tugged him toward the door. "Gabe has a meeting at the mine, so Macy and I decided to take A.J. out for lunch and make a day of it. What are you and Max up to?"

"I met with Bev, the real-estate agent, a few minutes ago."

"How did that go?"

"There isn't much for rent or sale right now." Unless Lucas counted the one place he *didn't* want. Unfortunately, his last resort was beginning to look like his only option.

"I'll ask around," Brooke offered.

"Thanks." With his free hand, Lucas caught Max lightly by the back of the collar as they stepped inside.

And Lucas fell through a crack in time.

The café looked exactly the same as it did the night he'd left town, from the straight-backed chairs, nicked and scarred from the heels of hundreds of cowboy boots, to the old-fashioned cash register perched on the counter.

"There's Macy. She's holding a table for us." Brooke angled toward the back of the café.

A low, guttural laugh came from the direction of the kitchen, stopping Lucas in his tracks. His head jerked around.

"Jerome Hicks is still—" *Alive?* "Around?"

Brooke wrangled A.J. into a booster chair next to a young girl who flashed a shy smile at him and Max. "Jerome *and* his brother, Gerald."

"Unbelievable."

"They're town icons," she said.

"Don't you mean historical landmarks?"

His cousin choked back a laugh. "I'm going to pretend I didn't hear that."

Lucas remembered the day Erin had hired the two brothers. Her mother had been in the hospital, forcing Erin to make a difficult decision and interview prospective cooks. That evening, she had laughingly told him that it felt more as if *she* were the one being interviewed.

Lucas had been indignant on her behalf. "You'll end up paying more if you hire both of them," he'd told her. "You're doing a great job. You don't need two stubborn, retired ranch cooks telling you how to run things when your mom isn't around."

"I do need them. But more than that, I think they might need the café," Erin had said simply.

"I get it. You're collecting strays again."

Erin had grinned but didn't deny it. The next day, Gerald and Jerome Hicks had taken over the kitchen of the Cowboy Café.

Max scrambled onto a chair and Lucas slid in beside him. A bottle of ketchup and mustard flanked the metal napkin holder like bookends, just the way he remembered. He ran his thumb over a set of initials etched in the corner of the table.

ST and LC.

The letters hit him like a spray of buckshot.

Susie Tansley and Lucas Clayton.

Clayton was too small. No matter how hard he tried to escape the past, there it was. Laughing in his face.

Someone might have linked his and Susie's initials, but they'd never been a couple. It had all been a lie, just like her pregnancy. He had a hunch it had been part of a coordinated effort by Susie and good old cousin Vincent to damage his reputation. The trouble was, that time it had actually worked.

For several weeks, Susie had followed him around, openly flirtatious and telling anyone who would listen that they were a couple.

Erin believed Lucas when he'd said that he wasn't cheating on her. She wanted to squelch the rumors once and for all by letting everyone know they had been secretly dating for the past six months, but Lucas wouldn't let her.

He'd dug in his heels and told Erin that anyone who really knew him would realize he wouldn't get involved with a girl as phony as Susie.

Maybe he wouldn't have been so stubborn if he'd known that his own mother would be one of the people who believed the worst.

He could still see the expression on Lisette's face when he'd walked into the kitchen after school and found her and Susie sitting at the kitchen table together.

Disappointment—not disbelief. As if he'd suddenly become the person his father had predicted he would be...

"Hey!" A menu waved in front of his face. "Earth to Lucas. Come in, Lucas."

"Are you always this sassy?" he growled, even though he was grateful that his cousin's teasing comment momentarily chased the shadows away.

"I'm the youngest. I can get away with it," Brooke said smugly. "Have you met Macy yet? Her mother, Darlene Perry, was the part-time secretary at Clayton Christian Church."

"I don't think so." Lucas aimed a polite smile at the young girl sitting next to Brooke and felt a ripple of shock. It was like looking at a miniature version of his cousin. Long blond hair. Hot-pink glasses framed eyes as blue as a summer sky.

"It's nice to meet you, Macy. I'm Lucas and this little guy is Max."

"Hi." The girl's wide smile coaxed a dimple out of hiding.

His gaze cut to Brooke and she shook her head in a subtle warning. So, he wasn't the first one to notice the resemblance.

Was that the reason he'd been hearing Macy's name come up in conversation over the past week? His mother had mentioned that Darlene Perry was terminally ill. He'd assumed everyone had taken the girl under their collective wing out of Christian duty.

But maybe it was because they suspected she was *family*.

"Hey, Kylie!" His cousin waved to someone behind him. "We need a few more menus."

One of the knots loosened inside of Lucas's chest.

Maybe Erin wasn't here—

"Can I take your order?"

She was here.

"Erin!" Without warning, Max clambered over Lucas and launched himself into her arms.

Erin recovered faster than the rest of them.

"Hey, cowboy." Her cheeks turned pink, but Lucas wasn't sure if it was from embarrassment or the fact that Max was clinging to her neck like a stuffed hanging monkey with Velcro hands, reducing the flow of oxygen to her brain. "What can I get you today?"

"French fries," Max said promptly.

"Coming right up." Without missing a beat, Erin shifted Max to her hip and pulled a note pad out of her apron pocket. "What would the rest of you like?"

Friendly but businesslike. And careful not to make eye contact with him.

Who could blame her, after the way he'd rejected her attempt to comfort him the night before.

She'd reached out to him and he had pulled away.

Over the years, Lucas hadn't let himself harbor regret, convinced that leaving Clayton after graduation had been the best decision. Not only for him, but for Erin.

Looking at her now, it occurred to him that maybe the move hadn't been as bold and daring as it seemed at the time.

Maybe he'd been exactly what Erin had accused him of the night he'd packed his bags.

A man who wasn't embracing the future, but rather running from the past.

The thought didn't sit well.

"Lucas?" The toe of Brooke's boot connected with his shin. "You haven't even opened the menu yet."

"A double hamburger, pickles, mustard and extra ketchup," he said automatically.

Brooke grinned up at Erin. "I guess he didn't need to look at a menu."

"I'm sure it hasn't changed, either," Lucas muttered. He realized how that sounded when Brooke's eyebrows shot up into her hairline.

And then he saw Erin's stricken expression.

Erin jotted down Lucas's order, careful to keep her smile in place.

She knew he'd spoken the words without thinking.

That was the trouble. In that simple statement, Lucas had revealed what he thought about the café.

It hadn't changed a bit.

He probably thought the same thing about her.

She still wore her hair in a ponytail. Preferred jeans and cotton shirts over dresses and high heels. No doubt Lucas looked at her in the same way he'd looked at the café and found both of them wanting.

She'd never attended college. Never experienced life outside of Clayton. She owned a café that catered to roughneck cowboys and locals who were more interested in food that "stuck to their ribs" rather than teased their palate.

After her mother passed away, Erin had thought about remodeling. Updating the menu. She'd come to the conclusion that her customers wouldn't want that. They didn't scoff at the familiar—they cherished it. Like it or not, the Cowboy

Café fit the tiny community like a favorite pair of boots. Not much to look at but comfortable. Reliable.

So instead of replacing the old display case and tables, Erin had bought a ramshackle place outside of town with plenty of room for the horses she planned to rescue.

It wasn't her original dream—Erin refused to let her gaze drift back to Lucas—but it was something to reach for.

"Erin." Dorothy Henry, proprietress of the Lucky Lady Inn, the local boarding house, waved her napkin to get Erin's attention as she made her way toward the kitchen. "The apple pie is delicious, as usual."

"Delicious. Simply delicious," sang the other two women at her table.

Erin paused to greet the trio of lively seniors who had been meeting at the café for lunch since she was a teenager. "I'll be sure to tell Arabella."

"I think we're due for another snowstorm," Edna Irving spoke up. "I've had a pain in my knee the past few days."

"Don't listen to her, honey. Edna always has a pain in her knee," Dorothy said.

Erin laughed with them, knowing it was expected.

"Excuse me, Erin." Someone hailed her from the table behind them. "I'd like a refill on my coffee."

Erin recognized the smoky voice without turning around. Katrina Clayton Watson, Arabella's mother, had drifted into town a few months ago after a ten-year absence. She'd moved in with Arabella, Jasmine and the triplets but Erin wasn't sure how her friend truly felt about the situation. Arabella had hinted that the relationship with her mother had always been strained but hoped her mother's return meant she wanted to start over.

"I'll be right back with a fresh pot, Kat," Erin promised.

She'd had a difficult time warming up to the woman, too. More than once, she'd heard Kat openly critique her daughter's parenting skills. She also made no attempt to hide her disapproval over Jasmine's upcoming wedding, and Erin had the feeling that Kat was jealous of the close relationship between Arabella and the younger woman.

Kat's gaze lit on Erin as she returned with the coffeepot. Something in the woman's pale green eyes always reminded Erin of a cat ready to pounce.

"You don't seem like your cheerful self today, dear." Kat tilted her head to the side, setting the faux rubies in her chandelier earring swinging like a pendulum. "Is something wrong?"

"No. Everything is fine." Erin might have gotten away with the claim if her hands hadn't been shaking. And she hadn't sloshed coffee over the side of the cup.

"Mmm." Kat made a point to blot up the spill with the corner of her napkin. "I thought Lucas had complained about something. You looked a little flustered when you left their table just now."

"Can I get you anything else besides a refill on your coffee?"

Kat wasn't so easily distracted. She glanced over at Lucas's table. "It appears that my nephew hasn't changed a bit, has he? Still as restless and brooding as ever, like a bronco trapped in a holding chute."

The tinkling laugh that followed the statement set Erin's teeth on edge. She would have moved on but it was obvious that Kat wasn't finished chatting yet.

The woman picked up a spoon and idly began to stir her coffee. "Arabella shooed me out of the house today so she and Jasmine can discuss the wedding plans. I told them I'd be willing to help but…" She shrugged. "They don't need me."

Knowing how sweet-tempered Arabella was, Erin doubted that she had "shooed" her mother out of the house.

"Trust me, Kat," she said quietly. "A girl always needs her mother."

To her astonishment, Kat reached out and patted her hand. "I was sorry to hear that Gloria passed away."

"Thank you—"

"Although to be honest, I'm surprised you didn't sell the café and get out of Clayton while you had the chance."

Erin didn't hold that against her. In all fairness, a lot of people had been surprised when she'd stayed on.

Herself included.

"Clayton is my home. I can't imagine living anywhere else."

"How sweet." Kat bared her teeth in a smile. "Some people are so…easy to please."

Two insults in the space of five minutes.

Help, Lord.

Rescue came a second later in the form of a familiar bellow from the kitchen.

"Order up!"

"Please excuse me, Kat."

"Of course, of course." Kat took a delicate sip from her coffee cup and dismissed Erin with a casual wave. "I wouldn't want to keep you from your work."

That's exactly what she'd been doing, but Erin smiled. And then she walked back to the kitchen and hugged Jerome, who began to sputter and spit like grease on a griddle. "Hey now! What's all this?"

"This—" Erin straightened the frayed collar of the cook's chambray shirt. "—is about remembering that God answers our prayers."

Jerome snorted. "Was there any doubt?"

Erin pressed a kiss against the grizzled cheek. "No. Not really. But it's always good to be reminded."

Brooke waited until Erin was out of earshot before leveling both barrels at Lucas. "Okay, what was that about?"

It was about him trying not to let Erin know how much

she affected him, that's what it was about. But Lucas couldn't tell Brooke that. She was engaged to Gabe Wesson, caught up in the whole notion of happily-ever-after.

"I didn't mean to insult Erin," Lucas muttered. "I think this town brings out the worst in me."

He was surprised he said the words out loud. Even more surprised when Brooke nodded as if she understood.

She slid a look at Macy, who was entertaining the boys with a herd of tiny plastic horses she'd emptied out of a bright pink purse.

"At first I hated the thought of coming back, too," she said in a low voice, her expression serious. "But now I thank God that Grandpa George drew up that will—"

"And dangled a large sum of money and all that land in front of everyone like a carrot," Lucas interrupted.

To his surprise, Brooke didn't scold him for being cynical.

"Everyone came back to Clayton for different reasons. Just like we all stayed away for different reasons," she said softly. "All I remembered were the bad things that happened. I blamed myself for Lucy's death. Losing my dad in the accident and then Mom a few years later…it cast a shadow over everything."

Lucas shifted his weight in the chair, not sure what to say. Brooke's little sister, Lucy, drowned in a tragic accident when they were kids, but he'd had no idea she blamed herself. His cousin had been a child herself at the time.

And caught up in his own grief over his father's death, Lucas had sometimes forgotten that the accident had also claimed the life of his uncle, George Jr. The brothers' deaths rocked the foundation of both families. The pain that should have bonded them had sent the cousins scattering as soon as they were old enough to leave.

"That's why I don't look back. It's better that way."

"I used to think so, too," Brooke admitted softly. "But then I realized I was also closing the door on the good things. Reverend West said that Grandpa changed when he found out he was dying. He made things right with God and he wanted to make things right between us."

Too little, too late, Lucas wanted to argue. Some things were so damaged, they were beyond fixing.

Lucas found his gaze drifting back to Erin.

Even if a man wanted to.

"Me and Zach and Viv, we all had our reasons for coming back and maybe they weren't so noble in the beginning," Brooke admitted. "But now it's less about getting something and more about discovering what we already *have*. Over the past six months, I've fallen head over heels in love."

Brooke saw his expression and chuckled. "Not only with Gabe. With the town…and the people." She slipped her arm around Macy's shoulders. "Maybe you will, too, Lucas."

"If I remember correctly, falling in love wasn't listed in the terms of the will," Lucas said drily.

"Not in the will, no," Brooke agreed. "But you never know what *God* has planned."

Chapter Seven

"The closed sign is in the window. We are officially off duty and my feet are officially killing me." Kylie was already untying her apron as she breezed into the kitchen. "I think everyone in Clayton stopped by today for a cup of coffee and one of Arabella's cinnamon rolls."

Not everyone, Erin almost said. She hadn't seen Lucas for several days.

Not that she'd been looking for him.

"When she stops in tomorrow, tell her we have orders coming in for her Christmas tea cakes." Erin added a pumpkin pie to the picnic basket on the counter.

"That looks good." Kylie took a peek inside the wicker container. "Are you giving out samples?"

"Not this time." Erin smiled. "Reverend West called early this morning and asked if I'd put together a meal on behalf of the Church Care Committee. I'm going to drop it off at the Halversons on my way home tonight."

Kylie stripped off her apron and hung it on a hook near the sink. "I thought Archie and Lorraine were selling the house and moving down south."

"I thought so, too, but Lorraine didn't bounce back right away from her last treatment of chemo. Maybe they decided to wait until after Christmas." Erin tied a red satin bow around the handles of the basket. The elderly couple were not only regulars at the café, they happened to be her closest neighbors. Erin hoped the added touch would brighten their day, especially if Lorraine wasn't feeling well.

"Let me know if there's anything I can do," Kylie offered.

"Mmm." Erin tilted her head. "Between waitressing, planning Jasmine and Cade's wedding and spending time with a certain deputy sheriff?" she teased.

"Hey, I learned to multitask from the best," her friend shot back.

"Who would that be?"

"I wonder." Kylie rolled her eyes as Erin turned off the overhead light and they made their way to the front of the café.

As they reached the door, a dark figure loomed in front of the glass, blocking the glow of the streetlamp.

Vincent?

Erin's heart skipped a beat until she recognized Zach Clayton's ruggedly handsome features.

"It looks like you get a police escort home."

Kylie laughed. "He's off duty. We're going to Darlene's house to help Macy decorate their Christmas tree this evening."

"That sounds like fun."

"It will be. We promised her that we would make this Christmas extra special for Macy."

There was no need to ask why. Everyone hoped she would be able to spend the holiday with her daughter, but Darlene's health continued to decline rapidly.

"Good evening, ladies." Zach's smile encompassed both of them but the light in his eyes was for Kylie alone.

After Erin locked the door, he stepped forward and gave the knob a twist to make sure it was secure for the night.

"I thought you were off duty," she teased him.

"Sorry." Zach shrugged. "Habit."

"That's what he says when I accuse him of keeping me under surveillance." Kylie heaved a long-suffering sigh but Erin could tell she didn't mind the attention.

And Zach didn't appear the least bit guilty. "You better get used to it," he murmured. "I plan to keep an eye on you for the rest of my life."

Kylie stood on her tiptoes and pressed a kiss against his rugged jaw. "Promise?"

The look that passed between the couple was warm enough to melt the snow on the ground.

Erin coughed. "Ah, well...good night, you two."

Kylie tore her gaze away from her fiancé and gave Erin a sheepish smile. "See you tomorrow."

"Give Macy a hug for me."

"Sure thing."

Zach's arm went around Kylie's waist and he tucked her against his side as they walked to his vehicle.

Erin tried not to feel envious. She'd never thought Vincent was good enough for Kylie and had prayed often that God would somehow reveal his true character.

Mr. Jones, Kylie's father, had been swindled by Vincent's grandfather after he'd partnered with him in a business deal. When Kylie dropped out of college and returned to Clayton to help her family, Vincent had hinted that if she'd agree to marry him, her family would no longer struggle financially. Kylie had tried to convince herself that she could learn to love Vincent, but when she'd caught him kissing another woman on their wedding day, she realized she couldn't spend the rest of her life with him.

Kylie had been cautious about Zach Clayton at first, but after watching them interact, Erin knew without a doubt that her friend and the handsome deputy were meant to be together.

She, however, had packed dreams of romance away a long

time ago. The cowboys who frequented the café flirted with her, and once in a while one of them would gather the courage to ask her out. Erin always declined, using the excuse that she didn't have time to go out, her schedule was too crowded.

And her heart was too crowded with memories of Lucas Clayton. They took up so much space, Erin doubted there was room for anyone else.

It was dark by the time she pulled up to the log home, but lights glowed in the windows. Retrieving the wicker hamper from the backseat, she lugged it up the shoveled walkway to the front door.

The front door that was usually bedecked with an evergreen wreath this time of year.

A frown pleated Erin's forehead. She hoped that didn't mean that Mrs. Halverson's health had taken a turn for the worse. Her husband had retired the year before and the couple was anxious to relocate to Florida to be closer to their daughter.

Because, unlike Lucas Clayton, there were people who *wanted* to be near family.

Erin made a fist inside of her mitten and rapped on the door.

"Merry—" The rest of the greeting died in her throat when the door swung open.

Lucas stood on the other side.

"It's you." His expression changed from irritation to relief. Before Erin could blink, Lucas had yanked her inside the cabin. "I need your help."

"I'm supposed to deliver a meal to the Halversons."

Now it was Lucas's turn to frown. "That's going to be a long drive. They left for Florida yesterday."

Had she misunderstood Reverend West's message? When he'd asked her to deliver the meal to her neighbors, Erin had assumed he'd been talking about the Halversons, but it was possible he had meant the Morgan family, who lived a few miles farther to the north.

"Something smells good." Lucas reached for the basket.

Erin took a step back and tightened her grip on the basket.

"This isn't for you. I'm on the Church Care Committee and we deliver meals to people who are sick. Or new—" To the community.

Oh. No.

It was a distinct possibility that Reverend West might consider Lucas Clayton a newcomer.

"I'm sick of peanut butter and jelly sandwiches—that has to count," Lucas said. "You can leave but there's no way I'm letting you take that basket with you."

Erin was dimly aware of Lucas wrestling the picnic basket from fingers that had suddenly gone numb.

"I didn't know you'd moved in." *Next door. To me.*

"Everything happened pretty fast." Lucas strode across the room with his prize, set it on the counter and lifted the lid.

"The condo the Halversons bought in Florida was completely furnished, so they took their personal possessions and left the rest. The real-estate agent told me they wanted to settle into their new place before Christmas."

Erin began to inch toward the door and her foot landed on something hard. A siren went off. She looked down and saw a plastic police car at her feet, tiny red-and-blue lights blinking.

For the first time, she noticed the mountain of toys heaped in the center of the rug. It wasn't the end-of-the-day roundup, either. Most of the toys looked to be in their original packaging.

Lucas followed her gaze. "Arabella insisted that Max spend the evening with her and the triplets so I would have time to wrap these gifts. The way it's been going, I'm tempted to call and tell her not to bother bringing him back until tomorrow."

"Max isn't here?" Erin tried not to let her disappointment show. She didn't know why the little boy had taken what Gerald Hicks would have called "a shine" to her, but the feeling was mutual. Max was adorable.

"This stew is still hot." Lucas looked ready to swoon. Maybe he hadn't been exaggerating when he said he'd been living on peanut butter and jelly sandwiches.

Erin refused to let herself feel sorry for him. Or smile. "You have to share it with Max."

Lucas looked up and somehow his blue eyes looked even bluer. "Max is eating supper with Arabella and Jonathan. And the—" he winced as if he had a difficult time even saying the word. "—triplets."

"Then I guess it's all yours."

Lucas met her eyes. "Or I could share it with you."

Had he just invited her to stay for dinner?

Erin fumbled with a button on her coat. "I don't think—"

"And you could help me wrap these presents before Max gets home."

So that was it. Lucas wanted her help, not her company.

"I really should get home." She wanted to stay. "Winston is waiting for his daily walk."

"Winston doesn't walk," Lucas said bluntly. "I can tell."

Erin lifted her chin. "Are you hinting that my dog is overweight?"

"No. As a veterinarian, I'm giving you my professional opinion. Your dog *is* overweight." Lucas peered into the basket again. "If you stay, I'll throw in a piece of pumpkin pie."

Erin couldn't help it. She laughed. "You're terrible."

"And you're a member of the Church Care Committee, right?" He arched a golden eyebrow.

"Yes."

"So start caring," he retorted.

"Fine. I'll help you wrap Max's presents."

"And I'll make dinner." The Clayton dimple made an appearance.

It was hard—no, impossible—to keep her emotions in check when Lucas was standing three feet away from her with that roguish smile on his face. And a piece of tape stuck in his hair.

With his guard down, he looked more like the Lucas she remembered from high school. The young man who'd shared his thoughts and dreams, vented his grief and frustration.

The Lucas Clayton who had shared his heart and stolen hers in the process.

The worst part?

Erin wasn't sure she wanted it back.

After the thoughtless comment he'd made in the café, Lucas hadn't expected Erin to speak to him again, let alone show up at his door. But now that she was here, he wasn't about to let her get away.

When Arabella arrived to pick up Max, she'd left a large sack of toys along with whispered instructions to wrap them before they got back. She'd even put tape and several tubes of wrapping paper adorned with skating penguins in the bag with the toys.

He'd used up half the tape in his first attempt and somehow ended up with a misshapen package that looked as if it had been run over by a herd of wild mustangs.

Erin shook her head and the movement set her ponytail into motion. "It looks like you bought out the entire store."

"What you are looking at is a coordinated effort by my meddling cousins and their significant others to make sure that Max has a decent Christmas."

"That's sweet."

Sweet? To Lucas, it only proved his family wasn't convinced he had this whole "dad thing" down yet. He might be upset—if it wasn't the truth.

Every day—no, every hour—he was hit with the magnitude of his decision to adopt Max. He had no idea how Arabella coped with being a single parent, to *triplets* no less, and yet she somehow managed to juggle a home-based business and family while adding him and Max to the mix.

Lucas had put in a full day administering vaccinations at one of the nearby ranches and then went to pick up Max from Brooke's house. On his way home, Arabella had called his cell phone and informed him that she wanted Max for the evening.

He didn't know whether to be relieved or offended by his family's intervention.

"What time do you expect Max back?" Erin was asking.

Lucas glanced at his watch. "Fifteen minutes ago."

Her golden-brown eyes widened. "Then I better start wrapping." She plopped down on the rug and began to separate the toys into piles.

Lucas decided the safest place to be at the moment was somewhere Erin wasn't. Did she realize what an enchanting picture she made sitting cross-legged in front of the fire, her forehead puckered in concentration?

He took his time searching the cupboard for dishes until a ripple of laughter washed over him, melting his defenses like a warm Chinook wind coming down from the mountains.

"What's so funny?"

"I think you're right about everyone chipping in." Erin held up the police car. "This one has to be from Zach...and Jack must have picked out the action hero on the four-wheeler."

Maybe setting the table could wait. Lucas wandered over and lowered himself onto the rug beside her. He picked up a tiny plastic grocery basket filled with fake food. "Vivienne?"

Out of all the cousins, Vivienne's return had been the most surprising. Years ago she had shed her small-town roots along with her cowboy boots and studied to be a gourmet chef, eventually settling in New York City. As far from Clayton as Venus is from Mars.

Erin's eyes sparkled. "Bingo."

Something pink snagged his attention. Lucas leaned closer to investigate and unearthed a tea set. He hadn't known there were so many different shades of pink in the world. "Zach always did have a twisted sense of humor."

"I don't think it was Zach." Erin grinned. "My guess is that Arabella's triplets want to have something to play with other than trucks when they visit."

Erin said the words as if his family dropping by for a visit would be a natural occurrence now that he was back in Clayton.

Lucas had expected his cousins would feel the same way he did about Grandpa George sentencing them to a year in Clayton. They would serve their time, then pack up and move on.

From what he'd witnessed, the opposite was true. His cousins weren't simply surviving—they appeared to be thriving.

If Lucas didn't know better, he'd think there was something in the water.

"Aww, look at this." Erin scooped up a teddy bear and pressed it against her cheek. "Macy must have picked it out. She loves stuffed animals."

Knowing how Lucas had reacted over the tea set, Erin waited for a biting comment while she studied the adorable toy. The bear's fur was soft as down and a patchwork heart had been stitched on its chest.

She glanced up and was amazed to see a wave of color creeping up his neck and surging over the blade of his jaw.

"It's from me." Lucas reached over and plucked it out of her hand. "I thought that maybe having something to sleep with would…"

"Stop the nightmares," she finished.

"It's worth a try."

The casual shrug that accompanied the words didn't fool Erin for a minute.

His family had bought gifts they thought would entertain a four-year-old boy. Lucas had picked out something he thought that Max *needed*. Whether or not Lucas was ready to admit it, he wasn't simply Max's guardian, a role he had taken on with the stroke of a pen. Max had grabbed hold of his heart.

"It's a great idea," Erin said softly.

"You think so?" The flash of vulnerability in Lucas's eyes was further proof he wasn't as impervious to human emotions as he pretended to be. "All this stuff is so…new."

"New can be good." Erin immediately regretted the words. "Never mind. I know what you're thinking," she added in a rush. "That statement is funny coming from someone who never left Clayton and who works in the same place she did in high school and still wears her hair in a ponytail…"

She ran out of breath. Because Lucas had suddenly shifted his weight, shrinking the distance between them.

His expression underwent a subtle change as he reached out and gave Erin's glossy ponytail a gentle tug.

"That's not what I was thinking."

Chapter Eight

Erin's heart stopped as Lucas's fingers continued their exploration, grazing a path down the curve of her jaw…

"Lucas, I'm back…guess what!" The door burst open and Max charged in, Jonathan Turner a step behind him.

Erin vaulted to her feet, sure that her face matched the color of her hair.

Max spotted her and changed direction. "Erin's here!" He dashed around the presents she and Lucas had just finished wrapping and hugged her.

"Sorry we're late," Jonathan said. Unlike Max, he didn't appear the least bit surprised to discover Erin in Lucas's living room. "We had an errand to run."

As far as Erin was concerned, Jonathan's timing had been perfect.

Erin didn't know the doctor very well, but over the past few months he had made an impression on the citizens of Clayton. And Arabella.

Jonathan had shown up in town a few months earlier, searching for the eighteen-year-old niece he hadn't known existed. That girl turned out to be Jasmine Turner, an at-risk teenager Arabella had taken into her home and who soon would be marrying Cade Clayton. Jonathan had wanted to meet his late brother's child and convince her to return to Denver, where he practiced, but had ended up staying in Clayton instead.

Erin knew the man had been vocal in his opinion that Jasmine not get married so young, but she'd eventually won him over. And Arabella had won his heart.

"Presents," Max breathed, finally noticing the mound of gifts they hadn't had time to hide. "Jessie an' Jamie an' Julie gots presents under their tree."

"Right. A tree," Lucas murmured.

"Ours is bigger." Max hopped up and down, his boots depositing clumps of snow onto the rug.

"Ours?" Lucas's eyebrows dipped together.

Max nodded vigorously. "A'bella said we have a house now so we needa tree."

"Is that what Arabella said?" Lucas looked at Jonathan for confirmation.

The doctor shrugged. "Hey, I'm just the chauffeur. And the tree delivery guy."

"You brought it *with* you?" Lucas stared at Jonathan.

"That's right." Jonathan stared right back.

Max appeared unaware of the subtle undercurrents in the room. He stood patiently while Erin knelt down and unzipped his coat. "We gotta decorate it. Like Erin's tree."

Erin didn't have time to feel flattered.

"No tree," Lucas said under his breath, "is going to look like Erin's tree."

Not fair! Erin thought.

Since Jonathan wasn't looking her way, she crossed her eyes and made a face at Lucas.

Leave it to Erin to lighten the moment.

She had always been good at diffusing volatile situations. Lucas remembered there'd been a lot of those in the eight months they'd dated.

But you aren't dating anymore, Lucas reminded himself sternly.

So why had he touched her? No, why had he almost *kissed* her?

He focused his attention on Max, who'd detached himself from Erin's side and flopped on the floor, staring at the presents as if he'd never seen such a bounty.

It struck Lucas that given Max's home environment most likely he hadn't.

Discouragement rolled through him. There were so many things Max needed. How did a guy even begin to fill those holes?

And now he had to disappoint Max again.

"We can bring the tree in but I'm afraid we won't be able to decorate it, buddy," Lucas said. "I don't have any ornaments or lights."

Jonathan cleared his throat. "As a matter of fact, you do."

"A'bella had extra," Max chimed in.

Good old cousin Arabella, Lucas thought, as he left Max in Erin's capable hands and followed Jonathan out the door.

Lucas stopped dead in his tracks, tracing the dark shape of a mammoth tree strapped to the top of Arabella's vehicle. "You've got to be kidding."

"Talk to Max." Jonathan flashed what could only be described as a wicked smile. "He picked it out."

"Maybe I should talk to Arabella," Lucas muttered.

Jonathan's smile faded. "Your family cares about you, Lucas. They want to help. My advice? Let them."

That was easier said than done. After severing ties with Clayton, Lucas had gotten adept at avoiding commitment. He might be alone at the end of the day, but there was no one to disappoint, either.

Jonathan retrieved a box of ornaments from the backseat while Lucas untied the tree. The two men dragged it up to the cabin. Once they got it inside, Jonathan said goodbye and fled.

The traitor.

Lucas had faced angry cattle, crabby horses and even the occasional bull-headed rancher, but a fragrant evergreen in the middle of the living room had him at a loss.

Max came to his rescue. "You should put it over there." He pointed to the corner near the window.

Erin nodded. "That's a great idea, Max. Then I can see the lights when I drive home at night."

Erin and Lucas wrestled it into place while Max pulled a string of lights from the box of decorations.

"These go on first." He shook them at Lucas, who bore the full weight of the tree against his shoulder.

Lucas grunted. "Not yet, buddy."

"Ah…do you have a tree stand?" Erin's eyes twinkled at him between a gap in the fragrant branches. "Not that you're not doing a great job, but you might get tired of holding it in place for the next two weeks."

Max giggled.

"Knowing Arabella, I'm sure we do," Lucas said drily.

"I'll be right back." Erin returned a moment later holding the tree stand up like a trophy. "You were right."

Lucas knelt down to secure the tree in the stand. Surrounded by the sweet scent of the needles, he tried to remember the last time he'd put up a Christmas tree.

He didn't have to go back further than his freshman year of high school.

"Lucas, you have to help me put up the tree," his mother had said, taking on the wounded expression that never failed to open a floodgate of guilt. *"You're the man of the house now."*

Seven little words that struck a match against the anger simmering below the surface of his emotions.

"I'm tired of you saying that," he'd shouted. *"I'm not the*

man of the house. I'm not Dad. I'm not going to be a doctor. I'm not going to church and pretend that I buy all the stuff the pastor preaches about peace and goodwill to men, either."

He'd stormed out of the house and slept in his truck that night.

Merry Christmas.

Lucas hadn't celebrated Christmas for years, but he had to change that. For Max's sake, he had to do this right.

Lucas slid out from under the tree just in time to see Erin reaching for her coat.

Max rushed to her side. "Where ya goin', Erin?"

"I have to go home now, sweetheart. It's getting late."

Max tugged on her sleeve, his expression earnest. "But you gotta help us put on the lights. And the oranments."

Erin smiled but didn't correct him. "I think that's something you and Lucas should do together."

"But we *want* you to stay, don't we, Lucas?" Max looked to him for confirmation.

Maybe it was a mistake to spend time with Erin. Maybe her smile fanned a flame that had never quite burned all the way out. Maybe he was being a nostalgic idiot...

But he wanted her to stay.

"I promised you dinner, remember?"

Erin caught her lower lip between her teeth, an outward sign of the inward battle he'd fought and lost a split-second ago.

"We'll let you put the star on top." Max was smart enough to know when someone was teetering on the edge of a decision. "Jessie says that's the most important job."

Lucas was impressed with the way Max operated. Especially when Erin hugged the boy and brushed a kiss against his downy head. "In that case," she whispered, "I'd love to stay."

An internal alarm began to ring, pushing Lucas into gear. He tore his gaze away from Erin. "How about I string the lights while you two find out what else Arabella thought we needed?"

"Okay. Come on, Erin." Max dropped to his knees beside the box and began to sift through the contents.

Lucas could hear their soft giggles as he threaded the lights through the branches.

They formed an assembly line of sorts. Max took the ornaments from the boxes and brought them to Erin, who handed them to Lucas to hang on the tree.

Max kept up a cheerful, rambling monologue of the evening spent with the Arabella and the triplets, detailing everything from the chicken and mashed potatoes they'd eaten for dinner to driving to Jones Feed and Supply to pick out a tree.

"This is a gigantic one!"

"That one doesn't go on the tree," Lucas heard Erin whisper.

Why had she whispered?

Lucas glanced down. Standing on a kitchen chair provided him an aerial view of the comical goings-on below. And right now he wished he had a camera to capture the expression on Erin's face while Max dangled an enormous ball covered in plastic mistletoe two inches from her nose.

"How come?" Max wanted to know. "It was in the box of dec'rations."

"You hang this one in a doorway."

"Why?" he asked in confusion.

"Because it's mistletoe."

Max's face brightened and Lucas knew what he was thinking. He'd been a boy once upon a time.

"Not a missile," he said swiftly. "Mistle*toe*."

Max's disappointment was palpable as he studied the prickly ball of artificial greens. "Then what's it for?"

Lucas raised a brow at Erin, whose blush continued to deepen with every innocent question.

"Just to look…pretty. See the cute red bow tied on the top? It's meant to enjoy."

Max looked as if he'd enjoy pitching it across the room more than hanging it above a doorway, but he handed it to Erin.

Out of the corner of his eye, Lucas saw her discreetly tuck it back into the box.

If only he could put aside memories of kissing Erin that easily.

"I think we're done." Erin arranged the last present under the tree and stepped back to admire it.

"And I think someone is…" Lucas stifled a yawn. "Tired."

Erin grinned. "I think so, too."

"I meant him." Lucas nodded at the sofa, where Max had curled up with his blanket while they straightened up the living room. "Time for bed, buddy."

Max didn't even protest when Lucas picked him up and draped him over his broad shoulder.

"Erin, too," Max murmured.

Erin didn't know how much more she could take. The last two hours had been…a gift.

Her sides hurt from laughing at Max's antics and her heart was…well, it was *full*. That's the only way she could describe it.

The tree shimmered in the corner, the lower branches—the only ones Max could reach—drooping from the weight of the ornaments. The trunk was a little crooked. Some of the lights blinked and some of them didn't.

Erin thought it was perfect.

She followed Lucas up the stairs to the loft. While he took Max into the bathroom to brush his teeth and change into his pajamas, Erin turned back the covers.

The bedroom was small but cozy, with knotty pine paneling and a wool trapper's blanket decorating one wall. The twin bed had been handcrafted from peeled logs and Lucas's battered Stetson hung on the bedpost.

Max's favorite blanket, folded neatly, crowned the pillow.

A half smile touched Erin's lips.

Lucas might think he wasn't equipped to take care of a small child, but his actions said something else.

He had been awkwardly sweet with Max while they decorated the tree. Patiently answering his questions. Whistling along with the Christmas carols on the radio. And after the last ornament was in place, Lucas had held Max up so he could help her put the star on top of the tree.

It hadn't escaped Erin's notice that Max absorbed any amount of attention like a desert flower soaked up the rain. The boy needed a stable home. Parents who loved him—and each other.

Erin closed her eyes, reliving the gentle glide of Lucas's hand through her hair.

"I thought only horses slept standing up."

Erin's eyes snapped open as Lucas sauntered back into the room, a drowsy Max cradled in his arms.

"I must be tired, too." Erin decided that part was safe to admit.

Downstairs, Lucas's cell phone began to ring.

"That's work." He shook his head. "I'm on call tonight."

"Go ahead and answer it," Erin said, knowing an after-hours call could mean anything from a simple question to an outright emergency. "I'll finish tucking Max into bed."

"Thanks." Lucas shot a grateful look over his shoulder as he jogged out the door.

Erin pulled the covers up to Max's shoulders and watched his eyelids drift shut, his lips pursed in a smile.

She didn't have to close her eyes to imagine her and Lucas as a team. The three of them—a family.

Erin padded down the stairs and heard Lucas talking on the phone. She hesitated, not wanting to intrude on his conversation but it was difficult in the great room, with no walls between them for privacy.

"Everything is great so far, Bev," Lucas was saying. "No, that shouldn't be a problem but try to give me a little advance notice if you book a house showing. My work schedule is kind of crazy…okay, thanks for calling."

Erin's vision blurred even as everything became clear.

"Max is already asleep." She fought to keep her voice steady as she collected her purse and coat.

Lucas frowned. "You're leaving?"

"I have to take care of the animals."

He beat her to the door and held it open. "Thanks for helping out tonight. It meant a lot to Max."

Did it mean anything to you?

Erin didn't ask the question, though, because she already knew the answer.

Lucas hadn't bought the cabin from the Halversons, he'd *rented* it.

Because he had no intention of staying in Clayton.

Chapter Nine

Returning to Clayton had been difficult. Avoiding it was proving downright impossible.

Lucas would have thought that getting a place on the outskirts of town and working as a large animal vet would have taken him outside the city limits more often than in, but his family apparently had other ideas.

As Lucas parked the truck, he saw Mei's face framed in the window of one of the cottages located on the property of their childhood home. By the time he released Max from the booster seat, his sister was waiting for them at the door. At her side, stood an enormous dog with shaggy white fur.

"Don't worry about Moose," she called out. "He's as gentle as a lamb."

Lucas shook his head as Max grabbed his hand. "And as big as a Shetland pony."

Mei grinned. "That, too."

"I'm surprised Mom agreed to let you keep him. She's pretty fussy about these cottages."

"Moose won her over—and Mom's dog, Albert, too," Mei said. "He's just that kind of guy."

"I see that."

Max, who'd been clinging to him as they approached

the door, giggled in delight as Moose's pink tongue swiped his chin.

Lucas wrapped an arm around his sister's shoulders and pulled her against him in a quick hug. She clung to him for a moment.

"Thanks for stopping by, Lucas."

He lifted a brow. "You sent me three texts and left two voice-mail messages. I didn't think I had a choice."

His sister smiled sweetly. "You always have a choice. Fortunately, you made the right one."

Given the fact that Mei wouldn't tell him *why* she wanted him to stop by after work, Lucas decided he would be the judge of that.

"You gotta tree!" Max shouted as they followed her inside. "So do me an' Lucas."

"I heard about that." The knowing look Mei slanted in his direction told Lucas that he'd been the topic of conversation at someone's dinner table. Probably Arabella's. He should have been used to it by now. "Would anyone like a cup of hot chocolate?"

"I do!" Max peeled off his coat and dashed across the room to admire the tree, Moose at his heels.

"I'll get us each a cup." Mei nodded toward a chair at the kitchen table. "You. Sit."

Lucas got the feeling this wasn't going to be a quick visit.

"What's up, sis?" he asked bluntly.

"You don't have to look so suspicious. I just need a favor. A *small* one."

"Sure." Lucas pushed the word out, a little afraid of what a favor from one of his family members might involve. Not that he was in a position to protest. Several times over the past week, his sister had taken care of Max. Hopefully, it was something simple. Like hanging a picture on the wall. Or a minor car repair...

"I'm supposed to take Macy out to Erin's tomorrow afternoon to see the foal, but Jasmine and Cade have a premarital counseling session with Reverend West," Mei explained. "They asked Jack and I to go with them. I thought maybe you could take Macy and Max in my place. Max talks about Erin a lot, so I thought he might enjoy spending some time out at her place, too."

Lucas ignored the question in Mei's voice. No way was he going there.

"Tomorrow afternoon?" he repeated, only to gain more time. Before he said no.

"The whole family is invited to Arabella's for dinner after church, so it would be after that."

Lucas had a sneaking suspicion that he and Max were included in that invitation. But church? He hadn't stepped foot in the door of Clayton Christian Church since his father's funeral.

Mei topped each cup with a handful of miniature marshmallows. "Do you already have plans?"

Plans to avoid Erin, yes.

"Actually…" He hesitated, not sure how he could explain why spending time with Erin wasn't a good idea without bringing up the past—and the fact they had one.

When they'd decorated the tree with Max, Erin had seemed at ease. Patient with Max. Teasing Lucas about the way he handled the ornaments as if they were grenades that were about to explode in his hands. Lucas had forgotten how much he had always enjoyed her company.

As they got Max ready for bed, her presence seemed so right in his home. In his life. Almost as if the years they'd been apart had never existed. Her abrupt departure had taken him by surprise.

Lucas had come to the conclusion it was better this way. The more time spent in Erin's company, the greater the possibility that Max would become too attached to her.

And so would he.

But he set his misgivings aside in the face of Mei's obvious disappointment.

"I suppose I could."

A smile lit his sister's onyx eyes. "Thanks, Lucas. I really appreciate it. Christmas Eve is right around the corner and everyone is so busy, but I didn't want to let Jasmine and Cade down. Or Macy, for that matter," she added.

Lucas thought about the little girl with the bright smile. "How is Macy's mother doing?"

"Not good at all but we're doing everything we can to help Macy get through it."

"We" meaning the community? Or the Clayton family?

"She had lunch with Brooke at the café the other day," Lucas said slowly.

Mei nodded. "Brooke promised Darlene that she and Gabe would adopt Macy."

"Brooke? She's only twenty-three years old."

"She and Macy have gotten really close over the past few months," Mei said in their younger cousin's defense. "And Brooke might be young, but she's great with kids. So is Gabe Wesson, her fiancé. You should see him with A.J. He's a great dad."

"I'm sure that's true, but wouldn't it be better if Macy is adopted by family?"

Mei's expression clouded.

"What?"

"She...might be. Adopted by family, I mean" came the quiet response.

The air emptied out of Lucas's lungs. "I guess I shouldn't be surprised that someone in Samuel's family could turn their back on their own child," he muttered.

His sister remained silent.

"Mei?" Lucas regretted the sharpness of his tone when Max looked up.

Mei flashed him a warning look and took one of the cups

of hot chocolate over to Max, who'd discovered the carousel music box on the coffee table. "It's hot, sweetie, so take little sips," she said.

Lucas drummed his finger against the table, waiting for Mei as she walked over to the stove and poured two more cups. He had the distinct impression she was stalling.

When she sat back at the table, he found out why.

"This time it might not be one of Samuel's clan."

Lucas could only stare at her. "What are you talking about?"

"Mom…she thinks that Dad might have had an affair with Darlene Perry, Macy's mother, ten years ago."

Dad? Their dad?

"That's crazy," Lucas snapped.

"I thought so, too. At first." Mei took a deep breath. "But she found a note in his pocket after Dad and Uncle George were killed. It had Darlene's name and address written on it. And the word baby."

"That doesn't mean anything." Lucas couldn't believe she was actually willing to explore the idea. "Dad was involved in all kinds of charity work at the church."

"I know." Mei caught her lower lip between her teeth. "But a few weeks ago, Mom confided in me…told me that it wouldn't have been the first time Dad was unfaithful. He'd had affairs before. I remember them arguing at night after we'd gone to bed and Mom always seemed so distant."

Lucas remembered, too, but he'd assumed that he was the cause of the tension in the household.

He flattened his palms against the edge of the table, trying to absorb the impact of what he'd just heard.

Their father, always quick to point out the flaws in others, may have had an affair. And a child out of wedlock.

Vern Clayton's reputation had meant everything to him. How many times had Lucas heard the question "What will people think?" cross his father's lips?

So many that Lucas had eventually stopped caring.

But as difficult as it was to believe his father had broken his vows more than once and gotten involved with Darlene Perry, Lucas couldn't imagine his uncle, George Jr., straying from his marriage vows, either. He and Aunt Marion had always seemed happy together.

But Brooke must have her suspicions if she'd agreed to take Macy in.

"Did anyone ask Darlene? I mean, this would be—" he hesitated, not wanting to sound insensitive to the woman's failing health "—the time to be honest if Macy is a...Clayton."

"I don't know what to think, but I feel bad that Mom carried this burden alone for so many years," Mei said softly. "It helped me understand why she's been so distant. Mom must have been blaming herself."

"And here all this time I thought she blamed me."

Mei saw right through his wry attempt at humor. "Mom's changed, Lucas. She wants things to be different."

"You can't change the past."

"No, but you can learn from it." Mei reached across the table and took his hand. "I'm sorry, Lucas. I didn't mean to drop the news on you like this, but you've been so busy since you came back. We haven't had much time to talk."

As usual, his sister was cutting him way too much slack.

Since his return, Lucas had deliberately tried to keep his family at arm's length, telling himself that he didn't want to get caught up in all the drama surrounding George Sr.'s will. He'd let phone calls go to voice mail and used his new job as an excuse to turn down dinner invitations.

"Yeah, well, I'm not used to talking," Lucas said. "At least not to people, anyway. The animals I work with don't demand much."

Mei smiled. "You better brush up on your skills before tomorrow then, brother."

"Why?"

"The dinner at Arabella's?"

Lucas's eyes narrowed. "What about it?"

"It's a welcome home party," Mei whispered, as if she were afraid someone would overhear them. "For *you*."

"Be patient, Winston. I'm almost finished," Erin scolded as her dog turned three circles and flopped down in the straw with a long-suffering sigh. She deposited a scoop of grain into Diamond's feeder before closing the stall door.

She'd put in a full day at the café, waiting on the steady stream of Christmas shoppers who stopped in for a cup of coffee or a piece of pie. However, when she returned home, the thought of heating up a bowl of leftover chili and curling up on the sofa—alone—held no appeal.

Erin had changed into her work clothes and spent the last several hours in the barn, mucking out the stalls and sweeping the floor. Changing the bedding where the kittens slept.

If she wasn't mistaken, there was a light bulb that needed to be replaced...

Winston rolled to his feet and barked at her, almost as if he'd read her thoughts.

Erin chuckled. "Okay, okay. I get it. You want to go inside." The trouble was, Erin wasn't ready to go back to the house yet.

Before he'd returned to town, thoughts of Lucas had only dominated her memories. Now they invaded both her heart and her home.

Especially since he showed up *everywhere* these days.

Whenever Erin was in the kitchen, she remembered the vulnerable expression on Lucas's face when he told her what had happened to Max. When she walked into the living room, she didn't see the Christmas decorations, she saw Lucas on the sofa, his arms wrapped protectively around Max as if he could somehow shield the boy from his fears.

And now, when she looked at her Christmas tree, images of the wonderful evening she'd spent decorating with Lucas and Max returned to torment her.

Why had she been so surprised to discover that he'd rented the cabin next door? Lucas made no effort to conceal how he felt about Clayton. He'd stayed away for years, hadn't he?

Lucas had no intention of returning to his roots. His decision to rent proved he'd only come back to satisfy George's last wishes and claim his inheritance.

And Erin was never going to make it through the next year. Not if that meant seeing Lucas on a regular basis.

And Max.

When he'd planted a kiss on her cheek after she'd tucked him into bed, she'd wanted to hug him and never let go.

Max, she told herself sternly, *not* Lucas.

Lucas she wanted to…shake silly. And *then* hug.

It was obvious that neither time nor a change of scenery had healed the wounds of his past.

What had made her hope that *she* could?

Standing in the doorway of the barn, Lucas saw the weary slump of Erin's slim shoulders and tamped down a surge of anger. At himself.

In the past, he'd always gotten on her case about her overdeveloped sense of responsibility and yet here he was, about to add more weight to the burden she already carried.

Lucas took a step backward, intending to sneak out the same way he had come in. A floorboard creaked, alerting Winston that there was an intruder in the barn. The corgi barked once and trotted toward him, tongue unfurling in anticipation of an impending saliva bath.

Erin's head snapped up and she whirled around to face him.

"Hey." No escaping now. "I saw the lights on."

"Lucas." She didn't move. Didn't even smile.

Lucas found himself wanting the woman that had been at his house the night before. The one who'd blushed at the sight of mistletoe and helped him tuck Max into bed.

He bent down to scratch Winston's ears. "I'm on my way home from Frank Clayton's place."

"I'm sorry," Erin said automatically. She flushed and caught herself. "Now I'm sorry again. I shouldn't have said that. He is your relative."

"Don't worry about it. He likes to forget that little detail, too." Lucas smiled when Winston flipped over onto his back, exposing his belly for more attention.

"Is Max with you?"

"Not yet. Viv and Cody's sister Bonnie offered to watch him for a few hours while I stopped out at Frank's. One of his geldings went lame and he wanted me to put it down."

Erin's expression went from guarded to dismayed. "But you could save it."

Lucas had to admit he was touched by Erin's confidence in him. It was a lot more flattering than Frank's blatant skepticism that he'd actually earned the title of veterinary doctor.

The man had trailed him to the barn, asking questions about Lucas's new job and dropping veiled references about George Sr.'s will. How it would have been nice if Lucas's grandfather had rewarded the family members who'd stayed in town rather than those who'd left.

It was ironic that Frank didn't realize the ones who had left did so because the ones who'd stayed had made life for George's offspring unbearable.

"Frank didn't want me to." Lucas saw the toe of Erin's boot tap the floor twice and realized she was waiting for an answer. "When I told him it was a degenerative condition, he didn't want to be bothered with the cost and fuss of medication."

"So…you came over to tell me that you had to put Frank's horse down," she said slowly.

"Not exactly. I came to tell you that I bought him." At twice the cost of what a lame horse was going for these days.

"You *bought* him?"

Confession time. "For you."

"For me!" Erin squeaked.

"Don't worry, it'll be joint custody. I'll pay for feed and provide free medical care. If that's okay," Lucas added.

"Frank said he'd drop him off whenever its convenient." For an additional fee, but Erin didn't need to know that.

"But…" Erin's voice trailed off.

"I remembered you said you wanted to rescue more horses like Diamond. I was thinking about it, and while I'm here, I can donate my services for any animals you adopt." Lucas had come to that decision on the drive to Erin's.

He'd already talked to Tweed and got his boss's permission to rip up the bill for delivering Diamond's foal.

Erin's shoulders straightened beneath the bulky coat. "That's very nice of you," she said politely. "I'll call Frank in the morning."

"Great." Lucas knew when he was being dismissed and felt the sting of Erin's less-than-enthusiastic response to what he'd thought was a generous offer.

What did you expect, a hug?

Her quick exit the night before had proved that Erin didn't want to spend time alone with him for old times' sake. She'd agreed to stay and help wrap gifts because she liked Max, not because of any residual feelings she might still have for Lucas.

Apparently she had room in her life for little boys who wanted to decorate Christmas trees and lame horses that needed a home. But not him.

And Lucas had no one to blame but himself.

Erin spent another hour in the barn, getting the empty stall next to Diamond's ready for the new arrival.

"Thank you, Lucas Clayton," she muttered under her breath.

Not that she minded the extra work that another horse would bring. She welcomed it, especially if it took the poor animal away from Lucas's uncle, whose hard-handed methods of "training" his horses were well-known in the area.

No, what she minded was Lucas sauntering back into her life with the full intention of sauntering right back out again.

While I'm here I can donate my services for any animals you adopt.

If Tweed had made the offer, Erin would have been thrilled. But she doubted that Lucas had even realized what he'd said.

The same way he hadn't cared how she would interpret the conversation she'd overheard between him and the real-estate agent.

She sighed and Winston pushed his wet nose against her knee in sympathy.

"Men can be so clueless sometimes," she said. "Present company excluded."

Winston cast a hopeful look at the door.

"We're done for tonight."

Erin flipped off the lights in the barn and stepped out into the moonlit night. Stars winked overhead in the black velvet sky.

If she was lucky, one of them would fall on her head and erase every memory of Lucas Clayton. Then whenever he showed up, she would stare right into those blue eyes…and probably fall in love with him all over again.

The crunch of tires against snow broke the silence.

Winston's tail began to wag. For one heart-stopping moment, Erin wondered if Lucas had returned. Until she saw the red-and-blue light bar on top of the vehicle.

When she saw who hopped out of the driver's side of the

squad car, Erin's pulse returned to its normal rhythm and she smiled. "Hey, Zach."

"Erin." Zach returned the greeting but not the smile. "Can you take a ride with me?"

"That depends. Are we going down to the department for questioning?" Erin was teasing but something in Zach's solemn expression ignited a spark of fear. "What's wrong?"

"There's been a fire. At the café."

Chapter Ten

"A fire?" Erin searched the deputy's face, waiting for Zach to admit that he'd been teasing her, too.

"It started in the Dumpster out back," Zach explained. "There's minimal damage to the building itself but I'd like you to come with me and take a walk around the inside so we can see if anything's missing…"

The words dissolved in Erin's ears as she tried to make sense of what he was saying.

Fire. Minimal damage.

Erin swallowed hard against the lump swelling in her throat and making it difficult to breathe.

Emptying the trash was the last responsibility of the day. Had something she'd thrown away accidentally ignited a fire?

"…want to make sure there's no sign of vandalism."

Vandalism?

"What?" Erin's voice thinned. "You think someone set the fire on purpose?"

Zach nodded, his expression grim. "One of the volunteer firefighters found a bunch of rags mixed in with the trash. And it looks as though an accelerant may have been used to start the blaze."

"I'll put Winston in the house and meet you in town." Once she could force her feet to move.

"Maybe you should ride with me," he suggested.

Erin assented with a jerky nod. Zach must have realized that she was too shaken to concentrate on driving. She put Winston in the house and found the deputy sheriff waiting for her just outside the door.

His hand cupped her elbow, steadying her as she got into the squad car. The warm air pumping out of the vents in the dashboard couldn't permeate the chill that had settled in her bones.

Zach was silent for several moments, as if he sensed that she needed time to think. To pray.

"It must have been some kids goofing around. Playing with matches." Erin eventually broke the silence. "They probably didn't mean to start a fire. Right?"

She waited for Zach to agree but he answered her question with one of his own.

"What time did you close up tonight?"

"Seven. The same as always."

"Were you alone?" he asked.

"Kylie got off work at six but Jerome and Gerald left at the same time I did."

"Do you remember who your last customers were?"

Erin tried to visualize the faces of the people who'd sat at the tables she'd cleared. There'd been so many people in and out that day, running errands and doing their last-minute Christmas shopping.

"A few of the guys from the Lucky Lady mine. Mayor Pauley—" Out of the corner of her eye, Erin saw Zach's jaw tighten, an outward sign of how he felt about his distant relative.

The Clayton family had been divided—split down the middle by the animosity that had existed for years between George Sr. and his brother, Samuel. If Lucas and his cousins had refused to return by Christmas and make Clayton their home for a year, the inheritance from their grandfather would have passed to Samuel and his offspring.

That alone would have been enough to cause the rift to widen, but Jasmine and Cade's engagement had added additional fuel to the resentment smoldering between the two sides of the family.

"He was alone for a while, until Charley and Billy Dean Harris joined him. They weren't together long. A few people came in and bought bakery items." Erin tried to match tables and faces. "Your Aunt Kat. She stopped by looking for Arabella."

The woman had also unloaded a litany of complaints about her daughter in the ten minutes she'd lingered at the counter, but Erin saw no reason to mention that.

"You parked in the alley behind the café?"

"Yes." Erin shifted in the seat, uncomfortably aware that this was a police interview, not the polite conversation she and Zach had exchanged in the past.

They reached the city limits and Erin leaned forward, her shoulders tense. Zach had said there was minimal damage, but what exactly did that mean?

"Would you like me to call Kylie and ask her to meet us there?" Zach murmured. "She'd be waiting at the door before I put the car in park."

Erin smiled, knowing it was true. The thought of having her friend close by was tempting but there was no sense in having both of them lose sleep.

"I'll be all right." Erin sent up a silent prayer for strength as Zach pulled up in front of the café.

He held out his hand and Erin dropped the key into his outstretched palm. As soon as Zach disappeared, she sank against the worn upholstery and closed her eyes.

Arson.

Erin could hardly wrap her mind around the word. This

was Clayton, Colorado. The people who lived in the area didn't lock their vehicles or their houses. It had to have been some bored kids, messing around the Dumpster with matches.

And an accelerant.

Erin pressed her forehead against the glass, waiting for Zach to reappear. Finally, he appeared in the window and waved at her to come inside.

Shadows danced on the walls as Erin walked through the café. She was comforted by Zach's solid, reassuring presence beside her while she looked around. Nothing appeared to be out of place. No windows had been broken. The safe in her office hadn't been tampered with.

She followed Zach out the back door to the alley where the acrid scent of smoke burned her nostrils. Wet rags littered the snow around the Dumpster. On the exterior wall behind it, black soot had left an ominous stain.

Erin's gaze followed its path to the wooden overhang above the back door and her stomach pitched. If left unchecked, the flames could have spread to the rest of the café.

Zach nodded, as if she'd spoken the thought out loud. "An anonymous call came in," he said carefully. "They told dispatch about the fire and then hung up. Normally when a person calls, they identify themselves and stay on the line until help shows up."

Erin realized that Zach was waiting for her to comment, but she couldn't think straight. She could barely think at all. She imagined the faces of the customers who had come in that day, their pleasant banter rising over the Christmas carols playing on the jukebox.

"I can't believe someone did this deliberately."

"If you can remember anything," Zach urged. "No matter how trivial it might have seemed at the time."

"You're asking me if I remember burning someone's biscuits?"

Zach's lips quirked in a lopsided smile so reminiscent of Lucas's that it suddenly hurt to breathe. He shook his head. "Since I know that doesn't happen on Gerald and Jerome's watch, try to think of something else. Someone who might want to get your attention. Someone who might have a... grudge."

"A grudge? Of course not..." Erin's voice trailed off as Vincent's mocking laughter danced in her ears.

"I want what's mine and Lucas isn't going to cheat me out of it this time."

No.

Erin instantly rejected the thought.

Vincent might have a list of grievances against Lucas, but what would he possibly have against her?

"You thought of someone." Zach had been watching her closely.

"No...it's silly."

"Let me be the judge of that," he said.

She sighed heavily, feeling as if she were back on the playground, tattling on a bully. "Vincent came in around closing time a few nights ago."

Zach's lips flattened. Although the breakup with Kylie had been Vincent's fault, he hadn't made it easy on her after she broke off the engagement. His resentment had continued to grow when it became evident that Zach and Kylie's friendship was developing into something more.

"Did he harass you?"

"Some of the things Vincent said...he made it clear that he's still got it in for Lucas." Erin decided not to mention that Vincent had grabbed her wrist. "But I'm sure it wasn't him. What would he have to gain? I mean, we're not exactly friends, but he has no reason to target me or the café. Lucas and I...there's no connection between us."

"Are you sure?" Zach pressed.

This time, Erin couldn't prevent a thread of bitterness from weaving through the words.

"I'm sure."

"Look, Lucas! There's a Bob in here."

Lucas groaned.

Max understood that to mean he was awake and scrambled onto the bed. "See?"

At that moment, the only thing Lucas could see was the inside of his eyelids. By sheer will he forced them open and squinted several times. Gradually, the blurry object clutched in Max's hand turned into a Christmas ornament. Inside the cavity was a miniature nativity scene and, sure enough, a trio of tiny camels.

"Camels. Right." Lucas yawned and sat up.

Max studied the ornament cupped in his hands. "Baby Jesus is sleepin' in there." He looked at Lucas for confirmation.

"Yup." Lucas cleared his throat. "That's who it is."

Max looked pleased. "He loves me."

Lucas drew in a careful breath and not because Max's elbow was digging into his ribs. "Did your Grandma Lisette or Aunt Mei tell you that?"

"Uh-uh." Max snuggled closer and the sweet scent of bubblegum shampoo drifted into the air. "Erin."

So, not only had she baked cookies with Max that day, she'd also taken time to share the Christmas story with him. And it was just like Erin to wrap the entire gospel message into three simple words.

He loves me.

As the son of Vern Clayton, missionary doctor, Lucas knew the Christmas story inside out and upside down. He'd memorized verses and played the part of Joseph in the children's Christmas pageant.

For years he'd tried to do everything right. Grades. Sports.

Church activities. Every time he would accomplish something, he would look to his father for approval. Approval he never received.

The day Lucas had given up and stopped trying, he'd turned his back on everything his father had stood for. He had tried to pray, but every time he thought of God, it became blocked by an image of his father, arms crossed, glaring down at him.

You disappoint me, Lucas.

"That's Mary and…" Max peered at the tiny figures inside the stable. "Joe."

Lucas choked back a laugh. "Joseph, Max. His name is Joseph."

"Jesus' daddy?"

This was *not* the conversation a man should have with a four-year-old before his first cup of coffee in the morning.

Maybe, Lucas thought darkly, he should call Erin and let her do the explaining. "God is Jesus' father. He's everyone's father, really—"

"'Cause He made us," Max interjected.

"Right." Lucas blew out a relieved sigh, momentarily grateful that Erin had covered that part, too. "God made us. He made everything." Lucas had never stopped believing that, he just doubted he could ever measure up to God's standards. Not when he hadn't even been able to please his earthly father. "But He lives in heaven, so Joseph took care of Jesus and Mary and kept them safe."

"From the bad guys?"

"From the bad guys." Lucas guessed that was a pretty accurate description of King Herod's soldiers.

"An' Joseph 'dopted him?"

Lucas should have been surprised that Max knew the word, but then again, knowing they were the main topic of conversation around his family's dinner table, maybe not.

"Sure, I guess you could say that."

"Like you 'dopted me."

Lucas felt the room tilt.

Over the past few months, he'd been Max's rescuer. His protector. He'd signed his name on some legal documents and become his guardian.

But Max didn't care about promises or legal documents. He didn't need a guardian...he wanted—no needed—a father.

If only Lucas knew how to *be* one.

Winging it is what parents do, Erin had said. If only it were that simple.

"Are you hungry?" Fortunately Max was too young to recognize the tactics of someone desperate to change the subject.

"We're goin' to Aunt A'bella's now? I'm gonna tell Jessie we decorated our tree."

"I meant hungry for breakfast," Lucas said. "We're not going to Arabella's until lunchtime."

Max deflated against him like a punctured balloon. "How come?"

"They won't be home until after church."

Max tilted his head. "What's church?"

Another wave of guilt crashed over Lucas. If he and God had been on speaking terms, Lucas might have thought He was trying to tell him something.

Lucas sighed. "It's where we're going after breakfast."

Chapter Eleven

Erin felt a tug on the hem of her skirt. She glanced down, expecting to see one of Arabella's triplets, but it was Max who stood there, grinning up at her.

"Hi, Erin!"

"Max." Erin bent down and hugged him, while at the same time searching the faces of the people in the sanctuary for Mei or Lisette Clayton, who must have lost track of the little boy when the service ended. "How are you?"

"Hungry."

Erin laughed and ruffled his hair. "The café is closed today, but I'm sure someone will make lunch for you."

"We're going to Aunt A'bella's house to eat. I'm gonna tell Jessie an' Julie an' Jamie—" Max paused to take a breath "—that our tree is bigger than theirs."

Our tree. Erin was touched that he included her but she wouldn't let her thoughts drift to the evening she'd spent at Lucas's. "I'm sure you'll have fun."

"Are you coming, too?"

The innocent question pulled at the loose threads of her emotions. Zach had invited both her and Kylie a few days ago but after the night she'd had, Erin knew she wouldn't be good company.

"Not today, sweetie." Erin straightened while keeping a protective hand on Max's shoulder. "Where's your Auntie Mei?"

"I don't know."

"Didn't she bring you to—" The next word stuck in Erin's throat and her heart took a slow tumble when a man emerged from the crowd.

Lucas.

He'd replaced his usual jeans and flannel shirt for a pair of tan cargo pants and a moss-green button-down shirt that enhanced the color of his eyes the way the leaves of a cottonwood complimented a summer sky.

Erin had volunteered to work in the infant nursery that morning, so she hadn't seen him come in. As far as she knew, Lucas hadn't stepped through the doors of Clayton Christian Church since his father's funeral.

So what had brought him here today?

"Lucas?" She lifted her hand to flag him down.

The frantic look in Lucas's eyes faded when he saw Max safely tucked against her side.

"Max," Lucas's voice came out in a low growl. "You were supposed to wait for me."

"I was. I'se just waitin' with Erin," Max said reasonably.

Lucas glanced at her. "Thanks for keeping an eye on him. Again. I was talking to Vivienne and Cody Jameson and the next thing I knew Max was…gone."

"They're quick at Max's age." Erin refused to smile at the look of utter bewilderment on Lucas's face that a four-year-old could disappear so quickly.

In fact, it was probably best not to look at Lucas at all, given the fragile state of her emotions. Whether lack of sleep or the stress of knowing how close she'd come to losing the café, tears had been simmering just below the surface all morning.

"Hey, Lucas!" Arabella's voice rose above the hum of conversation in the church foyer. "We're leaving now."

"Okay. Be there in five."

Knowing Lucas would be joining the rest of his family for lunch made Erin even more relieved that she'd turned down the invitation.

"Bye, Erin. Wait for me, Aunt A'bella." Max dashed toward his aunt.

Lucas, however, remained at her side, his eyes shadowed with concern as he stared down at her. "Is everything all right?"

Erin didn't want Lucas to be sensitive. Or kind. It made it that much harder to keep her distance. "I'm fine."

"You look…tired."

Erin forced a smile. "What every woman wants to hear."

"I'm serious."

And she seriously needed to get away from the man before she launched herself into his arms and released the emotions bottled up inside of her.

Erin had tossed and turned for hours after Zach dropped her off at home. She'd been counting on the fact that a cup of coffee and an extra layer of foundation would hide the damage of a sleepless night.

No one, not even Reverend West, had commented on the shadows underneath her eyes. No one except Lucas—the last person Erin had expected to notice.

Mei swept toward them, stunning in a dress made of mistletoe green velvet. "Are you two setting up a time to get together this afternoon?"

Erin's gaze bounced from Lucas to his sister and back again. "A time to get together?" she repeated.

"Jasmine asked Jack and I to attend a premarital counseling session with her and Cody this afternoon, so Lucas offered to bring Macy out to your place after dinner."

Erin cast a sideways glance at Lucas. "You didn't mention that last night."

"You were together last night?" Mei asked, her eyes alight with interest.

Lucas shifted his weight. "I had to stop by Erin's. It was a...professional call."

"I see." Mei grinned.

No, you don't, Erin wanted to say.

"I was actually planning to come into town later today to buy some more grain at the feed store," she said, grateful for the excuse. "I can swing by Arabella's and pick up Macy on my way home."

A tiny frown marred Mei's smooth forehead. "Are you sure it's no trouble? Lucas doesn't mind."

Even if that were true, which Erin suspected it wasn't, *she* minded. Macy's company would be a nice distraction from her troubles but Lucas would simply be a...distraction. "It's no trouble at all. I'll be there about two o'clock."

Mei linked her arm through her brother's. "I guess you're off the hook."

"I guess so."

The smile Erin aimed at Lucas fell short of its mark when she saw a shadow skirt across his face. If Erin hadn't known better, she would have thought it looked like...regret.

But she *did* know better. Even if Lucas had regrets, it was time to face the truth, once and for all, that Erin Fields wasn't one of them.

There were so many vehicles parked outside Clayton House, Arabella's turn-of the-century Victorian, that her yard resembled a used-car lot.

If Max hadn't been so excited about seeing the triplets again, Lucas might have turned the truck around and headed back to the cabin.

A mittened hand battered against the window. "We're here!"

"We sure are," Lucas muttered. He nosed the truck around until it faced the road, in case a quick getaway was in order.

The door opened as soon as his foot hit the top step of the wide, wraparound porch.

"Hi, Lucas. Max. Come on in!" Jasmine Turner stood on the other side of the door. She wore jeans, a hooded sweat-shirt and a wedding veil as delicate as a butterfly's wing over her straight brown hair.

Lucas tilted his head. "Did you change the date?"

The young woman grinned at his confusion. "No, it's still Christmas Eve. Macy and the triplets insisted I model my veil for them...and then you knocked. And everyone else is in the kitchen." Jasmine gave a helpless shrug. "Come in and join the chaos."

Chaos was a good word for it, Lucas thought as he peeled off Max's coat and set him loose. He charged down the hall toward the den, where the pint-size members of the Clayton family had gathered in front of the television.

"The triplets couldn't wait for Max to get here." Jasmine took their coats and tried to squeeze them into a narrow closet already bulging with outerwear. "Until recently, a man in this house was a bit of a novelty."

"I'm going to tell Jonathan you said that." A guy in his late teens wandered into the hall. He tucked one arm around Jasmine's slender waist and stuck out his hand. "It's good to see you again, Lucas."

Lucas hesitated a split second before extending his own.

"Same here." Lucas gripped his younger cousin's hand, amazed at the transformation. The last time he'd seen Cade Clayton, the boy had been nothing but arms and legs and missing his two front teeth.

Because of the animosity that divided their families and the difference in their ages, Lucas had never gotten to know

Cade, or his step-brother, Jack McCord, very well. But Cade's smile appeared genuine and he lacked the aura of discontentment that seemed to cling to Samuel's side of the family like smoke from a campfire.

His great-uncle had to be as mad as a rabid coyote at the thought of his grandson marrying Arabella's foster daughter.

A high-pitched screech, followed by a loud crash, made all three of them cringe.

"My turn," Cade said and jogged toward the living room.

"We're taking turns?" Lucas muttered.

"It's only fair." Instead of following her fiancé, Jasmine fell into step with Lucas.

"I just wanted to tell you that I think it's great how you took Max in and gave him a home," she said in a low voice. "I don't know what I would have done without Arabella over the past few years. And now I have Jonathan in my life, too. And of course, Cade. God keeps blessing me with family."

Lucas didn't know what to say. He hadn't really thought about family being a blessing before and he certainly hadn't considered that description for himself when it came to Max.

Communication with his parents had been almost non-existent unless Lucas was getting lectured. His relationship with Mei was complicated. Even though his sister was older, she'd been shy and withdrawn, always in the background of the family portrait. They'd been close as children but time and distance had worked against them. Over the years she'd tried to reach out to him, but Lucas had gotten better at letting go than holding on.

Maybe there had been some good times, but looking for them was like mining for gold. So rare that Lucas wasn't sure it was even worth the effort.

Arabella poked her head out of the kitchen and crooked a finger at him. "There you are, Lucas. Come with me. Real men congregate in the kitchen."

"Because that's where the food is." Jasmine smiled and

gave him a playful push in Arabella's direction. "You go and enjoy some adult conversation. Cade and I will keep an eye on Max."

Lucas wasn't sure whether to thank her or not as he walked into the kitchen and immediately found himself surrounded, not only by immediate family, but also their significant others.

Brooke and Gabe Wesson were putting together a relish tray while Vivienne and Cody Jameson sat together at the counter, peeling potatoes. Cody, a local rancher, was Vivienne's new fiancé, according to Mei.

Vivienne's head came up as Lucas entered the room. Her blue eyes sparkled below a fringe of blond bangs and the Clayton dimple came out in full force. "There's our guest of honor now."

"Shh." Brooke shook a carrot stick at her. "He's not supposed to know."

Lucas rolled his eyes. "I know."

"All right. Who told him?" Arabella's eyes narrowed as she made a slow sweep of the room, searching for the guilty party. "Jonathan?"

The doctor's eyes twinkled. "Not me. Doctor-patient confidentiality, you know."

Over Arabella's shoulder, Mei pinched her fingers together and made a zipping motion over her lips. Jack McCord, stationed beside her at the double sink, simply grinned.

"Zach?" Arabella speared him with a look.

"Don't look at me," Zach said. "I've been trained to withhold information."

"You certainly have." Kylie marched into the kitchen with a casserole dish in her hands and sparks in her eyes. "I had to hear about the fire at the café from Dorothy Henry!"

The sudden uproar from the group drowned out the sound of Lucas's heart hammering against his rib cage.

"What fire?"

"What happened?"

"Was anything damaged?"

"Is Erin all right?"

Zach ducked his head as the questions peppered the air like buckshot and held up his hand in a bid for silence. "The fire started in the Dumpster behind the café last night so there was no damage to the building. Erin was home at the time but I picked her up and took her down to the café. We took a walk through. Nothing appeared to be damaged or stolen."

"Why did you think there would be?" Lucas asked.

All eyes turned in Lucas's direction and the sudden silence proved more unnerving than their questions. Not quite the response he had expected.

"There've been a few—" Jack paused, searching for the right word "—situations lately."

"Situations?" Lucas looked at Zach and dread pooled in his stomach. "What kind of situations?"

"You know what happens if one of us breaks the terms of the will," Zach finally said.

"None of us inherits a thing." Lucas pushed the words out through gritted teeth. "That's why we came back."

"But if life gets…difficult…here and one of us leaves, Samuel's side inherits," Vivienne added.

Lucas knew that, too. "So?"

Brooke sighed. "So life has been getting difficult."

"Define difficult." Lucas kept a tight rein on his impatience.

Vivienne looked at Arabella.

"Jasmine's wedding dress disappeared. We found it later, completely shredded," their older cousin said.

"It sounds like someone doesn't want them to get married." No matter what Lucas's opinion on Cade and Jasmine's upcoming wedding, he couldn't imagine anyone going to such extreme lengths to prevent it.

"There's more," Zach told him.

More? Lucas had already heard enough.

"Zach's gun and badge were stolen a few months ago," Arabella said. "Someone wanted him to look bad."

And Samuel Clayton's side of the family excelled at making others look bad, Lucas knew.

"A bunch of Cody's hired hands got food poisoning. Since I was the cook, I got blamed for it," Vivienne added. "I almost gave up and went back to the city."

The rancher took her hand.

"It wouldn't have mattered," Cody murmured. "I would have brought you back."

Vivienne smiled but it was the last thing Lucas felt like doing.

As the list of offenses against his family increased, so did his anger. He couldn't believe they'd kept all this from him. He shot Mei an accusing look.

"You've had a lot on your plate since you got back." His sister's dark eyes flashed a mute apology, leaving Lucas to wonder if that was the only reason they hadn't kept him in the loop.

"We think someone on Samuel's side of the family has been looking for a...weak link," Brooke explained. "One of us who won't stick it out if things get tough."

Lucas didn't have to ask who they thought that might be. The family prodigal, who'd made no secret of the fact that he would never return to Clayton.

"The fire at the café could have been an accident, though," Arabella pointed out.

"Or it could be my fault." Kylie's shoulders slumped. "I work at the café and Vincent hasn't forgiven me for breaking our engagement."

"That's a definite possibility," Zach agreed. "I can't think of another reason why the person who's been trying to run us out of town would suddenly turned their attention to Erin."

A cold trickle of fear worked its way down Lucas's spine. He could.

Chapter Twelve

Erin sat in her car, trying to work up the courage to walk up to the door. Even with the windows closed, she could hear peals of childish laughter coming from the house.

Maybe if she honked the horn...it would bring everyone running.

Instead of going home after the worship service, Erin had sought refuge in the café. She'd opened the windows to air out the lingering smell of smoke and tried not to imagine a shadowy figure lurking in the alley.

If Vincent wanted to send out a warning to Lucas, he would have found a better way. She meant nothing to Lucas. Why target her?

The curtains lifted and an elfin face framed in light brown curls appeared in the window and disappeared just as quickly. One of Arabella's triplets was about to sound the alarm.

Erin got out of the car and fought the wind for control of her scarf. To her relief, it was Kylie who answered the door when she knocked.

And enveloped her in a bone-crushing hug.

"We missed you today," she whispered in Erin's ear. "I heard about the fire. Are you all right?"

"Yes." Erin gasped the word.

Kylie stepped back and eyed her critically, taking in the lavender brushstrokes beneath Erin's eyes.

"You don't look fine," she said with brutal honesty. "We're just finishing dessert but I'm sure there's a piece of Arabella's chocolate cake with your name on it."

Erin backed up. "Thanks, but I think I'll take a rain check. Is Macy ready?"

"I'll round her up. The kids have been playing hide and seek." Kylie grinned. "I guess we'll see if I'm as good as I used to be at that game. Don't you want to wait inside where it's warm?"

"No." Erin said the word so forcefully that Kylie blinked. "I left the car running."

"Okay." Fortunately, her friend didn't push the issue. "I'll send her out."

Erin was almost to the vehicle when she heard footsteps behind her.

"Erin?" Lucas's husky voice stopped her in her tracks.

She worked up a smile and turned around to face him. "What is it?"

Lucas's gaze swept over her with the critical eye of a doctor looking for symptoms. She had no doubt he saw them all. The shadows under her eyes. The pallor of her skin. Evidence of a sleepless night.

He took a step forward and for one heart-stopping moment, Erin thought he was going to take her into his arms. He thrust his hands into his pockets instead.

"Why didn't you tell me about the fire when I saw you at church this morning? I even asked you if something was wrong." As he spoke, he glanced toward the house.

The meaning behind the gesture was clear. He didn't want anyone to see them together.

Erin blinked back the tears that clawed at the back of her eyes and lifted her chin.

"Because it didn't concern you."

* * *

Lucas watched Erin's car drive away and resisted the urge to jump in his truck and chase after her. But that would really give people a reason to talk.

The fallout from the bomb his cousins had dropped right before dinner continued to overshadow his thoughts. It was no surprise that someone on Samuel's side of the family wanted to get their hands on the inheritance, but it was the lengths that person was willing to go that concerned him.

He ignored the cold gnawing its way through his shirt as Erin's car turned the corner and disappeared from view.

When Kylie announced that Erin had arrived to pick up Macy, Lucas had assumed she would come inside to say hello to Kylie and his family. But she hadn't. From the window, Lucas watched her trudge away from the house, a slight figure that didn't look strong enough to withstand a gust of winter wind pushing down from the mountains, let alone some unknown aggressor who might have chosen her café to send out a warning.

But why Erin?

As far as Lucas knew, none of their family or friends knew that he and Erin had secretly dated their senior year of high school.

Lucas frowned as his thoughts turned down another road. It was possible the person who'd been creating the "situations" his cousins had mentioned witnessed the exuberant hug that Max had bestowed upon Erin at the café the day he'd had lunch with Brooke. The affection between them would have been apparent even to a casual observer, making it obvious they had spent time together.

If someone was afraid that Lucas might actually decide to stay in Clayton, a woman with roots in the community as deep as Erin's would be determined a threat.

Whoever was responsible for the attacks against his family didn't want Lucas to have a reason to stick around.

And Erin, Lucas silently admitted, would be a reason.

The first few times their paths had crossed, he'd blamed the feelings she stirred in him on the memories of a teenage crush. Now he had to wonder if those feelings had never completely died.

Erin hadn't changed. She was still the sweet, kindhearted girl he'd fallen for. The girl who had made him believe there was something in Lucas Clayton worth loving.

But her feelings for him had definitely changed.

Did she blame him for the fire? Or for something else?

Lucas shook that thought away. He'd asked Erin to go away with him and she'd refused. Maybe the spark of anger he'd seen in her eyes wasn't because he'd left but because he'd returned and caused trouble for the people she cared about.

It didn't concern you.

That might be true, but it didn't change the fact that Lucas *was* concerned.

He strode back to the house and realized his absence had created some attention. A trio of little faces tracked his movement like flowers turning toward the sun. He hoped no one else had witnessed his conversation with Erin.

Mei met him in the front hall. "Mom just called. She wants you to stop over for a few minutes."

"Did she say why?" Lucas hadn't seen their mother since Mei had told him that Vern might have had a relationship with Darlene Perry.

"Maybe she just wants to visit with you and Max for a while."

Lucas didn't bother to hide his skepticism. "Maybe."

"Give her a chance," Mei urged. "You aren't the only one who's had to deal with some tough things."

Lucas bristled at the unexpected attack. "I never said I was."

"I want you to think about the fact that maybe it wasn't Grandpa George who brought us back to Clayton."

That might be true, but at the moment, Lucas was more interested in finding out who was trying to get them to leave.

"And Lucas?"

He tried not to sigh. "Yes?"

"Think about it on the way to Mom's house."

Lisette looked surprised when she opened the door and saw Lucas standing on the other side. As if she hadn't believed he would really show up. She tucked Albert, her temperamental Maltese, in the crook of her arm. "Please, come in."

"Hi, Mom." Lucas forced a smile, still not sure he was ready to face his mother in the light of what Mei had told him about their father.

Life had been easier in Georgia, where his emotions could remain safely on autopilot. Lucas wasn't forced to look at Erin Fields and wonder what might have been—or if he'd made the biggest mistake of his life when he'd left her standing in the driveway on graduation night.

He didn't have to drive through a town that kicked up memories like dust devils, making it difficult to discern the truth from the lies.

"Mei mentioned you wanted to talk to me." Lucas held Max's hand as they followed Lisette into the living room, where a small artificial tree sprouted from the center of the drum table in the corner.

The lights drew Max's eye like a shiny penny in the street. A wide grin split his face.

Lucas might have dismissed it as a hallucination if Max hadn't seen it, too.

"Mei mentioned how excited Max was about her tree the last time you visited, so I thought I should put one up this year." Lisette's smile turned pensive. "It always seemed like a lot of trouble when it was just me."

"Max, no!" Lucas saw the little boy reach for one of the

candy canes that decorated the lower branches. "Those are decorations."

"They're also to eat" his mother shocked him by saying. She took one off the tree and handed it to Max. "We can hang another one in its place."

Max hooked the candy inside one pudgy cheek and beamed at her. "Thank you."

Give her a chance, Mei had urged. Lucas took a deep breath. "Mei said you wanted to talk to me," he repeated.

His mother tugged at the strand of matched pearls around her neck. "Mei said the cabin is furnished, but I went through the closets, looking for some odds and ends that I thought you might need." Lisette gestured toward a cardboard box on the floor next to the sofa. "And I had some things of yours packed away until you..."

You came back.

Lisette didn't say the words out loud, but Lucas heard them anyway. Had she expected he would someday return to Clayton? Had she *wanted* him to come back?

Over time, Lucas had convinced himself that his mother's life would be easier if he simply disappeared. He didn't want to consider that maybe the person whose life had been easier might have been him.

Uncomfortable with the direction his thoughts were taking, Lucas dipped a hand inside the container. The first item he pulled out was a box with tiny silver hinges, hand-crafted out of pine.

"I found that on the shelf in your closet." Lisette sat down beside him. "Do you remember it?"

Unfortunately, yes. "Grandpa George gave this to me for Christmas when I was twelve."

"Your father and I weren't sure why your grandfather singled you out that particular year. He had a reputation in the family for being quite the Scrooge."

What Lucas remembered was that his initial excitement

over the package that his cantankerous grandfather had handed him quickly faded.

"What's the problem, boy?" Grandpa George had barked. *"You look disappointed."*

Lucas had scraped up the courage to tell him the truth. *"It's a...box."*

An *empty* box, to be exact.

Instead of becoming angry, George's booming laugh rattled the windows. *"I said the exact same thing when my father gave it to me. And I'll tell you what he said. It's a family heirloom. Jim Clayton made that box from a tree that grew on his claim. He built a cabin out of the rest of it. Whoever gets that box gets to decide who to pass it on to. I picked you."*

"Why?" Lucas asked even though he knew the answer. His grandfather would drone on about his good grades or the sports trophies he'd been awarded for basketball that year.

George had poked a thick finger a quarter inch from Lucas's nose. *"Because* you, *Lucas Clayton, will understand its value."*

Understand it? Lucas had stashed the box in his closet and forgotten about it.

His thumb absently traced the smooth grain of the wood. At the age of twelve, he hadn't appreciated the craftsmanship. Or the history.

"That box is as old as this town," Lisette murmured.

Another unwelcome reminder that his last name bound Lucas to a place he had never felt he belonged.

"I'm still not sure why he gave it to me. Why didn't he give it to Dad? Or Uncle George?" Someone worthy of a family heirloom.

"Their relationship was...complicated," his mother said carefully. "George Sr. was a difficult man to please. Much like your father."

Lucas had never heard her say anything negative about

his father. She had always been a staunch supporter of Vern's rules, no matter how unreasonable. After his death, Lisette had pushed and prodded Lucas to become a doctor.

Lucas opened his mouth, ready to unleash a cutting "I didn't think you'd noticed." The two words that came out were, "I tried."

"So did I." Lisette shocked him by saying. "Your father was a gifted physician but he began to rely on himself rather than God. He wanted to do things his own way. When a person becomes proud, it gets easier to pull away from people and more difficult to forgive. Even the people you love."

Lucas stared at the box cradled in his hands.

How many times had he told Erin that he refused to become like his father? What he'd meant was the kind of man whose inner life and outer life didn't match.

Now Lucas realized he was just as guilty of "going his own way." And he'd refused to forgive his father for his harsh demands.

Refused to forgive himself for not making things right before his father died.

He tried to hand the box back to his mother. "You should give it to Mei." His sister had every intention of making Clayton her home once she and Jack were married.

"It's yours." Lisette put it back in the cardboard box. "Maybe Max will like it. Little boys need a place to keep their treasures."

Lucas was too stunned to comment. It was the first time he'd seen any indication that his mother was willing to accept Max into the Clayton family. And the first time since he'd returned to his hometown that he saw a hint of a smile, rather than disapproval, in her eyes.

Maybe Mei was right. Maybe their mother did want things to be better between them.

A loud, staccato thump started at the front door and vibrated through the house.

Lisette rose to her feet. "Excuse me."

She turned a few moments later, Tweed at her side. Lucas automatically rose to his feet at the sight of his boss.

"I saw your truck," the vet said breathlessly, his British accent more pronounced than usual. "A horse trailer slid into the ditch a few miles outside of town and the stallion trapped inside is trying to kick its way out. Come on."

Lucas's pulse spiked. "I have to find someone to watch Max first."

"No!" Max flew across the room and his thin arms came around Lucas's waist like a grappling hook.

Lisette stepped forward. "I can take Max back to the cabin and stay with him until you get home."

Lucas's mouth dropped open. "But—"

"The lady is willing to take a shift," Tweed barked. "Let's go."

Lucas managed to peel Max off his leg. "I'll be home as soon as I can, buddy."

A low whimper was all he got in return.

"We'll be fine, Lucas."

"Are you sure, Mom?" he asked.

"I'm willing to try."

Warmth bloomed in Lucas's chest as he met her uncertain gaze.

Impulsively, he hugged her.

"So am I."

"Is this Erin?"

Erin's hand tightened around the phone as she recognized the breathless voice. "Mrs. Clayton. What can I do for you?"

"I'm sorry to call so late but I'm over at Lucas's. He went out on an emergency call late this afternoon and I offered to stay with Max for a few hours."

Erin glanced at the clock. It was almost ten. She had dropped Macy off at home more than an hour ago and was just getting ready to take a long bubble bath and turn in for the night.

"Is everything okay?" she asked cautiously.

Lucas had hinted that he'd moved out because his mother wasn't used to small children in the house. Erin had tried not to pass judgment on the woman but Max was such an adorable little boy, she had a difficult time believing that Lisette hadn't immediately fallen in love with him.

The way she had.

"No, it's not." Lisette's voice trembled. "He fell asleep about an hour ago but he just woke up…sobbing. I can't get him to stop and Lucas isn't answering his cell phone."

In the background, Erin could hear a muffled wail. No matter how conflicted her feelings for Lucas, she couldn't turn her back on Max. "I'll be right over."

"Thank you." There was no mistaking the relief in Lisette's voice.

When Erin arrived at the cabin ten minutes later, the door was thrown open before she had an opportunity to knock and Lucas's mother practically yanked her inside.

"He won't stop crying." Lisette, always so put together, appeared completely frazzled.

Hadn't Lucas told his mother about Max's nightmares?

With Lisette at her heels, Erin followed the sound of Max's cries to the small bedroom in the loft. He was huddled beneath the comforter, the heart-wrenching wail punctuated by ragged sobs.

Erin flipped on the switch for the overhead light. The scene that greeted her seemed different from the one she'd witnessed in her living room only a few weeks ago. The terror in Max's eyes had been locked on some unseen horror. Nothing had existed but fear. Now, his eyes tracked her approach, telling Erin that he was aware of his surroundings.

Remembering what Lucas had done, she settled more comfortably against the headboard and drew Max into her arms.

He snuggled closer, resting his head in the cradle of her shoulder. "Do you want to tell me what all these tears are about, cowboy?"

"Lucas is…gone."

Erin nodded. "He had to take care of an injured horse."

"Like Diamond?"

"Uh-huh. And he asked your grandma to stay with you until he got back."

Max's lower lip trembled. "He's…coming back?"

Now Erin understood. It wasn't one of Max's nightmares that held him trapped in the past. This time, it was the future that had him terrified.

"Of course he is," she whispered. "Sometimes he has to go to work but he'll *always* come back."

Max sniffled. "He didn't say goodbye. My dad didn't say goodbye when he left, either."

Lord, give me the right words to say.

"Your dad loved you very much," she said softly. "So much that he asked Lucas, one of his very best friends, to take care of you. Forever. Lucas won't leave you."

"He promised?"

"He promised." Erin's throat tightened. "And Lucas keeps his promises."

No matter that he'd broken the ones he'd made to her, when it came to Max, Erin knew she spoke the truth.

"Can I hava glass of water?"

Erin pressed a kiss against his damp forehead. "Coming right up."

Chapter Thirteen

Erin found Lisette downstairs, standing in front of the stone fireplace, her fingers pressed against her temples.

"Is he all right?"

"I think so. He got scared when he woke up and Lucas wasn't here." Erin suddenly noticed the unshed tears glistening in Lisette's eyes. "Are *you* all right?" she asked tentatively.

"I can feel a migraine coming on," Lucas's mother said. "Do you mind staying until Lucas gets back? My medication is at home and if I don't take it right away, the headache will get worse."

"I'm not sure that's a good idea, Mrs. Clayton—" Especially given the tension between her and Lucas.

"Please," Lisette interrupted. "Kat mentioned the other day how much Max likes you. I'm sure Lucas won't mind."

Erin wasn't sure about that at all. But when she heard Max call her name, it suddenly didn't matter what Lucas would think. Max needed her.

"All right. I'll stay."

Lucas tried not to panic when he noticed that his mother's car was no longer parked in the driveway.

Had she taken Max back to her house for the night? He had assured her that he wouldn't be gone longer than a few hours but it was close to midnight.

He didn't even take the time to shrug off his coat as he strode inside. "Mom?"

No answer.

The fire cast a bronze glow around the room, illuminating two figures curled up on the sofa.

Max, sound asleep. In Erin's arms.

For a moment, all he could do was stare. Erin's neat ponytail was gone, her hair a fiery cloud around her sleep-flushed cheeks.

"Erin?" He bent down and touched her arm.

She came awake with a start and struggled to sit up. "I'm sorry."

Why did Lucas get the feeling that he should be the one apologizing? Especially because she should have been home, sound asleep in her own bed by now.

Lucas reached for Max. "Stay here. I'll put him back to bed—" his mouth went dry as Erin began to finger-comb the wayward strands of copper hair framing her face "—and you can explain why you're here and my mother is gone."

He gathered Max into his arms and carried him upstairs. The boy's puffy eyelids and tearstained cheeks made his heart sink.

Max stirred as Lucas tucked him into bed. His eyes opened a crack and a sleepy smile lifted the corner of his lips. "Erin said you'd come home."

Home.

Lucas nodded, unable to trust his voice.

"G'night." Max drifted off again, a smile on his face.

He found Erin standing in front of the fireplace. She looked rumpled and worried. And beautiful.

"Max had another nightmare," Lucas guessed. Although why his mother had turned to Erin for help was a mystery.

"It wasn't a nightmare," Erin said slowly. "Not like last time."

Lucas frowned. "Then what was it?"

"When Max woke up and realized you weren't here, he got scared."

Lucas read between the lines. And he didn't have to wonder how his mother had reacted when she'd been unable to console Max. Not when she'd called Erin for backup.

"Your mom felt a migraine coming on and asked if I'd stay until you got back."

"I don't understand." Lucas raked a hand through his hair. "Max was right there when Tweed stopped by my mother's house. He knew I went out on a call."

"He thought you'd left him for good," Erin hesitated. "Like his father."

The color drained from Lucas's face even as his doubts festered. "What was I thinking? I don't know how much longer I can do this," he muttered. "I'm not cut out to be a father. Max should have someone who understands what he needs."

"He needs *you*."

It that were true, it was a terrifying thought. "You make it sound so simple."

"And you try to make it complicated."

Lucas blinked, taken aback by the edge in her voice. He was used to seeing Erin calm. Serene. There was only one other time she'd appeared this ruffled.

Looking at her flushed cheeks and blazing eyes, Lucas suddenly felt as if they'd fallen through a crack in time. The years melted away and they were eighteen again, squaring off against each other like pieces on a chessboard.

"What's that supposed to mean?"

"It means it's late and I'm leaving." Erin's coppery locks got caught in the collar as she struggled to put on her coat. Lucas reached out to help and their hands tangled.

Both of them went still.

They were practically nose to nose. Lucas could see the faint dusting of freckles across her nose. And the weary lines fanning out from her eyes. The faintest hint of smoke clung to her coat.

How could he have forgotten the reason for the weariness that marked her features?

Guilt broadsided Lucas. The last thing he wanted was for Erin to get caught in the crossfire of a feud that didn't involve her.

Unless she got involved with him.

No matter how he felt about her, Lucas couldn't take a chance that whoever had attacked his family would set their sights on Erin.

"I'll do what I think is best," he said.

"Oh, that's right." Erin parked both hands on her hips. "I forgot that *you* get to decide what that is. For everyone." She pivoted away from him.

"You can't make a statement like that and then walk away."

"Watch me."

Erin headed toward the door but Lucas got there first.

He blocked her path. "Tell me why you're so angry."

"How much time do you have?" Erin muttered.

"That does it." He set his back against the door.

She glared up at the underside of his unshaven jaw. "What are you doing?"

"Something we've never had. It's called closure." Lucas folded his arms across his chest.

"I don't *need* closure."

"Dr. Phil would argue that."

Under different circumstances, Erin might have laughed. She rolled her eyes instead. "It was a long time ago."

"It doesn't *feel* like a long time ago," Lucas snapped.

Erin's pulse sped up. Was it his way of admitting that he still felt the connection between them?

"Lucas—"

"I heard about the things that have been happening to my family over the past few months. I don't want you to become collateral damage because someone thinks we're…involved."

She deserved this for dropping her guard, even for a moment.

"And we can't have that, can we?"

"Why are you angry with me for trying to protect you?" Lucas asked, his voice gritty with frustration.

"I'm angry that after seven years you can't come up with some new material."

Lucas looked shocked. Erin was a little shocked, too, that she'd blurted that out.

"I have no idea what you're talking about."

Erin felt tears sting her eyes. "That was your excuse when we were dating. You didn't want anyone to know about our relationship because you were *protecting* me."

"It wasn't an excuse."

"Sure it was." Erin couldn't stop the words from tumbling out. "Your mother would have loved it if she knew we were dating. You would have done something Lisette might have approved of, and you couldn't have that, could you? Not to mention that you didn't want the kids at school to know you were spending time with sensible, responsible, *boring* Erin Fields."

Lucas's eyes darkened. "That's crazy."

"I'm sorry." Erin marched over to the window to put some distance between them. "Make that sensible, responsible, boring *and* crazy."

"I was protecting your reputation—"

"You were protecting *yours*."

"Where is all this coming from?" Lucas ground out.

"You left!"

"And you *stayed*." Lucas stalked toward her and Erin scooted around the back of the sofa.

"You didn't give me a choice." Erin looked up at the ceiling, as if appealing for help.

"Aren't you forgetting something?"

"No."

"I *proposed* to you," he said gruffly.

"You showed up at my door after midnight, told me you were leaving Clayton for good and asked me to go with you."

"She remembers." He looked at the ceiling, too.

"I remember we argued—"

"*After* you rejected my proposal."

Erin didn't know whether to laugh or cry. "That wasn't a proposal. I would have remembered if there was an, 'Erin, I love you more than life itself. Will you marry me and make me the happiest man on earth?'"

"You're saying I didn't do it right?"

"I'm saying you didn't do it at all!"

Lucas's lips parted but no sound came out. And then, "It was…implied."

"Implied! It was implied?" Erin's voice cracked. "How do you *imply* a marriage proposal?"

"You should know. You were there." The Clayton dimple made a brief but telling appearance.

Was he actually trying not to smile? Erin was overcome by the urge to hurl a cushion at his handsome face.

And she might have, if his next words hadn't stolen her ability to breathe, let alone move.

"I knew your heart, Erin. Your beliefs. When I showed up at your door that night, I wasn't asking you to go for a cross-country joyride with me. I was asking—in my own bungling way—for you to spend the rest of your life with me."

"No." She rejected the words because to believe them would scrape at a wound that had yet to heal. "You never even looked back. You just…left. There must have been something wrong with me—something that made it easy."

Lucas was silent for a long moment. And then, "Do you remember the first time we talked?"

Remember? The day remained pressed in her memory like a flower.

"You were in detention."

"And Ms. O'Leary saw you in the hall and asked you to keep an eye on the room while she took a phone call."

"You referred to me as 'the warden.'" Erin could still see Lucas in her mind's eye. A blond James Dean in cowboy boots. Long legs stretched out in the aisle. Blue eyes that tracked her every movement below the brim of a battered Stetson that, according to the school handbook, should have been kept in his locker during the school day.

"You weren't the least bit intimidated by me."

"No." Because she'd seen what no one else seemed to be able to see. The grief banked behind the simmering anger in Lucas Clayton's amazing blue eyes.

She'd prayed for him since the night his father and uncle died in a car accident, but they didn't talk. Until that day in seventh-hour detention.

"And I helped you with an English assignment." Erin didn't understand where this side trip down Memory Lane was going to take them any more than she understood the tender look in Lucas's eyes.

"You bullied me into working on my English assignment," he corrected her. "And then I dared you to meet me at the creek that night."

"Only because you didn't think I would."

Lucas had to admit she was right about that. But he'd hoped. Oh, he'd hoped.

Lucas wasn't sure what had stunned him more. Extending the reckless invitation or the fact that Erin had actually shown up.

He'd waited twenty minutes past the time he'd arranged, mentally chiding himself for sticking around. If he was the poster child for teenage rebellion, God kept a picture of Erin Fields in His wallet. When she wasn't at the library working on her GPA, she was helping her mother at the café.

In detention that day, Lucas couldn't help but be intrigued by her. She didn't call attention to herself the way girls like Susie Tansley did, with heavy makeup and clothes that accentuated their curves. Erin's copper hair hung in a neat braid down her back and she didn't need eyeliner to highlight a pair of big brown eyes a guy could get lost in and never find his way back.

They'd passed each other in the halls, she'd waited on him and his friends at the café, but he hadn't really noticed Erin until that day.

He'd wanted to get to know her better, so he'd tossed out a teasing challenge. His fear that she would show up was equal to his fear that she wouldn't.

Lucas had skipped a rock across the creek, ready to call it a night when a shadow moved through the trees. His heart had done a triple somersault in his chest when Erin came and sat down beside him. Right then and there, he should have known that although Erin Fields might not be trouble according to the population of Clayton, she was trouble for *him*.

They'd talked for two hours. And met the next night. And the next.

Erin had a way of getting to the heart of things—and staked a claim on his in the process.

Now, watching the play of emotions on her beautiful face, Lucas couldn't believe Erin had doubted the depth of his feelings.

He couldn't let her go on thinking that he'd left her behind because of some sort of flaw in her, instead of the ones in him.

"And just so we're clear on this, I was *never* ashamed of you."

"Sure." Erin folded her arms across her chest. "That's why you wanted me to keep our relationship a secret. You could have cleared up the lies Susie told if you'd just been honest about us. That was when I realized that you'd rather let your mother think the worst of you than let people see us together."

The undercurrent of bitterness made him wince. Lucas had convinced himself that breaking off all ties between them had been in Erin's best interests. Now he was beginning to realize how much he had hurt her.

He would have shouted his love for her from the top of Pike's Peak if he'd known what she was thinking.

"Because what we had was…amazing. Special. You know how people like to talk. I didn't want anything to ruin it." Lucas wanted—no, needed—her to understand. "Your mom was pretty strict and I was afraid that if she knew, she would pressure you to break up with me.

"You were the only person who didn't judge me. Who didn't look horrified when I questioned why God would take two fathers away from their families at the same time." And why He hadn't given Lucas the opportunity to make things right between him and his dad. "When I was with you, I wasn't Lucas Clayton, I was just…Lucas." He sighed heavily. "If I'm guilty of anything, it was being an eighteen-year-old guy who wanted to keep the woman he loved all to himself."

Erin's eyes were huge in her face. For the first time, Lucas had no idea what she was thinking. If she even believed what he was saying.

Maybe it was time to show her instead. And admit that pride—and fear—had played a role in his actions on graduation night. And over the past two weeks while he'd battled his feelings for her.

In one fluid gesture, Lucas vaulted over the sofa and landed next to her. Erin's lips parted in a gasp that turned into a squeak when he reached out to trace the delicate curve of her jaw.

Before she had time to shy away, he drew her into his arms and bent his head, taking her lips in a searching kiss that had nothing to do with the past but hinted at the promise of a future. When Erin's hands looped around his shoulders and skimmed down his back, everything else disappeared.

When they finally broke apart, Erin stared up at him. "That didn't feel like closure," she whispered.

Lucas smiled. "Finally I got something right."

He bent his head and kissed her again.

Chapter Fourteen

Kylie poked her head in the doorway to Erin's office. "Can you come out front for a second?"

The aggravated expression on her friend's face warned Erin that something was wrong. "Sure. What's going on?"

"Billy Dean Harris is at the counter. He insists on talking to you."

Erin released a ragged breath.

Vincent's brother-in-law was the kind of person who liked to "stir the pot" as her mother used to say. Erin closed the computer program she'd been working on and rose to her feet.

Feet that hadn't quite touched the ground since Lucas's unexpected kiss the night before.

Twelve hours later, her lips still felt tingly.

They hadn't had an opportunity to talk because Max appeared at the top of the stairs, wide-eyed and in need of assurance that Lucas hadn't left again.

Which was fine with Erin because she'd been rendered speechless by that unexpected kiss. A kiss that, amazingly enough, hadn't made her think of the past at all, but opened her eyes to the possibility of a future.

Because they both needed time to think about what had

happened—and what it might mean—Erin had gone home, treasuring the memory of Lucas's smile like a keepsake.

He had put to rest the lingering doubts about why he'd kept their relationship a secret.

But he'd still left. And he hadn't made any promises for the future other than the one to his cousins—that he would stay in Clayton for a year.

Lucas might be attracted to her, might still have feelings for her, but it didn't mean he would make the town his permanent home. Or take her with him when he left.

Erin followed Kylie into the dining area. The breakfast rush was over but there'd been a steady stream of customers for the past hour, taking a break from their shopping to get a cup of coffee or hot chocolate.

Billy Dean turned as Erin walked toward him. She was used to him trying to chisel down his bill or get something for free, but the sneer on his grizzled face caught her off guard.

He hooked his thumbs in the grimy suspenders of his bib overalls and glowered at her. "What kind of kitchen you runnin', Erin?" he said without preamble, making no attempt to keep his voice down. "I ate here yesterday and got sicker than a dog a few hours later. I had to take the rest of the day off from work and stay in bed."

Conversations at the surrounding tables faded, leaving his accusation to echo in the sudden silence.

Erin prayed for patience. "I'm sorry about that, Mr. Harris," she said evenly. "But if you didn't feel well, I'm sure it wasn't from eating at the café."

"Well, Doc Turner thinks different," Billy Dean retorted. "I stopped at the clinic this morning because I still didn't feel right and told him my symptoms. He said it sounded like food poisoning."

Erin's cheeks burned. It was embarrassing that Jonathan Turner might think that something on her menu had made

Billy Dean ill. "Even if that's true, I'm sure the meal you had here wasn't the only one you ate yesterday."

"It's the only one that made me sick afterward," Billy Dean roared.

Jerome charged out of the kitchen and skidded up to Billy Dean, slashing a wooden spoon in the air like a fencing sword several inches from the man's bulbous nose.

"I don't know what you're implying, Harris, but on its worst day, my kitchen is cleaner than Marsha's—"

"Now you wait a second, don't you be insulting my wife—" Billy Dean sputtered.

Erin saw an elderly couple exchange concerned looks before they put their coats on and hustled out of the café. "*Please.* Billy Dean. I'd like to offer you a coupon for a free meal—"

A snort followed her offer. "No, thank you, miss. I don't want a free meal *here.* I can't afford to miss another day of work!"

Erin tried not to flinch as the insult hit home.

"Then why stop in and make a fuss?" Jerome hissed.

"Because I thought she'd want to know." Billy Dean's chin jutted forward as he turned to Erin. "Might persuade you to keep a closer eye on things around the place. If business goes down, you might have to shut down."

Erin felt a rush of fear.

Was he trying to warn her? Had Billy Dean set the fire that night? As the husband of Pauley Clayton's daughter, Marsha, he stood to gain a share of George's inheritance if Lucas or one of his cousins didn't abide by the terms of the will.

"Jerome." Erin was surprised her voice sounded normal. "You have some orders to fill. I'll see Billy Dean out."

"I can find my own way well enough." Billy Dean whirled around and stalked out the door.

Erin couldn't help but notice that several other customers followed him. She hoped the timing was coincidental and not a response to the claim that he'd gotten sick from eating at the café.

Kylie, who'd been standing behind the counter through Billy Dean's tirade, lifted the coffeepot, a question in her eyes.

Erin nodded. "Refills on the house."

Her knees wobbled as she went into the kitchen, where Gerald and Jerome were squared off, crooked nose to crooked nose, in front of the ancient stove.

"...got to tell her," Gerald was saying.

"Tell me what?"

The elderly cooks whirled around.

"Nothing." Jerome's knobby elbow jabbed his brother in the side.

Erin looked at Gerald. "Your ears are red. That means you're hiding something from me."

"Our ma used to say the same thing." Jerome glared at his brother.

Gerald glared back and Erin sighed. "You may as well tell me. I'd rather not get another surprise like the one Billy Dean just delivered."

That seemed to convince them.

"I ran into Dorothy Henry on my way in to work this morning," Gerald said. "Two of her guests at the boarding house complained they didn't feel right after they ate here last night, but I figured Dorothy's chocolate-chip cookies were the culprit. She gives them out at check-in."

"And they sit in a man's stomach like bricks," Jerome felt obligated to add. "Nothing like the ones Arabella makes."

Erin was too dismayed to scold the cook for his less than flattering description of Dorothy's baking skills. "And she said they got sick from eating at the café?"

Gerald studied the floor. "You know Dorothy. The 'thinking' don't always come before the 'saying.'"

Erin couldn't argue with that. Dorothy Henry was a sweet

woman but she also happened to be the biggest gossip in town. Any rumors she started would far outdistance Billy Dean's public announcement by the end of the day.

"No one has ever gotten sick from our food," she said faintly.

"That's a fact," Jerome agreed. "And no one will. Could be a flu bug going around for all we know."

In the cook's flannel-gray eyes, Erin saw both anger and hurt. For Billy Dean to announce to everyone within earshot that he'd gotten food poisoning had the potential to damage more than business. The two cooks prided themselves on their reputation for turning out simple but delicious home-style meals.

Kylie appeared in the window.

"Order up?" Erin said hopefully.

The waitress shook her head. "Order canceled, I'm afraid. The couple who came in after Billy Dean muttered something about an appointment and left."

Erin tried to smile. "That's all right. Business will pick up over lunchtime."

"Don't worry, Erin." Gerald's liver-spotted hand clamped down on her shoulder. "Arabella drops off some more of her pies later on and people will be coming down from the mountains to get themselves a piece."

Jerome harrumphed. "Plus we got chicken and dumplings on special today. They'll be standing in line come noon, don't you worry."

Erin lifted her chin. "I'm not worried."

She repeated those words over the next few hours and wondered when she was going to start to believe them.

As the morning wore on and people passed by the window without so much as a glance inside, she silently recited a verse from the Psalms, one that had brought her comfort in the past.

When Kylie walked through the dining room, wiping

down the spotlessly clean tables she'd wiped down three times in the past hour, Erin stepped into her path.

"I can cover the rest of the shift, Kylie. I know you have a lot of last-minute wedding details to take care of for Jasmine."

"It's almost twelve o'clock," her friend protested. "What about the lunch crowd?"

Erin scraped up a smile. "I don't think there's going to be one." Or a supper crowd, for that matter.

"This isn't fair." Kylie's indignation matched the furious swipes of her dishcloth against the countertop. "It has to be a coincidence. Think about it—how many bake sales and holiday dinners have taken place over the past few days? There could be tainted meat in a bowl of chili. Sour mayonnaise in a salad."

"Unfortunately, it's a matter of perception, not truth," Erin reminded her. "Billy Dean announced to everyone that Dr. Turner said it sounded like food poisoning. Because he ate here yesterday, the café is suspect."

Kylie looked her right in the eye. "Well, I suspect something—or someone—else."

So, they'd had the same thought. But it was beyond Erin's comprehension that Billy Dean had made up a story in the hope that her business would suffer.

"If Billy Dean was lying, I don't think he would have gone to the doctor. And wouldn't Jonathan have found out when he examined him?"

"Dr. Turner isn't from around here. He doesn't know how crooked the branches are on Samuel's family tree. The whole bunch could have made a fortune on the stage," Kylie pointed out. "And, Erin, we might have to consider the alternative. That someone *did* get food poisoning here."

Erin stared at her friend.

A lie was one thing, outright sabotage another.

"No one would have access to the kitchen. Not with Gerald

and Jerome standing guard," she protested. "And I don't think anyone in Samuel's family would stoop that low."

"I know one of them who would," Kylie shot back. "Vincent is a snake. I wouldn't put anything past him."

"Neither would I."

Both women turned at the sound of a familiar voice behind them.

The grim expression on Lucas's face told Erin that he'd been standing there long enough to hear his cousin's name. And he planned to find out why.

Lucas kept his gaze trained on Erin as Kylie grabbed her coat and scooted out the door with a breathless, "I'll leave you two alone. See you tomorrow!"

"What," he asked softly the moment they were alone, "did my cousin do now?"

"Nothing...for sure." Erin caught her lower lip between her teeth.

Lucas's gaze swept the empty tables, pausing to linger on the lone customer sitting near the window and up to the clock on the wall. He had a break between appointments but hadn't wanted to bother Erin, knowing the hours between eleven and one were some of her busiest.

Lucas would have driven past the café if he hadn't felt something. An inner nudge. Now he was glad he had paid attention to it.

He took Erin's hand and tugged her into the office, closing the door behind them.

"Okay. Spill it."

Instead of obeying, Erin began to inch toward her desk.

"If I can scale the sofa, I'm pretty sure that flimsy little desk isn't going to be a challenge."

Erin blushed.

Lucas hadn't meant to remind her of the night before. Even if he hadn't been able to stop thinking about it.

That kiss had lingered in his thoughts through the sleepless night that followed and dogged his trail all morning. The truth was, he'd stopped in because he had to see her again. What he hadn't expected to find was Erin and Kylie Jones in the middle of a conversation about his cousin. He hadn't heard much—just Vincent's name—but it was enough to set off warning bells in his head.

"Billy Dean came in a little while ago and said that he'd gotten sick after eating at the café yesterday."

"He's lying," Lucas said flatly.

"I thought so, too…until Gerald told me that two of Dorothy's guests felt sick last night after eating supper here."

"And Kylie thinks Vincent is responsible." Lucas mentally made the jump from Vincent to his brother-in-law, Billy Dean Harris. It wasn't difficult. Not with Great-Uncle Samuel's family as close as stepping stones.

"After Kylie broke their engagement, Gabe fired him from the mine. He's been going from job to job ever since."

"So Kylie is the one that Vincent wants to get back at?" he asked.

"I don't know…for sure."

"Please tell me what you *do* know." Lucas had to fight to keep the frustration from creeping into his voice. "Because my family has been leaving a lot of blanks about what's been going on lately."

"Vincent stopped in here last week. He seems to hold you responsible for coming back and jeopardizing his chance to inherit George's estate."

His cousin held him responsible for a lot of things. Other than the broken nose Lucas had given him in retaliation for calling Mei a derogatory name when they were kids, most of the slights had been a figment of Vincent's imagination.

"You overheard him telling someone this?"

"Actually, he told me," Erin said reluctantly. "Somehow,

Vincent found out about us. You know how he likes to play mind games with people."

Lucas's back teeth ground together. "He threatened you?"

A shadow crossed Erin's face. "No."

Lucas didn't know if he should believe her. Maybe Vincent hadn't threatened her outright, but whatever he'd said had obviously upset her.

"I'll be back later."

Erin caught up to him at the door. "Where are you going?"

"I think it's about time that I paid my cousin a visit. For old times' sake."

Not knowing which rock to turn over to find his cousin, Lucas made a quick stop at Jones Feed and Supply.

A slow burn had worked its way through him as he remembered the empty tables he'd passed on his way out. First the fire and now an accusation of food poisoning at a time when business at the café would normally be booming.

He'd been avoiding Vincent for two weeks but now Lucas found himself looking forward to seeing the man again.

He threw out a few questions to the cowboys hanging around the coffeepot near the cash register and hopped back in the truck.

Erin was waiting for him on the passenger side.

"I'm coming with you."

Her tone left no room for argument. Lucas almost smiled. "You have to work."

"I'm the boss. I can take the afternoon off." Her lips curved. "I just had to ask Jerome if that was okay with him."

Lucas's heart tripped over that smile.

He'd kicked himself for crossing a line with Erin. A line that he'd been responsible for drawing between them in the first place.

Over the course of a sleepless night, he'd tallied the reasons why resuming his relationship with Erin would be a mistake.

He'd come up with an even ten. But with Erin sitting next to him, a smile on her face and a stubborn gleam in her eyes, Lucas couldn't seem to remember a single one of them.

Erin misinterpreted his silence.

"Lucas Clayton, don't you dare tell me that my staying behind is for the best," she warned.

"I wasn't going to."

Because under the circumstances, he figured the best thing to do was keep Erin close.

"Someone saw Vincent turn down Garvey Road about half an hour ago." Lucas put the pickup in gear and backed out of the lot.

Erin's brow furrowed. "The old salvage yard is the only thing on Garvey but Al Hutchins moved away over a year ago. Maybe he hired Vincent to do some plowing or a few odd jobs around the place."

Lucas hoped so. He was tired of Vincent slinking around in the shadows, waiting for the right moment to attack. And he was done letting his cousin use Erin or other members of his family to get to him.

A few miles outside of town, the old farmstead came into view just over a rise.

Erin leaned forward. "That looks like Vincent's truck." She pointed to the snubbed nose of a black pickup, barely visible between the two outbuildings.

On impulse, Lucas pulled into the cluttered salvage yard, thankful that his reliable but battered truck would blend in with its surroundings. He cut the engine.

Not a minute later, a movement caught his eye. Two men emerged from one of the buildings.

Vincent's muscular frame was unmistakable but it was the other man's hulking form that stripped the air from Lucas's lungs.

Erin was frowning. "There's Vincent but I don't recognize the man with him."

"His name is Maurice."

"You know him?"

"Not personally. The last time I saw him, the police were pushing him into a squad car. He's one of the men who abducted Max."

Chapter Fifteen

Erin stared at him in disbelief.

"But…why is he here? With Vincent?"

"He must have posted bond." Lucas's gaze remained fixed on the two men as they approached Vincent's truck. "When the police picked him up, Maurice claimed he didn't know anything about Scott's murder or a kidnapping. He said he was asked to 'protect' Max during a nasty custody suit."

"Then why follow you to Clayton?"

"I'm not sure if he followed me, or if he was invited." Lucas's jaw tightened. "Vincent wants me out of Clayton. If Max would happen to disappear again, he knows I'll follow."

Everything inside of Erin rebelled against the notion that Vincent was capable of tearing Max away from Lucas and turning him over to the bald, heavily tattooed man whose flat features looked as cold as a mountain spring.

She couldn't suppress a shudder as she imagined sweet-natured little Max at his mercy. No wonder the boy continued to have nightmares.

"Call Zach," Erin whispered.

"There isn't time for that."

Fear spiked in Erin's throat as Lucas's hand fumbled with the handle on the door. Without thinking, she flung her arm across his broad chest in a futile attempt to hold him in place. "You can't confront them alone."

Lucas tensed, the muscles in his forearm turning to iron beneath her fingers. Erin couldn't physically prevent him from leaving but she hoped that he would realize the danger.

Vincent hopped in his truck and gunned the engine a few times for show. For the first time, Erin noticed the nonde-script sedan in its shadow.

As Vincent drove past them, Maurice lifted his nose to the wind like a coyote on a scent trail as he made a slow, thor-ough sweep of the land before getting into his vehicle.

The sedan started up, the engine settling into a rough purr. A moment later, curls of smoke from a cigarette drifted through a crack in the window.

Lucas's fist smacked the steering wheel.

They couldn't leave without drawing attention to Lucas's truck. Which meant that Vincent had a head start into town.

"Where is Max right now?" Erin whispered.

"With Jasmine." Lucas's throat convulsed, as if he real-ized the path her thoughts had taken. "Arabella is running errands today so Jasmine is staying home to watch the trip-lets. They invited Max over to play with them."

Erin opened her purse and began to rummage around for her phone. "I'll call Jasmine and warn her while you let Zach know what's going on."

"So Vincent can worm his way out of this, too?"

"So Zach can *help* you," Erin said. "You don't have to do this alone, Lucas. Zach isn't going to let anything happen to Max, but if you don't do this the right way, someone could get hurt."

She saw the battle going on in the denim-blue eyes before he nodded.

While he dialed Zach's cell, Erin punched in Arabella's number, silently urging Jasmine to pick up. If Lucas was right about Vincent plotting to have Max kidnapped again, then most likely he would be the one to try to sweet talk Jasmine into letting him have Max.

Erin prayed the girl would see through any story that Vincent would concoct to persuade her to release Max into his care. According to Arabella, Jasmine and Cade had been trying to mend fences between their two families for months. Her fiancé didn't approve of his family's behavior, but there was no getting around the fact that Cade was Charley Clayton's son. Vincent wouldn't hesitate to use that relationship if it served his purpose.

"...I'm sure it was him," Lucas was saying in a terse whisper. "I'll meet you at the corner of Waxwing Road in ten minutes. Ask Jack to come with you. He can ID the guy. Maurice was following us the day Jack tracked me to the hotel...right. You, too."

Lucas snapped the phone shut without saying goodbye.

"Jasmine isn't picking up." Erin answered the unspoken question in his eyes.

Lucas's gaze cut from her to the shadowy figure inside the sedan. The butt of a cigarette flew out of the window.

"He's leaving."

Weak with relief, Erin watched the car creep forward and disappear behind the back of the house.

"He's finding a better place to hide." Lucas's fingers trembled as he turned the key in the ignition. "We have to go. Now. It won't take Vincent long to find out where Max is."

"Drop me off at Arabella's on your way to meet up with Zach," Erin said.

"No." Lucas's foot stomped on the gas pedal, causing the tires to buck in the deep snow. "I'm going to drop you off at the café."

"Someone has to be with Jasmine if Vincent shows up at the door."

"I've caused enough trouble for you."

So, they were back to that again.

"I can handle Vincent," she insisted.

"You and whose army?"

"God's."

To Erin's amazement, a smile touched Lucas's lips. "He does seem to look out for you."

"He looks out for you, too," Erin said. "It wasn't a coincidence that you stopped by the café this morning...or that we saw Vincent with Maurice. God takes care of his children."

"His children?" Lucas's lips twisted into a parody of a smile. "You really think He wants to claim me?"

"He already did. And He doesn't let go."

"Jasmine must be home. The lights are on." Lucas pulled up in front of Arabella's house.

"And no sign of Vincent." Erin couldn't hide her relief.

Lucas wasn't ready to celebrate yet. Not when his cousin was making deals with the guy who visited Max in his dreams.

Maurice had left Max in the care of his girlfriend, a flighty twenty-something whose idea of "watching" Max had been to lock him in a closet while she got stoned.

Bile rose in Lucas's throat when he'd watched Vincent thump Maurice on the back as if they were best buddies. He and his cousin had had their differences in the past, but he could hardly fathom that Vincent's hostility and greed ran so deep that he would get involved with a guy like Maurice.

"I'll be back as soon as I touch base with Zach and Jack."

"All right." Erin opened the door and hopped out.

There was so much Lucas wanted to say to her but all he could manage was a grating, "Be careful."

"You, too." Erin flashed a smile over her shoulder.

Lucas watched her auburn ponytail swing between her shoulder blades as she sprinted toward Clayton House.

Heat scratched at the back of his eyes.

*God, I don't deserve Your attention, but Erin and Max...
keep an eye on them, okay?*

It was the first prayer Lucas had uttered in years.

Jack McCord's car was parked on a side street a block from
Arabella's. The squad car, with Zach at the wheel, pulled up
a moment later.

With Pauley lurking around city hall during the day, they
couldn't risk him overhearing their conversation. If Pauley
got wind of the fact that his son was in trouble, he wouldn't
hesitate to warn him.

Lucas filled them in as quickly as he could, not leaving
out Billy Dean's accusation or spotting Vincent's cozy conversation with Maurice.

"I ran Maurice Blanchard," Zach said. "He served time for
burglary a few years ago. Crossing state lines is a violation
of his parole."

"That will take care of him, but what about Vincent?" Jack
put in. "If Blanchard won't talk, Vincent will deny any involvement with him. It will be Lucas and Erin's word against
his."

"And we know how well that's worked in the past," Lucas
said cynically.

"I have an idea how we can get both of them."

Something in Zach's eyes told Lucas that he wasn't going
to like this idea.

"Let's hear it," Jack said, a little too cheerfully under the
circumstances as far as Lucas was concerned.

He had to remember this was the guy who'd tracked him
and Max down in the Florida everglades, one step ahead of
Maurice and his cohorts.

"We have to set a trap for Vincent," Zach said.

But to set a trap, you had to have bait.

Lucas was already shaking his head. "No way. Max and

Erin are with Jasmine and the girls. That's putting too many people at risk."

Jack and Zach exchanged looks.

"I called Erin on my way here," Zach said slowly. "She's willing."

Lucas's heart kicked against his ribs. "Willing to do what?"

"Whatever it takes."

Erin glanced in her rearview mirror every few seconds but all she could see was the top of the black Stetson perched on Max's head.

Which meant that Vincent wasn't following them. Yet.

Jasmine had been given instructions that if Vincent showed up, she was to tell him that Erin had picked up Max and taken him home with her for the evening.

Moments earlier, Erin had tried not to let fear overtake her while Lucas stood in tight-lipped silence as Zach laid out his plan.

Now the snow continued to fall as she helped Max out of his booster seat. "We're going out to feed Diamond and then I'll make supper for us."

"Okay," Max chirped.

Her jumbled thoughts tried to form a prayer but Erin gave up. For now, she had to trust that God knew where she was. Knew what she was feeling.

Erin took Max's hand as they walked to the barn, her gaze straying to the access road that ran adjacent to her property. Were Lucas and Jack already there, waiting?

Just the memory of Maurice's cold expression made her knees wobble. Erin would do anything in her power to protect Max from the man who had abducted him but she also knew that her own power wasn't strong enough.

God, protect us. And protect Lucas.

She had no idea what Vincent's latest betrayal would do

to a man who'd spent years running from his past. But would Lucas turn away from God again—or run into His arms?

Erin had seen the glimmer of longing in Lucas's eyes when she'd told him that God had claimed him long ago. Like the prodigal son, all he needed to do was come home.

No matter how bad this situation looks, use it for good, Lord.

"I'm gonna see the kittens." Max scampered away while Erin retrieved a piece of straw from the bale near the stall.

"Don't go too far," Erin cautioned, keeping one eye on him as she tossed the hay inside the stall.

The barn, which had always offered a quiet sanctuary to work and to pray, now seemed threatening in the fading afternoon light. Shadows moved on the walls and the creak of the wind through the boards produced a sound that was eerie rather than comforting.

Over Max's giggling, Erin heard a soft thud in the mow above her head. Bits of hay and dust rained down through the cracks.

Zach.

Against Lucas's objections, the deputy had decided that he would be the closest one if Vincent made a move toward Max.

"I'm the only one authorized to arrest a person," Zach had said, reminding Erin how potentially dangerous the situation could be.

"This one likes me!" Max had a round-bellied kitten snuggled in his lap while another batted the laces on his boots.

"I think all of them like you—" Erin's breath stalled in her throat as a low rumble came from inside Diamond's stall. She'd only heard the mare make that sound one other time—when a snake had slithered into the barn.

Erin glanced up. Maybe the mare had sensed Zach's presence.

Max frowned. "Diamond sounds mad."

The sound of the horse's hoof connecting with the wall made both of them jump.

"It's getting dark in here," he whimpered.

"I know, sweetie." Erin bent down and hugged him. "We'll go up to the house now."

Where Lucas and Jack would be waiting.

Maybe they'd been wrong about Vincent. Maybe after talking to Maurice, he'd backed out of whatever plan the two had been concocting.

Please, God.

With one arm around Max's thin shoulders, Erin pushed on the heavy door. The wind whipped in and gave it a yank that almost jerked Erin's shoulder out of its socket.

Max squeaked and wound his arms around her hips.

"It's okay." Erin glanced down to comfort him but Max wasn't looking at her. The hazel eyes had locked on something behind them.

"Who's that?" he whispered.

Relief sifted through Erin, bringing peace to her initial panic. Zach must have come down from the loft. "Your uncle—"

"Yeah, kid. It's your Uncle Vincent."

Erin whirled around, keeping one arm around Max. Fear turned her mouth to cotton. How had Vincent managed to arrive ahead of them? His pickup had been nowhere in sight when she'd brought Max home with her.

"You scared me half to death." Erin met his gaze without flinching. "What are you doing here?"

Surprise skittered through Vincent's eyes.

Good. Erin didn't want the man to know she was afraid of him. As far as Vincent was concerned, she knew nothing about his meeting with Maurice.

"I got to thinking it's a shame the kid doesn't know the other side of his family." Vincent sauntered toward them, shoulders hunched, thumbs hooked in the belt loops of his jeans. His casual posture belied the sly glint in his eyes. "Thought it was time I did something about that."

"I'm cold, Erin." Max tugged on her sleeve.

Vincent's gaze shifted to the boy and he smiled. "I'm Lucas's cousin. I was hoping you and I could take a ride and see the Christmas lights. Maybe stop for some hot chocolate afterward."

"You're crazy if you think I'm going to let you take Max anywhere." Erin took a step backward and came up against the door. Even if she grabbed Max's hand and tried to make a break for it, Vincent would catch up to them before they made it to the house.

"So protective," Vincent mocked. "But you're not the kid's mother, Erin, anymore than Lucas is your—" He tilted his head. "What's the word they use in those romantic comedies? Oh, I remember now. *Your knight in shining armor.* Those guys are supposed to rescue a damsel in distress, not run off on her."

Erin wet her lips, struggling to maintain her composure. "Lucas had to get out of Clayton," she murmured. Vincent loved to taunt, so all she had to do was keep him talking until help arrived. "It was the right thing to do."

"So noble and self-sacrificing." Vincent shook his head. "And so deluded."

"You're the one who is deluded if you think Lucas is going to let you take Max anywhere."

"I'm doing him a favor." Vincent smirked. "He doesn't want to be tied down with a kid anymore than he wants to be tied down with you. Thanks to his old man, Lucas isn't wired for that.

"He'll spend the rest of his life running. Now me, I stick by my family." Vincent's eyes narrowed. "You and I both know Lucas only came back for the money."

"So you're trying to force him out of town."

"Hey, it worked last time, didn't it?"

It was the opening Erin had been hoping for. "You mean when you convinced Susie to tell everyone she was pregnant with Lucas's baby?"

"She had a thing for him and needed some cash. All I did was come up with a plan so Susie could have both."

"You think you're so smart," she snapped.

"I am. Smart enough to make sure George Sr.'s inheritance goes to the right people."

I hope you're listening, Zach, because it's the closest thing to a confession you're going to get, Erin thought.

Vincent held out his hand. "Come on, kid. Time to see those Christmas lights. And, Erin, don't try to interfere or you'll be waiting tables at someone else's café instead of your own."

"You started the fire," Erin breathed.

"Arson is a crime, Erin." Vincent pressed a hand against his heart in mock affront.

"So is being a party to kidnapping."

Vincent's right eye began to twitch. "I don't know what you're talking about."

"You met with Maurice Blanchard." Erin prayed she wasn't bringing more harm to the situation but she could see that Vincent's patience was wearing thin. Physically, the man outweighed her by about a hundred pounds, all of it muscle. "Zach is arresting him right now."

"You're lying."

"No, I'm not." Erin swallowed hard. "And Maurice is going to turn on you, the same way you turned on Lucas and the rest of the family."

Vincent look undecided for a moment and then his expression turned dangerous. "Give me the kid. Now."

Erin heard the crunch of footsteps on the snowy path leading up to the barn.

A few more seconds…

"He's scared, Vincent. He doesn't know you."

"We'll get to know each other."

Erin lifted her chin. "You'll have to take me with you."

"Now that's the best idea I've heard all day."

Max went limp in Erin's arms as the door of the barn flew open and Maurice Blanchard stalked in.

Chapter Sixteen

Lucas closed his eyes when he heard Blanchard's voice.

What had happened?

Maurice should have been in custody by now. Zach and Jack should be riding in like the cavalry.

Through a crack in the ceiling, he could see Max sheltered in the protective circle of Erin's arms. It took everything he had not to leap down from the loft and take Vincent out. Except now he had Blanchard to deal with, too.

"So, Maurice is under arrest, huh?" Vincent pushed up to Erin. "I knew you were bluffing."

"Lucas—"

"Will thank me for getting rid of both of you," Vincent interrupted. "It'll save him the energy of having to do it himself."

"If you don't think Lucas will try to find Max, then why take him?" Erin pointed out, a note of desperation creeping into her voice.

"Because from what I hear, Lucas has been getting a little too cozy with you lately. We can't have you two playing house, decorating Christmas trees and going to church together. He might forget he's not a family man."

Anticipating Vincent's next move, Erin scooped up Max

in her arms. The little boy, who had been silent up until now, began to cry.

"Shut him up while I think," Maurice snarled. "What's going on, Clayton? You said you had a plan."

"And part of that plan was for you to stay put until I brought the kid to you." Vincent stood over Erin, who was trying her best to comfort Max. "I did my part. Now take him and go."

"I like Plan A better." Maurice leered at Erin. "Taking them both."

"Vincent!" Erin shrank back.

His cousin chuckled. "Don't worry—you'll be fine. Maurice is going to tuck you somewhere safe for a while."

Lucas's fist silently pounded his knee. Vincent couldn't be that naive.

Forget the odds. He'd take on both men before he allowed Erin and Max to get into a car with Blanchard.

He scanned the walls for anything he could use as a weapon. Being in the loft put him at a distinct disadvantage. The only way down—a ladder built into the far wall—was in full view of the people clustered near the door.

Erin thought Zach was in the loft but Lucas had talked his cousin into letting him take up position there. He'd needed to be close to Max and Erin if anything went wrong.

And things are going wrong, Lord.

Lucas froze, realizing this was the second time a prayer had slipped out, as naturally as he'd taken his next breath. He tried another.

Erin and Max need Your help. I need Your help.

Below him, Vincent pushed the door open. The motion sensor on the barn flicked on, sending a shaft of light through the loft. Falling on the fire extinguisher attached to a beam on the wall.

Lucas smiled.

He had forgotten that sometimes God's response could be very swift. And extremely practical.

Erin tried to comfort Max as Vincent opened the door and the wind enveloped them in an icy hug.

"Wanna go home!" Max cried.

"I know, baby." Erin's heart threatened to beat right through her chest.

She was not only afraid for herself and Max—she also was afraid for Zach, Jack and Lucas. The bulge in Maurice's coat pocket had the distinct outline of a handgun.

"Wait." Erin tried to appeal to Vincent's conscience one last time. "Max is going to need clothes. And his blanket."

Maurice grabbed her roughly by the arm and gave her a shove. "No more stalling. Hit the lights, Clayton. We're out of here—"

A dull thud followed by Vincent's sudden howl drowned out Max's sobs and Winston's frantic yips.

Vincent crashed to the floor and curled into a fetal position, hands clamped around his head.

Maurice let go of Erin.

"Erin. *Run!*"

Lucas?

Erin didn't wait to find out. She stumbled out of the barn, shielding Max the best she could.

Shadows in the darkness around the barn took on human form as men converged on the scene. Erin recognized Zach as he charged past her, gun drawn.

Jack tackled Maurice before he reached his vehicle.

Oblivious to the cold, Erin sank to the ground, Max still cradled in her aching arms.

The next half an hour was a blur. Zach and a fellow deputy loaded Vincent and Maurice into separate squad cars while a female officer escorted Erin and Max back to the house.

"Would you like a cup of tea?" The officer, a sweet-faced

young woman who looked as if she would have been more suited teaching a kindergarten class than police work, offered her a cup of tea. "You look half frozen."

"I c-can g-g-get it." Erin's teeth were chattering as she pushed the words out.

Max had already fallen asleep on the sofa beside her, wrapped in a cocoon of blankets.

"You might want to wait a minute," the officer cautioned. "Zach is doing a…debrief in your kitchen."

"A debrief?"

"With Jack McCord and his cousin, Lucas." Laughter sparkled in her eyes. "But trust me, you don't want to go in there yet…"

Erin was already on her way to the kitchen. She paused in the doorway at the sound of a familiar growl.

"What I want to know is what took you so long?" Lucas was demanding.

"We had to get something on Vincent."

"So we were waiting for the right moment." Jack clapped a hand against Lucas's back.

"Like a fire extinguisher hurtling down from the loft to bean Vincent in the head," Zach said with a weary grin. "Nice aim, by the way. You should consider joining the men's baseball league this summer."

Erin clapped a hand over her mouth but couldn't prevent a weak laugh from slipping through her fingers.

Lucas spun around. "It isn't funny…you're *crying*."

Was she?

Erin pressed her fingertips to her cheeks and felt a jolt of surprise when they came away wet.

In two strides, Lucas was at her side. He swept her against his chest and held her close.

"It's over, Erin. You and Max are safe. It's over." He rocked her in his arms and spoke soft words of encouragement that for some reason made Erin cry even harder.

Jack and Zach looked on in amazement.

"Did you see this coming, Deputy Clayton?" Erin heard Jack whisper.

"No" came Zach's amused response. "It looks like I'm going to have to ask my witnesses a few more questions. Just for the record."

"Someone's here to see you, Erin."

Erin looked up. "The state health inspector?"

Kylie grimaced. "Very funny. No, it's not the health inspector."

Erin pushed away from her desk. She needed a break from the books. After two days, business had been slowly picking up. Very slowly. She had wanted to give her employees a Christmas bonus but now the only thing Erin hoped to give them was their weekly paycheck.

News of Vincent's arrest had swept through the small community, but no one knew the extent of his involvement in the plot to chase Lucas and his cousins out of town. Erin knew the Claytons wanted to keep it that way.

She was glad it was over and they'd found out who was responsible for all the attacks. Maybe now Lucas would finally give himself permission to leave the past where it belonged and embrace the family God had given him.

"Wait! Let me fix your hair."

"Fix my—" Erin batted Kylie's hands away. "What's wrong with my hair?"

"Nothing. Except that it looks like you combed it with a branch from your Christmas tree this morning." Kylie grinned.

Erin paused in front of the mirror. Her neat ponytail had been abused by the constant shuffling of her fingers while she was going over the books.

Kylie plucked at the strings of her apron as she walked toward the door. "You don't need this."

Erin rolled her eyes in exasperation. "Who wants to see me? A celebrity food critic?"

Her friend closed one green eye in a saucy wink. "Better," she whispered.

A split second later, Erin had to agree.

Because Lucas and Max stood by the counter. Both wore jeans, flannel shirts and matching Stetsons on their heads.

A curious lightness began to build in her chest.

"What's going on?"

"A date!" Max shouted.

Now Erin understood. "Oh, you two are having a boys' night out."

Behind the counter, Kylie let out a delicate but audible snort.

"The last I heard—and correct me if I'm wrong—a date involved a guy and a girl," Lucas drawled. "Or on occasion, a guy and a girl and a four year old."

Max nodded happily at having been included.

"You're asking me out on a…date?" Erin ventured, not quite able to believe it. Sure, she'd dreamed about it. Longed for it. But never believed it would ever happen.

Especially given the fact that she hadn't seen Lucas for two days. They'd talked briefly on the phone the evening before but he'd made no move to see her. Until now.

Lucas looked up at the ceiling. "I'm still not getting this stuff right, am I?" Then he turned back to Erin. "Yes, Max and I are taking you out on a date."

"To your house!" Max wasn't about to be left out.

"My place?" Erin echoed.

"And we—" Kylie swept up with a picnic hamper "—supplied the dinner."

Erin's eyes met Lucas's. "I accept."

"Hamburgers and french fries." Max bounced in place, causing the cowboy hat to list over one dark eyebrow.

Erin sent a silent prayer of thanks that he didn't seem to

be affected by their harrowing ordeal. It was possible Max hadn't understood exactly what was happening when Maurice showed up at her barn.

She wished she could say the same. Images of the man's leering expression coupled with the drop in business had taken a toll on her peace of mind.

"For Max." Kylie couldn't stop smiling, a proud accomplice to this particular secret. "For you and Lucas, two T-bone steaks, baked potatoes, salad and one of Arabella's famous apple pies."

"Thank you, Jerome and Gerald!" Erin called.

A duet of grunts and coughs followed.

"Go on, get!" Jerome finally hollered back. "You've been puttin' in too many hours as it is."

"Here's your coat." Kylie thrust it at her. "See you tomorrow."

Erin climbed into the pickup next to Lucas and then almost climbed right back out again when she saw the bouquet of red-and-white roses on the seat.

"Those are for you," Max informed her. "Lucas said you haveta give a girl flowers on a date. I'd rather have Legos."

Lucas chuckled. "It's my way of saying thank you. For… everything."

"Thank you." Erin hugged them against her, burying her face in the fragrant petals. "I love them."

I love you. I never stopped.

But gratitude wasn't the same as love. And a date was…a date. It was two people spending the evening together, not a lifetime commitment.

Lucas won't stop running…

Erin pushed Vincent's taunting words aside. He'd already caused enough damage. Tonight she was going to enjoy the company of her two favorite men and not worry about the future.

Max disappeared into the living room to play with Winston moments after they arrived at her house.

Lucas joined her in the kitchen. "You sit down. I've got this."

"Unpacking a picnic basket?"

He responded to her teasing with a smile that made her weak at the knees. "Hey, we all have our talents."

For a moment, Erin enjoyed the sight of Lucas Clayton in her kitchen. *Her* kitchen. She pinched herself under the table, just to make sure she wasn't dreaming.

"How is Max doing?" Not one to remain idle for long, Erin started to put together a tossed salad from the ingredients Kylie had packed in individual containers.

"He took a long nap yesterday afternoon."

"No nightmares?"

"No." Lucas opened the oven and put the steaks under the broiler. "What about you?"

Erin evaded the question. "I still can't believe Vincent was ready to put Max in danger like that."

"None of us can," Lucas admitted. "Zach said Vincent asked for a lawyer right away and he's refusing to talk. But as far as I'm concerned, it's guilt by association. He and Maurice were together. It stands to reason that Vincent was responsible for the attacks on the rest of the family."

"Including the café."

Lucas's expression changed. "It's only been two days, Erin," he said quietly. "Give it some time."

Erin wished she felt as confident. "Vincent won't admit to tampering with the food, so there's no way to prove it wasn't my fault."

"You know it wasn't."

"Yes." But that wasn't what had kept her awake the previous night. "If I ever needed the perfect excuse to close the doors of the café for good, I'm pretty sure this would be it."

Erin couldn't believe she'd actually voiced out loud the thought that continued to plague her.

"Is that what you want?"

"I thought it was. All this time I thought I was keeping Mom's dream alive, honoring something that was important to her..."

"But now it's important to you," Lucas finished.

He had put into words what Erin hadn't been able to.

"A few of my regular customers came in this morning as if they hadn't heard the rumors. When I walked into the kitchen this morning, Jerome and Gerald were wearing Santa hats to cheer me up. The truth is, for years I wanted to be a veterinarian, but now I can't imagine doing anything other than what I'm doing."

"That's funny. The last thing I wanted to be was a veterinarian, and now I can't imagine doing anything else. Thanks to you."

Erin couldn't hide her shock. "To me?"

"For almost a year, I was under the influence of a woman who loved animals," Lucas said. "Some of it rubbed off. The weird thing is, my father would have approved. He claimed that being a doctor was in our blood and since he didn't specify that I had to heal *people*..."

"The family legacy continues," Erin teased.

A troubled frown settled between Lucas's eyebrows before he turned away. "There are some things a man doesn't want to pass on. Look at my father. And Grandpa George. What does it say about a man who has to bribe his family to get them to return to their hometown?"

"It says that it's never too late to change. That he made things right with God and the people he loved."

Lucas opened his mouth but Erin wasn't sure whether he was about to argue or agree with her because Max appeared in the doorway, a wooden camel in each hand.

"I'm hungry!"

"So am I, sweetie." Erin laughed. "We're just waiting for the steaks."

Max's nose wrinkled. "I'd rather have a burger."

"I hope you feel that way when you're sixteen," Lucas said drily. "It'll save on the grocery bill."

Erin drew in a breath.

That didn't sound like a man who was planning to shirk his responsibility. It sounded like a man who was making room for Max in his future.

But would that future be in Georgia? Or a rustic town at the foot of the Rocky Mountains?

That's what Erin was afraid to ask.

Chapter Seventeen

Erin's alarm went off at six the next morning. She fumbled to shut it off, pressed a hand against her forehead and closed her eyes again. A jackhammer pounded against her temples and her stomach pitched like a raft in whitewater rapids.

What on earth?

She'd felt fine when she went to bed that night. She and Lucas had played a game with Max until his eyes could barely stay open. After they'd left, Erin had stayed up another hour reading.

She reached for her cell phone and saw three missed calls from Kylie. Her friend must be anxious to hear all the details of her date with the two most charming men in Clayton. Pushing herself into a sitting position, Erin punched in the number.

"Thank goodness," Kylie said by way of a greeting.

Erin tried not to groan as the words ricocheted around in her head. "I'm sorry I missed your calls. I guess I overslept. Is everything okay?"

"Zach called me a few minutes ago. Max is in the hospital."

Fear shot through Erin. "What happened?"

"We don't know for sure. He got the news secondhand

from Arabella. Jonathan said it sounded like a severe case of food poisoning so Lucas took Max to the emergency room about 2:00 a.m. The pediatrician on call admitted him because they're worried about dehydration."

"Food poisoning." Erin collapsed against the pillow.

It couldn't be. Not again.

"Lucas has a mild case, too," Kylie continued. "But he won't leave Max's side."

"I'm on my way." Erin tried to sit up but it felt as if her stomach stayed in place. She stifled a groan but Kylie heard it.

"Hey, you don't sound too good, either. Are you feeling okay?"

Erin avoided the question. "I don't understand how this could have happened. Lucas and Max were with me last night. We had dinner together."

Kylie was silent as she processed the news. "The dinner we prepared for you—"

"At the café." Erin's breath caught. Everything except dessert. "We had one of Arabella's pies, too. Lucas and I shared a piece but Max ate a whole slice."

"This has got to stop." Kylie's voice shook with emotion.

"But Vincent is in jail." Erin ignored her roiling stomach as she slid from the bed and reached for a pair of jeans. "He couldn't have done it."

"Not Vincent, no," Kylie agreed.

But if he wasn't responsible, then who was? Every member of Samuel's family stood in line to inherit. Marsha and Billy Dean Harris. Charley and Frank Clayton. Even Pauley, the mayor.

As Erin drove to the county hospital a half hour away, she prayed for Max. And for Lucas. The blessing he'd said at dinner made her hopeful that he was back on speaking terms with God. She could tell the prayer hadn't been for Max's benefit but had come from Lucas's heart.

Was his shaky faith strong enough to stand another attack?

Erin made her way to the pediatric unit, pausing to ask a nurse which room Max was in.

"Room 204." A pretty, dark haired nurse pointed to a door at the end of the hall.

Max was alone when Erin slipped into the room. Sound asleep, with his hand tucked against his cheek, he looked even smaller in the hospital bed. His legs moved restlessly beneath the thin blanket.

Erin took his hand and gently traced Max's fingers, careful not to touch the plastic tube in his arm.

A shadow fell over the bed. "How is he doing?" Zach whispered.

"I don't know yet. Lucas isn't here."

"He's around here somewhere. I just talked to him about fifteen minutes ago." Zach exhaled. "He didn't look too good."

"Will you sit with Max for a few minutes?" Erin asked. "I'll find him."

"Sure." Zach caught her lightly by the arm as she took a step toward the door. "This isn't your fault, you know."

He'd talked to Kylie.

"I don't know what else to think." Erin bit her lip. "Vincent was arrested with Maurice. If it wasn't him, then who's responsible?"

"I don't know," Zach said tightly. "But I plan to find out."

Erin walked to the nurses' station and waited until she got the attention of a nurse sitting at the computer.

"Can I help you?"

"I'm looking for Lucas Clayton. His son, Max Cahill, is in a room just down the hall."

"Blond hair? Blue eyes? Cowboy hat?" At Erin's nod, she pointed to a small hallway on the right. "I think he's in the chapel."

"Thank you." Erin had seen the small gold sign on the door as she'd walked off the elevator.

The door was closed. Gathering up her courage, Erin turned the knob.

"If you don't mind, I'd like to be alone."

Erin stopped. The sight of Lucas, sitting on the bottom step of the small altar, his shoulders set in a rigid line, fractured her heart. The night before, he had laughed with her. Challenged her and Max to a french-fry-eating contest. As the evening wore on, Erin didn't even feel as if she and Lucas were settling back into their old relationship. This had felt different. New.

Better.

Now she could see that any ground they'd gained was gone. But Erin wasn't going to give in without a fight.

Lucas held his breath, waiting for the door to close behind her. He couldn't face Erin. Not now, when the softest glance or slightest touch would cause him to crumble.

Over and over, his mind played through the past six hours. Watching Max doubled over, his eyes glazed with pain, had been worse than waiting out one of his nightmares.

Lucas, so calm and efficient on the job, had felt totally helpless in the face of the boy's misery. He'd wanted to break down and cry right along with him.

The early hours of the morning blurred together. Lucas had called Jonathan and woke him out of a sound sleep. The doctor had listened to Max's symptoms and suggested that Lucas take him straight to the hospital to find out what they were dealing with. The clinic he'd opened in Clayton wasn't equipped to handle cases like the ones Lucas had described.

The pediatrician had admitted Max immediately. Lucas called his sister and asked her to get a message to Tweed that he wouldn't be at work that day.

Mei must have called the rest of the family to let them know what had happened...

He snapped back to the present when the door closed, snuffing out the light from the hall.

For a moment, Lucas thought Erin had left. Until she sat down beside him.

This was the reason he hadn't called her to tell her that Max was in the hospital. It would be more difficult to stick to his decision while looking into Erin's compassionate brown eyes.

So he just wouldn't look at her.

"I'm going to call Mark Arrington, George's attorney. There has to be a loophole in that will. If he can't find one, I'll find a way to come up with my share of the inheritance and divide it among them." Lucas had already thought it through. He had some money saved, and the rest he might be able to borrow.

"Your family wants you to stay—and not because of the money or the land," Erin said evenly. "Your grandfather's will wasn't to divide his assets. It was meant to bring his family back together."

"Tell that to Samuel," Lucas said bitterly.

"You'll hurt your family more if you leave."

He refused to back down. "I'm not going to stay here and put everyone at risk."

"Or yourself," Erin said softly.

"What's that supposed to mean?"

"If you walk away, you're in control. If you stay, you might have to change." Her knuckles rapped the top of his Stetson. "No more Lone Ranger. You'll have to open up your life and your heart to the people you care about."

And disappoint them?

No, thanks.

Lucas still hadn't recovered from the image of Max's accusing eyes when he'd bundled him into the pickup and driven him to the hospital. It was bad enough to know that he couldn't take the pain away. Worse to know that in a sense, he was the one who'd caused it.

"You don't understand."

"That's where you're wrong. I know what it's like to have expectations placed on you. What it's like to lose a parent. I even know what it's like to have life take an…unexpected turn." Erin linked her fingers through his. "God understands, too. That's why He promised that no matter what we go through, He never leaves us or forsakes us."

Lucas stared at Erin.

Until this instant, he had never realized how closely their lives paralleled each other. The difference lay in how they had handled the things that had come their way.

From the moment Erin had walked into detention that day in high school, Lucas had been drawn to the peace in her eyes while refusing to recognize its source. Faith. Erin had clung to hers while Lucas had walked away from his.

And he'd been lost ever since.

Maybe Brooke had been right when she'd said that it was God—not Grandpa George—who had brought them all home.

Brought *him* home.

Lord, if You've been waiting all this time for me to come to my senses, thank You. I'm tired of doing things my own way. Your plan, whatever it is, has to be better than mine. Mine's taken me on a path to nowhere.

He let out a slow breath as the weight in his chest lifted. And then it disappeared completely. Erin had been right. New *was* better.

"I should check on Max." Maybe he hadn't been a good son, but with God's help, he just might be a good father.

Lucas rose to his feet. "Are you coming with me?"

"Do you want me to?"

Lucas could have kicked himself when he saw uncertainty

flicker through Erin's eyes. He was responsible for her doubting herself. And his feelings.

He vowed to make it up to her somehow. He nodded.

As they walked down the hall to Max's room, Lucas glanced through the doorway of the waiting room.

And stopped so abruptly Erin was three steps ahead of him before she realized he'd stopped moving.

The family lounge was crowded with…family. *His* family.

Not only Lisette, but Mei and Jack. Brooke and Gabe were pouring cups of coffee. Kylie and Zach had taken their place by the telephone. Arabella and Jonathan. Vivienne and Cody. Even Jasmine and Cade were there.

Zach wore his uniform and Jonathan was in a pair of rumpled scrubs. Cody and Cade looked as if they were fresh off a cattle drive. It was clear that everyone had dropped what they were doing to make the drive to the hospital.

Erin had been right about that, too.

The doctor stopped just inside the doorway. "Mr. Clayton? If you'd step out into the hall with me for a moment."

"That's all right, Dr. Platt. Whatever you have to say, you can say it in front of my family."

Erin's hand tightened in his.

"All right," the pediatrician said briskly. "The initial tests for E. coli and salmonella came back negative. The lab is checking for a few other things, but Max is resting comfortably now."

Lucas and Erin exchanged looks. "What does that mean?"

Dr. Platt smiled. "It means he can go home as soon as he keeps some fluids down. Which should be in a few hours."

"Thank you, Doctor." Lucas stretched out his hand and the doctor shook it.

"Go on." Arabella motioned toward the door. "We're not going anywhere."

Lisette took Lucas's face in her hands and pressed a kiss

smack dab in the middle of his forehead, the way she had when he was Max's age. "We'll be here when you get back."

There was a commotion in the hallway as he and Erin made their way back to Max's room. A nurse went scurrying into one of the rooms but it was Erin's soft gasp that pushed him into high gear.

Erin was a step behind Lucas as he rounded the doorway into Max's room.

"I'm sorry, Mr. Clayton." The dark haired nurse raised her voice a notch above the muffled sobs from the boy thrashing around beneath the thin white blanket. "A minute ago he was sound asleep."

Lucas sat on the edge of the mattress. "Hey, cowboy," he murmured.

"Daddy!" Max wailed.

Lucas's heart plummeted, because he knew Max had asked for the one thing he was unable to give him.

But there was one thing he could—the same thing he'd done the last time Max had been caught in a nightmare. And the time before that. He wrapped his arms around the thin frame and settled him against his chest.

"Da—" a long shudder "—ddy."

Lucas held on tight. His eyes met Erin's over Max's head to see if she was praying. Unshed tears glistened in her eyes and she was…smiling.

Smiling.

The mattress dipped as Erin sat down on Max's other side and stroked his damp hair away from his cheek. They sat that way for the next half hour, linked together by the little boy in the center of the bed.

When Max finally fell back to sleep, they slipped out into the hall. The minute the door closed behind them, Lucas leaned against the wall and closed his eyes.

"He's going to be okay, Lucas," Erin said.

"Physically, yes." Lucas pushed away from the wall and

shoved his hands into his pockets. "I thought…he hasn't had a nightmare in days. I thought he was healing."

"He is healing."

"You heard Max. He was calling for his dad."

"Yes, he was."

"Then how can you say that?"

Erin slipped her arms around his waist and tipped her head to look at him. "Don't you understand? He was calling for *you,* Lucas."

"We have a plan," Brooke announced the moment they returned to the family lounge. "And it's a good one."

"That's what Zach said a few days ago." Lucas scowled at the deputy sheriff.

"I'm in," Erin said promptly.

"You don't know what it is yet," Lucas muttered.

"Whatever it is, it has to better than the one you came up with."

"Let me guess," Mei said. "Did his plan involve a suitcase?"

"That was Plan A," Lucas admitted with a sideways look at Erin. "Plan B is staying put for a while."

For a while.

Erin tried not to read too much into the words.

"Vincent isn't talking," Zach said. "So it's up to us to figure out who's willing to go to such desperate measures to get us to leave Clayton."

"And how do we do that?" Lucas looked skeptical.

"We make it easy for them," Jack drawled.

Chapter Eighteen

"It's almost time." Erin drew in a ragged breath, her chest as tight as the knot in her apron. "Is everyone here?"

Kylie nodded. "I think so. Lucas just drove up."

The knot tightened.

Erin hadn't spoken to him since Max was released from the hospital the day before, but she hadn't stopped praying that Lucas had reached a turning point in his relationship with God. And his family.

She could tell he'd been touched by the fact that no one had budged from the waiting room until Max was released from the hospital later in the afternoon.

Oddly enough, Erin was the one who'd felt out of place. No one questioned her right to be at the hospital, but the curious glances cast her way let Erin know that everyone was wondering what—if anything—was going on between her and Lucas.

They weren't the only ones.

"Sorry I'm late." Lucas shucked off his coat as he walked through the door. "I had to play a quick game of Candy Land with Max and my mom before I left."

"Quick?" Arabella laughed. "That game can last all day."

"I should have remembered that before I agreed" came

the wry response. "Erin and I played two games with him the other night. I've performed surgeries that didn't take as long."

Once again, Erin felt the weight of those curious eyes upon her.

Zach came to her rescue.

"Arabella is going to give each of us a job," he said. "We have two hours until we meet up with Reverend West for Christmas caroling."

Each of them had a job to do—and a part to play—in their plan to catch a criminal.

Kylie had taken advantage of her six-hour shift to tell anyone who would listen how excited she was that all the Claytons were going to meet at the Cowboy Café that evening to prepare the food for Jasmine and Cade's reception dinner. Zach was confident the local grapevine would take it from there.

After Erin closed up for the day, Arabella and Vivienne had hauled in their state-of-the-art baking supplies and cookware to boost Jerome and Gerald's meager supply.

"Everyone smile for the camera," Jack said.

Erin appreciated the man's attempt to lighten the moment but the reminder that they'd met for more than a social get-together weighed heavy on everyone's mind. Zach had hidden two video recorders inside the café. One in the kitchen and one in the dining room.

Everyone had been willing to put their own schedules on hold for the moment. If Zach's plan didn't work, then another case of food poisoning would be attributed to the café and more attempts would be made to "persuade" the Claytons to leave town.

Arabella stepped forward. "I think we should start with prayer."

As if by silent agreement, everyone gathered in a circle.

One by one, everyone spoke a few simple words, straight from the heart.

There was a moment of silence after Erin finished praying. And then it was Lucas's turn. For a second, she thought he would pass. Even though she'd sensed that he was on speaking terms with the Lord again, it was another thing to speak to Him out loud, with his family listening.

"Lord." Lucas's husky voice seemed to catch on the word. "Thank You for bringing us together tonight. Thank You for…family. But most of all, thank You for loving us no matter what. Amen."

A familiar, tinkling laugh followed Lucas's quiet benediction.

"Well, look at this! For a second, I thought I accidentally walked into church instead of the Cowboy Café."

"Mom." Arabella twisted her hands together as Kat sauntered in. "I didn't expect to see you here."

"I suppose that's because no one remembered to invite me." Kat shed a red leather coat a shade lighter than her hair and tossed it over the back of a chair, a good indication that she intended to stay.

"Jasmine said that she and Cade were babysitting my granddaughters tonight because all the Claytons were meeting at the café to make food for the reception. And since I'm a Clayton…" Her green-eyed gaze swept the faces of the people gathered in the kitchen, almost as if she were waiting for someone to challenge the statement.

"That's great," Vivienne said with forced cheerfulness. "We need all the help we can get."

Kat patted her niece's cheek. "Of course you do, dear. Now, what can I do?"

"There's a box of petit fours on the table." Arabella stepped in and pointed to one of the tables. "You can attach a frosting rose to the top of each one."

Erin hid a smile. Arabella had put her own mother in the corner to keep her out of trouble.

Brooke, Mei and Kylie sat together, putting together sprays of colorful silk flowers and greenery to form centerpieces for the reception tables.

Under the supervision of Arabella, Vivienne and Erin, the men filed into the kitchen to help with food preparation.

"Jasmine and Cade wanted a fun reception with a Western theme, so we're going with chicken and ribs and all the fixings," Erin said.

"And the best part is, we get to sample as we go," Cody said with a grin.

The men pitched in like troupers, their banter dispelling the tension that continued to mount as the evening wore on.

"This is going to work," she heard Zach tell Lucas at one point. "We'll find out who's been causing all this trouble and then all you have to do is finish out the year."

Erin left the kitchen, afraid to hear Lucas's response.

Erin was avoiding him.

Lucas tried to catch her eye several times over the course of the evening but she flitted from person to person like a butterfly, never staying in one place for more than a few minutes.

Smiling at everyone but him.

Lucas wasn't sure what had caused the change in Erin, but he knew they needed some time to sort things out. Alone.

"Erin? I think Lucas needs a lesson in making gravy," Kylie sang out.

Lucas pretended to be offended. "What's wrong with adding some texture?"

Erin left her station to examine the contents bubbling in the pot. "See this wire whisk? It's your new best friend."

She would have moved on, but Lucas caught her arm. "Max wants to see you."

That earned a smile. "How is he doing?"

"Feeling well enough to beg for a candy cane off Mom's tree," Lucas told her.

A faint smile touched Erin's lips. "I'm glad he's feeling better."

Lucas was aware of the looks and smiles being exchanged between the kitchen crew.

Was I thanking You yesterday for my family, God? Because right now I could use a few minutes alone with Erin...

A tap on the window drew everyone's attention.

"That's our cue," Vivienne said.

Lucas saw Reverend West, his wife, Laura, and several members of the congregation waiting for them on the sidewalk.

"And just in time." Cody sighed. "Those little frosting roses were staining my fingers *pink*. A guy has a reputation to uphold, you know."

Vivienne batted her eyelashes. "Don't worry, honey. With that five o'clock shadow, you still look like a tough cattle wrestler."

"Wrangler." Cody heaved a sigh. "The word is *wrangler*. What did New York City do to you, sweetheart?"

"It made me appreciate Clayton, Colorado, even more." She gave him a radiant smile.

"I can't remember the last time I did this," Lucas muttered as he shrugged his coat on.

"I do," Mei said. "But you weren't singing with the carolers. If I remember correctly, you were caught *pelting* them with snowballs."

She was right.

"I didn't stay away long enough," Lucas complained. "You still remember all of my stupid mistakes."

"Not all of them." Vivienne sashayed past, knotting a colorful scarf around her neck.

"She's right." Zach thumped him on the back. "There's waaay too many."

"But the past is in the past. And we love you." Mei linked her arm through his.

Lucas felt his throat tighten.

Maybe his family was willing to forgive him, but he had a lot to make up for.

Starting with the slender redhead who had managed to slip out the door when he wasn't looking.

A half a block from the café, Erin realized she'd left her mittens in her office.

"I'll be right back," she whispered to Kylie as the carolers crossed the street.

"Hold on." Someone snagged her arm. "If I can't sneak away, neither can you."

Erin felt Lucas's touch all the way to her toes. "I forgot my mittens," she said. "I'll be right back."

"Do you want me to come with you?"

"No." *Yes.* "I'll catch up in five minutes." Erin didn't give Lucas a chance to argue. With a quick smile, she broke free and jogged down the sidewalk toward the diner.

She skirted around the back of the building and unlocked the door. All the lights were off, but the mouth-watering scent of BBQ lingered in the air.

Erin was about to enter her office when she heard a noise. Her heart jumped into her throat.

As far as she knew, everyone in their group was still caroling with Reverend West.

She took a few careful steps toward the kitchen, listening intently even as she scolded herself for having an overactive imagination. There was no way Samuel or one of his cohorts would choose to break into the café now. Not with the other side of the Clayton family gathered a block away, singing around the Christmas tree in the town green.

It's an old, creaky building, Erin told herself.

The confrontation with Vincent and Maurice had her spooked, that was all. But it still didn't prevent a cold shiver from racing down Erin's spine as she heard the noise again.

She peeked around the doorway and her knees went weak with relief.

Kat Clayton stood in front of the row of pies, still warm from the ovens. Erin wasn't that surprised to see her, given the fact the woman had turned up her nose at the idea of caroling. Kat had started out with the group and must have doubled back at some point to take shelter from the cold.

But Erin couldn't let the woman's presence mess up the trap that Lucas's family had gone to such lengths to set, either.

"Kat?"

Kat jumped a foot in the air and dropped whatever she was holding onto the floor. It spun out of her hand and stopped at Erin's feet.

"What are you doing here?" Kat squawked.

"I forgot something." Erin automatically bent down to retrieve the object Lucas's aunt had dropped.

"Leave that alone." Kat charged toward her, her face twisting with something akin to panic.

"What…" Erin's mouth dried up as she stared at the tiny glass medicine dropper in her palm. "What is this?"

Kat's nostrils flared. "It's mine, if you must know. My medicine."

Erin looked at the clear liquid in the dropper. And then at the food they'd spent the last few hours preparing. "You put something in the food."

"Don't be ridiculous." Kat drew herself up and glared at Erin. "Why would I do that?"

"Because you don't want Jasmine and Cade to get married." It was beginning to make sense. Jasmine's wedding dress. Everyone had assumed one of Samuel's relatives was responsible, but to cause trouble in Lucas's family, who better than a member of that family?

"You are so naive." Kat's shrill cackle echoed through the empty diner. "I don't care about the wedding. Although, I could buy them a nice gift with the money I earned. Especially now that we don't have to split it with Vincent."

The money she'd earned?

Erin took a step back and slipped the dropper in her pocket, unnerved by the almost gleeful expression on the woman's face. "You were helping Vincent."

"Helping him?" Kat snorted. "Vincent is all muscle and no brains. He was helping *me*."

"But…you're Arabella's mother."

"Thank you for the reminder" came the cutting response. "But I don't owe my darling daughter a thing. Arabella made her choice to stay in Clayton. Just like you did." She shrugged. "A woman has to do what a woman has to do."

And this woman had definitely come unhinged.

"You put poison in people's food!" Erin remembered Max lying in the hospital bed, so small and fragile, and felt physically ill. "You're crazy."

"Like a fox." Kat winked at her as the front door opened and a familiar voice called her name.

Lucas.

Thank You, God.

Before she could open her mouth, Kat beat her to it.

"We're in the kitchen, Lucas," she wailed. "Please, hurry!"

Lucas rounded the corner at a run, his gaze sweeping over the room and settling on Erin.

Kat latched on to his arm. "I came back to get my purse and caught Erin putting something in the food."

Chapter Nineteen

Erin stared at Lucas's aunt, dumbfounded.

"That's not true." Her voice barely broke above a whisper.

"Check her coat pocket if you don't believe me," Katrina cried. "I saw her hide the vial when I came in."

"What's going on?" Zach appeared in the doorway, flanked by Jack and Cody. The rest of the Claytons crowded in behind them.

Erin didn't get an opportunity to speak as Kat appealed to her other nephew now. "Arrest her, Zachary. She's the one who has been causing all the trouble. She and Vincent deserve to sit in jail together."

Erin felt as if she were living one of Max's nightmares. She turned to Zach. "Kat is lying. She teamed up with Vincent. She admitted it a few minutes before Lucas came in."

Arabella's gasp drew Kat's attention. "She's trying to frame me, sweetheart. Can't you see that? Samuel and Vincent promised her a cut of the inheritance."

"Why would Erin do that, Mom?" Arabella's voice shook.

"Revenge," Kat said without missing a beat. "Erin never forgave Lucas for walking out on her seven years ago. He made her all kinds of promises he didn't keep."

The cousins exchanged looks.

"Is that true, Erin?" Zach asked. "You and Lucas were dating and he broke up with you?"

She nodded before Lucas could say anything.

A triumphant gleam appeared in Kat's eyes. "Check her pocket," she demanded. "You'll see that I'm the one telling the truth."

Zach didn't move. Erin withdrew the dropper from her pocket and handed it to him.

Silence descended on the room.

The way Kat had neatly turned the tables on Erin had sent her reeling. She wasn't even sure what she could say in her defense.

To her absolute astonishment, Lucas slipped his arm around her shoulders.

"Erin isn't that kind of person. She would never hurt anyone. Not for money. Not for *any* reason."

The quiet confidence in his voice gave Erin strength. If Lucas believed her, maybe the others would, too.

"He's right." Arabella faced her mother. "But you would."

Katrina, in a performance worthy of an Academy award, pressed a hand against her heart. "You're my daughter. How can you accuse me of that?"

Arabella shook her head. "That's why you came back," she said slowly. "Not to reconnect with your family. You want the same thing as Samuel. The money and the land. And this proves you were willing to do anything to get it."

"She's the one holding the vial. It's my word against hers." Kat cast a malevolent look at Erin.

"No, it isn't." Zach raked a hand through his hair, his expression weary rather than victorious.

Cade pointed to the clock.

"Smile for the camera, Aunt Kat."

Her features contorted into a mask of rage and accusation. "You set me up!"

"You set yourself up," Zach said evenly. "Samuel and Vincent were using you—"

"Using me?" Kat sneered. "Oh, please. I was using *them*. My father taught me all about blackmail and payoffs. Ask Darlene Perry if you don't believe me."

"You can explain everything," Zach said. "In the police report."

"I've got nothing to say to you." Kat tossed her head. "You're just as guilty as I am. None of you came back here to reconnect with your roots."

"Not at first," Brooke murmured.

"You're as bad as her." Kat pointed at Arabella. "I don't need a sermon. I need the money that should have been mine to begin with. But no, my father, the man who'd been controlling and self-centered all of his life, had to perform this great noble act before he died. I don't know what he hoped to accomplish."

"He wanted to change things." Vivienne stared at her aunt as if she'd never seen her before.

Mei linked her arm through Arabella's in a show of solidarity. "He *did* change things."

Kat's lips twisted in disgust. "You're all weak. Every one of you. I'd rather sit in jail than listen to this."

Jonathan wrapped Arabella in a protective embrace as she fought to hold the tears back.

"I can take care of that." Zach took his aunt by the arm and began to lead her away. "Erin?" He paused as he reached the doorway. "I'm going to need that vial. And I'll need a statement from you, too."

The stress from the past ten minutes had left her feeling a little shaky. All Erin could manage was a brief nod.

"I'll walk with you over to the station," Lucas said.

"No." Erin carefully extricated herself from the warm refuge of his arms. "Your family needs you right now."

"Don't worry. We'll clean up." Kylie wrapped Erin in a tight hug. "I'll lock up here when we're done."

"We'll have to throw away all this food now," Vivienne said in a low voice. "What are we going to do?"

Arabella summoned a shaky smile.

"We're going to give them a wedding to remember."

"Whatcha doin'?"

Lucas felt a tug on his leg. Max had joined him at the window, where he'd been staring at the smoke curling from Erin's chimney for the past fifteen minutes. She hadn't returned his phone calls that morning, but when he'd called the café, Kylie said that Erin hadn't come in to work yet.

"Thinking," Lucas said truthfully.

"Okay." Max pursed his lips together and frowned in what Lucas realized was a parody of his own expression. "I think we should go to Erin's house."

"You know something, Max?" Lucas grinned. "You read my mind."

He was anxious to talk to Erin. She'd looked shaken by Kat's accusation...and even more surprised that he hadn't believed Kat's lies.

It was becoming clear that Erin still harbored doubts. Not about him—about herself.

That blew him away. How could she not see what everyone else saw in her? The perfect blend of sweetness and spunk.

The perfect woman for him.

Lights shone in the windows of the barn so Lucas parked outside the door and helped Max out of the truck.

Frank Clayton's gelding poked its nose out of the stall, the velvet lips tugging at Lucas's sleeve when he paused to say hello.

In the chaos of the past few days, he had forgotten about the horse. But Erin hadn't. The door next to Diamond's stall sported a red velvet bow.

"I'm gonna find the kittens." Max broke away from him, not the least bit hesitant to revisit the place where the man from his nightmare had come to life again.

Lucas had Erin to thank for that, too. Sometime in the past twenty-four hours she had transformed the barn into a wonderland of twinkling lights. They were everywhere. Tacked along the walls. Fashioned into the shape of a star above the bales of hay where the kittens played.

Erin didn't want Max to remember the darkness. She wanted him to laugh and play and feel safe, surrounded by lights.

The barn looked a lot different than it had a few nights ago, when he'd been lying on his belly in the loft, listening to his cousin coolly transfer Erin and Max into Maurice's keeping.

And the woman who had willingly put herself in danger for his son was singing along with a familiar Christmas carol, her lilting voice joining the chorus in a stirring rendition of "Emmanuel" that vibrated the speakers of a dusty radio plugged into the wall.

God with us.

Lucas could finally accept that as truth.

Thank You.

Talking to God was getting easier, too. Maybe, Lucas thought ruefully, because the last few days had given him ample opportunity for practice.

Erin's solo abruptly stopped as Max dashed past her, chasing after one of the kittens. A second later, she peeked around the corner of the empty stall.

Lucas's heart crashed into his rib cage, a familiar response whenever he saw Erin. "Hi."

Very smooth, Clayton. Maybe you should stick to charming horses.

"Hi." She blew a few strands of copper hair off her forehead and smiled down at Max. "Hey, cowboy. You're up bright and early."

"That's 'cause I gotta secret."

Erin looked at Lucas but he appeared as mystified by Max's announcement as she was. She went down on one knee, bringing them to eye level.

"A secret? That sounds serious."

Max nodded, as if he expected Erin would understand.

After everything that had happened, Lucas didn't appear quite so understanding. "Who told you a secret, Max?" he demanded.

Max's eyes went wide at his tone. "M-Macy did."

"Macy?"

"Uh-huh." Max scraped the toe of his boot against the floor. "She wants a kitten for Christmas."

Erin looked at Lucas and saw her relief mirrored in the blue eyes. "A kitten."

Max pursed his lips. "It's okay that I told, isn't it? 'Cause how is she gonna get a kitten if you don't give her one?"

"Mmm. That's a good question." Erin rocked back on her heels. "You did the right thing."

"So we can give her one?"

Erin hesitated. It was only a matter of time before Macy moved in with Brooke Clayton. She didn't want to cause trouble if Lucas's cousin didn't want a furry livewire in her home, but she didn't want to pass up the chance to brighten Macy's Christmas, either.

"What do you think?" Lucas asked.

"I think Macy must like Max an awful lot if she's willing to tell him a secret." Erin stood up and brushed her hands off. "So, I say we make Macy's Christmas wish come true. Would you like to pick one out, Max?"

"I know which one!" Max dropped to his knees in the swarm of kittens and picked one up, draping it over his arm like a furry purse. Instead of trying to scramble away, the calico closed its eyes and began to purr, its soft paws kneading the sleeve of his coat.

The perfect choice for a ten-year-old girl.

"I'm sure she'll love this one," Erin said in a husky voice.

Max beamed. "Let's go."

"Right now?" Erin slanted a look at Lucas. Under the circumstances, she didn't know if they should show up at Macy's house unannounced. "I received a prayer request this morning about Darlene."

Lucas understood. "I did, too. Maybe it would lift Macy's spirits if we stopped over and surprised her," he said quietly.

"It will." Max snuggled the animal. "Can I have one, too, Daddy?"

"That's up to Erin."

Erin's gaze shifted from the sparkle in Max's eyes to the tender look in Lucas's and knew at that moment, there wasn't anything he wouldn't give the boy to put a smile like that on his face.

She might as well use it to her advantage.

"Butterscotch has six kittens. I think I can part with one. Or two."

Max's face lit up. "Two?"

"You're going to pay for that," Lucas whispered in her ear.

"Mmm." Erin tipped her head. "Think of it as *payback* for the horse in the stall behind you, Dr. Clayton."

Max sang to the kitten in its carrier on the way out to Darlene Perry's. Erin stared out the window and Lucas knew she was thinking about how difficult the coming days would be for Macy.

"She has family."

Lucas was just beginning to understand the value of those words.

"I know." Erin gave him a tremulous smile. "I was remembering how hard it was when Mom died. She was sick for a long time, too."

And he should have been there for her.

It would take Lucas a lifetime to make up for the last seven years—but he was looking forward to it.

Jonathan Turner greeted them at the door. He'd exchanged his shirt and tie for jeans and a cream-colored fisherman's sweater but there was no doubt he was the acting physician.

"Good morning." A hospice nurse with warm brown eyes and a smile to match ushered them into the living room.

Macy wandered in, looking as forlorn as they'd ever seen her. "Hi, Max."

"We gotta kitten," he said.

"I know." Macy smiled. "I've seen them in the barn. You know which one is my favorite? The little orange calico with the black patch over her eye."

Lucas could tell by the look on Erin's face that she'd had no idea the little girl *had* a favorite. But the slow smile that drew up the corner of her lips was a sure sign that Max had chosen the right one.

Max jumped up and down. "That's the one we bringed."

Macy looked to Erin for an explanation.

"I don't think we're going to be able to keep this a secret very long," she laughed. "Max, why don't you take Macy into the kitchen and introduce her to her Christmas present?"

Max didn't need to be asked twice. He grabbed the older girl by the hand and ran from the room.

Darlene Perry lay in a hospital bed, her features ravaged by the disease that had slowly won the battle. "Come in and sit down."

Lucas looked at Jonathan, who nodded. "I have to make a phone call. I'll be back in a few minutes."

Jonathan excused himself from the room while Lucas and Erin took a seat on the worn sofa.

"Sweet of you, Erin," Darlene rasped, her breathing labored. "Macy talks about your animals all the time."

"I enjoy having her visit."

"Brooke said she would stop by this morning." Darlene's head rolled toward the window. "She and Zach are going to pick Macy up later this afternoon and take her skating."

Lucas cleared his throat, wondering how much he should say. "I'm sure Brooke will be here, but Zach has to…work."

Darlene's sunken eyes clouded. "Did something happen?"

Lucas hesitated. He didn't want to cause undue stress on Darlene, yet it seemed to him there'd been enough secrets in the family. Like Reverend West had said in his sermon, maybe it was time to let some light in.

"He had to arrest his aunt, Katrina Clayton, last night. It turns out that she was responsible for planning the attacks against my family the past few months."

Darlene began to tremble violently and Erin went to her side. Lucas inwardly kicked himself.

"I'm sorry, Mrs. Perry." Once again, it appeared he'd made the wrong decision.

"No." Darlene gasped. "I'm glad you told me. I thought I was doing the right thing…I made a promise." Her legs moved restlessly beneath the blankets.

Erin took Darlene's hand and comforted her in the same way she'd comforted Max.

"Is there anything we can do?" Lucas asked, feeling responsible for causing the woman more pain.

"Call Reverend West," Darlene whispered. "And the rest of your family. They need to…hear."

Lucas wasn't sure he understood. "My family?"

"Yes…ask them to come." Darlene struggled to sit up. "Soon."

"All right." Lucas met Jonathan in the doorway and pulled him aside. "Darlene wants Reverend West here. And the rest of the family. I'm not sure that's a good idea—"

"Yes, it is," the doctor interrupted. "Something has been weighing on that poor woman since I met her. If I were you, I'd do what she said. As soon as possible."

That was all Lucas needed to hear. "I'll start making phone calls."

Chapter Twenty

One by one, cars began to line up along the snow-covered driveway as the Clayton family gathered in Darlene Perry's living room.

The festive Christmas decorations were at odds with the somber mood. Reverend West moved from couple to couple, his presence easing the tension that had begun to permeate the air as members of the family arrived.

"I asked you all to come here today…" Darlene looked at Reverend West, who nodded encouragingly. "I made a promise ten years ago. I shouldn't have…but I thought I had to keep it. I didn't know if it was right but I prayed about it. When Lucas told me about Kat, it was an answer to my prayer."

Gabe slipped his arm around Brooke's shoulders. The gesture wasn't lost on Darlene. Tears pooled in her eyes.

"I don't want this to cause anyone pain…I want it to bring healing. What Kat did…it was wrong. What I did was wrong, too. I hope she finds the forgiveness that I have." Darlene released a ragged breath. "Ten years ago, I had an affair…"

Across the room, Mei's eyes met Lucas's. He braced himself to hear his father's name, suddenly grateful their mother wasn't in the room. It would be better hearing the news from one of them rather than from Darlene.

"With George Clayton Jr."

Brooke's audible gasp sounded like a gunshot in the quiet room. Vivienne turned her face into Cody's broad shoulder. Zach didn't look surprised by the admission, leaving Lucas to wonder if he hadn't suspected this all along.

"It's all right," Reverend West murmured. "Take your time."

Darlene nodded, tears tracking her hollow cheeks. "Georgie and I dated in high school, but your grandfather said I wasn't good enough for him. No one stood up to George Clayton Sr., so he broke up with me."

"Your father—" Her gaze touched on Zach, Brooke and Vivienne. "He loved you—and your mother. George was going through a difficult time after Lucy died and he turned to me for comfort. It was a mistake. We both knew that. When I found out I was pregnant, neither of us knew what to do. George didn't want to lose his family, but he was a good man. He wanted to do the right thing."

Darlene's gaze bounced from Mei to Lucas. Lucas sucked in a breath, knowing that somehow this situation involved his father, too.

"He confided in his brother. Vern was…furious. He didn't want a scandal in the family."

Bitterness swelled in Lucas. Of course his father hadn't wanted a scandal. His reputation had become the most important thing in his life, more important than his family or even the God he served.

"Uncle Vern and my dad were on their way to your house when the accident happened, weren't they?" Vivienne asked in the silence that followed.

"I think so." Everyone had to strain to hear Darlene now. "After they died, I didn't know what to do. I finally got the courage to tell your grandfather. He didn't want to have anything to do with me or the baby."

Reverend West moved to Darlene's side and took her hand, giving her the strength to continue. She gave the minister a grateful look. "George offered me money if I kept the name of Macy's father a secret. I didn't know what else to do. I was pregnant and alone. George Jr. was gone. I didn't want to cause your family any more grief—your mother deserved the good memories she had of her husband. It wouldn't have been right to take those away."

"You had to think of Macy," Brooke said. Her face was as white as Darlene's, but already the warm light of forgiveness kindled in her eyes.

"Where does Kat fit into all this?" Zach asked, his expression still guarded.

Lucas had harbored no illusions about his father, but this had to be tough on his older cousin, too. George Jr. and Zach hadn't been close, either, but the news of his father's infidelity still had to cut deep.

"I thought a woman might be more sympathetic to my situation," Darlene confessed. "I met with Kat and poured out my heart to her. She said she would see what she could do—but what she did was look out for herself."

"She tried to extort money from her own father." Arabella, who had been silent up until now, dashed at the tears welling up in her eyes. "She wanted cash in exchange for her silence."

"Yes." Darlene took a sip of water from the glass Laura West offered her. "Kat left town after that. I bought this house with the money George Sr. gave me and raised Macy the best I could. When I got sick, I knew that my daughter would need a family. I prayed about what to do. I didn't want to hurt anyone, but Macy needed you. All of you. I'm so sorry to cause you more pain."

"I'm sorry, Darlene." Arabella moved across the room and sat down next to Macy's mother. "Sorry for what my mother did. Sorry the family wasn't there for Macy—or for you—a long time ago. If we'd known, we could have helped."

A murmur of agreement rippled around the room.

"You may not agree with George's methods, but his motives were good," Reverend West said. "He acknowledged his mistakes and got right with God." A hint of a smile touched the man's lips now. "I think as far as the will is concerned, George would say that the end justified the means. You're all in Clayton. Now each one of you has to decide where to go from here."

Darlene's head rolled back against the pillow. "George wanted to make things right before he died. I—I wanted to do the same thing. If it isn't too late."

"It's never too late." Arabella leaned down and embraced Darlene. Vivienne and Brooke followed suit, offering the forgiveness that Darlene longed for.

Watching his cousins, Lucas felt the last of his defenses crumble. In spite of Kat's negative influence, Arabella was a wonderful mother to her girls. If she could overcome the past, maybe he could, too.

Darlene's eyes fluttered closed, and Jonathan quickly moved to her side. "I think Darlene should rest now."

Arabella looked at him, a question in her eyes. Jonathan nodded and took Darlene's hand. The woman's peaceful smile rivaled the lights on the Christmas tree. "You'll all stay…for a while?" she asked in a broken whisper.

Brooke smiled through her tears. "We're family. I'm afraid you're stuck with us."

It was almost eight o'clock when the headlights from Lucas's truck cut a swath through the darkness.

"Daddy's here?" Max looked up from the puzzle they'd been putting together.

Ever since Max's stay in the hospital, he no longer called

Lucas by his first name. That day had been a turning point for both of them.

"I think so." Erin brushed the curtain aside, her heart in her throat. It had been a difficult afternoon, waiting for him to return. Wondering why Darlene had asked Lucas's family to gather at her home.

She and Max had eaten supper hours ago. When the house began to cool, Erin started a fire and supervised Max while he took a bubble bath.

Erin had been drawing the bedtime routine out, hoping Lucas would make it home before she tucked Max in bed for the night.

Max heard Lucas's footsteps and bounded to the door. "Weputapuzzletogetherandplayedgamesandbuiltatower…"

"Whoa. Take a breath, bud. My ears can't keep up." Lucas flashed a weary grin before turning to Erin. "I'm sorry I'm late. Again."

"It's all right. Max and I have been having fun."

Lucas picked up his son and hugged him until he squirmed. "I can't breathe, Daddy!"

"I know it's a little past his bedtime, but he wanted to see you before he fell asleep."

"I wanted to see him, too." Lucas fumbled with the buttons on his coat. Without thinking, Erin brushed his cold hands aside and took over, unfastening them the way she would have done if it were Max standing in front of her.

"I'm gonna brush my teeth and pick out a story." Max scrambled up the stairs.

Erin waited until she heard the bathroom door close. "Darlene?"

"She passed away an hour ago."

Tears sprang into her eyes. "Was Macy…?"

"Not at the end. It was what Darlene wanted. They spent some time together and then Jasmine and Cade took her and the triplets and A.J. Wesson back to Arabella's house. The rest of us stayed with her."

The lump in Erin's throat expanded. "It must have been so hard to say goodbye to her daughter."

"Yes…and no." Lucas cleared his throat. "She was an amazing woman. Darlene told us that she had peace knowing she would be safe in the Lord's arms and Macy…Macy would be safe in ours."

Lucas reached out and brushed a tear off her cheek with the pad of his thumb. "That was everyone's response," he murmured.

Erin knew there was more he wanted to say, but Max galloped down the stairs and flew into Lucas's arms. "Can we open a present tonight?"

"I'll tell you what." Lucas tucked Max under his arm like a football. "Saturday night is Christmas Eve. You can open one present after Jasmine and Cade's wedding. How does that sound?"

Max's face lit up. "Really?"

"Really. Now up to bed."

"Are you going to open one, too?" Max asked.

"Sure."

"Is Erin goin' to open one?" Max looked concerned.

"Erin's presents are under her tree at home," Lucas pointed out.

Max thought about that. "You can open one anyway," he whispered. "Santa won't mind."

"I just might do that." Erin swept Max into her arms and planted a kiss on top of his head, breathing in the scent of bubblegum shampoo.

"Okay." His little feet barely touched the floor when he danced up the stairs.

"Darlene wanted a small, private memorial service," Lucas said. "Reverend West is making the arrangements for the day after tomorrow. She made Arabella promise that Jasmine and

Cade wouldn't postpone the wedding. Darlene said it was another step toward healing for our family—and for Macy."

"I wish I would have known her better," Erin murmured. "She must have been a very strong woman."

"So is Arabella, considering what she's been through the past few days. Finding out her mother was behind everything hasn't been easy on her."

Erin nodded. "I know. We've been working almost round the clock to get things ready. Kylie, Vivienne and I are finishing up the food tomorrow."

"But aren't you going to the wedding?"

"Since I'm not family, I offered to take charge of the reception dinner. I'm needed more there."

Something in Lucas's expression caused Erin's breath to catch in her throat. "But I need—"

"Daddy!" Max appeared at the top of the stairs. "I found a book about a cowboy!"

Erin smiled. "I'll let myself out."

"Are you sure you don't want to stay longer?"

"I'm sure." Erin turned down the invitation even as she silently acknowledged the truth.

She *wanted* to stay. Forever.

Chapter Twenty-One

Luminaries lined the snow-covered sidewalk as the wedding guests arrived.

Over the course of the day, Clayton Christian Church had been turned into the setting of a fairy-tale wedding with hundreds of tiny lights, lush poinsettias, white roses and miles of white netting.

Lucas saw Kylie slip in through the front doors and join Zach in the foyer. There was no sign of Erin. He'd been lurking in the hallway for almost half an hour, hoping she'd changed her mind about attending the ceremony.

"Is Erin still setting up the buffet?" He had to ask.

Kylie's pert nose wrinkled. "She made me leave but she insisted on staying to keep an eye on the food. She said, and I quote, 'I'm your boss so you have to do what I say.' Unquote."

"She should be here," Lucas muttered.

Kylie gave him a look. "Then convince her. I'll keep an eye on Max for a few minutes."

Lucas was out the door and across the street to the town hall, already formulating a list of reasons why Erin should attend the wedding.

I'm not part of the family, she'd said.

Well, if Lucas had his way, she wouldn't be able to say that again after tonight.

He pushed open the door and saw her fussing with a centerpiece on the table. A white apron skimmed her trim frame but couldn't completely conceal the filmy black dress that clung to her slender curves. Instead of a ponytail, silver filigree combs caught up her hair in a loose topknot.

"You look beautiful."

Erin started at the sound of his voice. "Isn't the ceremony about to start?" she asked, a blush staining her cheeks.

"That's why I'm here. Come on."

She balked. "I can't. I've got to stay—"

"Everything looks great. And it will still look great a half hour from now when the reception starts." Lucas took a step toward her and Erin took a step back.

"Max was asking where you were." Okay, so it was low to use his son to get his way, but Lucas knew Max wouldn't mind. And he *had* been asking about Erin.

"I suppose." Erin started to fumble with the strings on her apron and Lucas gently pushed her hands aside.

"Let me." He worked the knot free, overwhelmed by the urge to take her into his arms again.

But then they'd both be late for the wedding…

Five minutes later, they were seated in the back of the church, Max perched on his lap and Erin at his side.

Jack and one of Cade's friends from high school took their place at the front of the church next to Reverend West. Most of the groom's family was missing—Lucas had heard that Samuel and a few key members of his family had taken an extended vacation—but the George Clayton side was there in full force.

As the prelude began, Arabella's triplets, adorable in emerald-green velvet, danced up the aisle, each carrying a basket of rose petals. Macy followed at a more sedate pace, the hem of her satin gown swishing around her ankles.

"There's Julie an' Jamie an' Jessie!" Max sang out before Lucas could shush him.

Erin bit her lip to keep from smiling as laughter rippled through the church.

Everyone rose to their feet as Jonathan and Jasmine appeared in the doorway. The young bride looked stunning in a floor-length gown glistening with seed pearls. A veil covered Jasmine's face but Lucas could see her wide smile beneath it.

"Please be seated." Reverend West came to stand in front of the bride and groom and opened a small leather Bible. "I'd like to read from the book of Isaiah this evening.

"'Therefore the Lord himself will give you a sign. The virgin will be with child and will give birth to a son, and will call him Emmanuel,' which means God with us.

"This is a familiar passage read at Christmastime, but maybe you're wondering why I chose to read it tonight, as Jasmine and Cade exchange their wedding vows."

Reverend West closed the Bible and his warm smile encompassed the people who were listening. "Because both are about promises. Tonight, Jasmine and Cade are making promises to each other. To love one another. To forgive one another. To forsake all others. Love is more than a feeling—it's a promise.

"In Isaiah, almost seven hundred years before Jesus was born, God promised the world a Savior—His only son. God promises He will never forsake us. Never. Emmanuel. God *with* us. The promise of that first Christmas." Reverend West nodded at the young couple. "With God as the center of your marriage, you will be able to get through the ups and downs that every couple faces as they journey together. He'll help you keep the promises you make tonight—because He's a God who keeps His."

He gave Cade a reassuring nod as tears streamed down

Jasmine's face. Cade took her hand and offered a watery smile of his own.

Reverend West smiled. "Let's pray and ask God's blessing on this young couple."

Lucas finally cornered Erin after the reception meal. Her cheeks were flushed and tendrils of hair had escaped from the combs, but she had never looked lovelier.

"I think we're going to call it a night." Lucas hoisted a giggling Max over his shoulder. "Would you like to stop over for a while?"

"Max is probably tired. And he's going to have a busy day tomorrow."

Lucas hiked a brow. "Does Max *look* tired?"

As if to underscore the point, Max wiggled around until he was facing her. "You haveta watch me open my present."

"I wouldn't want to miss that."

There were a lot of things Lucas didn't want to miss, either. Like every moment with Erin.

"So, that's a yes?" Lucas prodded gently.

"Sure." Erin smiled at Max. "Arabella hired a cleanup crew, so I don't think they need me anymore."

That was good. Because *he* needed her.

Erin's car pulled in a few minutes after his. Max had brushed his teeth and prepared for bed in record time. Lucas put on an instrumental Christmas CD and pulled a plate of cookies Arabella had given him out of the freezer.

He was as nervous as the proverbial cat on a hot tin roof when Erin walked in. Max didn't have the same issues. He raced over to Erin, grabbed her hand and tugged her toward the Christmas tree, his patience finally at an end. Lucas knew the feeling!

Max flopped down and retrieved a lumpy package. "This one's yours." He handed it to Lucas. "A'bella helped me wrap it."

Lucas carefully opened the present under Max's watchful eye. Inside was a framed photograph of him and Max...and Erin. One of his sneaky cousins must have snapped it at the reception.

"That's..." Erin's voice trailed off in a squeak.

Max leaned in to see what all the fuss was about. "Us," he said matter-of-factly.

"Which one are you going to open?" Her cheeks pink, Erin redirected the attention back to the gifts.

"This one!" Max wrapped both arms around the largest present and hauled it out from under the tree. He unwrapped it and tunneled through a thick layer of red tissue paper.

"Cowboy boots!"

"Every cowboy needs one to go with his hat," his dad said.

Max hurtled himself into Lucas's lap. "I love them." The tip of his nose touched Lucas's and brought them eyeball to eyeball. "I. Love. You."

"I love you, too." Lucas somehow managed to get the words out.

"Where's Erin's?" Max tilted his head, looking at Lucas expectantly.

"I don't—"

Lucas cut her off with a smile. "It's the one with the pink bow."

The one with the pink bow?

Erin slanted a look at Lucas, feeling self-conscious. She didn't want him to feel obligated to give her a present because he'd allowed Max to open one.

"It's a new tradition. One present on Christmas Eve," Lucas said.

"Yup." Max nodded vigorously. "You gotta open it."

"All right." Erin slid her fingernail through the tape and unwrapped layers of gold paper until she found a plain pine...

box. Obviously old. And judging by the whittle marks in the wood, handmade.

She gave Lucas a questioning look.

"It belonged to my great-grandfather, Jim Clayton," Lucas explained. "Grandpa George gave it to me when I was twelve years old. I have to admit, I was disappointed."

"So you…regifted it?"

"In a way." Lucas didn't smile in response to her teasing. "I didn't appreciate what it meant at the time. Grandpa George said he was passing it on to me because I would understand it's value. It took me long enough, but now I do.

"In his will, my grandfather asked each of us to think of one good memory of him. I realized it was the day he gave me this gift because it reminded me of what was important."

Erin couldn't hide her confusion. "If it's a family heirloom, shouldn't you keep it?"

Lucas shook his head. "My cousins think God brought us back here to reconnect with our roots, but I don't believe that."

Erin's heart sank. "You don't?"

"I've been thinking—and praying—about this a lot over the past few days. And I believe God brought me back to Clayton for *you,* Erin. Because He meant for us to be together." Lucas took the box from her numb fingers and opened the lid.

Tucked in a nest of gold tissue paper was another box. A very small, velvet box.

Erin couldn't move. Couldn't breathe. Couldn't speak.

"You got another one, Erin!" Max wiggled closer. "Open it!"

But she *still* couldn't move. So Lucas lifted the cover. When he did, a diamond solitaire winked at her from its setting in a simple gold band.

"Erin Fields, I love you more than life itself," he said

softly. "Will you marry me and make me the happiest man on earth?"

She couldn't speak, either.

"Why's Erin cryin', Daddy?" Max said with a worried frown.

"I'm not sure." Lucas sounded just as worried.

Erin decided it was time to put their fears to rest. And hers, too. Their lives may have taken different paths for a few years, but Lucas was right. God had brought them back together.

"They're happy tears," she sniffled.

Max frowned. "What's that mean?"

Laughing, Erin launched herself into Lucas's arms with the same enthusiasm that Max had just moments ago.

"Yes," she whispered in his ear. "It means yes."

Epilogue

Christmas Eve—One Year Later

"Are you sure you're ready for this?" Lucas pulled up in front of Clayton House and managed to squeeze his pickup between a minivan and the deputy sheriff's car parked along the curb. "My family can be a little overwhelming, you know."

He didn't fool her a bit. Erin heard the undercurrent of deep affection in the teasing comment. "They're your family, Lucas. I love every single one of them."

"That's good." Lucas muttered. "Because every single one of them is here tonight."

"'Cause it's Jesus' birthday tomorrow," Max piped up from the backseat. "And we're goin' to have a party and cake and everything!"

"You're right, buddy. And I can't think of a better way to celebrate." Lucas wove his fingers through Erin's and gave them a warm squeeze, sending her pulse into a little skip. "Unless it's sitting in front of a blazing fire with my beautiful wife," he murmured.

"That part comes later," Erin promised in a whisper.

Lucas helped her out of the truck before releasing Max

from his booster seat. He sprinted up the path, the old black Stetson bouncing on his head and his cowboy boots churning up the snow.

Right before they'd left, Max had appeared at the top of the stairs wearing the pair of black corduroy pants and a crisp plaid shirt Erin had bought him for the evening service—and Lucas's old cowboy hat. Erin hadn't asked him to take it off. She'd taken his picture for next year's Christmas card instead.

The door flew open before they reached the top step. The triplets surrounded Max and for a moment Erin lost sight of him in the sudden flurry of sparkling taffeta and ruffles.

"Max, come see the birthday cake Auntie Viv made," Jessie said, grabbing her younger cousin by the hand.

"It's got lotsa frosting." A.J. Wesson, adorable in a white shirt and a necktie sprinkled with tiny gingerbread men, spun in a circle and almost took out the coatrack. "Macy helped dec'rate it."

Max paused long enough to shed his coat before chasing after his cousins through an obstacle course of discarded boots, hats and gloves.

"I think we better watch Max's sugar intake this evening or he'll be up all night," Lucas said.

"You're such a dad." Erin slipped her arm around his waist.

Lucas took advantage of the moment to turn her fully into his arms, dip her backward and press a kiss against her soft pink lips.

"Uncle Lucas and Auntie Erin are kissin' again!" Jamie announced as she scampered past.

"That's because they're newlyweds," Jasmine said when Erin and Lucas stepped into the living room.

Erin blushed. "We've been married eight months," she protested.

In spite of the number of engagements over the past year, she and Lucas had been the first couple to exchange vows after Jasmine and Cade's Christmas Eve wedding.

Lucas had informed his cousins they would have to wait their turn because he and Erin, with their "seven-year courtship," had been together the longest.

Erin knew exactly what he meant. Their love had never died—it had simply remained stored in their hearts until God had brought them back together again.

And Lucas Clayton had been worth the wait.

He and Max had moved into her house after the wedding and when Tweed retired, Lucas had taken over the practice. The first thing he'd done was hire a partner and a vet tech so that he could spend more time at home with his wife and adopted son.

It was one of the many changes Erin had seen in her husband. Little by little, Clayton's prodigal son had been drawn back into the fold. He'd even coached a boy's T-ball team the previous summer at the Lucy Clayton Recreational Center that Brooke had opened in memory of her sister.

"It's our first anniversary," Cade reminded them. "So technically, we are no longer newlyweds."

"I suppose that makes you an old married couple?" Lucas swept a herd of plastic horses aside to make room on the sofa.

"Of course," Jasmine said. "We can give the rest of you advice!"

A collective groan followed the cheerful statement.

"I knew we shouldn't have let them get married so young," Arabella told Jonathan in a stage whisper. "And they've got six months on us."

Arabella and Jasmine's uncle had married in June, the month Jonathan had officially relocated his practice from Denver to Clayton. Jasmine and Cade had stayed in the city while he attended college and she attended culinary school, but the couple often came home on weekends to visit.

"And four on Brooke and I," Gabe added. "So if seniority rules, we can give Mei and Jack advice. They aren't getting married until Valentine's Day."

"What are we talking about?" Vivienne swept into the living room with a cheese tray. She paused long enough to let Cody snag a handful of crackers.

"Weddings." Zach sighed but his eyes were twinkling. "What else?"

"And in spite of what *some* people might think," Mei looked pointedly at the men in the room, "they are not a competition."

Cody crossed his arms. "Everything is a competition."

"He's right." Jack grinned. "And we're going to come in dead last." He looked at Mei and lowered his voice to a stage whisper. "Unless we elope tonight."

"No way." Kylie entered the fray. "No one elopes on my watch. I love planning weddings and no one is going to cheat me out of the opportunity!"

"See what you started?" Arabella smiled at her foster daughter. "A whole *stampede* of Clayton weddings."

Jasmine performed a cute little curtsey. "You're all very welcome."

Brooke looped one arm around Gabe and the other around Macy. "I wonder if Grandpa George knew what he was starting when he wrote up that will."

"Oh, I think he *hoped*," Mei said softly.

The smile she and Lucas exchanged warmed Erin's heart.

Even though the conditions of the will had recently been met and everyone had received their inheritance, the past twelve months had connected the family in ways no one had quite expected.

George's will might have forced them to return to Clayton, but it was their love for each other that made it *home*.

* * *

"Are you looking for another piece of cake, Lucas?" Vivienne held up a plate.

Lucas winced and patted his flat stomach. "If I eat another piece of cake, I'll have to roll myself to the church. Actually, I'm looking for Erin."

He'd lost track of his wife at some point between the children's roof-raising Happy Birthday chorus and the cake-cutting, picture-taking, cleaning-frosting-off-the-walls event that followed.

"I think she went thataway." Vivienne pointed a chef's knife in the direction of the small sitting room located off the kitchen.

The room was washed in shadows, the only light coming from the streetlight shining through the window. Lucas started to back up when he saw a faint glimmer of copper.

Concern propelled him across the room. He dropped to his knees in front of the chair Erin was sitting in.

"What's the matter?"

"Nothing at all," Erin said quickly. "I'm just feeling a little tired tonight, I guess. It's been a busy week."

"I heard A.J. tell Brooke that the triplets were making his *ears* tired." Lucas was rewarded with a wan smile. "A family get-together can have that effect on people."

"I love your family."

"I know, but at times like this, don't you wish it were smaller?"

"Not for a moment." Erin paused and a smile played at the corners of her lips. "Do you ever wish it were bigger?"

Something in her eyes made Lucas catch his breath. "Erin?"

She looped her arms around his neck. "My Christmas present to you is that by this time next year, Max will have a brother or a sister."

His heart expanding at the unexpected news, all Lucas could do was stare at her. A baby. By next Christmas.

"I know we didn't plan on having a baby so soon." Erin bit her lip. "You aren't upset, are you?"

"Are you kidding? You know what this means, don't you?"

"What?"

A slow smile spread across Lucas's face. "We're in the lead again."

* * * * *

Dear Reader,

I enjoyed being part of the Rocky Mountain Heirs series because it combines two things that are very special to me—faith and family.

Proverbs 13:22 says, *"A good man leaves an inheritance for his children's children…"* That's what Lucas's grandfather, George Clayton, wanted to do. He took steps near the end of his life to make sure his family could have a new start. A new start that involved forgiveness, commitment and, of course, love!

It's my prayer that after reading this series, you will have a new and deeper appreciation for your own family. With God's help, we can all leave a wonderful legacy to the next generation.

I love to hear from my readers! Check out my website at www.kathrynspringer.com and sign up to receive my free quarterly newsletter. And until we meet again in the pages of my next book, keep smiling…and seeking Him!

Blessings,

Kathryn Springer

Questions for Discussion

1. Did you support or disagree with George Clayton Sr.'s plan to convince his grandchildren to return to Clayton? What was his motivation?

2. What factors influenced Lucas's decision to leave Colorado at the age of eighteen? How did they compare to Erin's reasons for staying?

3. The Clayton family had been divided for years because of a long-standing feud between George Sr. and his brother Samuel. How did this affect other relationships? Have you ever experienced this kind of difficulty in your family? What did you do to solve it?

4. Whether real or imagined, both Erin and Lucas struggled with the expectations their families placed on them. How did they respond? Which of them can you relate to the most in that regard?

5. What qualities did Erin possess that Lucas admired? Why do you think she didn't see those things in herself?

6. It was clear from the moment they met that Erin and Lucas still had feelings for one another, but what was the turning point in their relationship?

7. Lucas felt inadequate when it came to being a good father to Max. If you are a parent, what is the issue you struggle with the most? What is an area in which you feel confident when it comes to raising your children?

8. Erin's mother told her to "look for the good" that was right in front of her. Do you think that was good advice? What does it mean to you?

9. In what ways did Macy Perry bring the Clayton family back together?

10. Katrina Clayton allowed a root of bitterness to grow in her heart. Compare and contrast her character to Darlene Perry, who turned to God to find healing. What lessons can we learn from these two women?

11. How did you feel about Jasmine and Cade marrying so young? What are some of the challenges they might face? What will they need to overcome them?

12. When did you figure out who was responsible for the attacks on the Clayton family? What hints led you to that conclusion?

13. Which couple in the Rocky Mountain Heirs continuity series did you relate to the most? Why?

14. What was your favorite scene? Why?

15. What does the word *legacy* mean to you? What kind of legacy do you want to pass on to the next generation? What steps will you take to do this?

INSPIRATIONAL

Wholesome romances that touch the heart and soul.

Love Inspired

COMING NEXT MONTH
AVAILABLE DECEMBER 27, 2011

SEASIDE REUNION
Starfish Bay
Irene Hannon

LONGING FOR HOME
Mirror Lake
Kathryn Springer

DADDY'S LITTLE MATCHMAKERS
Second Time Around
Kathleen Y'Barbo

THE DOCTOR'S SECRET SON
Email Order Brides
Deb Kastner

MONTANA MATCH
Merrillee Whren

SMALL-TOWN SWEETHEARTS
Jean C. Gordon

Look for these and other Love Inspired books wherever books
are sold, including most bookstores, supermarkets, discount
stores and drug stores.   LICNM1211

REQUEST YOUR FREE BOOKS!

2 FREE INSPIRATIONAL NOVELS
PLUS 2
FREE
MYSTERY GIFTS

Love Inspired

YES! Please send me 2 FREE Love Inspired® novels and my 2 FREE mystery gifts (gifts are worth about $10). After receiving them, if I don't wish to receive any more books, I can return the shipping statement marked "cancel." If I don't cancel, I will receive 6 brand-new novels every month and be billed just $4.49 per book in the U.S. or $4.99 per book in Canada. That's a saving of at least 22% off the cover price. It's quite a bargain! Shipping and handling is just 50¢ per book in the U.S. and 75¢ per book in Canada.* I understand that accepting the 2 free books and gifts places me under no obligation to buy anything. I can always return a shipment and cancel at any time. Even if I never buy another book, the two free books and gifts are mine to keep forever.

105/305 IDN FEGR

Name	(PLEASE PRINT)	
Address		Apt. #
City	State/Prov.	Zip/Postal Code

Signature (if under 18, a parent or guardian must sign)

Mail to the **Reader Service**:
IN U.S.A.: P.O. Box 1867, Buffalo, NY 14240-1867
IN CANADA: P.O. Box 609, Fort Erie, Ontario L2A 5X3

Not valid for current subscribers to Love Inspired books.

**Are you a subscriber to Love Inspired books
and want to receive the larger-print edition?
Call 1-800-873-8635 or visit www.ReaderService.com.**

* Terms and prices subject to change without notice. Prices do not include applicable taxes. Sales tax applicable in N.Y. Canadian residents will be charged applicable taxes. Offer not valid in Quebec. This offer is limited to one order per household. All orders subject to credit approval. Credit or debit balances in a customer's account(s) may be offset by any other outstanding balance owed by or to the customer. Please allow 4 to 6 weeks for delivery. Offer available while quantities last.

Your Privacy—The Reader Service is committed to protecting your privacy. Our Privacy Policy is available online at www.ReaderService.com or upon request from the Reader Service.

We make a portion of our mailing list available to reputable third parties that offer products we believe may interest you. If you prefer that we not exchange your name with third parties, or if you wish to clarify or modify your communication preferences, please visit us at www.ReaderService.com/consumerschoice or write to us at Reader Service Preference Service, P.O. Box 9062, Buffalo, NY 14269. Include your complete name and address.

After surviving a devastating tragedy, combat reporter Nate Garrison returns home to Starfish Bay. But his reunion with lovely Lindsey Collier is nothing like he's dreamed. Lindsey is now a sad-eyed widow who avoids loss and love. Knowing he's been given a second chance, Nate sets out to show her faith's true healing power.

Seaside Reunion
by Irene Hannon

Available January wherever books are sold.

www.LoveInspiredBooks.com

LI87715

In the exciting new FITZGERALD BAY *series
from Love Inspired Suspense, law enforcement siblings
fight for justice and family when one of their own
is accused of murder.*

*Read on for a sneak preview of the first book,
THE LAWMAN'S LEGACY by Shirlee McCoy.*

Police captain Douglas Fitzgerald stepped into his father's
house. The entire Fitzgerald clan had gathered, and he was
the last to arrive. Not a problem. He had a foolproof excuse.
Duty first. That's the way his father had raised him. It was
the only way he knew how to be.

Voices carried from the dining room. With his boisterous
family around, his life could never be empty.

But there *were* moments when he felt that something
was missing.

Some*one* was missing.

Before he could dwell on his thoughts, his radio crackled
and the dispatcher came on.

"Captain? We have a situation on our hands. A body has
been found near the lighthouse."

"Where?"

"At the base of the cliffs. The caller believes the deceased
may be Olivia Henry."

"It can't be Olivia." Douglas's brother Charles spoke.
The custodial parent to his twin toddlers, he employed
Olivia as their nanny.

"I'll be there in ten minutes." He jogged back outside
and jumped into his vehicle.

Douglas flew down Main Street and out onto the rural
road that led to the bluff. Two police cars followed. His
brothers and his father. Douglas was sure of it. Together,

they'd piece together what had happened.

The lighthouse loomed in the distance, growing closer with every passing mile. A beat-up station wagon sat in the driveway.

Douglas got out and made his way along the path to the cliff.

Up ahead, a woman stood near the edge.

Meredith O'Leary.

There was no mistaking her strawberry-blond hair, her feminine curves, or the way his stomach clenched, his senses springing to life when he saw her.

"Merry!"

"Captain Fitzgerald! Olivia is…"

"Stay here. I'll take a look."

He approached the cliff's edge. Even from a distance, Douglas recognized the small frame.

His father stepped up beside him. "It's her."

"I'm afraid so."

"We need to be the first to examine the body. If she fell, fine. If she didn't, we need to know what happened."

If she fell.

The words seemed to hang in the air, the other possibilities hovering with them.

Can Merry work together with Douglas to find justice for Olivia…without giving up her own deadly secrets?
To find out, pick up
THE LAWMAN'S LEGACY by Shirlee McCoy,
on sale January 10, 2012.

SHLISEXP0112